The Ultimate Studio One Pro 7 Book

A step-by-step guide to recording, editing, mixing, and mastering professional-quality music

Doruk Somunkiran

‹packt›

The Ultimate Studio One Pro 7 Book

Copyright © 2025 Packt Publishing

All rights reserved. No part of this book may be reproduced, stored in a retrieval system, or transmitted in any form or by any means, without the prior written permission of the publisher, except in the case of brief quotations embedded in critical articles or reviews.

Every effort has been made in the preparation of this book to ensure the accuracy of the information presented. However, the information contained in this book is sold without warranty, either express or implied. Neither the author, nor Packt Publishing or its dealers and distributors, will be held liable for any damages caused or alleged to have been caused directly or indirectly by this book.

Packt Publishing has endeavored to provide trademark information about all of the companies and products mentioned in this book by the appropriate use of capitals. However, Packt Publishing cannot guarantee the accuracy of this information.

Portfolio Director: Pavan Ramchandani
Relationship Lead: Mohd Riyan Khan
Content Engineer: Mohd Hammad
Technical Editor: Vidhisha Patidar
Copy Editor: Safis Editing
Proofreader: Mohd Hammad
Indexer: Hemangini Bari
Production Designer: Ponraj Dhandapani
Growth Lead: Nivedita Singh

First published: July 2023

Second edition: April 2025

Production reference: 1170325

Published by Packt Publishing Ltd.
Grosvenor House
11 St Paul's Square
Birmingham
B3 1RB, UK.

ISBN 978-1-83620-097-0

www.packtpub.com

To my students, who inspire me every day with their curiosity, creativity, and perseverance.

– Doruk Somunkiran

Contributors

About the author

Doruk Somunkiran is a composer, music producer, and instructor with 20 years of experience in the industry. Graduating from Berklee College of Music with top honors in 2000, Doruk has since written and produced music for countless albums, commercials, movies, and TV programs. As a teacher, he's helped more than 5,000 students in defining and reaching their musical goals, and his hands-on, intuitive teaching style has earned stellar reviews from thousands of students around the globe.

I want to thank my family for always being there for me. You're the best!.

About the reviewers

Yeside Lawal has worked in the audio engineering field for 10 years, with 5 years specifically dedicated to mixing and mastering songs. She has worked with different sound engineering companies and mixed for various artists. She has received different certificates in audio-related courses. She is currently the lead engineer at LiquidSand Productions, where she provides consultation to clients and heads the post-production team. She also heads the training department of the company.

Valentino Vraneković is an audio engineer, musician, and IT specialist with over 15 years of experience in live performance, studio production, and sound engineering. As a keyboardist, he has played in multiple bands and worked as a session musician. His expertise includes live mixing, studio production, mastering, and forensic audio analysis. Throughout his career, he has contributed to numerous live events as a performer or sound engineer.

In addition to his music career, he is an IT specialist with a master's degree in Digital Forensics and Information Security, specializing in cybersecurity, cloud computing, and IT infrastructure. He is passionate about continuous learning, innovation, and sharing knowledge in both fields.

Table of Contents

Preface — xv

Part 1: Getting Started with Studio One

1

Choosing Your Flavor of Studio One — 3

Meeting the candidates – Perpetual, Annual, and Monthly	4
Choosing the right plan	5
Sifting through the additional content	5
Virtual instruments	5
Effects plug-ins	11
Loops and sounds	12
Summary	14

2

Installing and Configuring Your Studio One Environment — 15

Technical requirements	15
Installing Studio One and additional content	16
Installing Studio One	16
Installing additional content	18
Exploring online resources	19
Configuring Studio One	20
Filling in the artist profile and choosing a language	21
Configuring your audio device	22
Buffer size and latency	23
Configuring your external devices	26
Optimizing your system for best performance	31
Working with multiple disks	31
Configuring file locations	32
Summary	34

3

Exploring the Studio One Environment — 35

Technical requirements	35
Understanding the Song, Project, and Show pages	36
Touring the user interface	37
The Song page	38
The Project page	43
The Show page	44
Navigating the Studio One environment	46
Window management	46
Zoom levels	48
Extra navigation tips	51
Summary	53

Part 2: Creating in Studio One

4

Creating a New Song — 57

Technical requirements	57
Setting up your Song and exploring the Song settings	57
Name	59
Save location	59
Sample Rate	59
Resolution	60
Other New Document page settings	61
Changing the tempo, key signature, and time signature within the Song	63
Using the Tempo track to change your Song's tempo	64
Using the Signature track to change your Song's key or time signature	66
Summary	68

5

Recording Your First Audio Track — 69

Technical requirements	70
Setting up your hardware for recording audio	70
Setting up a microphone	70
Setting up an instrument	72
Setting up Studio One for recording audio	73
Creating an audio track	73
Setting recording levels	76
Applying effects during recording	78
Setting up the metronome	81

Understanding different recording modes	83	Loop recording	85
		Recording best practices	86
Basic recording	83	Summary	88
Auto Punch	84		

6

Adding Virtual Instruments and Recording MIDI — 89

Technical requirements	90	Recording a live performance with MIDI	96
Introducing MIDI	90	Inputting MIDI notes manually	99
Connecting devices to Studio One	91	Using Melodyne to convert audio to MIDI	107
Adding and configuring MIDI instruments	92	Choosing the right type of audio material	107
Adding a software instrument	92	Audio-to-MIDI-conversion walkthrough	108
Adding a hardware Instrument	93	Summary	109
Inputting and recording MIDI	96		

Part 3: Editing in Studio One

7

Editing and Rearranging Your Song — 113

Technical requirements	113	Understanding Snap and various Snap modes	126
Exploring the editing tools	114	Snap To Grid	126
Arrow tool	114	Relative Grid	127
Range tool	120	Snap To Cursor & Loop	128
Split tool	121	Snap To Events	128
Eraser tool	121	Snap Event End	128
Paint tool	121	Snap To Zero Crossings	129
Mute tool	123	Using the Arranger Track to edit a song	130
Bend tool	124		
The Listen tool	125	Using the Launcher to try out new ideas	131

Summary	134

8

Editing Audio — 135

Technical requirements	135
Mastering the audio editing tools	136
Transposing and tuning audio events	136
Strip Silence	137
Creating the perfect take from several layers	139
Working effectively with editing commands	140
Fixing and enhancing the timing of audio recordings	143
Understanding transients	143
Using the Audio Bend tool to fix errors manually	144
Quantizing audio to fix timing errors automatically	146
Extracting and quantizing to custom grooves	147
Using Melodyne to fix and enhance vocal recordings	148
Fixing an out-of-tune vocal performance with Melodyne	149
Using Melodyne to create background harmony vocals	153
Using stem separation to isolate audio events	154
Summary	155

9

Editing MIDI — 157

Technical requirements	157
Using basic editing tools and quantization	158
Using the Arrow tool to perform basic editing tasks	158
Using the Select Notes window to make a precise selection	159
Quantizing MIDI notes to change the timing of a performance	161
Adjusting note lengths and applying half-time or double-time	163
Adjusting MIDI data to enhance a performance	166
Transposing notes	166
Adjusting velocity	168
Adjusting modulation and other parameters	172
Working in the Pattern Editor	174
Using Note FX to spark creativity	176
Loading Note FX plug-ins	177
Arpeggiator	179
Chorder	181
Repeater	183
Input Filter	184
Summary	186

10

Using Global Tracks — 187

Technical requirements	187
Using the Chord Track to control the harmonic content of a song	187
Getting started with the Chord Track	188
Detecting and extracting chords automatically	188
Entering chord information manually	190
Setting Instrument Tracks to follow the Chord Track	191
Setting Audio Tracks to follow the Chord Track	194
Using the Ruler, Marker, and Lyric Tracks to work more efficiently on a project	197
Keeping track of different time units with the Ruler Track	197
Using the Marker Track for easy navigation	198
Using the Lyric Track	200
Using the Video Track to add sound and music to a video	202
Importing video files	202
Navigating the Video Track and Video Player	202
Editing video	203
Synchronizing audio and MIDI events with video	204
Understanding Timebase	206
Exporting video	208
Summary	210

Part 4: Mixing and Mastering

11

Preparing for the Mix — 213

Technical requirements	213
Preparing a Song for the mix session	213
Optimizing hardware and software for the mix	214
Should I convert instrument tracks to audio?	215
Editing for perfection	217
Gain staging	217
Organizing tracks for better control	220
Setting levels, panning, and automation	223
Setting levels	223
Panning to create a stereo image	225
Adding automation to create a dynamic mix	228
Summary	232

12

Working with Effects Plug-Ins to Craft a Mix — 233

Technical requirements	233	Reverb plug-ins	239
Controlling level and frequency with dynamics plug-ins and equalizer	234	Delay plug-ins	242
		Adding color and character with plug-ins	**244**
Compressor	234	Distortion plug-ins	244
Limiter[2]	235	Modulation plug-ins	246
Expander	236	Combined mix plug-ins	250
Gate	236	**Using special tools and analysis plug-ins**	**253**
De-Esser	236		
Multiband Dynamics	237		
Tricomp	237	Special tools	253
Pro EQ[3]	237	Analysis tools	254
Adding depth and space with reverb and delay plug-ins	**239**	**Summary**	**254**

13

Optimizing Signal Flow and Elevating Your Mix — 255

Technical requirements	255	Using Splitter for precise targeting	270
Understanding Studio One's signal flow	255	Using groups for a faster workflow	273
		Customizing plug-ins	275
The anatomy of a mixer channel	256	**Exporting final mixes and stems**	**278**
Using the Inserts rack to add effects	258	Exporting final mixes	278
Using FX channels	260	Exporting stems	281
Using buses to control several channels	263	**Summary**	**283**
Using VCA channels to control volume	266		
Applying advanced techniques	**267**		
Sidechain processing	267		

14

Working with Spatial Audio — 285

Technical requirements	285	Mixing and exporting spatial audio	
Getting started with spatial audio	286	material	292
Understanding different types of spatial audio	286	Using the Surround Panner	292
The naming convention for speaker		Understanding beds and objects	293
configurations	286	Using the Object Panner	294
Hardware requirements for spatial audio	287	The Dolby Atmos Renderer	296
Creating a new Song for spatial audio	288	Exporting spatial audio material	297
Mapping speakers	289	Summary	298
Formatting tracks for spatial audio	291		

15

Navigating the Project Page and Producing Final Masters — 299

Technical requirements	299	Editing tracks on the Project page	307
Creating a new Project and		Adding effects plug-ins	310
navigating the Project page	300	Using the metering tools	312
Creating a new Project	300	Using automation on the Project page	317
Navigating the Project page	303	Rendering final masters for	
Integration between the Song and		publishing and delivery	318
Project pages	304	Creating final masters for digital release	318
Mastering the Project page	305	Creating final masters for release on a CD	319
Entering metadata	305	Summary	321
Sequencing tracks	306		

16

Using Additional Studio One Features — 323

Technical requirements	323	Exploring the Show page	325
Using Studio One in live		Working with players	326
performances with the Show page	323	Adding effects to a live performance	330
Creating your first Show	324		

Using the Arranger Track to define sections of song	332	Adding musical expressions and formatting the score	337
Performing live with the Show page	333	Finalizing and printing a score	340

Using the Score Editor — 334

Opening the Score Editor	334	**Creating and manipulating samples with SampleOne XT**	**341**
Exploring the Score Editor	335	Adding a sample	342
Entering notes in the Score Editor	336	Editing a sample	343
Editing notes in the Score Editor	337	Selecting Trigger modes	344
		Summary	**345**

Appendix

Customizing Studio One and Following Best Practices — 347

Technical requirements	**347**	Removing unused files	358
Customizing Studio One	**347**	Using autosave and recovery	358
Creating your own Smart Templates	348	Saving incremental versions	360
Working with Track Presets	350	**Sharing your files with others**	**361**
Using effects chains	354	Sharing with a collaborator who has Studio One	361
Understanding the file and folder system	**356**	Sharing with a collaborator who does not have Studio One	362
Exploring Studio One's file management system	356	Sharing tracks for mixing	362
Locating and copying missing files	357	**Summary**	**363**

Index — 365

Other Books You May Enjoy — 378

Preface

Music production is a fascinating and rewarding pursuit, but it can be daunting at times. With so many tools, techniques, and software options available, it can be difficult to know where to start. That's why I've written this book, to guide you through the process of making music with PreSonus Studio One.

Studio One is a powerful **digital audio workstation** (**DAW**) that offers a wide range of features and tools to help you create, record, and mix your music. Whether you're a singer-songwriter, a producer, or a composer, Studio One can help you achieve your musical vision.

In this book, I'll take you through the essential steps of creating music with Studio One. We'll start by looking at the interface and the basic tools you'll need to get started. We'll then move on to recording audio and MIDI, editing your recordings, and adding effects and virtual instruments to your tracks. Finally, we'll explore how you can use the mixing and mastering tools in Studio One to deliver professional-sounding final masters of your songs.

Throughout the book, I'll provide step-by-step instructions and practical tips to help you make the most of Studio One. Whether you're a complete beginner or an experienced musician, this book will help you take your music to the next level.

So, if you're ready to dive into the world of music production with Studio One, let's get started!

Who this book is for

This book is for musicians, bands, and composers who want to learn Studio One from scratch in order to create their own music on a professional level. It is also aimed at producers and audio professionals who already have experience in another DAW but now wish to switch to Studio One or include it in their workflow.

What this book covers

Chapter 1, *Choosing Your Flavor of Studio One*, provides an overview of the different versions of Studio One and is designed to help you choose the version that is right for you.

Chapter 2, *Installing and Configuring Your Studio One Environment*, walks you through the process of installing Studio One and its additional components. This chapter also explains how you can configure Studio One to get the best results for your system and production workflow.

Chapter 3, *Exploring the Studio One Environment*, provides a guided tour of the Studio One interface and describes the windows, panels, and other components that we'll be working on in the following chapters.

Chapter 4, *Creating a New Song*, shows you how to create your first Song in Studio One, with step-by-step instructions on how to set up initial song parameters such as sample rate, tempo, and key signature.

Chapter 5, *Recording Your First Audio Track*, walks you through the process of recording audio using a microphone or instrument. This chapter also provides a list of best practices that will help you make the most of every recording session.

Chapter 6, *Adding Virtual Instruments and Recording MIDI*, starts with a crash course on MIDI for beginners. Then, the chapter shows you how to add virtual instruments to a song and explores several alternative methods of recording MIDI, with or without a keyboard.

Chapter 7, *Editing and Rearranging Your Song*, provides an overview of Studio One's editing tools and their various modes of operation, which creates a foundation for the next two chapters.

Chapter 8, *Editing Audio*, shows you how to use audio editing tools to fix timing and intonation errors in audio recordings. This chapter also discusses several methods of using editing tools for creative purposes, such as changing the groove of an existing drum track or creating harmony background vocals.

Chapter 9, *Editing MIDI*, explores Studio One's extensive MIDI editing capabilities and discusses several ways in which these capabilities can be used to embellish your musical ideas.

Chapter 10, *Using Global Tracks*, provides an in-depth look at Studio One's global tracks and shows you how to harness their power to gain more control of your projects.

Chapter 11, *Preparing for the Mix*, walks you through several steps you can take to make sure that your mixing sessions run smoothly. This chapter also covers several best practices that will help streamline your production workflow.

Chapter 12, *Working with Effects Plug-Ins to Craft a Mix*, provides a tour of Studio One's effects plug-ins. The chapter then goes on to explain how you can choose the right plug-in for a given task and add it to your projects.

Chapter 13, *Optimizing Signal Flow and Elevating Your Mix*, provides an in-depth look at how signal processing works in Studio One and how you can harness the power of the Mix Console to present your songs in the best light. Then, the chapter discusses how to apply advanced mixing techniques in Studio One, and finishes by explaining how to export stems and final mixes of your songs.

Chapter 14, *Working With Spatial Audio*, explores Studio One's immersive audio capabilities and shows how to craft three-dimensional experiences for games, movies, and enriched music.

Chapter 15, *Navigating the Project Page and Producing Final Masters*, starts with an overview of the Project page, Studio One's unique mastering environment. The chapter then goes on to explain how you can work on the Project Page to master your songs to the specifications required by digital music platforms.

Chapter 16, *Using Additional Studio One Features*, explores exciting features in Studio One that fall outside the standard music production workflow, but deserve a special mention nevertheless. These features include the Show Page, which allows you to use Studio One on your live performances; the Score Editor; which allows you to input MIDI data using standard musical notation, and SampleOne, which allows you to create your own unique sound samples for unlimited creative options.

Appendix: *Customizing Studio One and Following Best Practices*, shows you how you can customize Studio One to match your workflow in the most effective way possible. The appendix also provides an in-depth look at Studio One's file and folder system and provides best practices for sharing projects with collaborators.

To get the most out of this book

To get the most out of this book, you should already have basic knowledge and experience of musical processes, such as arranging, recording, mixing, and mastering. However, you will learn how to perform these processes more effectively in Studio One.

Software/hardware covered in the book	Operating system requirements
Studio One Pro	Windows 10 22H2 or higher, macOS 12.4 (Monterey) or higher

You will need Studio One Pro version 7 to follow along with all the content in this book.

Keep in mind that this book aims to provide extensive coverage of the functions and features of Studio One. Therefore, depending on the version that you decide to work with, you may find that some of the features described in this book are not available in your system.

Conventions used

There are a number of text conventions used throughout this book.

Bold: Indicates a new term, an important word, or words that you see onscreen. For instance, words in menus or dialog boxes appear in **bold**. Here is an example: "Go back to the **Audio Setup** window, but this time, take specific note of the two tabs labeled **Audio Device** and **Processing**."

> **Tips or important notes**
> Appear like this.

Get in touch

Feedback from our readers is always welcome.

General feedback: If you have questions about any aspect of this book, email us at `customercare@packtpub.com` and mention the book title in the subject of your message.

Errata: Although we have taken every care to ensure the accuracy of our content, mistakes do happen. If you have found a mistake in this book, we would be grateful if you would report this to us. Please visit `www.packtpub.com/support/errata` and fill in the form.

Piracy: If you come across any illegal copies of our works in any form on the internet, we would be grateful if you would provide us with the location address or website name. Please contact us at `copyright@packt.com` with a link to the material.

If you are interested in becoming an author: If there is a topic that you have expertise in and you are interested in either writing or contributing to a book, please visit `authors.packtpub.com`.

Share Your Thoughts

Once you've read *The Ultimate Studio One Pro 7 Book*, we'd love to hear your thoughts! Scan the QR code below to go straight to the Amazon review page for this book and share your feedback.

`https://packt.link/r/1836200978`

Your review is important to us and the tech community and will help us make sure we're delivering excellent quality content.

Download a free PDF copy of this book

Thanks for purchasing this book!

Do you like to read on the go but are unable to carry your print books everywhere?

Is your eBook purchase not compatible with the device of your choice?

Don't worry, now with every Packt book you get a DRM-free PDF version of that book at no cost.

Read anywhere, any place, on any device. Search, copy, and paste code from your favorite technical books directly into your application.

The perks don't stop there, you can get exclusive access to discounts, newsletters, and great free content in your inbox daily

Follow these simple steps to get the benefits:

1. Scan the QR code or visit the link below

    https://packt.link/free-ebook/978-1-83620-097-0

2. Submit your proof of purchase
3. That's it! We'll send your free PDF and other benefits to your email directly

Part 1: Getting Started with Studio One

In the first part of this book, you will learn about the different versions of Studio One and how you can pick the one that best suits your needs. Then, you will learn how to install and configure Studio One to run smoothly on your system. Finally, you will take a guided tour of the Studio One interface and get to know the windows that we will be using throughout this book.

This part includes the following chapters:

- *Chapter 1, Choosing Your Flavor of Studio One*
- *Chapter 2, Installing and Configuring Your Studio One Environment*
- *Chapter 3, Exploring the Studio One Environment*

1
Choosing Your Flavor of Studio One

Competition is fierce in the world of **Digital Audio Workstations** (**DAWs**), with well-established major contenders having, over time, specialized in different aspects of music production. Although **Studio One**, the ever-popular DAW developed by **PreSonus**, is more than a decade old at the time of writing, it's still considered a newcomer. However, it has garnered a well-deserved reputation as the *program that does it all*.

As exciting as that may be, not everyone needs all the functionality that the full-fledged version has to offer. So, in the past, PreSonus came up with several alternative packages to choose from, offering different levels of functionality, complexity, and pricing.

Over time, the abundance of options made things complicated – at a certain point, there were as many as seven different flavors of Studio One. So, in order to make life easier for everyone, PreSonus adopted the tagline *One DAW for all* and dispensed with all the light versions of Studio One, leaving us with the full-fledged Studio One Pro only.

Having said that, as of the time of writing, there are still three different options for getting into Studio One Pro, which can be confusing for newcomers as well as veteran users seeking to upgrade from deprecated versions.

In this chapter, we will go over these options, analyze the differences between them, and discuss which user profile each option would be most suitable for. By the end of this chapter, you will have a solid understanding of which option will best meet your needs, and why.

In this chapter, we will cover the following main topics:

- Meeting the candidates – Perpetual, Annual, and Monthly
- Choosing the right plan
- Sifting through the additional content

Meeting the candidates – Perpetual, Annual, and Monthly

Currently, PreSonus offers two alternative methods for owning Studio One Pro: a **Perpetual** license, which is a one-time purchase for the core version of the software, or **Pro+**, a subscription-based plan that offers several additional features. Pro+ itself comes with further options of its own: **Annual** and **Monthly** subscriptions. At first glance, these options may seem confusing, but the key point here is to decide whether the additional features brought by Pro+ are suitable for your workflow, production style, and budget.

So, let's start by taking a deep dive into Pro+ and see whether it is the right choice for you.

Pro+ (formerly known as **PreSonus Sphere** and then, for a brief period, as **Studio One+**) is a subscription-based model that gives you access to Studio One Pro and almost every other software product developed by PreSonus. This includes **Notion**, a powerful music notation program that tightly integrates with Studio One, as well as a huge list of sound effects, virtual instruments, Sound Sets, and loops that are not available when you purchase Studio One Pro *normally*, that is, with a standalone Perpetual license.

Since the inception of Pro+ and its predecessor, Sphere, PreSonus has really beefed up the package to make it more attractive. Thus, a subscription will get you extra goodies, such as access to exclusive online events and educational materials, cloud storage, cloud exchange and collaboration tools, live streams, and so on.

Now that we know what a subscription-based plan will bring to the table, we are ready to talk about the alternative methods for owning Studio One Pro:

- **Perpetual license**: This is the basic, old-fashioned, one-time purchasing option. You pay the full price for Studio One Pro and it's yours forever. You get access to Studio One Pro's core set of plug-ins and content library. Any other add-ons offered through Pro+ will cost you extra. You will not be able to update your version of Studio One beyond minor maintenance updates or bug fixes. Select this option if you need the features of the core Studio One Pro software, but do not really care about the additional content offered by Pro+.

- **Monthly subscription**: This option gives you access to everything Pro+ has to offer with no long-term commitment. If you choose to end your Monthly subscription, that will be it. Since you're reading this book, I assume that you already have, or are considering having, a long-term commitment to Studio One, so let's just cross this option out to simplify our decision-making process.

- **Annual subscription**: This gives you access to all the goodies that are included in Studio One Pro+. At the end of your subscription period, even if you don't renew your subscription, you will have a Perpetual license for Studio One Pro, which will be yours to keep forever, for the version available at the time when your subscription ends. This is a great option if you want to have a wide selection of loops, sound libraries, and plug-ins at your disposal.

Armed with the preceding information, we are now ready to choose the best option for you.

Choosing the right plan

In deciding between a Perpetual license and a subscription, the first factor we need to talk about is the additional content that a Pro+ subscription brings to the table. Is this content relevant and useful to your musical style and production workflow?

The best way to decide whether a Pro+ subscription is the right choice for you is to take a close look at all the extras that come with it and see whether they will be useful for your productions. We will examine the main ingredients of this package in the following section (see *Sifting through the additional content*). Be sure to also visit PreSonus' website to listen to the demos and hear them in action.

Give yourself a couple of days to check out the extra content. If you think you would use at least 30% of the extra content in your productions, go with a Pro+ subscription. If not, purchase selectively.

The second factor we need to talk about in deciding between a Perpetual license and a subscription-based model is the price. At the time of writing, the cost of an Annual subscription to Studio One Pro+ is $179,99 and the cost of a Perpetual license is $ 199,99 for first-time users. So, keeping in mind the fact that you'll have a Perpetual license at the end of an Annual subscription period, going with an Annual subscription is a no-brainer at the time of writing. However, these prices are subject to change, so it's a good idea to do a bit of research before pulling out your credit card.

Up next, we will take an in-depth look at the additional content included in Pro+ to assist you in choosing between a Perpetual license or a subscription-based model.

Sifting through the additional content

PreSonus offers a plethora of additional content that can be used as plug-ins or extensions within Studio One. In this section, we will go over the main categories, since this will help you in choosing the right combination for your production style. However, keep in mind that there are far too many items to cover individually here. Once you have a clear understanding of content categories, it's a good idea to spend some time on PreSonus' website to go over the product catalog at `https://my.presonus.com/products` and see which ones will be useful for your production style.

Virtual instruments

The core version of Studio One Pro comes with a variety of virtual instruments that will cover all your basic needs to kick-start an arrangement—everything from sampled acoustic instruments to drums and synthesized sounds. When you outgrow these virtual instruments, Pro+ offers several alternatives that will take your productions to the next level. In this section, we will take a close look at each of these instruments to help you decide which of these alternatives will work best for you. All the core instruments listed here are available in Studio One Pro, with the exception of Lead Architect and Deep Flight One, which are only available through a Pro+ subscription.

Presence

Presence is the standard equipment that ships with all versions of Studio One. It is a sample player that triggers audio samples of actual instruments. Hence, the sound quality you'll get from Presence is directly related to the quality of the samples that you load into it.

Figure 1.1: Presence

Presence has its own sample file format, called **Sound Sets**. The standard Sound Set that ships with a Perpetual license for Studio One Pro contains hundreds of instrument sounds, which are mostly run-of-the-mill and nothing to get excited about. They can be used to create tracks for a demo, but are highly unlikely to make their way into a final, polished production.

Studio One Pro comes with another Sound Set, called **Presence XT Core Library**, which has higher-quality samples. A Pro+ subscription will allow you to get your hands on many other sound sets available in the PreSonus catalog, so there's plenty to explore.

Presence can also load and play samples in EXS, Giga, and Kontakt formats, acting as a gateway between the PreSonus ecosystem and other vendors such as Native Instruments. If you're switching from another DAW and already have a sample collection in these file formats, Presence has got you covered.

Impact

Impact is PreSonus' take on the ever-popular pad-based drum sampler, allowing you to program intricate drum tracks. A different sample is loaded into each pad, which can then be further tweaked and manipulated individually, allowing for granular control of your drum sounds.

One overlooked feature of Impact is its ability to act as an instant sample player. Just drag any audio clip or file, either from Studio One itself or from your desktop, Finder, Explorer, and so on, and drop it into any of its pads. You can use this method to create your very own custom kits and save them for your future projects as well!

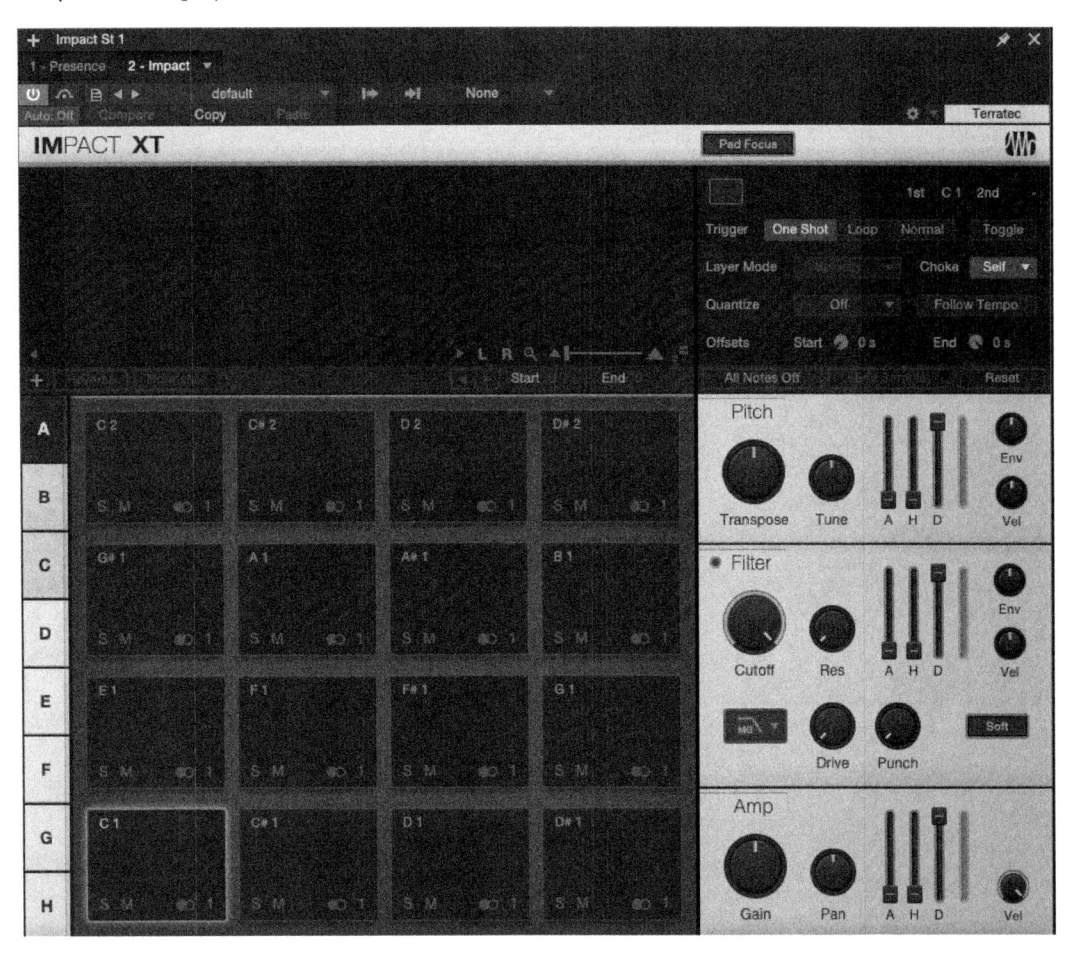

Figure 1.2: Impact

Impact comes with several drum kits, each of which is a collection of drum sounds tailored for a particular genre. EDM and hip-hop receive preferential treatment over acoustic drum kits in the standard package. A Pro+ subscription gives you access to around 100 GB of additional kits, loops, and sounds.

Mai Tai

A polyphonic, analog-modeling synthesizer, **Mai Tai** delivers an amazing variety of high-quality sounds and excellent presets, and comes with a simple user interface.

Figure 1.3: Mai Tai

Mojito

A simple, monophonic, subtractive synthesizer, **Mojito** is perfect for creating and tweaking bass and lead sounds. Unless you're going for deep-level music synthesis, Mojito and Mai Tai will have your bases covered for most EDM and pop styles.

Figure 1.4: Mojito

Sample One

Sample One is a powerful, feature-packed sampler that lets you trigger any audio recording with MIDI. It comes with a vast range of tone-shaping tools and onboard effects. If you're into electronic music or hip-hop production, this is something you definitely want to have in your arsenal.

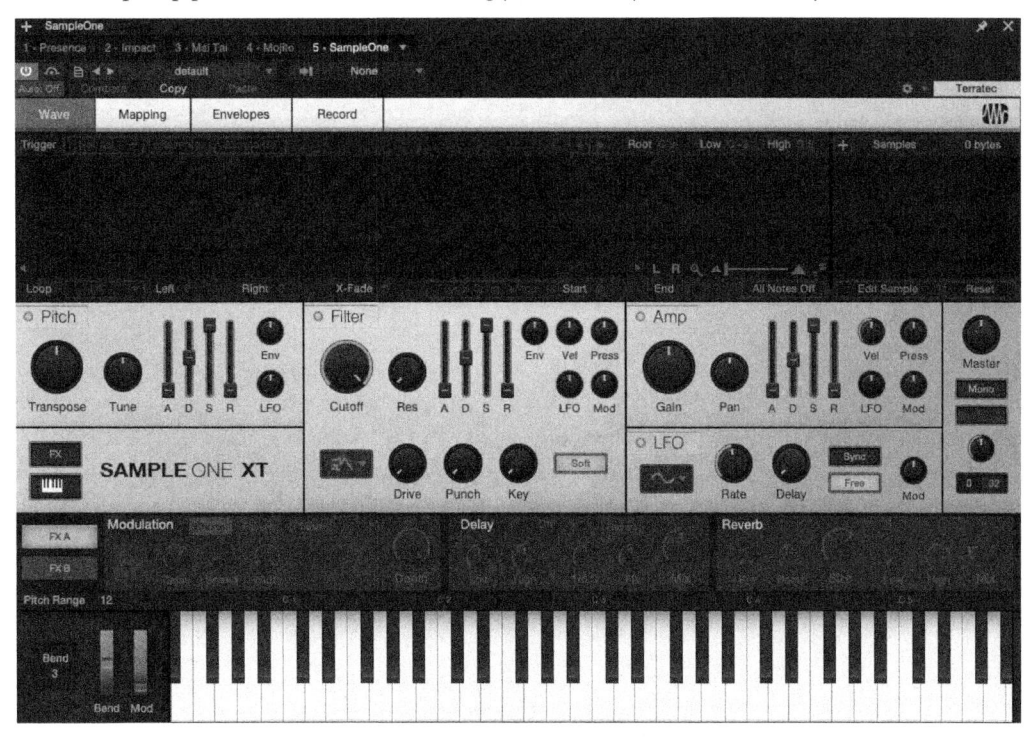

Figure 1.5: Sample One

Lead Architect

Lead Architect is the latest addition to the PreSonus family of virtual instruments, and is currently only available through a Pro+ subscription. It's a sample-based instrument with synth-style filtering and modulation. With sounds that lean toward the edgy and aggressive part of the spectrum, this instrument is guaranteed to deliver powerful lead sounds that will cut through any dense music arrangement.

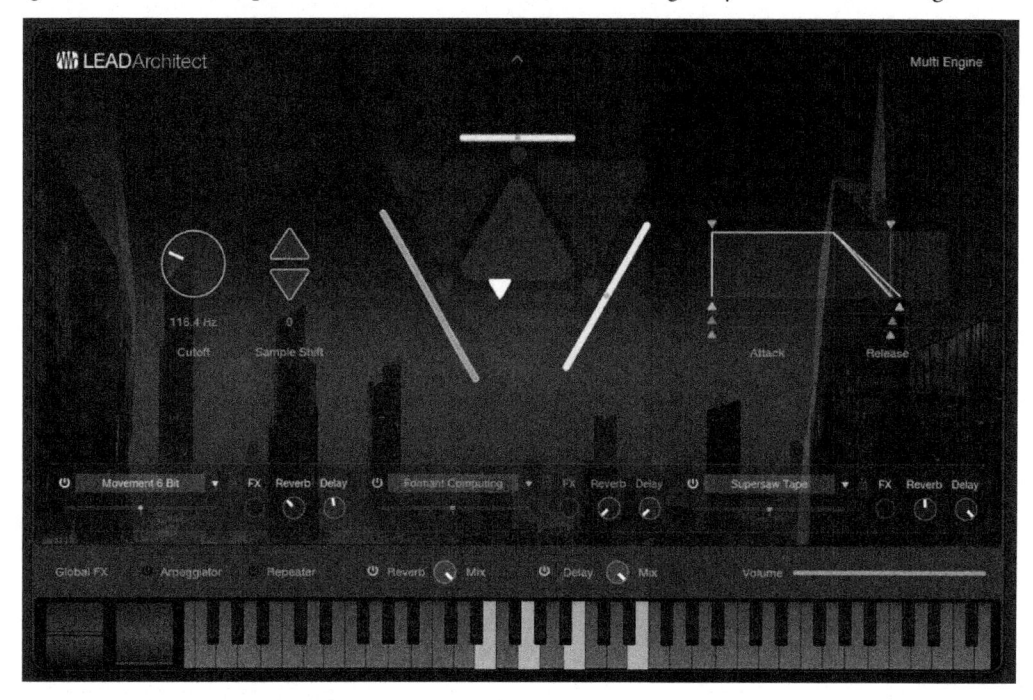

Figure 1.6: Lead Architect

Deep Flight One

Deep Flight One first came to life as a creative sound library for Presence XT, but soon evolved into a standalone virtual instrument in and of itself. It lets you combine and manipulate three layers of sound samples to create otherworldly soundscapes, drones, pads, and atmospheric textures. If experimental, creative sound design is your thing, then this tool has plenty to offer. Deep Flight One is currently available through a Pro+ subscription or can be purchased separately to add an element of otherworldliness to an existing Perpetual license.

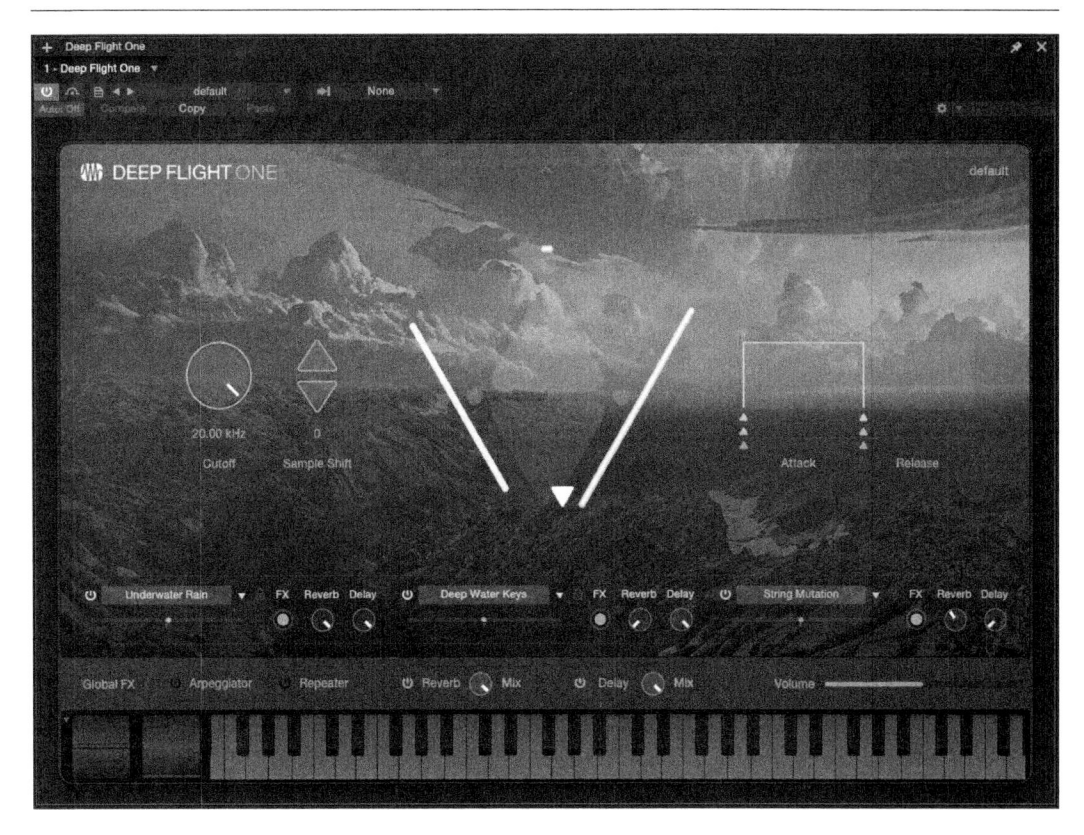

Figure 1.7: Deep Flight One

In this section, we reviewed the virtual instruments that come with a core Studio One installation and the extra instruments and features available through a Pro+ subscription. We will take a much closer look at these instruments when we work with them in *Chapter 6*. Now, let's focus on the wide selection of effects plug-ins available in the Studio One ecosystem.

Effects plug-ins

Studio One users have long been happy and content with its stock plug-ins. The only thing lacking in earlier versions was **analog flavor**: plug-ins designed to give that elusive analog character or warmth that many people feel is missing in DAWs. In recent years, PreSonus has boldly and successfully entered the analog-modeled plug-in market and released several successful products. Today, there is even less need for third-party plug-ins.

In this section, we will look at the plug-in selection that comes with each version of Studio One, so you can decide which particular version will best suit your needs.

Perpetual license

For most users, Studio One Pro's stock plug-ins (which include a generous selection of equalizers, compressors, reverbs, and modulation effects, a total of 45 plug-ins at the time of writing) will be all they ever need. There's a good amount of variety and the overall quality is more than enough for professional music production. PreSonus has chosen to exclude some new and/or unusual plug-ins from the list of plug-ins included with a Perpetual license, apparently to make Pro+ more enticing. However, if you fancy any of these, keep in mind that they can also be purchased individually and added to an existing Studio One installation.

Pro+

This is the way to go if you're looking for ultimate variety and a dazzling number of choices. As of writing, Pro+ will give you 15 different compressors to choose from, including RC-500, FC-670, and Everest C100A, all modeled after classic vintage analog hardware. At this point, it becomes a matter of personal preference, rather than musical style. Some people like to have many toys to play with (of which I've sometimes been guilty, but beware of the dreaded **Gear Acquisition Syndrome (GAS)**), whereas some people just select a couple of effects, stick with them, and focus on their music. If you're in the former group, Pro+ is guaranteed to keep you happy with its abundance of choices.

In this section, we saw that although there are a lot of plug-in options to choose from, identifying your production goals will narrow down the choices and make it easy for you to pick the best alternative. Up next, we will take a look at the final component of the vast collection known as **Additional Content**, and we will complete our tour of the Studio One ecosystem.

Loops and sounds

Loops and sounds are *production-ready* elements that can be used as starting points to spark that first flame of inspiration when you're creating a song, or to spice up and embellish a maturing project:

- Loops are pre-made audio recordings or MIDI clips. They can contain anything from a drum groove to a synthesizer arpeggio. When you drag and drop them into your project, they will automatically match your song's tempo and are constructed in a manner that allows you to repeat them over and over again in your arrangement, hence the name.

- Sounds, on the other hand, refer to the building blocks that virtual instruments use to generate complex sonic textures. For example, when you load **Prime Selection Sounds** into Presence, Presence will use that sound set to produce sounds unique to that collection.

Collectively, loops and sounds are organized into **production kits**, which are several musical elements comprising an entire song arrangement, that you can freely drag and drop into your own project. Then you can tweak them to your heart's content, or since they are royalty-free, you can leave them as is (and sound like ten thousand other songs on Spotify).

As of writing, the core version of Studio One Pro comes with 13 such production kits (with a preference skewed toward electronic music genres). This is a decent selection for home studio use, but if your production workflow relies heavily on using production kits, you will soon outgrow these and find yourself digging for more.

The real blast comes with Pro+. You gain access to a seemingly endless list of production kits, drum kits, loops, and sounds. If loops are the main ingredient of your production style, then this is a no-brainer; a Pro+ subscription costs much less than buying all (or several) of these materials separately.

If you feel that you might need an occasional loop or production kit every now and then, though, this might be overkill. It's a good idea to go over the catalog at PreSonus' website to see how much of this additional content may eventually find its way into your songs. Then you can make an informed decision on whether a Pro+ subscription is the right choice for you.

The table below summarizes and compares the main feature sets available for each version. Please note that new features and plug-ins are being added constantly, so it's a good idea to double-check PreSonus' website before reaching a final decision.

	Perpetual license	**Pro+ Annual plan**	**Pro+ Monthly access**
Price as of writing	$199.99	$179.99/year	$19.99/month
Included effects plug-ins	45 native plug-ins	Native plug-ins + all plug-ins from the Pro+ suite	Native plug-ins + all plug-ins from the Pro+ suite
Included virtual instruments	7 native instruments	Native instruments + Deep Flight One, Lead Architect, and instruments from third-party vendors	Native instruments + Deep Flight One, Lead Architect, and instruments from third-party vendors
Loops & samples	20 GB	20 GB + 15,000 loops and samples from the Pro+ Library	20 GB + 15,000 loops and samples from the Pro+ Library

Table 1.1: Comparison of main feature sets available in each version

This concludes our tour of the vast alternatives available in the Studio One ecosystem. While the sheer number of options may be daunting at first, focusing on your production goals and musical style will narrow down the choices and help you decide on which version is right for you.

Summary

In this chapter, we learned about the different versions of Studio One and took a close look at the functions, features, and content provided by each. Then, we examined the additional content offered by PreSonus and discussed which option would be the right choice for several different scenarios.

In the next chapter, you will configure Studio One to run smoothly on your system and learn about best practices that will save you tons of time further down the line.

2
Installing and Configuring Your Studio One Environment

Installing and configuring software is normally a simple task, but when it comes to audio production software, things can get really messy. Computers are designed to process data in chunks, and in between those chunks, they either process chunks from background tasks or wait patiently for your next command. Audio production, on the other hand, requires processing an uninterrupted flow of data at high volumes, something computers are not equipped to handle off the shelf.

In this chapter, we will take an in-depth look at the strategies you can use to optimize Studio One for your production environment and make sure you are getting the best performance possible out of your system. We will go over the process of selecting and downloading the software components and additional content that you will be using. Then, we will discuss several options available for different scenarios – all the way from a portable rig based around a laptop computer to a fully fledged music studio – and see how you can configure Studio One to run efficiently on each system.

By the end of this chapter, you will be ready to start producing music with Studio One, confident in the knowledge that it is running with optimum efficiency, and you will be well equipped to troubleshoot any configuration problems that may occur down the line.

In this chapter, we are going to cover the following main topics:

- Installing Studio One and additional content
- Configuring Studio One
- Optimizing your system for best performance

Technical requirements

In order to run Studio One, your computer must meet the following minimum system requirements:

- **Operating System**: macOS 12.4 (Monterey) or higher or Windows 10 or 11 (64-bit only)
- **Processor**: Intel Core i3/Apple M1 or better, or Intel Core i3/AMD A10 or better, processor

- **Ram**: 8 GB (minimum); 16 GB or more (recommended)
- 40 GB available hard disk space for installation, additional content, and projects
- A minimum monitor resolution of 1280 x 768 dpi
- An internet connection (required for installation, activation, and cloud-based integration)

Installing Studio One and additional content

Whether you purchase a perpetual license for Studio One or have subscribed to Studio One Pro+, your journey will begin by creating an account on PreSonus' website. This will be your hub for everything Studio One. Once you complete your purchase, log in at my.presonus.com. There is a lot to explore here, and lots of valuable content to help you make the most of your Studio One experience. We will take a closer look at these resources, but first, let's get Studio One up and running on your computer.

Installing Studio One

From the my.presonus.com home page, head over to the **Products** page. Here, you will see a list of all the software, virtual instruments, effects, samples, and loop libraries included with your purchase:

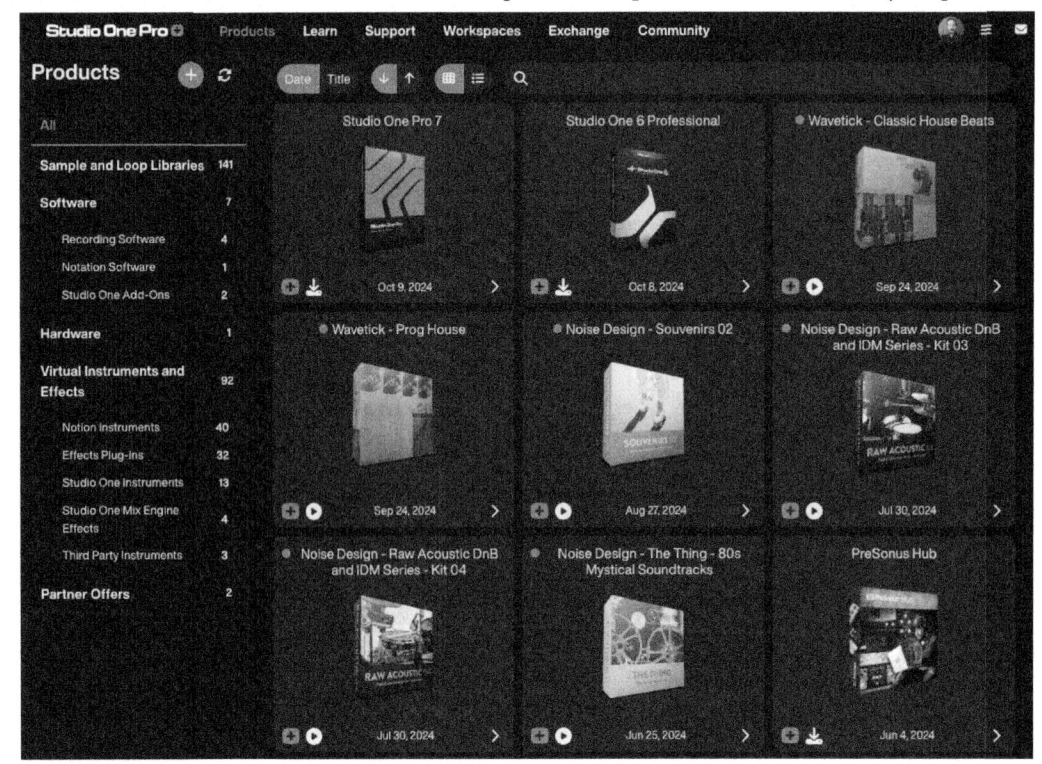

Figure 2.1: The Products page on PreSonus' website

At the top of the list, you will find the latest version of Studio One. Click on it and you will be taken to a page where you can find the installer:

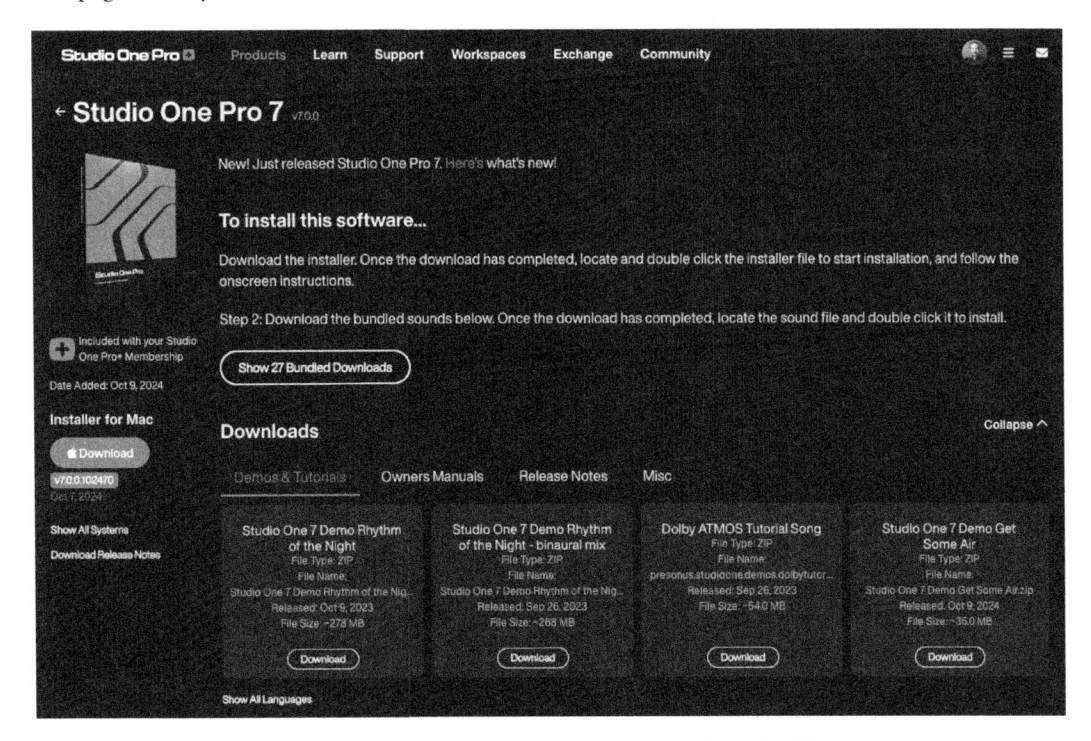

Figure 2.2: Studio One download page with Download links and additional content

Download the installer and run it on your computer. When the installation is complete, your shiny new Studio One will ask you to log in to your MyPreSonus account. Once you've done that, it will automatically retrieve the activation code and activate itself.

> **Tip**
>
> You can install Studio One on up to five different computers using the same activation code. This is an excellent – and very generous, compared to competitors – option for those who need to work on different platforms. So you can, for example, install Studio One on two different computers in your studio, on your home computer, your laptop, or your live rig, and share the same project across all of these computers using workspaces. It is important to note that these computers must belong to a single user; sharing an activation code between users is not permitted.

Installing additional content

You will notice that the core installer for Studio One is pretty lightweight. PreSonus has maintained a modular, open buffet approach, where you pick and install only the components that you will actually use, saving you time, bandwidth, and disk space.

Free extra content and plug-ins

If you go back to the **Products** page, you will find additional software, effects plug-ins, sound sets, and loops, which are not part of a standard Studio One installation but are available to you for free as part of your purchase. Take your time going through the options, checking out their demos on the PreSonus website and picking the ones that you would like to use.

I recommend that you install the following:

- **Ampire**: A suite of plug-ins comprising digital simulations of vintage guitar amplifiers, cabinets, and effects pedals. While targeted mainly at electric guitars, you can use it to add vintage color to just about any sound.
- **Fat Channel XT**: A collection of digital models of highly prized vintage analog effects processors found in top studios all over the world. These processors will be extremely handy when we talk about mixing your projects.

Once you've selected the materials you'd like to use, download them. Go ahead and run the installers for the effects plug-ins, but leave the sound sets and loops in your download folder.

Included sound sets

Back on the page where you downloaded the installer for Studio One (*Figure 2.2*), click on the button that says **Show n Bundled Downloads** (where *n* is the amount of additional content available for free depending on your version of Studio One). Click that and you will see a list of sound sets containing a large selection of instruments, ranging from symphonic strings to synthesized textures, as well as production-ready loops that you can use to kick off or spice up your production. Take your time going over each item. Listen to their demos on the PreSonus website and see whether they match your production style.

Regardless of your production style, I recommend that you download the following:

- Studio One Instruments Volume 1 & 2
- Impact XT Kits and Sounds
- Studio One Musicloops

These offer a generous palette of sounds that will cover your bases on a wide variety of genres (however, availability depends on your version of Studio One).

Though those are the ones I recommend, download any others that you like and leave them in your downloads folder for now. We will come back to them later in this chapter, in the section titled *Configuring file locations*.

Melodyne Essential

Further down the same page, you will see a section titled **Downloads**. Here you can download **Melodyne Essential**, a bundled third-party program that lets you do pitch correction on vocal recordings and convert audio recordings to MIDI. Download and run the installer; it will introduce Melodyne to Studio One and take care of all necessary configurations. We will talk about Melodyne in great detail in *Chapter 8*.

Exploring online resources

Now that we have installed Studio One and some additional resources, let's take a quick guided tour of the excellent resources available at `my.presonus.com`, so you don't miss out on any of the features:

- We've talked about the **Products** page already. It's a good idea to check back here every now and then – there may be some new goodies!

- On the **Learn** page, you will find a collection of videos that will show you how to perform specific tasks or use certain features in Studio One. An even larger collection is available for Studio One Pro+ members under the **Exclusives** section. (Since you're reading this book, it is highly unlikely that you will ever need them, but they may still be nice to have!)

- The **Support** page is where you will open and monitor tickets if you ever need assistance from the PreSonus support team.

- **Workspaces** is the gateway to an innovative feature available to Studio One Pro+ members only. It lets you share your mixes and stems with collaborators and communicate with them in real time using mark-ups and performance notes. This is a brilliant tool for collaborating with fellow musicians or receiving feedback from clients over a distance.

- The **Exchange** page is an excellent platform where users share resources that they have created for Studio One: everything from sound sets to drum patterns, and from FX chains to color schemes. If you ever need a feature that Studio One does not have, this is the first place to look; chances are someone else will have already needed that feature, written a macro for it, and shared it for other users to enjoy. All the content on this page is free!

- Finally, the **Community** page hosts a very active discussion board with a wide variety of topics. Thread topics are not limited to Studio One; you will find discussions on everything from woodwind instruments to video post-production. A MyPreSonus account will let you read the posts; however, in order to join the conversation, you'll need a Studio One Pro+ subscription.

Great! You have just completed the first step in your journey with Studio One. You have chosen and downloaded everything you will need for your Studio One-based production environment. You are now ready to customize Studio One and optimize it to run smoothly on your system.

Configuring Studio One

When you launch Studio One, the software will take a moment to familiarize itself with its new home – it will analyze your computer's hardware configuration, search for any friendly or unfriendly plug-ins you have installed (yes it does have a blacklist!), phone home to PreSonus, sniff out the peripherals connected to your computer, and then greet you with the **Start** page:

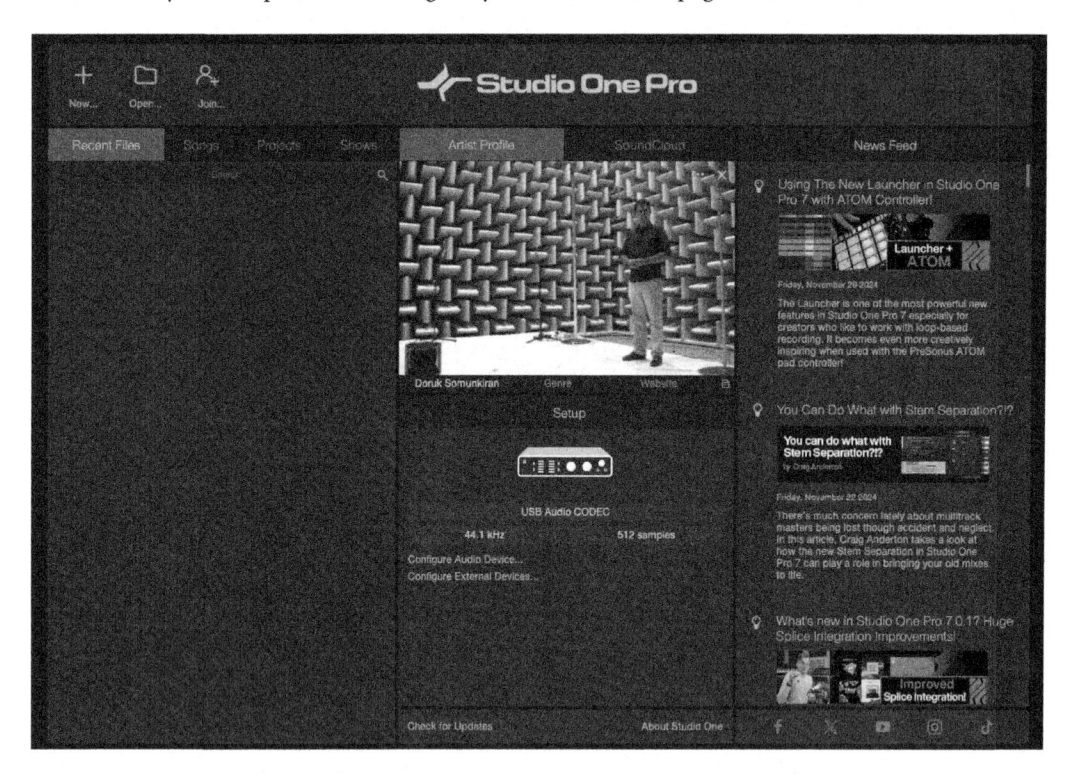

Figure 2.3: Studio One's Start page

Now, let's start configuring Studio One.

Filling in the artist profile and choosing a language

Right in the middle of the **Start** page is the **Artist Profile** window. When you installed Studio One in the preceding section, you logged in to your PreSonus account, so Studio One already knows who you are, and it will populate this section by pulling your photo, name, last name, and website link from your account info. If for some reason (e.g., due to a firewall) this section is still empty, go ahead and fill in the information manually.

Studio One will use this information to give you a warm welcome every time you launch it, but it's for much more than a friendly greeting; this information will also be used by Studio One to populate **meta tags** within the awesome audio files that you will soon be exporting. Ever wondered how additional information such as album name and year of release appears when you play MP3 files? That information is stored in meta tags contained in the MP3 files. So, the next time you export an MP3 to share a rough mix with a friend or client, your name and other info will be added automatically.

This is also a good time to ensure that Studio One is using the language you feel the most comfortable using. As of the time of writing, the Studio One user interface supports nine languages. If you'd like to use it in a language other than English, go to **Studio One** on the top menu and make your selection under **Language**:

Figure 2.4: Selecting your language

Now that Studio One knows who you are, it's time to introduce it to the other members of the team: the hardware devices in your studio.

Configuring your audio device

When you launch Studio One, it asks your operating system about the audio devices available on your computer and makes an educated guess about which one you will want to use. Now let's make sure that the correct device is selected and optimized for best performance.

Back on the **Start** page, right under your photo and name, you will see a section called **Setup**. Here, click **Configure Audio Device**, which will open the **Audio Setup** tab of the **Preferences** window:

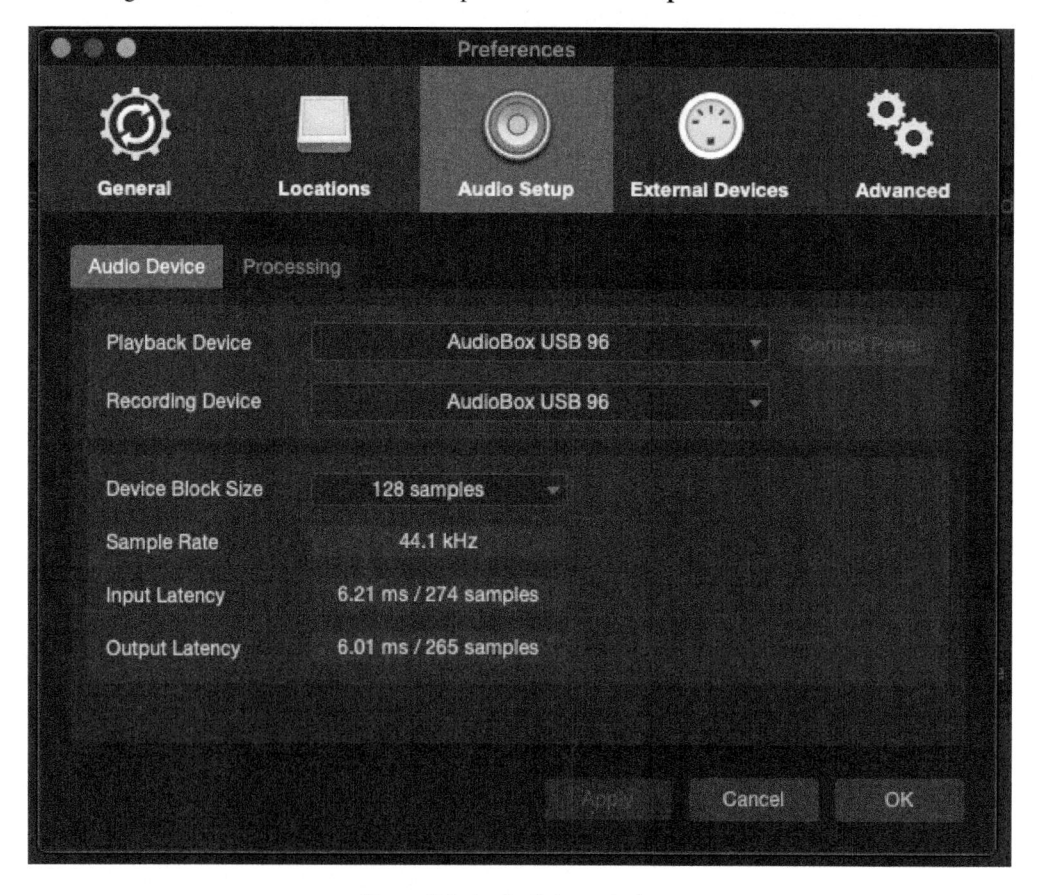

Figure 2.5: Audio Setup window

There are two drop-down menus on this tab:

- **Playback Device**: You can think of this as the audio output coming out of Studio One. The device you select here will be the device that you will be connecting your speakers or headphones to.

- **Recording Device**: This is the input going into Studio One. This is the device that you will be hooking up your sound sources to, such as microphones and instruments.

In most home studio environments, these two devices are one and the same; a typical audio interface will serve as both a playback device and a recording device. So, for the great majority of users, all you need to do here is to select your audio interface on both of these menus, and you will be good to go.

The same thing applies to USB microphones, which are becoming increasingly popular due to their ease of use. A USB microphone is basically a microphone with a built-in tiny audio interface that connects to a computer with a standard USB cable. If you have one of these, select it from the **Recording Device** drop-down menu, and it will be ready to go.

If your studio requires a more complex setup, you can get creative with the options on the **Audio Device** tab. Let's explore some options:

- If you have a more elaborate setup comprising discrete analog-to-digital and digital-to-analog converters, you can set them independently as recording and playback devices, respectively.
- If you'd like to route Studio One's audio output to a streaming or screen-capturing software (to play a project to a client in an online meeting, for example), you can set loopback software as the playback device.

For the purpose of this book, though, we will stick with the most typical home studio scenario and assume that you have selected the same audio device for both menus.

> **Important note**
>
> If your device is connected to your computer but you cannot see it in these lists, most likely the driver software for your device has not been installed or has not been recognized. Studio One uses the ASIO protocol to access audio devices, so go to your device manufacturer's website and download the ASIO driver that matches your operating system. After that, restart your computer and you should be fine. If a suitable driver is not available (it happens), you can try installing the free and generic ASIO4ALL driver on Windows machines.

Buffer size and latency

Audio production requires the uninterrupted flow and processing of a huge amount of data, and computers are not natively equipped to handle this. Digital audio workstations and audio devices work around this problem by using **buffers**.

You can think of a buffer as a water tank that protects a house from water outages. Working with buffers buys time for your computer's and audio device's processors to perform their tasks gracefully. A larger buffer means much better performance, even on a modest computer. But as with many things in life, there is a trade-off: **latency**. Simply put, latency is the time delay between when you sing into your microphone and hear yourself back on your headphones. Just like water going into and coming out of a water tank, it takes time for audio data to go through a buffer. There are several buffers along the signal path, and the delay introduced by each of them will add up.

When you hook up a microphone on your audio device and sing into it, the sound captured by your microphone must go through several buffers before you can hear yourself back on your headphones. This is the **roundtrip latency** imposed by your entire system, measured in **milliseconds** (**ms**). Anything above 10 ms will be very noticeable and distracting. You will not be able to record with a latency above that level. The solution is to decrease the buffer size. As you decrease the buffer size, the latency will decrease, but you will be placing a heavier burden on your system. You will start hearing clicks, cracks, and all sorts of artifacts as the computer struggles. Eventually, you may experience audio dropouts or system freezes.

This dilemma has existed for as long as digital audio workstations have existed. The classic workaround is to decrease the buffer size when recording (because that's when latency becomes noticeable) and to bring it back up when editing and mixing. But Studio One introduces an innovative and more effective approach by letting you adjust your audio device's and computer's buffer settings independently.

Here's how you can configure your system to work with minimum latency and maximum performance. Go back to the **Audio Setup** window, but this time take specific note of the two tabs labeled **Audio Device** and **Processing**.

The Audio Device tab

The **Audio Device** tab displays, and lets you adjust, the latency created by your audio device:

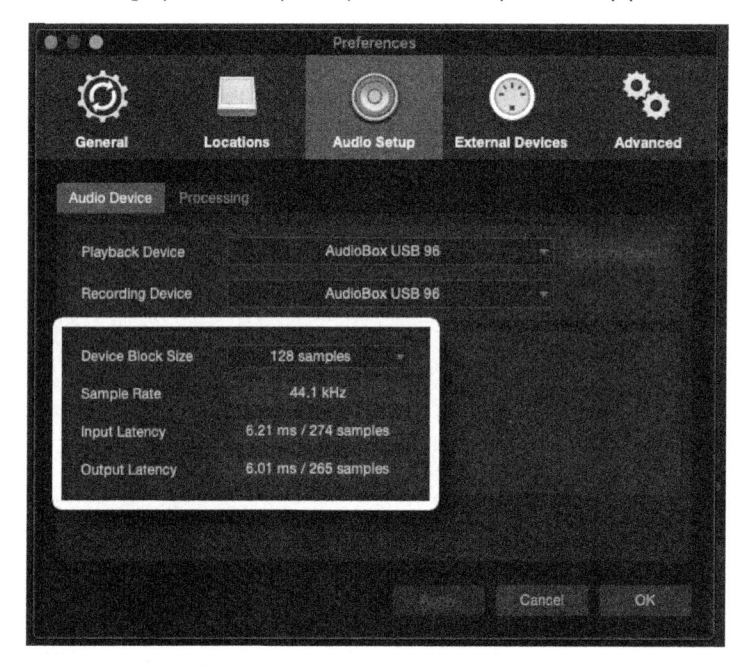

Figure 2.6: Latency measurements and settings for the audio device

When you sing into the microphone, converters in your audio device will convert the analog signal from the microphone into digital data. This conversion takes some time and is listed as **Input Latency** here on the **Audio Device** tab.

Once the computer does its magic and sends audio data back to the audio device, the digital-to-analog converters in the device will then convert this data back to analog signals so you can hear yourself on the headphones. The time spent for this conversion is listed as **Output Latency**.

Together, input and output latencies account for your audio device's total share in your system's overall latency. This can be adjusted by changing the **Device Block Size** value here on the **Audio Device** tab, but don't touch it just yet; we will come back to it after we have covered the **Processing** tab.

The **Audio Device** tab also has a specific option only available for Windows users: **Release audio device in background**. This controls whether or not Studio One will allow other programs to use your audio device when it's minimized. Let's say, for example, that while working on a project in Studio One, you decide to take a break, open your internet browser, and watch a video. The browser may change the settings of your audio device and this may cause problems when you switch back to Studio One. This option is disabled by default, meaning Studio One will not share the audio device with other programs when it's minimized, but you may experiment and enable it if you find that other programs are playing nicely.

The Processing tab

Now, head over to the **Processing** tab of the **Audio Setup** window:

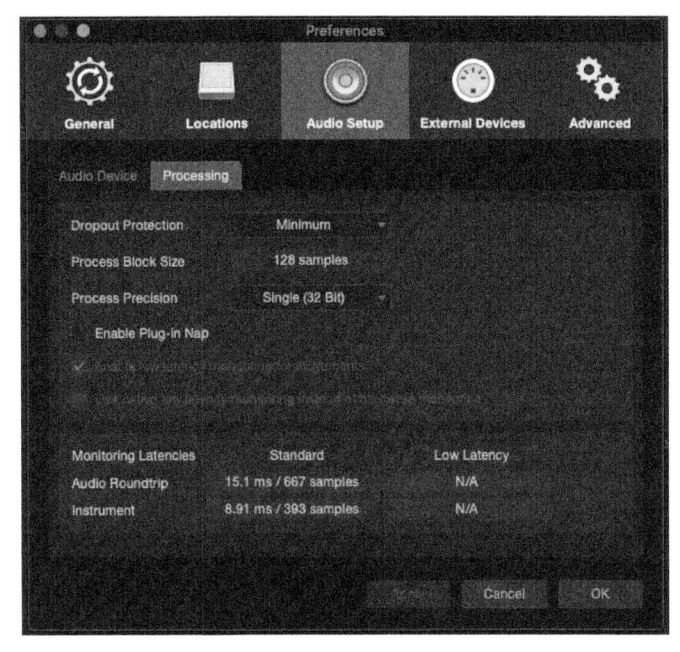

Figure 2.7: Processing tab of the Audio Setup window

This tab lets you monitor and adjust the latency added by Studio One itself. At the bottom of this tab, **Audio Roundtrip** gives you the exact time, in milliseconds, it takes for you to sing into the microphone and hear your voice in the headphones. Anything above 10 ms will be noticeable.

Here's how you can keep latency at a minimum while allowing your computer to run efficiently:

- On the **Audio Device** tab, set **Device Block Size** low enough that **Audio Roundtrip** in the **Processing** tab falls below 10 ms and leave it there.

- When you are recording and need minimum latency, set **Dropout Protection** on the **Processing** tab to **Minimum**.

- When you are finished recording, set **Dropout Protection** to a higher value. You will have higher latency but it will not be a problem (when you're mixing a song, waiting for an extra 20 ms when you press play is no big deal). You will need that extra buffer protection when you start adding plug-ins.

There are no hard and fast rules or fixed values for these settings; it all depends on your computer's processing power and your audio device's driver efficiency.

Configuring your external devices

Now let's introduce your MIDI controllers, keyboards, control surfaces, and other peripherals to Studio One. Most of these devices support plug-and-play operation, but you will need to configure them manually if you want to use them beyond standard MIDI functionality, which may be too basic for most purposes.

Studio One groups external devices under three categories. Let's go over these one by one, so that you can place your devices under the right category:

- **Keyboard** means a hardware MIDI device that is used for playing and controlling other MIDI devices and software instruments.

- **Instrument** is an external hardware device such as a synthesizer, sampler, or workstation. It uses incoming MIDI data to generate or manipulate sound.

- **Control Surface** refers to a hardware device with transport controls, faders, and knobs that can be used to manipulate functions and parameters in other devices or within Studio One.

Note that a hardware device may contain more than one of the device types listed here. For example, if you have an all-in-one hardware workstation that comprises a keyboard, a built-in synthesis engine, and transport controls, you will need to add it separately under each of these three categories.

Now, let's make sure your devices are configured properly so that you can get the best performance out of them.

Back on Studio One's **Start** page, click **Configure External Devices**. This will take you to the **External Devices** tab of the **Preferences** window:

Figure 2.8: External Devices window

Click **Add…**. You will be taken to the **Add Device** window:

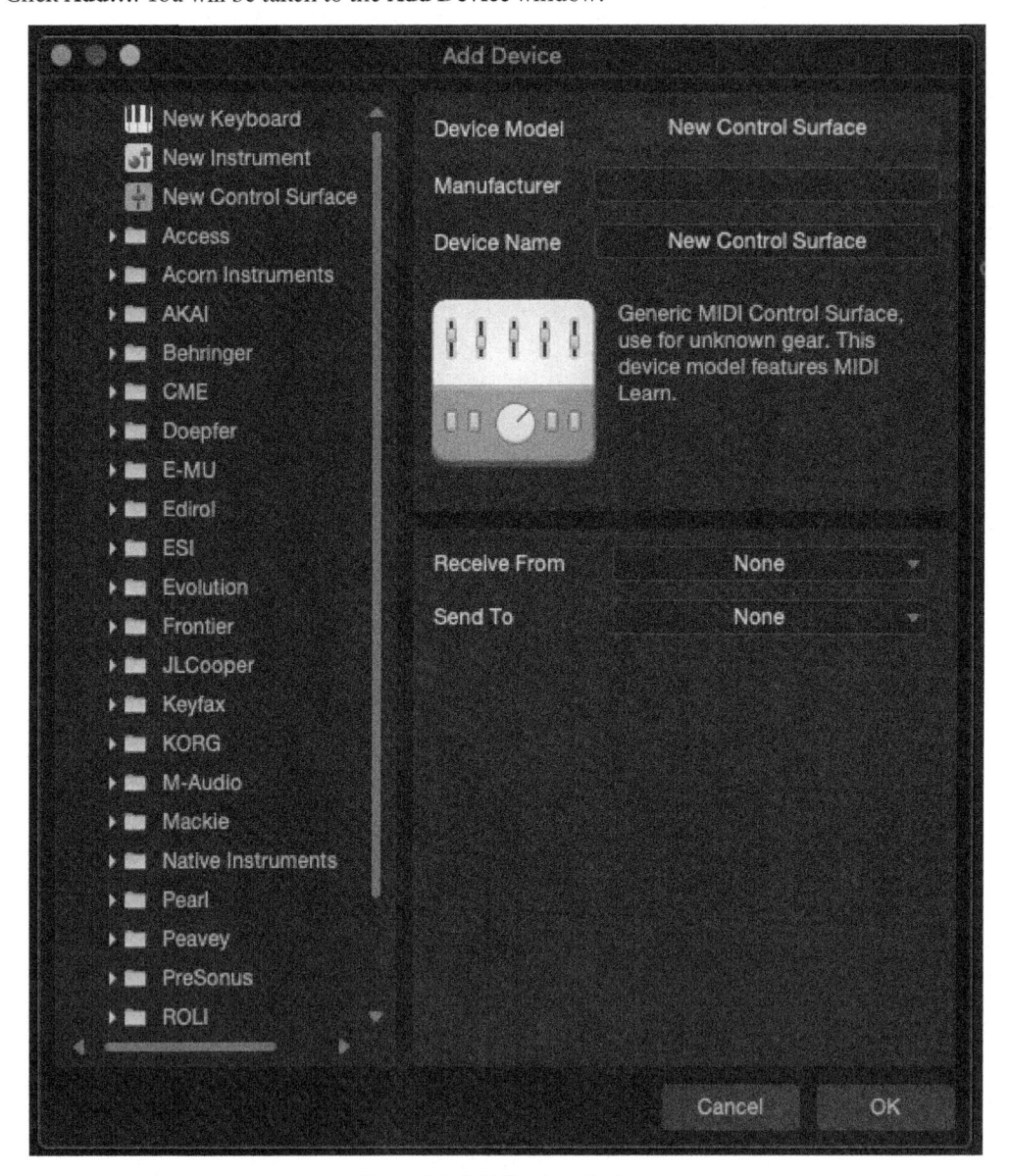

Figure 2.9: Add Device window

Use the following subsections and *Figure 2.9* to add as many devices as you need.

> **Tip**
> In this section, we will only cover the essential steps required for initial configuration. You will notice that we will skip some options listed in the menus as they require more context. Don't worry, we will get back to them in later chapters.

Adding a keyboard

To add a keyboard device, follow these steps:

1. On the left side of the **Add Device** window, you will see a list of device categories, followed by a list of equipment vendors. Scroll down and see whether you can find your device's manufacturer and model there. If you do, select it. If not, select **New Keyboard** at the top of this list.

2. In the top-right section of the **Add Device** window, provide a name for your keyboard under **Device Name**. This is the name you will be using to select this keyboard when working inside Studio One, so make it short and descriptive, especially if you'll be using more than one keyboard.

3. Underneath **Device Name**, select which MIDI channels will be active for this device. This is a powerful feature that lets you build flexible configurations.

   For example, if you have a keyboard and a separate pad controller, set your keyboard to use all channels except *Channel 10*, and set the pad controller to use *Channel 10* only. On your keyboard device, assign *Channel 10* to drum sounds. Now you can use the pad controller to play drum sounds and the keyboard to play everything else.

4. In the **Receive From** drop-down menu, select the physical connection that ties this device to the computer. If the device connects directly via USB, you will see its name here. Otherwise, it will be a generic name such as `USB MIDI Cable 1`.

5. In the **Filter** section, you may filter out unwanted MIDI messages emanating from this keyboard. Do not select anything here unless you are absolutely sure that you will not be using these MIDI messages.

6. The **Send To** drop-down list allows you to route the MIDI data from this device to another hardware device.

   For example, if you want *Keyboard X* to control *Hardware Synthesizer Y*, select *Keyboard X* for **Receive From** and *Hardware Synthesizer Y* for **Send To**. If you will only be using software synthesizers, you can leave this at its default setting: **None**.

> **Tip**
> **Send To** and **Receive From** can be confusing. Although we are configuring a keyboard device, these settings are named according to Studio One's perspective, and not the keyboard device's perspective. So, think of these settings as "Studio One will send to" and "Studio One will receive from," respectively. You want to select the device(s) that you'd like Studio One to send data to and receive data from.

This is all you need to do to make sure your MIDI keyboard is properly configured for Studio One.

Adding an instrument

Now let's take a look at how you can configure Studio One to work with your hardware instruments:

1. On the **Add Device** window, click on **New Instrument**.
2. Type a short, descriptive name for your instrument in the **Device Name** section.
3. In the **Send To** drop-down menu, select the physical connection that ties this device to the computer (most likely a MIDI interface or USB-to-MIDI converter).
4. You will probably not need to receive MIDI data from this device, so you can leave **Receive From** at its default setting: **None**.
5. You can select which MIDI channels will be used to communicate with this instrument. Set this to **All** if the instrument is multitimbral (capable of synthesizing several different instrument sounds simultaneously).

And that's how to configure instruments. Be sure to remember that if you have several instruments, you will need to repeat these steps for each of them.

Adding a control surface

Now let's add a control surface to use with Studio One:

> **Important note**
> If you have a MIDI keyboard that has knobs, faders, and transport controls and you'd like to use that keyboard as a control surface, you still need to add it as a control surface as described in this section, even if you already added it as a keyboard as per the earlier instructions.

1. On the **Add Device** window, click on **New Control Surface**.
2. Type a short, descriptive name for your control surface under **Device Name**.
3. Set the **Receive From** and **Send To** fields (as discussed in the preceding sections).

> **Tip**
> If you ever notice paranormal activity in Studio One, such as faders or knobs moving by themselves even when the project is not playing, your control surface is the first suspect. Some devices emit continuous MIDI data in the background, which Studio One may falsely interpret as legitimate commands. Refer to your device's user manual to see whether you can disable the offending data stream.

You have now properly introduced all your hardware devices to Studio One; they are optimized and ready to start working their magic on your first project.

In the next section, we will talk about disk performance, a serious issue that typically causes bottlenecks in most home studios.

Optimizing your system for best performance

Let's consider a common scenario: say you have a laptop computer with a conventional **hard disk drive** (**HDD**) and you're working on a modest project with 10 audio tracks and 10 virtual instrument tracks.

Now, if you want to record another audio track on top of that, here's what's going to happen: as soon as you click the record button, Studio One will try to simultaneously read audio data from all 10 existing audio tracks, retrieve sound sets for the virtual instrument tracks, and write data for the new track that you're recording on.

Keeping up with this amount of data flow is demanding even for a fast HDD, and it will become even more so as the project grows bigger. Add to this the fact that the operating system may need to use the disk for background tasks of its own, and we're pushing the disk way beyond its limits. HDDs are equipped with buffer memories to avoid this and they can continue to provide an uninterrupted flow of input and output for a limited time, but that's not enough for today's music projects with several high-resolution audio tracks.

Here's another scenario: say that you have a laptop computer with a **solid-state drive** (**SSD**). In contrast to an HDD, the SSD will be able to keep up with even the most demanding projects thanks to its instant, random access capability, but this time you will run into storage space limitations. As you grow your sound set, loop, and audio sample collection, you will find that you need terabytes of space, and it may become too expensive to store all of that material, as well as your projects, on an SSD.

Now let's talk about how you can configure disk usage to get the best performance out of your system. The steps we discuss here will not only optimize your system's efficiency but will also allow you to grow and upgrade your setup with minimum hassle in the future as well.

Working with multiple disks

The best solution is to distribute this load across several discs. Let's talk about the ideal scenario first and then we will focus on how to adjust this to fit your particular setup.

The ideal scenario offers excellent performance, is cost-effective, and comprises the following:

- **Disk 1**: A system disk that contains the operating system, programs, and plug-ins. This can be an HDD; it will not need to read and write huge bursts of data.

- **Disk 2**: A disk for your active projects. Think of this as your workbench. This will be an SSD and it will contain only the projects that you're currently working on. Since you will only have a couple of projects here at any given time, you won't need too much storage space, so an SSD with a smaller capacity (and lower price) will suffice.

- **Disk 3**: A disk for your sound sets, audio samples, and loops. As mentioned, your collection will inevitably grow, and you will soon find that you need terabytes of space to accommodate them. The good news is that this can be an HDD as well, just like your system disk; although it will be reading audio data, the demand for continuous output will not be as heavy as on the project drive, so any HDD with a speed of 7,200 RPM and above will be able to cope easily.

  If you choose to get an external disk for this purpose, you will have the additional benefit of using the same disk with all your computers. Just plug it in and you're good to go; there is no need to install the same terabytes of data on each computer. Just make sure that the disk (and each computer) supports USB 3.0. Earlier versions of USB may impose a bottleneck on transmission speed.

- **Disk 4**: A disk (or two) to back up and archive your projects. An external HDD with lots of storage capacity is ideal for this one.

If you have a desktop computer with a tower design, simply install disks 1 and 2 as internal disks. You can also install disk 3 as an internal disk if you don't plan to share your sound assets with other computers.

If you have a laptop computer, your best bet is to use the internal SSD as disks 1 and 2 and to keep disks 3 and 4 as external drives.

This takes care of the most severe hardware issue that hinders digital audio workstations. But we need to let Studio One know about our new configuration; otherwise, it will continue to save projects to default locations and look for assets in all the wrong places. Let's take care of that right now.

Configuring file locations

Follow these steps to tell Studio One where to look for existing files and where to create new files:

1. On the top menu, click **Studio One** and then **Preferences** (Mac) or **Options** (Windows). Then, select **Locations**:

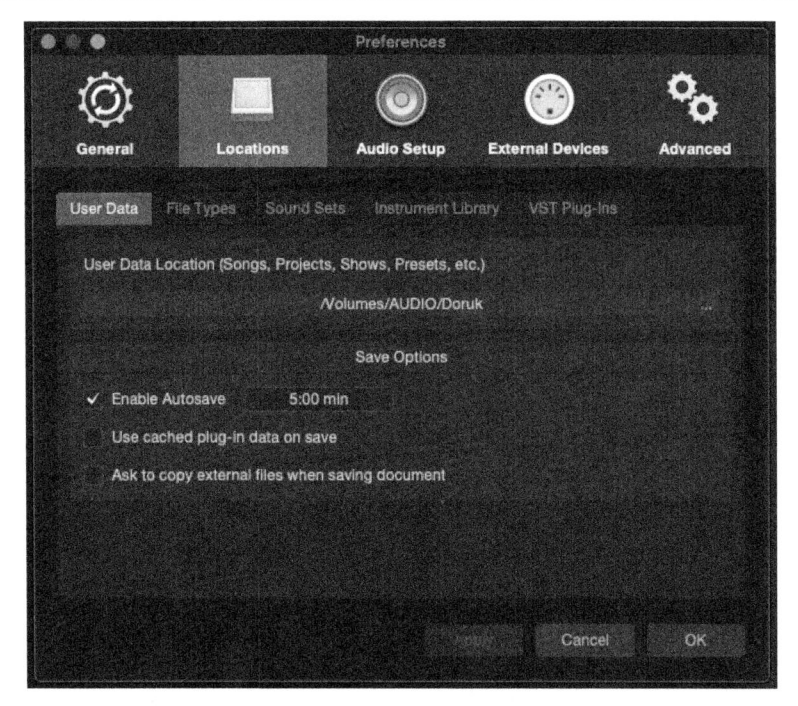

Figure 2.10: Locations window

2. The **User Data** tab of this window allows you to choose a default destination for your Songs, Projects, and Shows – basically anything you will be creating in Studio One. Here, select your *Disk 2* (discussed in the preceding section) as the default destination. From now on, all your work will be saved here, with each project or song automatically grouped under separate folders.

3. While in the **User Data** tab, make sure that the **Enable Autosave** option is active. When you're working on a project, this automatically creates backup copies of your project file at specified intervals (that you can set in the field to the right). These backup copies are stored in a folder called **History** that resides within your project folder. If something goes wrong (power failure, system freeze, or a wrong move that **Undo** cannot fix), you can open the most recent backup and continue from there. Studio One only keeps the 10 most recent backups, so this will not fill up your disk with unnecessary clutter.

4. You will remember that in the first part of this chapter, when you downloaded sound sets and loops, you left them in your **Downloads** folder, and I promised we would come back to them. Then, in the preceding section, we talked about where your sound sets should reside, and we called it *Disk 3*. Now, you can move all your sound sets and loops from your **Downloads** folder to *Disk 3*. Feel free to organize them under arbitrary folders to find them easily. It doesn't matter if *Disk 3* is external or internal – the procedure will be the same.

34   Installing and Configuring Your Studio One Environment

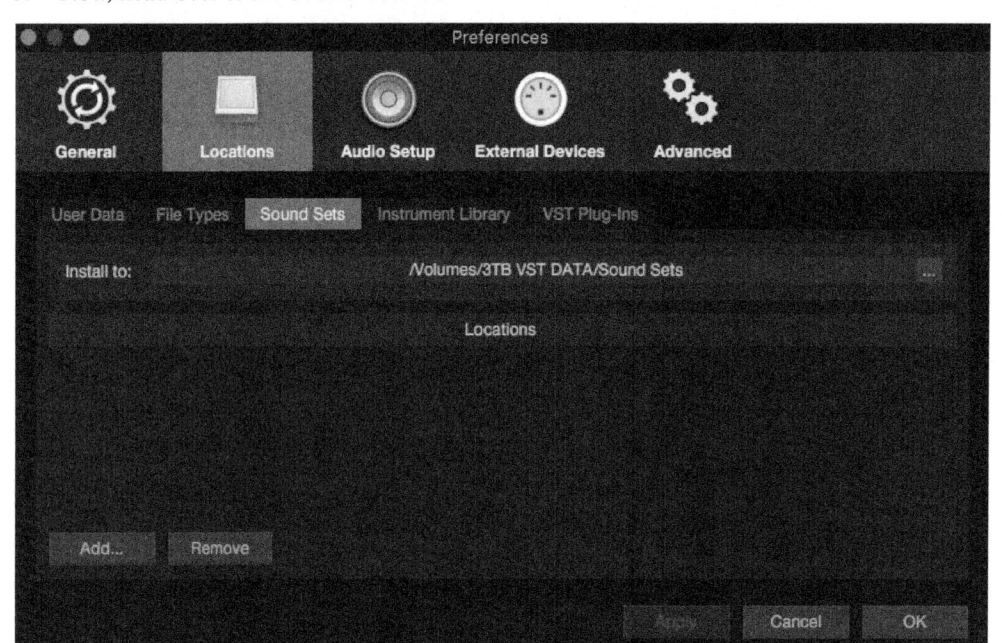

5. Now, head over to the **Sound Sets** tab:

Figure 2.11: Locations window | Sound Sets tab

6. Here, click **Add** and point the location selector to the top folder on *Disk 3* containing all your sound sets and loops. Click **Apply**, then **OK**. Studio One will scan this folder every time you launch it and assets located here will be available for use in your projects.

7. Then, click **Install to** and again point to the same folder. Click **Apply**, then **OK**. Any additional content you download after this point will automatically be installed in that folder.

Excellent! You have not only taken care of one of the biggest hardware issues but also future-proofed your system for a long time to come. Thanks to these best practices, your projects will stay organized and your workflow will be much smoother.

Summary

In this chapter, we downloaded and installed Studio One and all the additional content that you will need to get started with making music in your studio. We added and configured external devices and optimized Studio One to work as efficiently as possible.

In the next chapter, we will take a deep dive into the Studio One environment. You will learn about the **Song**, **Project**, and **Show** pages, how to navigate Studio One, and the tools that we will be using in the following chapters.

3
Exploring the Studio One Environment

Some DAW programs are packed with features but are very complicated. Others are more user-friendly but light on the feature set. And then there's Studio One. It's extremely powerful yet very easy to use, thanks to a brilliant user interface that simply lets you sit down and start creating.

Saying that, there is a lot to explore beneath the surface, and the interface can only help you if you know what to look for. In this chapter, we will take a deep dive into the Studio One production environment and learn about all the different pages, windows, and tools that we will use in the following chapters. You will gain a clear understanding of the function and purpose of each page and zone in Studio One, along with learning how to work effectively with the interface and make the most of your computer screen(s).

Music projects can become crowded very quickly, so an important part of taking command of your production software is being able to navigate confidently and effectively without getting lost among tracks on the timeline.

In this chapter, we will cover the following main topics:

- Understanding the **Song**, **Project**, and **Show** pages
- Touring the user interface
- Navigating the Studio One environment

Technical requirements

To follow along with this chapter, you just need to have Studio One installed and activated on your computer.

Understanding the Song, Project, and Show pages

Studio One has three separate environments, called **pages**, designed for three different but related tasks. They provide specialized workflows for creating and presenting your music projects. It is important to understand what these pages are and what they do, which is what we will do in this chapter. These three pages are the following:

- **Song page**: This is where you will do your actual music production, including recording and editing your audio tracks, programming and tweaking your virtual instruments, arranging sections of your song, and mixing your music.
- **Project page**: You will use this page to master the song(s) you created on the **Song** page.
- **Show page**: This page will allow you to use the Songs in a live setting. You can combine your Songs in setlists, use them for playback on stage, and add real and virtual instruments.

These pages are fully integrated and dynamically linked, so the changes you make on one page will be reflected on other pages instantly.

> **Important note**
>
> The use of the words "song" and "project" becomes confusing in Studio One terminology. In almost every other production software, you create a project to work on a song (which makes total sense). But in Studio One, you create an empty Song, and when it's completed, you move it over to a Project. In other words, what is normally referred to as a project in any other production program is called a **Song** in Studio One (which is kind of unfortunate, since the program is used for creating so much more than just songs). A collection of completed Songs is referred to as a **Project**. It is common practice throughout the music industry to use the words song and project interchangeably, so we will honor that practice in this book. When referring specifically to a Studio One Song or Project, we will capitalize the first letter, as in this sentence.

Now that we know what each page in Studio One is designed for, we can go ahead and take a close look at each of them.

Touring the user interface

To get to the three pages that will be discussed, go to the **Start** page and click on the large plus sign labeled **New…**. This will open the templates browser, as seen in *Figure 3.1*:

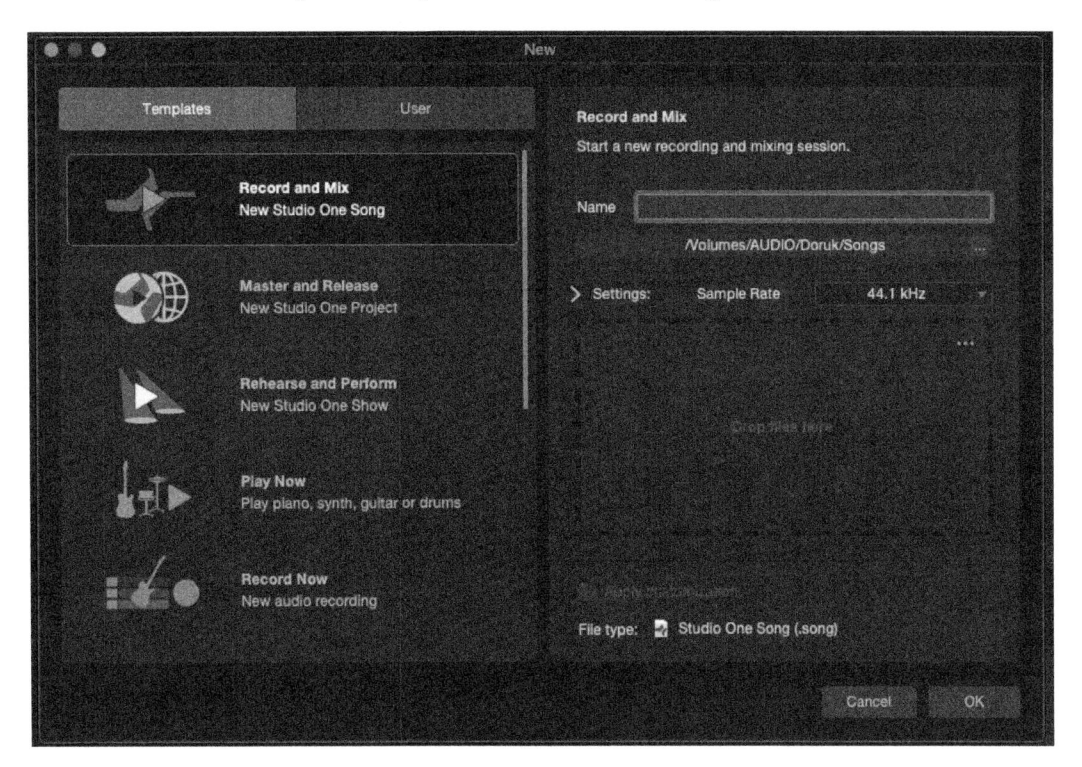

Figure 3.1: The templates browser

You can use the first three template buttons here to create a new Song, a new Project, and a new Show, respectively.

Please note that our aim in this chapter is to explore the Studio One environment and get acquainted with the windows and tools in the interface. You will learn more about the functions of these tools and windows as we progress through the book.

The Song page

The **Song** page is the heart of Studio One, where you will create and develop your projects. Here's an empty **Song** page:

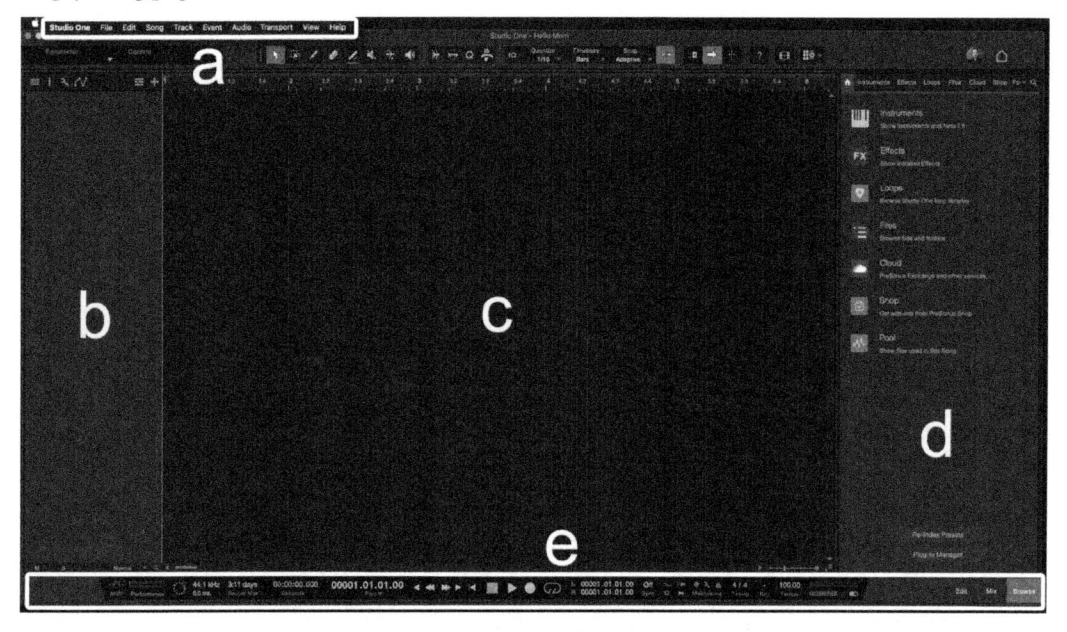

Figure 3.2: The main components of the Song page

Let's break it down. The **top menu** (*a* in *Figure 3.2*), as in any other software, hosts a multitude of commands and options at your disposal, all tucked under separate headings. We can get a closer look here:

Figure 3.3: The top menu

One of the coolest things about Studio One, however, is that you won't have to search through this menu to reach a particular function or setting. Instead, the brilliant smart contextual menus in Studio One place everything you need at your fingertips: just right-click on anything on the page – an event, an area, a clip, anything you like – and every possible command or setting related to that item will open in a floating window.

If you use keyboard shortcuts for basic file and transport operations, which is another excellent way of speeding up your workflow, you will rarely need to use the top menu at all (we will cover all these shortcuts throughout the book too).

Most of the real estate on the **Song** page is occupied by the **track window**, **arrange window**, **browse window**, and **lower panel**.

Track window

The **track window** (*b* in *Figure 3.2*) is where our audio, instrument, and other tracks will be stacked. At the top of the track window, there are a few buttons that we must mention:

Figure 3.4: Track controls

From left to right, they are as follows:

- The **Track List** button opens a window that contains a list of all the tracks in your project. As you add more and more tracks, your project will start to look crowded, and you will find yourself getting lost and distracted. You can use **Track List** to hide and reveal tracks; this allows you to just see the tracks that you are working on and helps to reduce clutter.

- The **Inspector** button opens the inspector window. When you select a track, this window will list the main parameters associated with it. So, you will be able to tweak those parameters without having to leave the arrange window (e.g., no need to go to the mix window to tweak the fader for a track).

- The wrench-shaped **Options** button opens a floating window where you can set the options for track layouts and determine what happens when you select a track.

- The **Show Automation** button tells Studio One to overlay automation curves on top of the audio waveforms in the arrange window. Displaying automation data tends to make the screen crowded, and you cannot edit audio and MIDI clips when this is active, so leave it disabled unless you are specifically working on automation.

- The **Global Track Visibility** button controls the visibility of global tracks. These tracks are always active in the background and either let you control global aspects of your project in relation to the timeline (e.g., change key or tempo at certain points on the timeline) or allow you to identify and manipulate sections of your project (by adding markers or defining song sections). Although they are always active, you do not always need them on your screen (e.g., you don't need to see the tempo track if your song will not change tempo). If you need to use a global track in your project, this is where you will find them and make them visible.

- The plus-shaped **Add Tracks** button lets you add actual tracks that you will be recording or working on. We will talk about different track types throughout the book.

Arrange window

The **arrange window** (*c* in *Figure 3.2*) is the heart of the **Song** page. This is where we will create and modify audio and MIDI clips, the basic building blocks of our song. This is also where we will arrange our song into sections (hence the name) and do most of our production work.

Above this window is the **tool selection panel**:

Figure 3.5: The tool selection panel

Here, you will find (listed from left to right) the **Arrow**, **Range**, **Split**, **Eraser**, **Paint**, **Mute**, **Bend**, and **Listen** tools. We will talk about the functions of each of these tools in detail in the following chapters.

Browse window

The **browse window** (*d* in *Figure 3.2*) can be toggled with the **Browse** button in the lower-right corner of the **Song** page and comprises several tabs that we will use quite frequently. Let's go over them:

- The **Instruments** tab is home to the virtual instruments you installed in *Chapter 2*, and any other third-party virtual instruments that you may already have on your computer. You can view them as a list or have Studio One group them under folders for easy classification. You can add a star to the instruments you use most often to place them in the **Favorites** section. To launch a virtual instrument, all you have to do is drag it from the **Instruments** tab and drop it anywhere on the arrange window.

- The **Effects** tab hosts the effects plug-ins installed on your system. Just like virtual instruments, you can have them grouped by category or by vendor and star your favorites. To add an effect as an insert to a track, drag it from the **Effects** tab and drop it on the name of that track in the track window. To add an effect on an FX channel (don't worry if this is new to you; we will come back to it in *Chapter 12*), drop it in an empty part of the arrange window.

- The **Loops** tab lists all the loops you selected and installed in *Chapter 2* (loops coming from outside the PreSonus ecosystem will not appear here; they will be under the **Files** tab). You can list loops by instrument and style and search for them using tags. There is a small player at the bottom of this tab that provides basic information on the selected loop and lets you audition it at its original tempo or your project's tempo. When you find something you like (you guessed it!), just drag and drop it on an empty part of the arrange window. Studio One will create an empty track, stretch the loop to match your project's tempo, and place it at the point where you dropped it on the timeline.

- The **Splice** tab opens a gateway to **Splice**, a sample library that offers millions of royalty-free samples and loops. This tab makes it super easy to search through Splice's vast sample database. Just drag audio or MIDI events from the arrange window and drop them on this tab, and you will receive several suggestions for material that matches your song's style. You can audition these materials directly, as Studio One will match them to your song's key and tempo. If you have a Splice membership, you get access to the entire sample library. If you don't, you still get a decent selection of loops and samples offered for free through the partnership between Splice and PreSonus.
- The **Files** tab gives you access to your computer's filesystem, just like Finder on Mac or File Explorer on Windows. If you have any loops or sounds installed on your machine that come from non-PreSonus sources, you can locate them here and drag and drop them into your project just like the **Loops** tab. This tab also has a mini player at the bottom so you can audition them and hear them at your song's tempo.
- The **Cloud** tab is your gateway to PreSonus Exchange and Studio One Pro+, which we talked about in *Chapter 1*. You can also use this tab to link to **SoundCloud** if you plan to upload your exported files directly to your account there.
- The **Shop** tab lets you peek into the PreSonus shop – it is always worth a look; there are free goodies as well.
- Finally, the **Pool** tab displays all the audio files referenced in your project. If you record something and delete it in the arrange window, the actual audio file still remains on your hard drive and is listed in this tab. In the heat of creative inspiration, you may record several takes of an idea that you later decide not to use; these will still take up space on your disk. Or you may add materials from other projects on other disks and lose track of them. This tab is a lifesaver in such situations. We'll talk about file management in detail in *Chapter 17*.

Lower panel

The **lower panel** (*e* in *Figure 3.2*) is located at the very bottom of the **Song** page and provides easy access to frequently used settings, transport controls, and global song parameters. On the far-right side of this panel, you can find toggle buttons for the edit, mix, and browse windows.

Edit window

You can open the edit window by double-clicking on any item in the arrange window, or by selecting the item and clicking on the **Edit** button in the lower panel. If you'd rather have the edit window as an independent, floating window (to maximize it on another screen, for example), you can do so by clicking the **Detach** button:

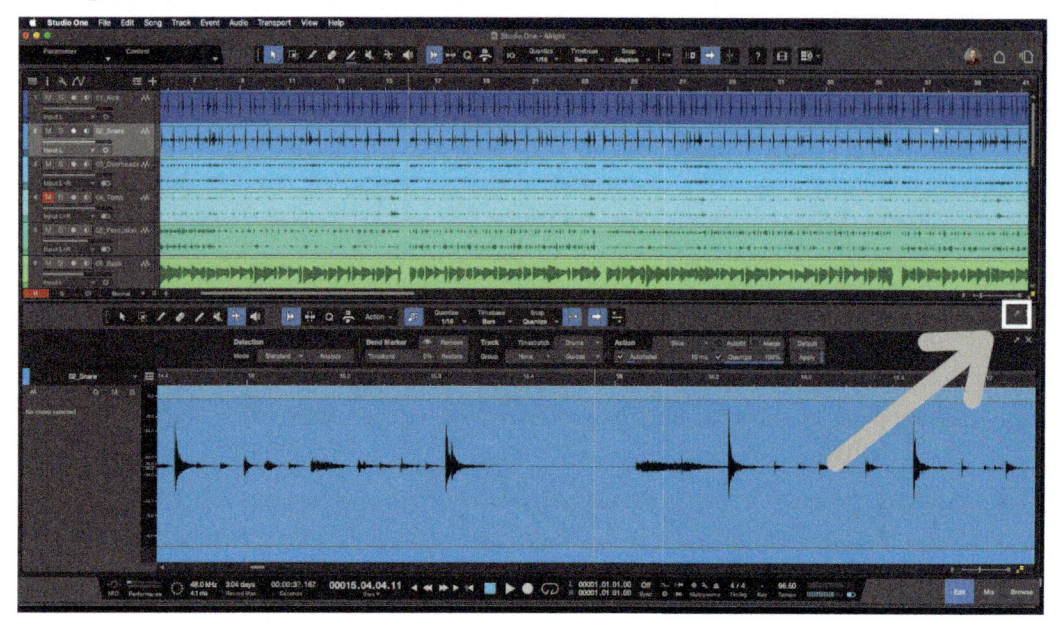

Figure 3.6: Song page with the edit window open on the lower half, with the Detach button marked

You will notice that the edit window has exactly the same set of tools and options as the top panel. It is important to remember that this window can be configured independently. So you can, for example, select the **Arrow** tool in the arrange window (upper half of the screen) and the **Bend** tool in the edit window (lower half of the screen). The tool will then change accordingly as you go back and forth between the two windows.

Mix window

Finally, you can open the mix window by double-clicking on any track or by using the **Mix** button in the far-right corner of the lower panel. The mix window also has a **Detach** button just like the edit window, but for some reason, this one is located on the far-left side instead:

Figure 3.7: The mix window and its Detach button

Although you will be doing most of your production work on the **Song** page, Studio One Pro offers two more environments, called the **Project** page and the **Show** page, which allow you to apply mastering to your tracks and perform music live on stage, respectively. We will put these environments through their paces in *Chapters 15* and *16*, but now is a good time to get acquainted with their interfaces. That's exactly what we are going to do in the next section.

The Project page

Studio One is the only DAW that offers a separate environment for mastering audio. The **Project** page provides a specialized and powerful workflow that streamlines the mastering process.

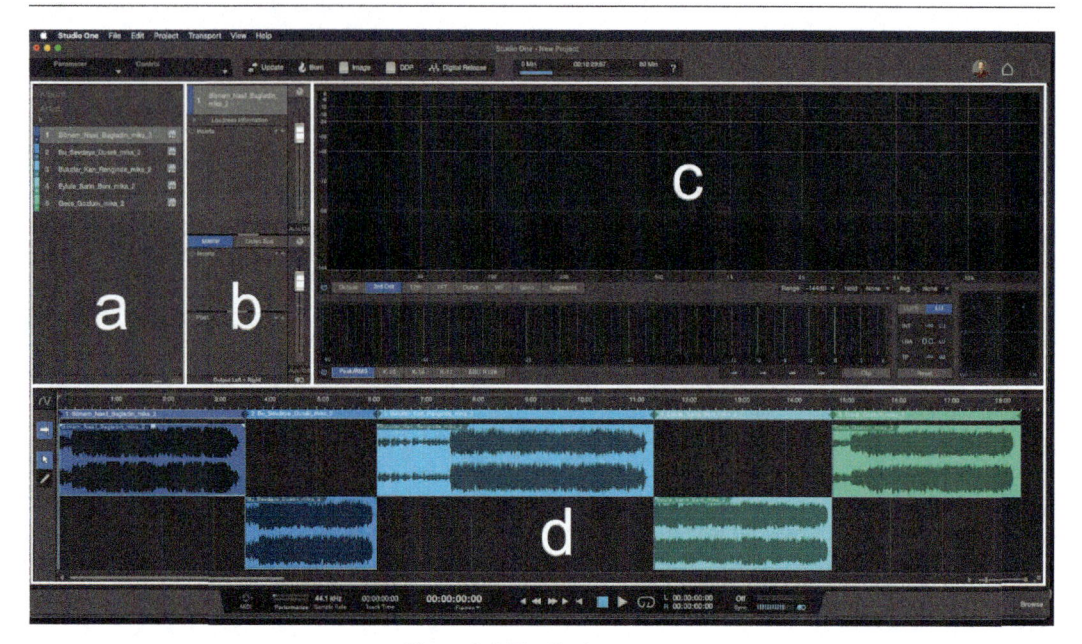

Figure 3.8: The Project page

Compared to the **Song** page, the **Project** page is very straightforward – there are no extra windows or hidden panels here:

- **Track column** (*a* in *Figure 3.8*): This is where your completed Songs – the Songs you want to combine within a Project – are displayed in the form of a playlist
- **Effects window** (*b* in *Figure 3.8*): This is used to apply effects to individual tracks or the entire Project
- **Metering window** (*c* in *Figure 3.8*): This comprises a host of analysis tools tailored for audio mastering
- **Work area** (*d* in *Figure 3.8*): This is where you get to fine-tune your songs for final release

Audio mastering is usually intimidating for beginners, but this unique workflow makes it much more accessible. We will have an in-depth look at this page and the mastering process in general in *Chapter 15*.

Up next, we'll take a look at a unique work environment that allows you to harness the power of Studio One Pro to deliver live performances on stage.

The Show page

With the **Show** page, Studio One has boldly stepped into the live performance territory, where **Ableton Live** has been the undisputed king for two decades. It's a brilliant idea: a DAW has all the tools needed for live music production – you can feed all your live instruments and vocals into it, apply effects and tweak them to your heart's content, add software instruments, and support your performance with backing tracks, all in real time. But a typical DAW interface is optimized for detailed production work, and trying to use it on stage is like digging a hole with a needle. On stage, you need access to only a handful set of features, and you need to have them right under your fingers.

The **Show** page is a simple, stripped-down interface that has only what you will need on stage. If you need to do detailed work, the **Song** page is one click away. The first thing you will notice upon entering the **Show** page is its simplicity:

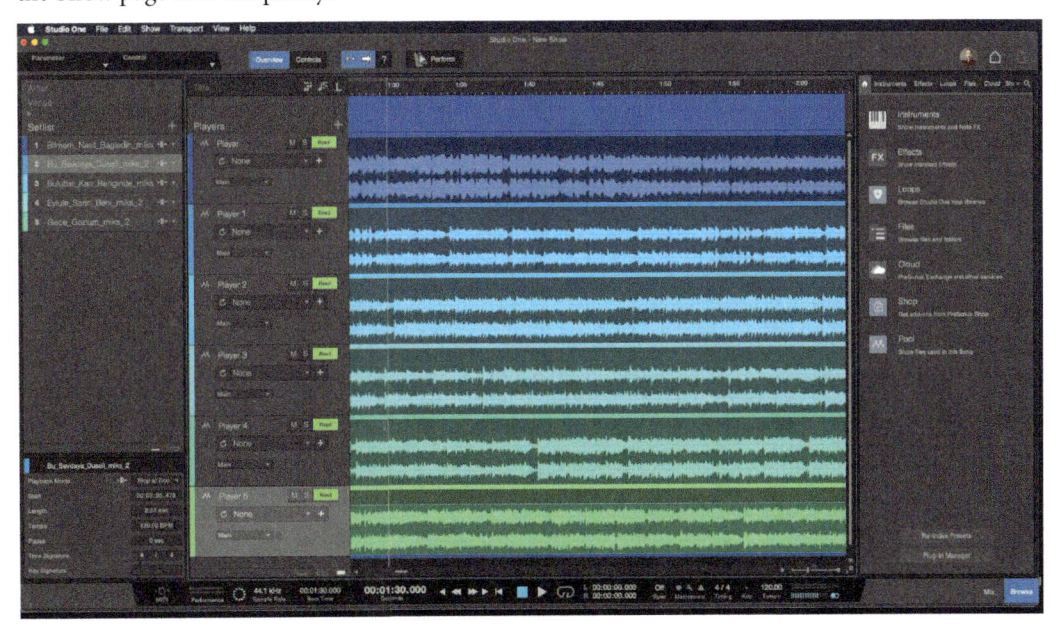

Figure 3.9: The Show page

There's a functional deviation from Studio One's design aesthetic: the controls on this interface are bigger and provide more contrast, for better visibility in poor lighting conditions and on smaller screens.

The **Show** page is extremely fun to work with: you can bring your Studio One Songs into your live set as stems and use them as backing tracks, add virtual instruments and live instruments on the fly, set them up exactly how you want them to sound throughout your live performance, and let Studio One handle everything while you simply focus on your performance. We will put the **Show** page through its paces in *Chapter 16*.

In this section, we took a close look at the Studio One environment and learned about the pages, windows, and tools that you will be using extensively in the following chapters. There's only one thing left to talk about before we actually start creating music in Studio One: how to navigate effectively in your projects. Following these best practices will save you time and speed up your workflow, allowing you to focus on the music rather than the software.

Navigating the Studio One environment

Music production requires a great deal of mental concentration. From the moment you start creating your first musical idea all the way to mastering a finished song, you need to be in the flow and fully focused on what you're trying to achieve. One common source of distraction is the DAW software itself. It's hard to immerse yourself in a project when the user interface keeps getting in the way.

Being able to navigate effectively inside a project is a crucial skill that most people tend to overlook. Time and again I see students getting lost amid the tracks in their projects and losing their concentration looking for something on the interface, only to miss a precious moment of inspiration.

This section will introduce a skill set that you will be using in the following chapters, and in all your future projects. So, make a point of coming back here from time to time to see whether you're up to speed with all the best practices we will be discussing.

Window management

When working in Studio One, you will spend most of your time on the **Song** page. As we saw in the preceding section, this page comprises several windows and panels; because of this, time and again, I see students struggling to find their way on a page like the one shown in *Figure 3.10*.

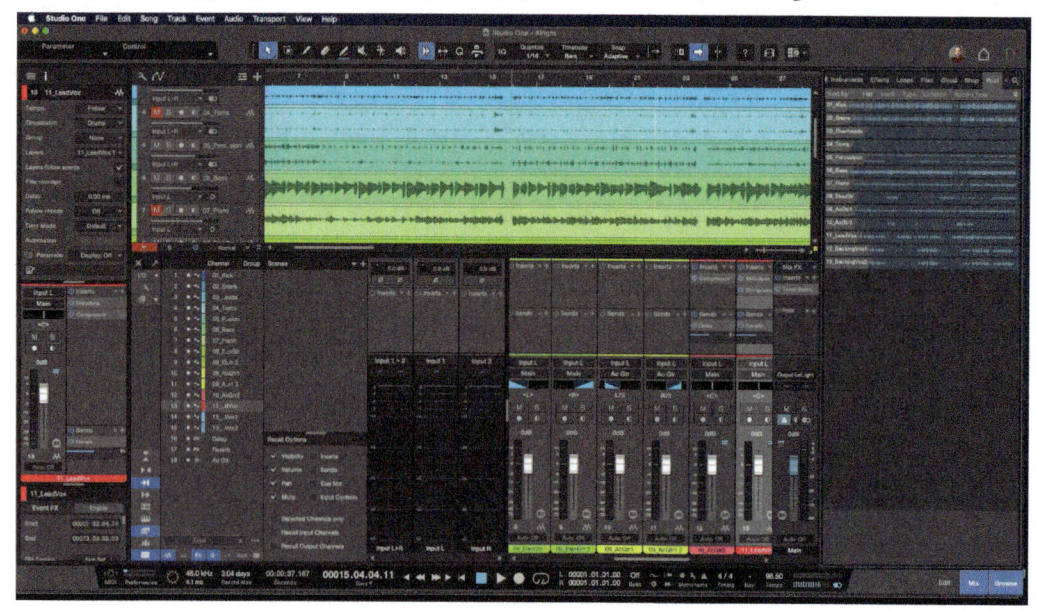

Figure 3.10: A cluttered screen

This window layout may be ideal for promotional content showing off Studio One's bells and whistles, but it's an ergonomic nightmare – there's no way you will ever need to have all these windows open at the same time. Not only does it make it hard to find what you're looking for, but it causes eye fatigue as well.

The first step, then, is to close all the windows that you don't need at any given time. Like any good habit, you might have to remind yourself to do this in the beginning, but it will soon become second nature.

The second step is to simplify the user interface to show you only the elements that you will actually need. Right-click anywhere on the toolbar and select **Customize**. This will open the **customization editor**:

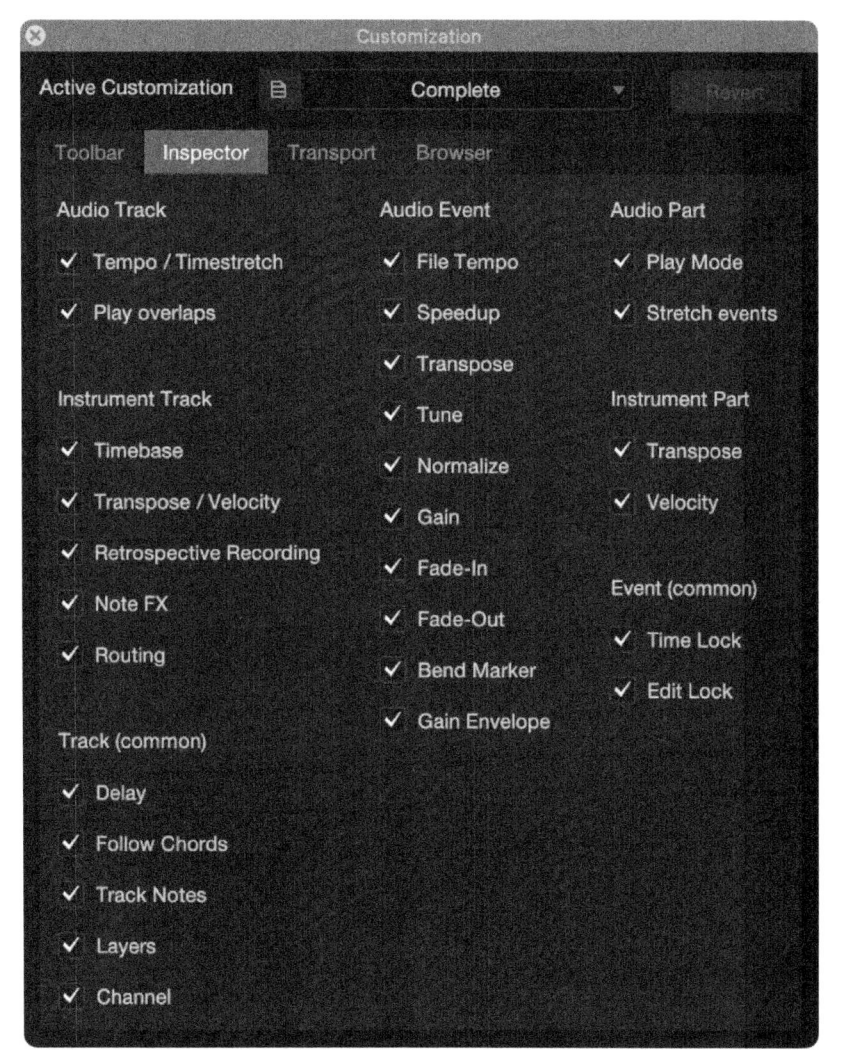

Figure 3.11: Customization editor

You can use this window to display or hide almost every element in the user interface. If you're new to Studio One, you may not be certain as to which elements you will need at first, so there are several presets to help you get started. Click on the **Active Customization** pull-down menu at the top of this window and select the preset that matches your current task – recording, editing, mixing, and so on.

> **Tip**
> If at any point you cannot find a button or display mentioned in this book or a tutorial, select **Complete** in the **Active Customization** menu. This will make sure that every available user interface element is being displayed.

Zoom levels

Studio One lets you zoom in and out of your project both horizontally and vertically. This is an obvious feature that many people overlook. Working at the correct zoom level and using the right tools to change it makes a big difference in your production efficiency. Here are some zooming best practices that will allow you to stay focused on your projects:

- Memorize and use these keyboard shortcuts: *E* will zoom in and *W* will zoom out horizontally, while *Shift + E* zooms in and *Shift + W* zooms out vertically. Alternatively, use the *Ctrl* key + mouse wheel for vertical zooming and *Ctrl + Shift* key + mouse wheel for horizontal zooming.
- Use the pinch gesture to zoom in and out if your computer has a touchpad that supports it.
- Zoom out to the song level (so you can see both the beginning and end of your entire song in the arrange window) and stay there unless you have a valid reason to zoom back in. This helps you to focus on the entirety of your song and reduces eye fatigue due to unnecessary scrolling.
- Don't use the arrange window for microsurgery. That's what the edit window is for. When you need to do delicate work on a part of your production, double-click that part to open it in the edit window. You can set zoom levels independently for these two windows, so you can go ahead and zoom in all the way to the sample level on the edit window if you like.
- A very practical way of zooming in in Studio One is to bring your mouse to the point on the ruler where you want to zoom in – for example, if you want to zoom in at the beginning of measure 9, point your cursor like so:

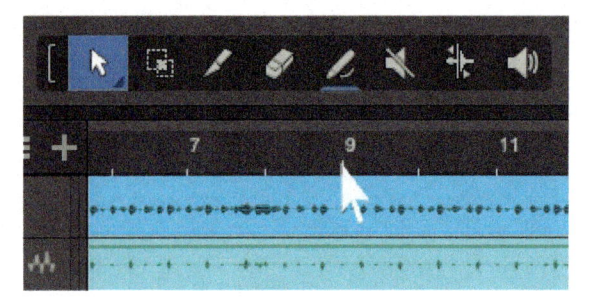

Figure 3.12: Zooming with a mouse

Then, click and drag the mouse down the screen to zoom in as much as you want. When you're done editing, click and drag up the screen at the same point to zoom back out. The edit window has its own ruler, so you can perform this trick there as well.

- Studio One has presets for vertical zoom levels, which can be accessed on the lower end of the track window:

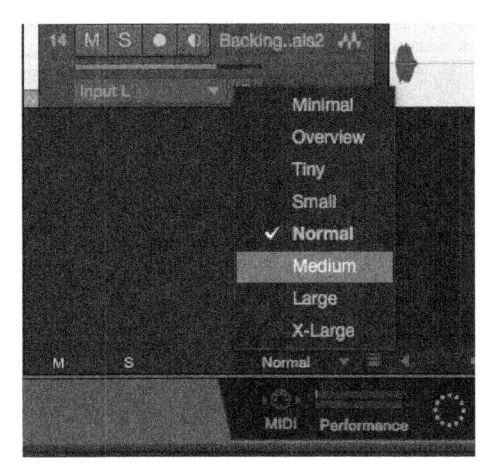

Figure 3.13: Track height or vertical zoom presets

- You can set keyboard shortcuts for these presets to quickly set all tracks to the same height. To do that, go to **Studio One** on the top menu and select **Keyboard Shortcuts**:

Figure 3.14: The Keyboard Shortcuts window

Then type `track height` in the **Search** box and select the track height you want to create a shortcut for (**Overview** is a good place to start). After that, in the **Enter key** field, type in the key combination you'd like to use for this shortcut. Studio One will warn you if that combination is already reserved for another shortcut. Once you find a key combination that both you and Studio One are happy with, click **Apply**, then **OK**.

- If you want to synchronize the zoom levels between the arrange window and edit window, you can do so by activating the **Synchronize Editor to Arrangement** button:

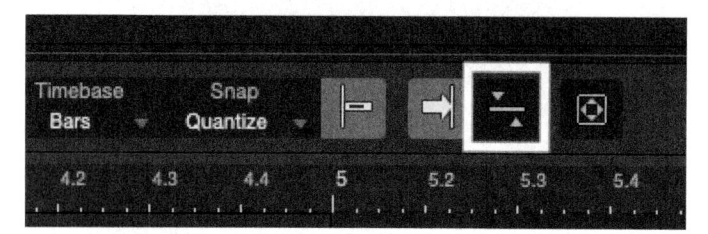

Figure 3.15: The Synchronize Editor to Arrangement button

- Always keep the **Autoscroll** button enabled so that when the project is playing, you can see where you are on the timeline:

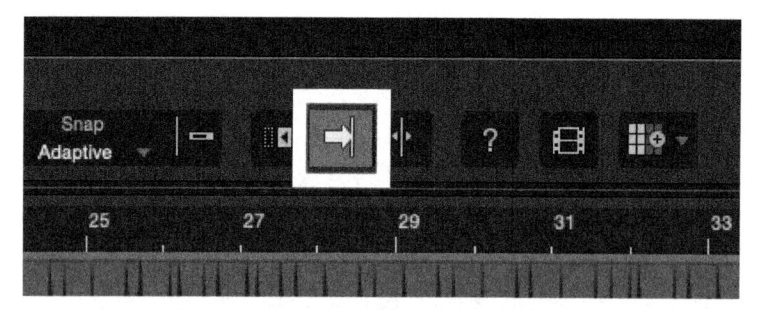

Figure 3.16: The Autoscroll button

The only time you want to turn it off is when you are zoomed in too closely and do not want to lose your position when you hit the **Play** button.

- If an audio track is recorded too quietly and you cannot see the waveforms, you can magnify them using the **Data Zoom** slider in the lower-right corner:

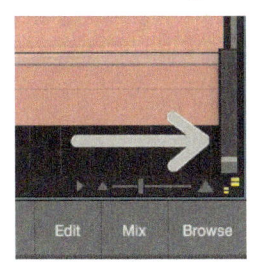

Figure 3.17: The Data Zoom slider

It will look like you're turning up the gain on all your audio tracks, but don't worry; you're only magnifying the audio waveforms for better viewing.

Working at the correct zoom level will make it easy enough for you to go anywhere you want in your project. Now let's take a look at some final tips that will make your sailing even smoother.

Extra navigation tips

Here are some finer tips and tricks to let you zero in on the essence of your project and stay focused, without getting distracted by details on the interface. Before we go on, you must promise that you will never, ever use the scroll bars for navigation:

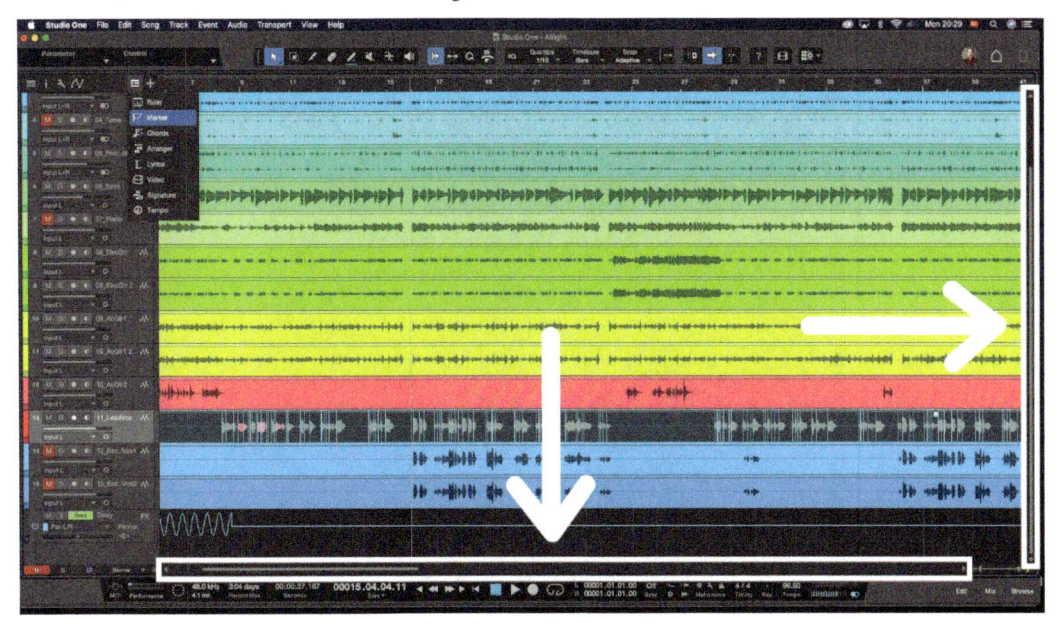

Figure 3.18: The horizontal and vertical scroll bars (don't use these!)

Scroll bar controls are jerky and imprecise; you will end up jumping all around the arrange window until you find the location that you're looking for. Instead, to scroll vertically, use your mouse wheel, and to scroll horizontally, press *Shift* and then use your mouse wheel. If you're on a laptop computer with no mouse, use the two-finger scroll gesture on your touchpad.

Now onto some pro tips for smooth navigation:

- Press . (the period key) on your keyboard to go to the beginning of your project (known as **return to zero**).
- By default, the only way to go to a specific time in your project is to click on the corresponding time on the ruler. But why limit yourself to the tiny ruler when you have plenty of space in the arrange window? Click the **Options** button on the track window and check **Locate when clicked in empty space**. Now, when you want to jump to a specific time in your project, just click on any empty part of the arrange window corresponding to that time and you'll be there instantly!
- Sometimes you want the timeline to return to its initial position when you stop playing or recording, and sometimes you want it to stay wherever it is. There is an option called **Return to Start on Stop**, which you can toggle by pressing the *Option* (Mac)/*Alt* (Windows) key and *0* on your numeric keypad. If you don't have a numeric keypad on your keyboard, just go to the **Keyboard Shortcuts** window and change the shortcut to something that works best for you.
- As your project becomes more and more complex, you will need to jump back and forth between specific points in your song. This is where **markers** come in. Markers are a convenient way to define and jump to specific points in a project, such as the beginning of a song's chorus. To start using markers, click on the **Global Track Visibility** button and select **Marker**:

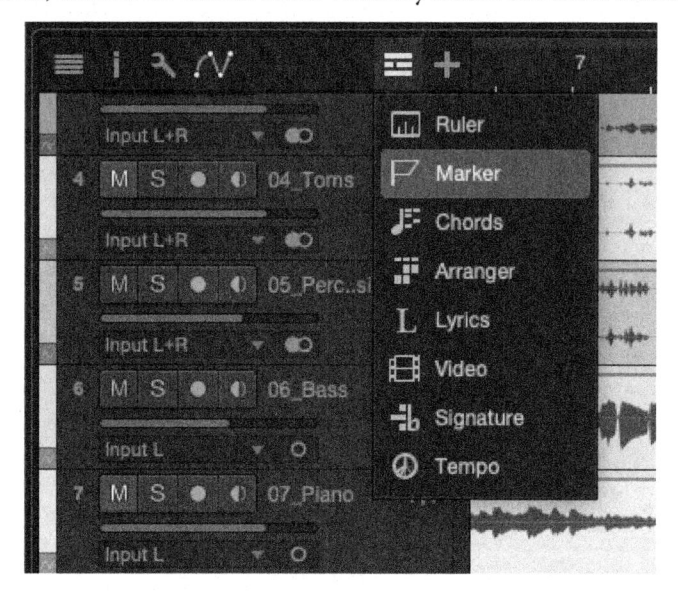

Figure 3.19: Opening the marker track

This will open the marker track at the top of the arrange window. Now click on any point in time that you want to enter a marker for (e.g., the beginning of the verse at measure 9). Then, click the + sign on the marker track to add a new marker at that point in time:

Figure 3.20: Adding a new marker

You can add as many markers as you need. Double-click on these markers to name them (*verse*, *chorus*, *build*, *drop*, etc.). You can easily jump between markers by using the numbers on your numeric keypad; keys *1* and *2* are reserved for loop-in and loop-out points (which we'll talk about in the following chapters), so markers will be automatically assigned to keys *3* and above.

You are now able to jump to any point in your project without even thinking about it and have full control of the navigation tools. The user interface is at your command.

Summary

In this chapter, we took a deep dive into the three main environments in Studio One: the **Song**, **Project**, and **Show** pages. We analyzed the user interface for each of these environments and introduced the terminology that will be used in the following chapters. Then, we discussed several best practices pertaining to project layout and navigation to help make your workflow smooth and efficient. Sticking to these best practices will help immensely when you start working on larger, more complicated projects.

In the next chapter, you will create your first Studio One Song.

Part 2: Creating in Studio One

In this part, you will create your first Song in Studio One. Then, you will learn how to record audio using a microphone or instrument. Finally, you will learn how to work with virtual instruments and record MIDI data to bring your musical ideas to life.

This part includes the following chapters:

- *Chapter 4, Creating a New Song*
- *Chapter 5, Recording Your First Audio Track*
- *Chapter 6, Adding Virtual Instruments and Recording MIDI*

4
Creating a New Song

A Song is the heart of Studio One. It's where you do most of your production work, including recording, editing, and mixing. In this chapter, we will create your first Song in Studio One together.

Music production is a highly creative process and each project is unique. You may create a new Song just to try out new ideas and see what comes out, or you may already have a fully arranged composition that you'd like to finalize. I will present a step-by-step workflow in this and the following chapters, but keep in mind that this is a flexible process and you are welcome to skip any steps that you are not ready to complete yet (you can always come back to them later).

In this chapter, we will take a close look at the options and settings available for creating a new Song. Some of these are controversial and often spark debates in studios and on the internet. This means that some technical discussion is in order, but I promise to keep it simple.

So, in this chapter, we will cover the following main topics:

- Setting up your Song and exploring the Song settings
- Changing the tempo, key signature, and time signature within the Song

Technical requirements

To follow along with this chapter, you need to have Studio One installed and activated on your computer.

Setting up your Song and exploring the Song settings

Studio One presents you with a plethora of options and settings while creating a new Song, but keep in mind that you don't have to adjust all these settings at this point. You can always come back and set them (or modify them) later. Experimentation is a huge part of music production, and at the time of creating a new Song, you may not even know what any of these settings will turn out to be. Feel free to skip any parameter that you haven't decided upon.

Now let's create your first Song together. On Studio One's **Start** page, click the large plus sign titled **New…**. This will open the **New Document** window:

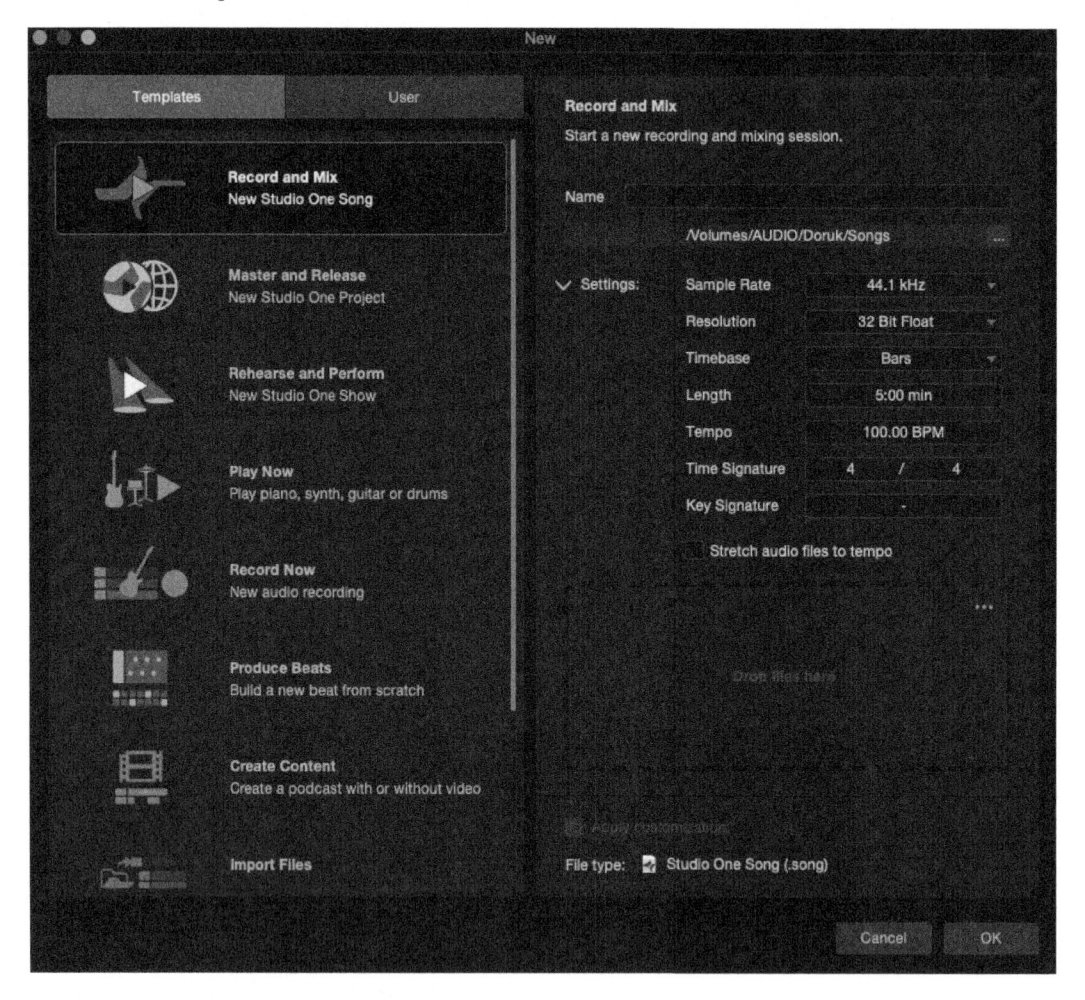

Figure 4.1: New Document window

The left column in this window holds a list of templates designed to get you started quickly even if you haven't used Studio One before. Feel free to explore these different options; however, we will be using the **Record and Mix** template here. When you select it, the right column of this window will now display a list of settings for the Song you're about to create, as seen in *Figure 4.1*.

Let's go through those settings now.

Name

It's always hard to come up with a name for a song when you're just starting out. Studio One takes care of that by automatically filling in the **Name** field with today's date and the name you selected on the Artist Profile on the **Start Page**. You can use this tentative name to create your Song now and change it later. If your song does have a name, go ahead and type it in.

Save location

The untitled field below the **Name** field lets you view and select the location where this new Song will be saved. In *Chapter 2*, we discussed the ideal location for your Song and Project files and configured Studio One accordingly. This box is now pointing to that folder.

The next two settings, **Sample Rate** and **Resolution**, are based on concepts that cause a fair bit of confusion and debate, so they merit some analysis here. Let's start with **Sample Rate**.

Sample Rate

When you connect a microphone or an instrument to your audio interface (commonly known as your sound card), the interface will convert the analog signal coming from these sources into **digital** data (ones and zeros) that the computer can work with. To do this, the **analog to digital converter** in your audio interface will **sample** the incoming analog signal at regular intervals.

This is similar to how a video camera operates; it captures still images (frames) of continuous movement at given intervals. When these still images are played back, this creates the illusion of continuous movement.

Audio interfaces work much faster than video cameras, though: whereas video cameras typically capture around 24 to 30 frames per second, audio interfaces typically sample the audio signal 44,100 times during the same period. This is called the **sample rate**. An audio interface that samples incoming signals at 44,100 times per second is said to have a sample rate of 44,100 Hertz (Hz) or 44.1 Kilohertz (kHz).

In the **New Document** window, the options available in the **Sample Rate** drop-down menu will depend on your audio device's capabilities. Most devices manufactured today support a wide variety of sample rates, all the way up to 192 kHz.

This is where the debate begins: some argue that higher sample rates deliver higher sound quality, suggesting, therefore that you should set this as high as your device allows you to. A detailed discussion of digital audio is outside the scope of this book, but if you'd like to know more about the science behind the technology, a good starting point is to look up *Nyquist theorem*, on which all our current digital audio technology is based.

> **Further reading**
>
> If you're curious to dig a little deeper into how digital audio really works, check out the article below – it's a great starting point: https://www.soundonsound.com/sound-advice/all-about-digital-audio-part-1

The fact of the matter is that a sample rate of 44.1 kHz provides perfectly adequate audio quality for music production (you can see I used this in *Figure 4.1*). Using higher sample rates will only result in larger audio files and a heavier load on your computer.

There are only two cases where a higher sample rate is called for:

- If you're producing audio material to be used in videos (soundtracks, sound effects, dialogues, etc.), use a sample rate of 48 kHz. This is the sample rate that video editing programs expect. If you deliver files at a different sample rate, video editing programs will convert them without complaint, but every conversion results in some degree of loss in quality, so it's better to start off with the correct setting.
- If you change the tempo of your song after recording audio, Studio One will have to apply **time stretching** (meaning it will have to stretch your audio material in order to keep it aligned with the new tempo). Although time stretching algorithms have improved significantly in the last couple of years, it's still a process that degrades sound quality, and recording with a high sample rate is the best way to minimize its artifacts. So, if you think you may change your song's tempo after recording audio, go for a high sample rate (88.2 kHz is a good choice here).

> **Important note**
>
> If you change the sample rate displayed in the **New Document** window, Studio One will initiate a sample rate change on your audio device. If the value you select here is not supported by your device or if your device does not allow third-party applications to change its sample rate, Studio One will issue a sample mismatch warning. You can still create a new Song with this warning and Studio One will try to resample incoming audio data as per your selection, but this may cause stability and performance issues. To avoid this, stick with sample rates that are supported by your audio device.

Now that we have discussed the sample rate, let's discuss resolution.

Resolution

Resolution determines how much detail will be used to express the difference between the softest and loudest parts of your recording. The difference is referred to as your recording's **dynamic range**.

At first glance, resolution and dynamic range may seem unrelated; the former is a digital term measured in **bits**, and the latter is an acoustic term measured in **decibels** (**dB**). For a quick conversion, each bit here corresponds to around 6 decibels. Hence, if you select **16 Bits** in the **Resolution** menu, this will give you around 16x6=96 decibels of dynamic range, which is more than enough for most music material. The next option, **24 Bits**, will give you around 144 decibels. It is common practice in almost every studio around the world to record at 24-bit resolution, and this is the setting that you should be using as well.

You will see that there are higher options available in the menu, and just like sample rate, there are people who argue that these deliver better sound quality. The fact of the matter is that these higher options are overkill; they deliver massive amounts of dynamic range that even falls beyond what is scientifically classified as sound on Earth. 190 dB is considered the loudest sound that air can handle; anything above that will result in a shock wave (that explosion-like phenomenon we experience when aircraft go above the speed of sound).

So, if these options are overkill, why are they available? The first reason is that some people do believe that these sound better, and are willing to use their credit cards for them. The second reason is more practical, though exceptional. If you're a sound recording professional and you're working in a very uncontrolled, unpredictable environment (e.g. you're recording a theater performance, the actors are whispering, you apply insane amounts of gain, and then they start shouting), the extended dynamic range provided by these options will provide an extra safety net. Other than that, there's no valid reason to use a setting higher than 24 bits.

So, to recap this section: for music projects, set **Sample Rate** to 44.1 kHz and **Resolution** to 24 bits. If you're producing audio material for use in videos, set **Sample Rate** to 48 kHz and **Resolution** to 24 bits.

Other New Document page settings

The following settings can easily and safely be modified later, so feel free to skip them if you're just starting to write your song and haven't decided on any of these yet.

Timebase

The **Timebase** setting adjusts how time will be displayed on the timeline ruler at the top of the **Arrange** window. Here are the options:

- **Bars**: Displays time in musical units (e.g. bars, beats, and then 8th notes, 16th notes, etc.), depending on your zoom level. This is very practical because it allows Studio One to assist you in aligning events in the **Arrange** window to musically meaningful places such as the beginning of bars and beats of a song. This is the default setting, and it's the one you'll want to use for music production.
- **Seconds**: Displays time in hours:minutes:seconds:milliseconds. Use this option if you're working, say, on a podcast recording and you want the ruler to display time in an absolute format.
- **Frames**: Displays time in hours:minutes:seconds:frames. Use this option when working with video in order to jump to specific frames.

- **Samples**: Displays time based on the sample rate we discussed in the previous section. Use this option for deep editing and microsurgery.

We will talk about timebase in detail in *Chapter 10* when we discuss working with different time units using **Ruler Track**. Now let's continue with our trip along the **New Document** menu.

Song Length

This setting lets you specify the length of your Song, which will be used to define the region to be exported once your production is complete. I have never had a reason to set this at the beginning of a project, nor seen or heard of anyone who has. Just skip this setting – you will be able to easily set your song length once your song is finished.

Tempo

First, bad news for those who are just starting out with music production in a DAW environment: you will have to record with a metronome. This is something most musicians coming from a traditional background are not accustomed to, but it's a necessary paradigm shift and you will have to get used to working with a metronome if you want to reap the benefits that made DAWs so popular in the first place. Everything in this environment is designed to work with a time grid, and if you work without a metronome, you will find it next to impossible to add instruments and use many of the editing features later on.

Now the good news: you don't have to decide on your Song's **tempo** just yet. You can create your song, experiment with different tempos, and then set it once you're happy. You can even change the tempo throughout the song and control tempo changes precisely, as we will see in the following section.

If you know what your song's tempo is, you can set it here now. If you don't, just skip this setting.

Time and key signatures

As with the tempo, you can set your song's time and key signatures at the time of creation, or you can set them later:

- Studio One uses **Time Signature** information to subdivide the timeline ruler in the **Arrange** window in accordance with your song's rhythmic structure. Setting this correctly is a prerequisite for properly using Studio One's excellent editing features, including aligning events perfectly across a musical grid. This information is also used by Studio One's metronome to place accented beats synchronized to your song's rhythmic pulse. Looking at *Figure 4.1*, the number on the left (known as the **numerator**) indicates the number of beats in a bar and can be set to any value. The number on the right (known as the **denominator**) shows the note value corresponding to each beat, and can only be set to common note values (4, 8, 16, and 32). So if your song is in 9/8, for example, set these values to 9 and 8, respectively.

- The **Key Signature** setting offers a more limited advantage: It affects the notes that can be selected in the **Score** view. So you need to fill this in only if you are going to use the **Score** view to display and/or print notes from within your song.

Now that Studio One knows the main parameters for the Song you're about to create, there's one last step we need to talk about before you hit the **OK** button.

Adding external files

If there are external files that you'd like to use in your project, you can import them at the time of creation by simply dropping them into the box titled **Drop files here**. Studio One will automatically create individual tracks for them and place them at the beginning of the Song.

If **Stretch audio files to tempo** is selected, Studio One will try to adjust these files to match the tempo you just selected in this window. Some audio files have tempo information contained in their meta tags. If they don't, Studio One will use its own tempo detection algorithm to make a guess. Deselect this option if you want to import audio material that should be left as is – dialogue, sound effects, and so on.

> **Tip**
> If you need to change the **Stretch audio files to tempo** setting after you have created a Song, go to the top menu, click **Song**, and then **Song Setup**.

Now we have covered all the settings available for creating a new Song. By clicking **OK** on the **New Document** window, you will be taken to your first Song in Studio One.

If you're planning to change tempo, key signature, or time signature through the course of your song, it's a good idea to map these out before you start recording, and that's what we are going to do in the next section. Again, keep in mind that you can always come back and complete these steps later.

Changing the tempo, key signature, and time signature within the Song

You can change the tempo, key signature, and time signature as many times as you like throughout your Song. Studio One handles these changes using the **Global Track** family. Global tracks by default span the entire arrangement and each of them controls a dedicated function, allowing you to view and modify the status of their respective functions throughout the arrangement. These tracks are always active, but by default, they are hidden from view. To reveal them, click the **Global Track Visibility** button:

Figure 4.2: Global Track Visibility button

In this section, we will work with two of these global tracks: **Signature** and **Tempo**. Let's start by looking at how you can change tempo throughout your song.

Using the Tempo track to change your Song's tempo

You may want to apply subtle tempo changes to breathe life into a recording that sounds mechanical, or you may want to introduce a radical tempo change in the middle of a song for dramatic impact. These are all very easy to accomplish in Studio One, and any element in your music that is synced to tempo will continue to remain synced.

To get started, click the **Global Track Visibility** button and select **Tempo**. This will reveal the **Tempo** track:

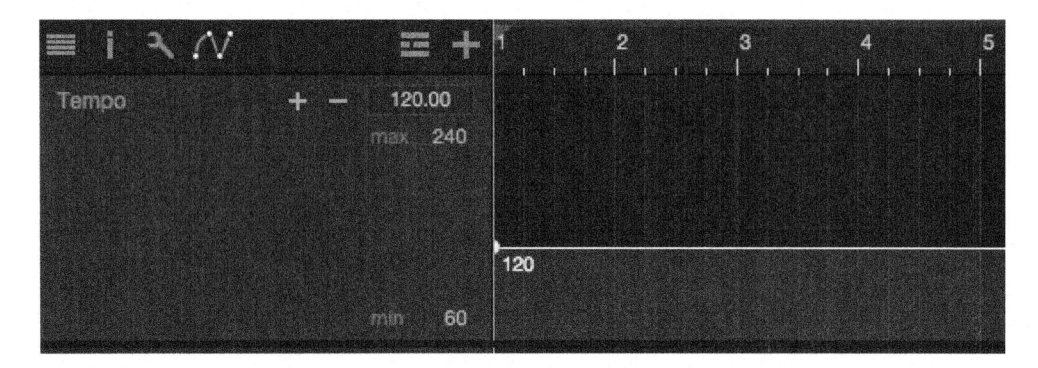

Figure 4.3: The Tempo track

From here, you have two options: You can change tempo gradually over time, or you can set the tempo to jump to a different value at a specific point in time (e.g., switch to a faster tempo in the chorus of the song). Let's explore both options.

Here's how to change tempo gradually over time:

1. Select the **Arrow** tool by pressing *1* on your keyboard.
2. Click anywhere on the **Tempo** track to insert a tempo change. Studio One will insert a dot at the location that you clicked on.
3. Drag that dot up and down to change the tempo to the desired value. You can also drag it left or right to adjust its position in time.
4. Repeat *steps 2* and *3* to enter as many tempo changes as you like.
5. Now hover your mouse over the ramp between any two dots. A hollow dot will appear. Drag this up or down, left or right, to turn the straight line into a curve (or parabola). Applying a tempo change with a parabola tends to yield a smoother result compared to a linear tempo change. In *Figure 4.4*, the tempo changes linearly between measures 1 through 4 and smoothly (with a curve) between measures 4 through 7:

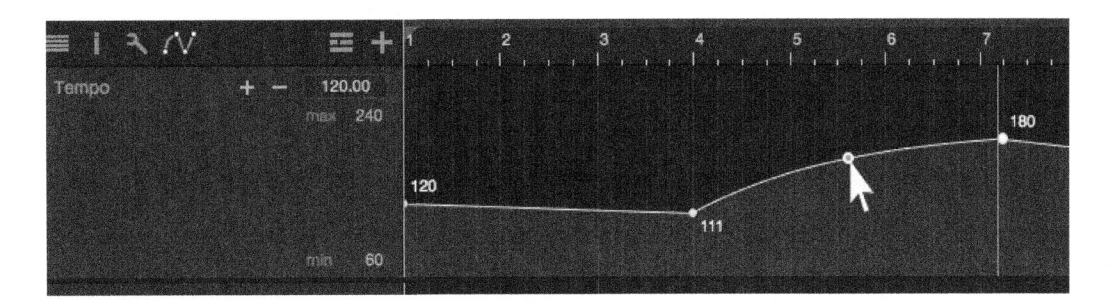

Figure 4.4: Applying a smooth tempo change with a parabola

Here's how to change tempo at a specific time in your song:

1. As an example, let's assume that your song has an 8-bar intro. You want the intro to play at 100 bpm and then jump to 135 bpm going from the intro to the next section of the song.
2. Make sure that the cursor is at the beginning of the song by pressing , (the comma) on your keyboard.
3. On the **Tempo** track, type *100* in the value field. This is the tempo you want at the beginning of your song.
4. Click on bar 9 on the timeline ruler to bring the cursor to the end of the 8-bar intro.

5. Then, on the **Tempo** track, type *135* in the value field. Now the tempo of your song will jump from 100 bpm to 135 bpm going from bar 8 to bar 9:

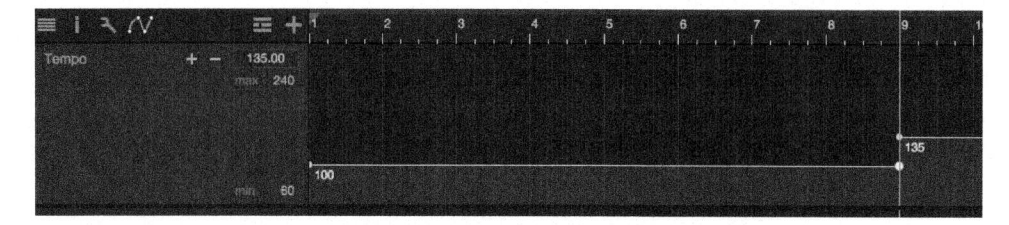

Figure 4.5: Applying instant changes in tempo

You can use any combination of these methods to inject fluid tempo changes into your song. The **Tempo** track will remain active even if you hide it using the **Global Track Visibility** button.

Using the Signature track to change your Song's key or time signature

The **Signature track** allows you to change both key and time signatures. You can reveal this track by clicking the **Global Track Visibility** button and selecting it in the list.

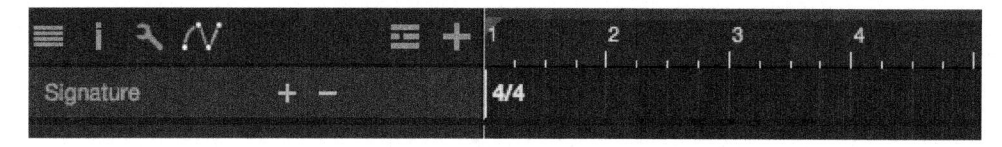

Figure 4.6: Signature track

Studio One uses key signature information to assist you in selecting the correct notes in the **Score View**. By default, a Song does not have a pre-selected key signature. To add or change key signatures, follow these steps:

1. On the **Signature** track, right-click on the bar number where you want the key signature to change. This will open a small dialog box asking you to choose between a new time signature or a new key signature. Click on **Insert Key Signature…**.

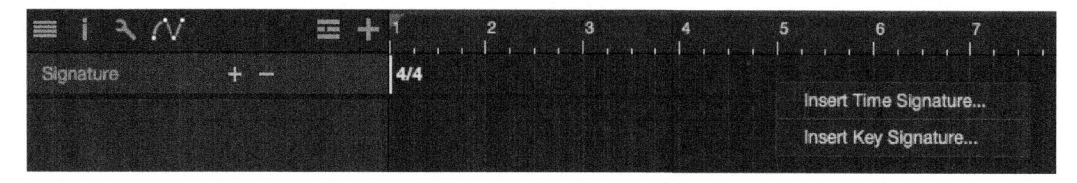

Figure 4.7: Inserting time and key signatures

2. Studio One will open a circle-of-fifths diagram, which is a visual representation of the relationships between different keys and their key signatures. Select your key from the diagram. Remember that major keys are listed on the outer circle and minor keys on the inner circle.

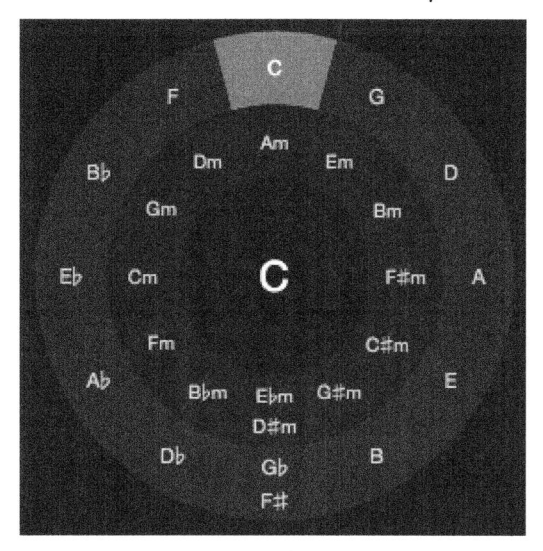

Figure 4.8: Key signature selection diagram

3. Repeat this as many times as you need to add key changes to your song.

Studio One uses time signature information to subdivide bars correctly in the timeline ruler. It also uses this information to place accents correctly in the metronome. It is essential that you set this up correctly if you're using any time signature other than the default 4/4.

Now, here's how you can add or change time signatures:

1. On the **Signature** track, right-click on the bar number where you want the time signature to change. This will open a small menu asking you to choose between a new time signature or a new key signature (see *Figure 4.7*). Click on **Insert Time Signature…**.

2. This will open a small window where you can set your new time signature. Use the **Numerator** and **Denominator** fields to set your time signature. **Numerator** indicates the number of beats in a bar, and **Denominator** equals the note value for each beat, so if your song is in 6/8, set **Numerator** to 6 and **Denominator** to 8:

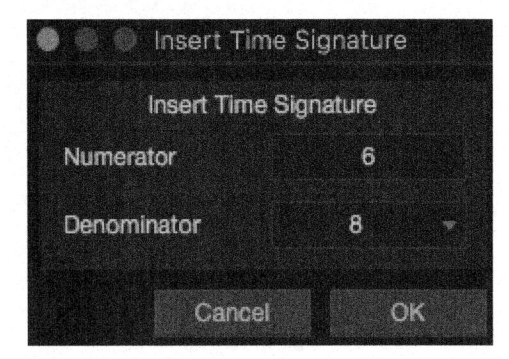

Figure 4.9: Insert Time Signature dialog box

Great! You have now mapped out all the important cornerstones in your song. This will make your life much easier when you start recording your music, and also facilitate your workflow when you're editing your material.

Summary

In this chapter, we created your first Song in Studio One. We took a detailed look at all the parameters that must be set on a per-Song basis and discussed how to change tempo, key signatures, and time signatures through the course of the arrangement.

In the next chapter, we will make our first audio recording. You will learn how to set up Studio One to capture the best possible take and you will have a command of several different recording methods that cover a wide range of scenarios.

5
Recording Your First Audio Track

One of the coolest things about music production is that there are no hard and fast rules on how to start creating. Sometimes you already have a song idea and you want to build on top of that. Sometimes you just want to experiment until you find a gem that inspires you. Studio One allows you to start your creative journey on any of these paths and work your way toward a fully produced final master.

This chapter and the next one are not sequential in terms of workflow. If you already have a song idea, you will want to record it as a scratch track and then start working on its arrangement. In that case, follow along with this chapter and then proceed to the next. If, however, you want to start with a blank canvas, explore the new sounds available in the Studio One ecosystem, and experiment till you find that catchy hook for your next hit, skip ahead to the next chapter and come back to this one when you're ready to add audio material.

In this chapter, you will learn how to record audio in Studio One and how to optimize your recording workflow to get the best results possible.

We will cover the following topics:

- Setting up your hardware to record audio
- Setting up Studio One to record audio
- Understanding different recording modes
- Recording best practices

Technical requirements

To follow along with this chapter, you need to have Studio One activated on your computer. You will also need a source for recording (a microphone and/or instrument) and cable(s) to connect your source(s) to your audio device.

Setting up your hardware for recording audio

Let's begin by connecting your source to your audio device. We will cover two common scenarios:

- Recording vocals or instruments with a microphone
- Recording instruments connected to your audio device with a cable

If you'd like to do both (e.g., sing into your microphone while, at the same time, playing an electric guitar hooked up via cable), simply implement both methods simultaneously.

Setting up a microphone

We can use microphones to both capture vocal performances and record instruments acoustically. There is a huge amount of technical literature based on microphones, and for good reason: picking the right microphone and using it correctly (or not) can make or break a recording. A microphone is by far the most important element in your recording signal chain.

While we cannot cover all the details pertaining to microphones, we want to make sure that you choose the right microphone and use it correctly, so a crash course is in order.

Getting to know your microphone

There are two main microphone types as far as construction and operation are concerned:

- **Condenser microphones** are generally more sensitive and capture more detail, so they are usually preferred in recording sessions. They require external power to operate the circuitry inside their casing. This is known as **phantom power**. Phantom power is supplied through the same cable that attaches your mic to your audio device; no external cable or power source is needed for most models. Just make sure that you switch it on your audio device (in some devices, phantom power is referred to as **48V**, short for 48 volts, which is the standard amount of electric power delivered for this purpose).

- **Dynamic microphones** are not as sensitive and responsive as condenser mics, but they have their shining moments as well: their reduced sensitivity makes them more forgiving of environmental noise and allows them to handle loud sound sources more gracefully. If you're recording in a noisy environment or recording a loud instrument, such as drums or an electric guitar amp, you'll get better results with a dynamic microphone.

All microphones use diaphragms to capture sound waves. There are two types of diaphragms based on size:

- **Small-diaphragm microphones** are about the size of whiteboard markers and are better at capturing high-frequency sound sources. So, they would be the microphone of choice for flutes, mandolins, and cymbals on a drum set, for example.
- **Large-diaphragm microphones** are heftier and have the edge in mid and low frequencies. If you can pick only one microphone, go with a large diaphragm. It will yield the best all-around performance on a wider variety of material. Large-diaphragm microphones almost always work better on vocal recordings as well.

If you've ever worked with microphones before, you already know that they are not equally sensitive to sound coming from different angles. A microphone's **polar pattern** describes how sensitive a microphone will be to sound waves coming from different directions. Most microphones have a **cardioid** pattern, meaning that they will be sensitive to sounds coming from the front and rejecting sounds coming from the back. It is essential that you know your microphone's polar pattern and place it so that your sound source falls within its sweet spot. Consult your mic's user manual; the information will be in there.

> **Tip**
> USB microphones are becoming increasingly popular due to their ease of use. A USB microphone is a microphone with a built-in audio interface. So rather than plugging a conventional microphone into your sound card and connecting the sound card to your computer, you simply connect a USB microphone directly to your computer using a standard USB cable. Apart from this, USB microphones work and behave just like conventional microphones, and all the different features we just discussed apply to USB microphones as well.

Positioning your microphone

Most home studios are not ideal environments in terms of acoustics, so a little extra effort here goes a long way. Your recording environment must be quiet, especially if you're working with a sensitive condenser mic, but that's only half the story. If there are audible sound reflections in the room, these will be captured by the microphone, and reflections in a sound recording are a big no-no unless you're in a space with excellent acoustics.

The good news is that this is usually easy and cost-free to fix. Fill your room with sound-absorbing materials; for example, use carpets to take care of reflections bouncing off the floor, hang thick curtains to dampen reflections from windows, and place sofas in front of bare walls. This will be enough for most rooms. If you still hear reflections, you can look up do-it-yourself sound absorbers and further treat your room acoustically.

If there are noisy fans on your computer and you're recording in the same room, take note of your microphone's polar pattern and place it so that these fans will be in the least sensitive spot and your singer/instrument will be in the most sensitive spot.

Maintain a distance of around 20 centimeters (8 inches) between your source (the singer/instrument being recorded) and your condenser microphone. Decrease this distance if the source is too quiet, or increase it if the source is loud. If you're working with a dynamic microphone, you will need to bring the source much closer. There are no exact recipes here; experimentation is key.

Working with microphone accessories

There are several types of microphone accessories available, ranging from essential to detrimental. Let's take a look at the most common ones:

- When recording, never hold a microphone in your hand. Doing so will cause the microphone to pick up vibrations from your hand, which will end up as a low-frequency rumble. While this is acceptable during a stage performance, we want to have as clean a recording as possible when recording. Use a mic stand instead.
- Use a **shock mount** to isolate any vibrations reaching the microphone via the mic stand.
- **Pop filters** are often used to cut **plosives**, the sudden burst of air produced by letters such as *p* and *b*. I'm not a big fan of pop filters, since they are, well, filters. You can easily tame plosives in a vocal recording by asking your singer to hold their head at a slight angle to the microphone so that the burst of air does not hit the diaphragm head-on.

In this section, we talked about choosing the right microphone, positioning it correctly, and using accessories selectively. Now, let's take a look at the steps you will need to take in order to record an instrument directly with a cable.

Setting up an instrument

Compared to microphones, instruments are straightforward to set up. There is only one classification that you need to know at this point:

- An electric guitar, bass guitar, and basically any instrument with a built-in pickup is called an **instrument-level source** (this is sometimes referred to as **Hi-Z**).
- A synthesizer, electric piano, drum machine, and any electronic hardware instrument is referred to as a **line-level source**.

A typical audio device will accommodate signals coming from both of these source types. Some devices detect the type automatically, some have separate input jacks for each of them, and some devices expect you to set a selector switch manually.

Go through your audio device's user manual and make sure that your device is set to expect the correct type of signal.

If you will be recording an instrument with stereo outputs and your audio device has two inputs available, use two separate instrument cables to connect the left and right outputs of your instrument to separate inputs on your audio device.

Now that you have connected your input sources, you are ready to hop into Studio One to make a few final adjustments before we start recording.

Setting up Studio One for recording audio

We will start our recording session with a blank Song.

1. On Studio One's **Start** page, click the large plus sign titled **New….** This will open the **New Document** window.
2. Select the **Record and Mix** template and adjust the settings for your new Song as we discussed in *Chapter 4*.
3. Click **OK**.

Now, let's create your first audio track and make the final adjustments before you hit the **Record** button.

Creating an audio track

The first thing you need to do inside the new Song is to create audio tracks that you will be recording on. Each physical source you connected to your audio device in the previous section must go on a separate track – that way, you will be able to process each element in your music separately. So if, for example, you're recording a singer, an electric guitar, and an electric piano simultaneously, you will need to create three separate audio tracks.

74   Recording Your First Audio Track

Repeat the following steps to add as many audio tracks as you need:

1. Click the **Add Tracks** button. This will open the **Add Tracks** menu:

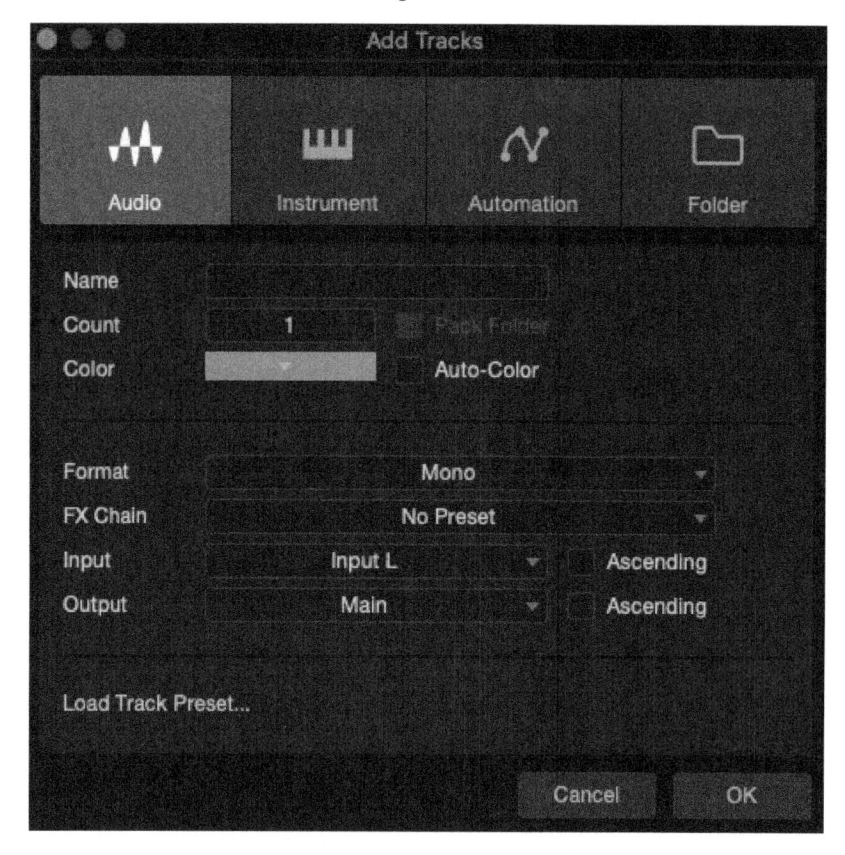

Figure 5.1: The Add Tracks menu

2. At the top of this menu, select the **Audio** tab if it's not already selected.

3. In the **Name** field, type a short, descriptive name for the track you're about to create. If you leave this field blank, Studio One will automatically assign a generic name to it, such as `Audio 01`, `Audio 02`, and so on. But as you add more and more tracks, it will become harder to keep track of your recorded material. Naming your tracks clearly will help immensely as your project begins to grow. Something as simple as `Elec. Gtr. Clean` will do.

4. The **Count** parameter can be useful if you want to create several tracks at once. But keep in mind that all these tracks will have the same attributes (same name, same input, etc.), which is not what we want here. Leave this at **1** (its default value).

5. Select a **Color** option for your track. This may look like eye candy at first, but color-coding your tracks is an effective way of navigating a large project. Come up with a color scheme for your tracks and stick with it in all your projects (e.g., blue for drum tracks, orange for percussion tracks, etc.). This will help you gain command of your material at a glance.

6. Under **Format**, select **Mono** for sources connected to a single input on your audio device (this includes microphones and guitars). Select **Stereo** for stereo sources connected to two separate inputs on your audio device (guitar effect processors with stereo outputs, synthesizers with stereo outputs, etc.).

7. Skip **FX Chain** for now. We will add effects manually in the section titled *Applying effects during recording*.

8. Under **Input**, select the physical input on your audio device that this track will be connected to. Note that input names listed on the faceplate of your audio device may be different from the generic names assigned by Studio One. For a typical entry-level audio device with two inputs, Studio One will label these as **L** and **R**, whereas the device itself will list them as **1** and **2**, respectively.

9. Leave **Output** as **Main** (its default setting).

10. Click **OK**.

Great! You've created your first audio track! Now, let's take a closer look at the controls located on it:

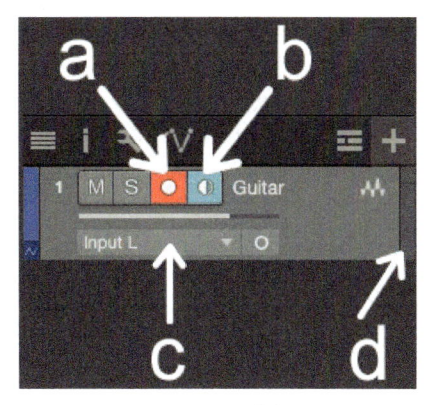

Figure 5.2: A track header

The **Record Enable** button (*a* in *Figure 5.2*) arms a track for recording. Make sure that this is enabled (red). You will need to deactivate this once you are happy with your recording and are ready to move on to another track.

The **Monitor** button (*b* in *Figure 5.2*) acts like a toggle switch that selects the input source for the track. When it's active (blue), you will hear the sound coming from the physical input that this track is connected to. When it's inactive (gray), you will hear what is recorded on the track itself. We have nothing recorded yet, so leave it active.

> **Important note**
>
> If your microphone is in the same room as your speakers, enabling the **Monitor** button may produce a very loud feedback sound, resulting in potential ear and gear damage. Use headphones instead of speakers when microphones are in operation in the same room.

Let's do a quick sound check:

1. Talk into the microphone or play the instrument connected to this track.
2. With the **Monitor** button active, you should be able to hear your voice/instrument on your speakers and see activity on the **VU meter** (*d* in *Figure 5.2*).
3. If you don't see any activity, open the **Input** selector (*c* in *Figure 5.2*) and switch to a different input.

> **Tip**
>
> If you notice a delay between when you talk into the microphone or play the instrument and hear it back on your speakers, decrease **Dropout Protection** as discussed in *Chapter 2*.

Setting recording levels

Setting the right recording level is essential for capturing clean audio. If this level is too low, your source material may get buried in the noise floor – inherent noise emanating from the environment, hardware circuitry, and so on. If it's set too high, this may exceed the maximum level that the system can handle, resulting in clipping and distortion. Here's how you can make sure that your levels are optimized before you hit the **Record** button:

1. Open the **Mix** window.
2. Click the **Inputs** button (*a* in *Figure 5.3*). This will open the **Inputs** section (*b* in *Figure 5.3*) of the **Mix** window, with a dedicated VU meter for each input on your audio device:

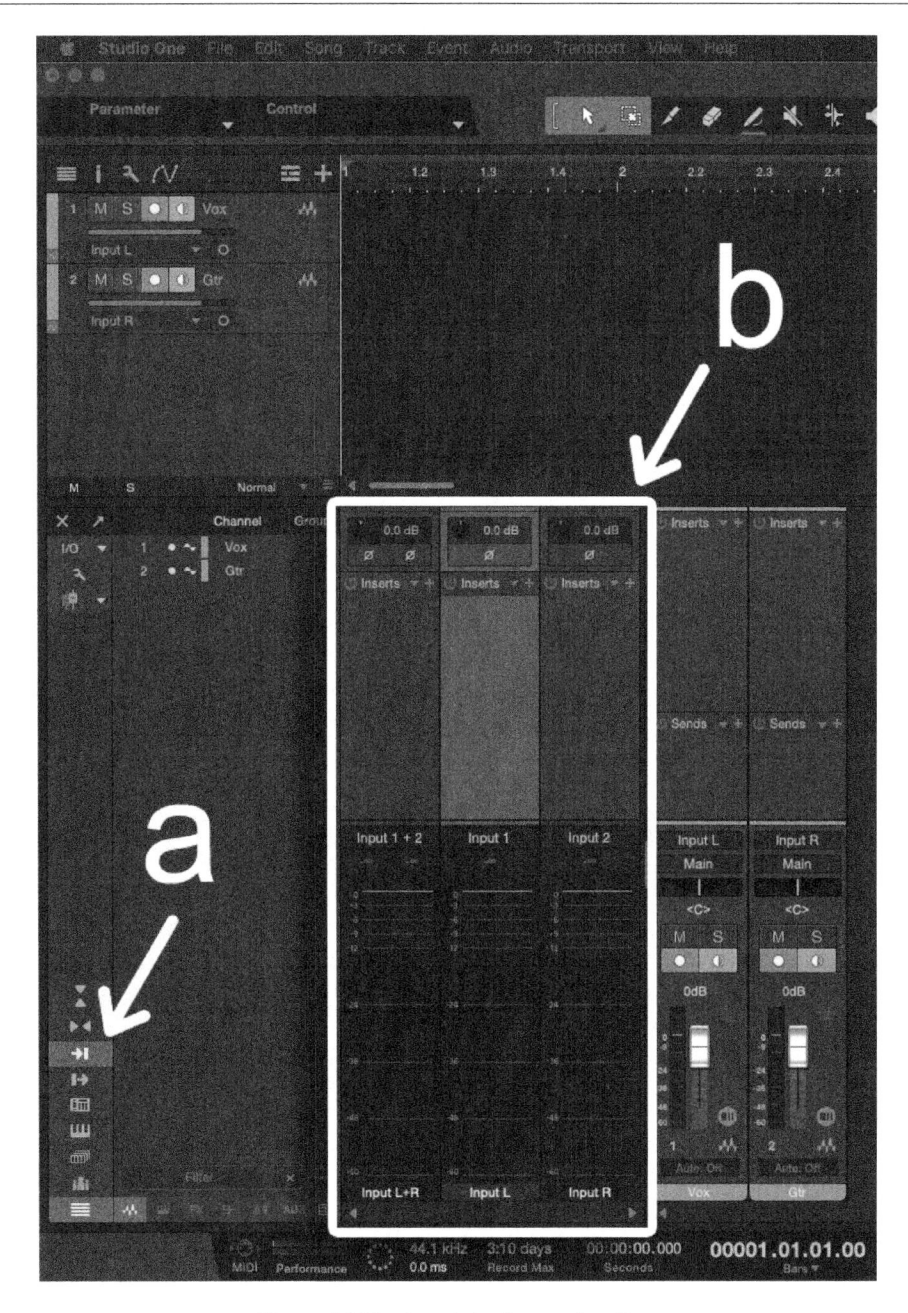

Figure 5.3: The Inputs button and section

3. Now, sing into the microphone or play the instrument that you will be recording. It is essential that you sing or play at the same volume that you will when you start recording in a few minutes.

4. Keep your eyes on the corresponding VU meter. Using the gain control on your audio device, set the level so that the VU meter hovers around -12 decibels as you sing or play (you don't have to be too precise, the vicinity of -12 decibels is a safe area).

5. Note that some audio devices, such as RME Babyface, do not have physical gain controls. If that's your case, then you will have to open the software mixer for your device and use the virtual gain knobs there.

6. Do not touch the faders on Studio One's **Mix** window at this point. They have no effect on the recording level. If you need to adjust your monitoring levels, use the output or volume knob on your audio device.

7. If you find that you have to turn up the gain excessively (past 3 o'clock), this brings the risk of introducing excessive noise from the mic preamplifier circuitry. Try to move closer to the mic instead.

8. If you find that you have to turn down the gain excessively (below 10 o'clock), you may be too close to the microphone. Try to move further away from the mic instead.

If your recording has a great dynamic range (some very quiet parts followed by some very loud parts), you may plan to record it in two takes (or more, depending on the song's structure), optimizing the level for each part, recording it, and then moving on to the next.

Applying effects during recording

For most people, hearing their bare voice on their headphones is not a very inspiring experience. The same goes for a raw electric guitar sound. Adding effects that pamper their voice or instrument tone will help musicians get into the mood of the song and encourage them to deliver a better performance. Capturing a good performance is your ultimate goal in recording, so feel free to indulge your performers with effects that will hype them up.

But as exciting as these effects are, we don't want to *print them to tape*, as studio professionals say. An effect that feels fantastic in the heat of recording may sound over the top when you start mixing the song a few days later, and if the performance is recorded with the effect baked into it, there is no turning back.

So, we use a method that gives us the best of both worlds: we can go crazy with effects that we feed into our performer's headphones while recording only the dry, unprocessed signal. Here's how it works:

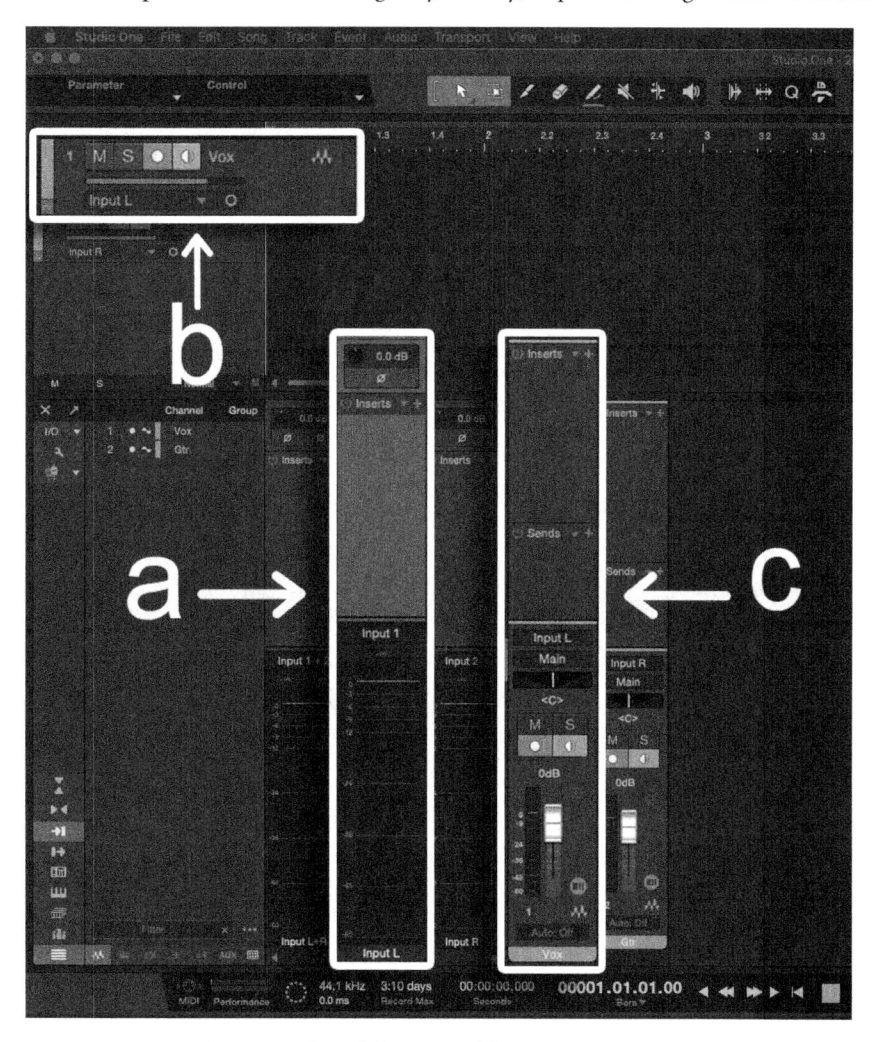

Figure 5.4: Signal flow to and from an audio track

Let's assume that you want to record your own vocal performance for a song you're working on. You connect your microphone to **Input L** on your audio device; the signal from your microphone is now reaching Studio One through the strip labeled **Input L** on the mixer console (*a* in *Figure 5.4*). Then, you create a new audio track and select **Input L** as the input source (*b* in *Figure 5.4*). Studio One automatically creates a new channel strip on the mixer console to represent the output coming from this new track (*c* in *Figure 5.4*).

A track is like a tape recorder. It's where the audio signal is recorded and played back. If we substitute the track in *Figure 5.4* (*b*) with the image of a tape recorder, the signal flow will be much easier to visualize:

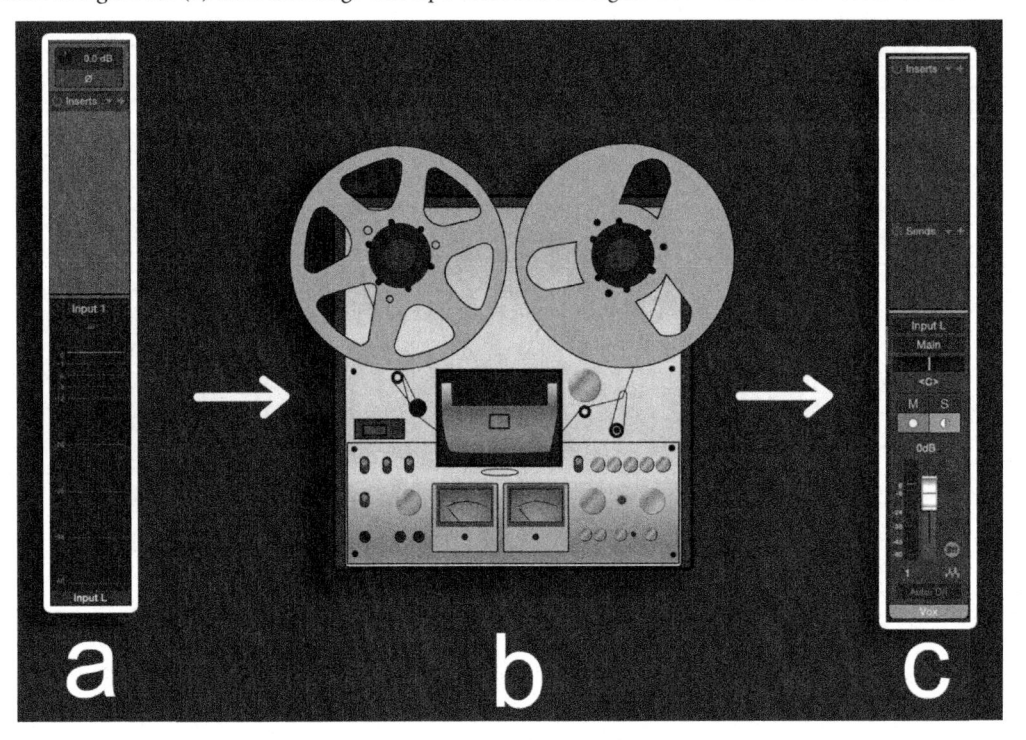

Figure 5.5: Another way of looking at signal flow

The signal coming from your audio device will first hit the **Input** channel (*a* in *Figure 5.5*) and then be recorded on the track (*b* in *Figure 5.5*). It will then be routed to the channel strip for the track (*c* in *Figure 5.5*).

You will notice that both of these mixer channels (*a* and *c* in *Figure 5.5*) have a section titled **Inserts**. **Inserts** are virtual slots on Studio One's mix console that we use in order to apply sound effects. So, for example, if you want to add reverb to give a sense of depth and ambiance to your vocals, you could apply a reverb plug-in on either of these **Inserts** sections and the end result would sound exactly the same.

The difference, however, is that any effect you insert on the input channel will be recorded to the track. Going back to our example, if you insert a reverb plug-in on the input channel, your vocal performance will be recorded with the reverb baked into it. You will not be able to remove it or modify it when you start mixing your song.

The solution is to apply effects on the **Inserts** section of the channel strip for the track. You can go ahead and try all sorts of effects here, without having to commit to them. Studio One will only record the dry, unprocessed signal coming from the input channel.

Here are some suggestions for effects plug-ins that you may try on your next recording session:

- Adding a **Compressor** plug-in with a gentle setting (with the **Ratio** parameter set to anywhere between 2 and 4) allows singers to hear themselves better in their headphones and helps them deliver a better performance.
- Everyone loves reverb in their own voice. Insert Studio One's own **Room Reverb** plug-in, select a **Large Hall** setting, and adjust the **Mix** parameter to taste.
- Use Studio One's **Tuner** plug-in to make sure the instruments you're recording are tuned correctly. Remember that the signal flows from top to bottom in the **Inserts** section of a channel strip; if you have several plug-ins inserted, the signal will first hit the plug-in at the top of the list and then travel toward the bottom. The **Tuner** plug-in may become confused by effects added by other plug-ins, so drag it to the top of the list.
- Use **Ampire** to add color and character to otherwise dull and dry sound sources. Although designed primarily for electric guitars, it works well on almost every instrument. This added tonal "attitude" will help you get into the right mood and deliver a better performance.
- Try **Redlight** to add some extra bite and brightness to dull vocals.

Great! By applying these effects, you have placed your performers in the best light, and everyone is excited to start recording. There is one final step left before you can actually hit the **Record** button.

Setting up the metronome

In order to reap the benefits of Studio One's stellar editing features, which we will cover in the following chapters, I strongly suggest that you record with Studio One's built-in metronome. If you prefer not to use a metronome at all (e.g., you're recording a classical piece with a free tempo), feel free to skip this section.

You can turn the metronome on or off by hitting C on your keyboard or by clicking its icon in the lower panel:

Figure 5.6: Precount, Metronome Setup, and Metronome on/off

If you activate **Precount**, when you hit the **Record** button, the metronome will count for one bar before the recording actually starts. This will give you time to get your instrument in position, take a breath, and get ready for recording (it's an invaluable feature, especially if you're recording by yourself).

For the most common recording scenarios, this will be all you need to know about using the metronome, but if you need to tweak it further, just click on the wrench-shaped **Metronome Setup** icon and you will be taken to this page:

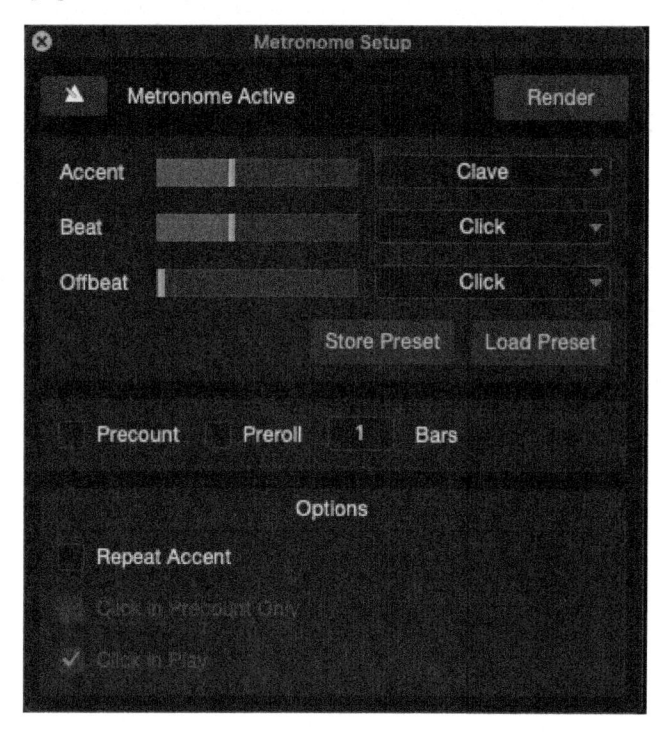

Figure 5.7: The Metronome Setup window

In this menu, you can set the metronome using three different sounds: **Accent** plays on the first beat of each bar and **Beat** plays on all other beats. So if your time signature is set to 4 / 4, **Accent** will play on the "1" of each bar and **Beat** will play on beats 2, 3, and 4.

Offbeat, which is turned off by default, will play halfway between each beat. You know how a 4/4 measure is sometimes counted as "ONE AND TWO AND THREE AND FOUR AND…"? **Offbeat** is responsible for sounding those ANDs. This could be useful if you're working at a very slow tempo and need to hear the metronome with smaller subdivisions.

This menu allows you to set the respective volumes of each of these three metronome sounds. You can even change the default sounds if they clash with other sounds in your arrangement.

Moving on down the window, **Precount**, as we mentioned, tells Studio One to count one measure before actually starting to record. **Preroll** is also designed to help you get ready for recording, but it's more useful when you want to start recording somewhere in the middle of the song. With **Preroll** enabled, when you hit **Record**, Studio One will go back one bar before the current position of the timeline, start playback, and then automatically start recording once the playback passes the cursor position.

You can change the **Precount** and **Preroll** times here if you need more time to get ready to perform.

Repeat Accent makes the metronome easier to follow if you're using a time signature with more than one accent per bar. For example, if your time signature is 12/8 and **Repeat Accent** is disabled, the metronome will put an accent on the first beat of the bar only. If you enable it, the metronome will place an accent on every fourth beat (ONE two three FOUR five six…) making it much easier to follow.

If you activate **Click in Precount Only**, the metronome will go quiet after the precount and will stay silent during the actual recording. This is useful if the metronome sound is leaking from headphones and reaching the microphone.

By default, the metronome only clicks when you're recording. **Click in Play** allows the metronome to be heard during playback as well – perfect for practicing the part before hitting the **Record** button.

Speaking of which, we are finally ready to hit the **Record** button! In the next section, we will talk about the various recording modes available in Studio One and how you can use them to capture the best performance in a variety of scenarios.

Understanding different recording modes

There are several different methods for recording audio in Studio One, each designed with a different purpose. Understanding these modes will make life much easier and make recording a much less stressful process.

Basic recording

Here's the basic method for recording audio:

1. Arm your track(s) for recording by clicking on the **Record Enable** button. If this button is red, then the track is armed for recording.
2. Set the playback cursor to the point where you want the recording to begin.
3. Press * on your numeric keypad or click the **Record** button on the **Lower Panel**:

Figure 5.8: Transport controls on the Lower Panel, including (a) Stop, (b) Playback, (c) Record, and (d) Loop

4. If **Precount** is enabled, the metronome will click for the number of bars you specified in the **Metronome Setup** window and then the recording will begin.

5. If **Preroll** is enabled, the playback cursor will jump back for the number of bars you specified in the **Metronome Setup** window, playback will begin, and Studio One will start recording once the cursor reaches the point where it was before you hit **Record**.

6. Recording will continue until you manually stop it by pressing the *spacebar* or clicking the **Stop** button.

Now, let's take a look at the other available recording methods.

Auto Punch

Imagine that you just recorded an amazing performance, with just one small mistake right in the middle. It would be a shame to have to ditch the entire take just because of that one mistake, right? By using the **Auto Punch** feature, you can re-record just that problematic part without affecting the rest of the take. Here's how to do it.

Let's assume that the problematic part in your recording extends from the beginning of bar 9 through the beginning of bar 11:

1. Activate **Auto Punch** by clicking on its icon. It will turn red when it's activated, as shown in *Figure 5.9*.

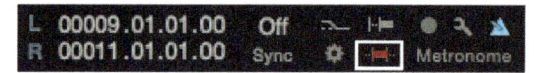

Figure 5.9: The Auto Punch button

2. Set **Left Locator** to where you want the recording to begin (for this example, you'll want to set it to the beginning of bar 9). You can do this by manually dragging it across the Timeline ruler or by entering a value in the **L** field shown in *Figure 5.9*.

3. Set **Right Locator** to where you want the recording to end (for this example, you'll want to set it to the beginning of bar 11). You can do this by manually dragging it across the Timeline Ruler or by entering a value in the **R** field shown in *Figure 5.9*.

   Your Left and Right Locators will now look like this:

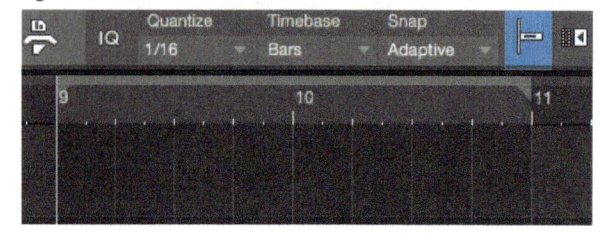

Figure 5.10: Left and Right Locators set between bars 9 through 11 for the Auto Punch recording

4. Now, set your playback cursor to where you want the recording to begin, and hit **Record**. Studio One will start in playback mode and it will begin to record when the playback cursor reaches the beginning of measure 9. It will stop recording automatically at the beginning of measure 11.

   Although Studio One will not start recording before measure 9, it's a good idea to start playing/singing in previous bars anyway so that you don't have to "start cold" when recording begins.

That's it! You have saved an otherwise perfect take by fixing a minor mistake.

Loop recording

This is an excellent feature that lets you loop a section of your song and record several takes without having to constantly stop and restart the recording. You can use this feature to try out new ideas or to create a perfect composite take by selecting the best parts from several different takes. Proceed as follows:

1. Go to **View** on the top menu and select **Record Panel**. This will open the **Record** panel right on top of the **Lower Panel**. *Figure 5.11* shows the part of this panel that lets you adjust **Record Mode**.

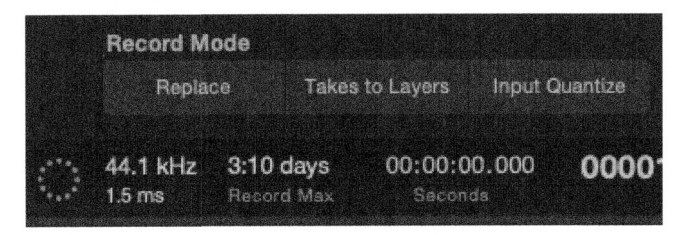

Figure 5.11: The Record panel

2. Click **Takes to Layers** to enable it. It will be blue when active.
3. Set your **Left** and **Right Locator** positions around the section of the song that you want to work on.
4. Click the **Loop** button to activate it (*d* in *Figure 5.8*).
5. Start recording.
6. When the playback cursor reaches the **Right Locator** position, it will jump back to the **Left Locator** position, creating a loop between the two points.
7. Each pass between the loop points will be recorded on a separate layer inside the track.
8. Recording will continue until you stop it manually by pressing the *spacebar* or clicking on the **Stop** button.

9. Once you stop recording, the recorded layers will be expanded automatically, labeled `Take 1`, `Take 2`, and so on, depending on how many times you let the recording loop between the two locators:

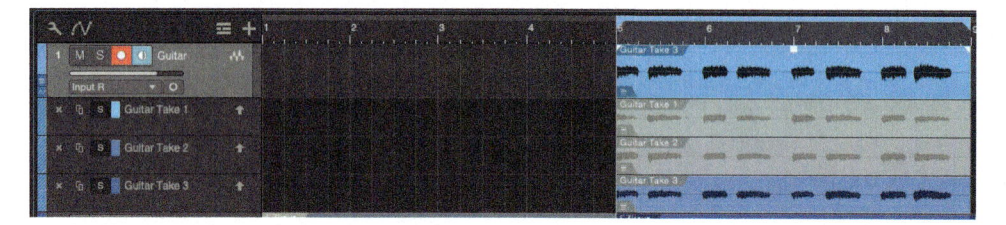

Figure 5.12: Track layers expanded after loop recording

In *Chapter 8*, you will be able to work with these layers to select the best part of each take and create a perfect composite take.

So far in this chapter, we have focused on the technical side of recording audio. But recording is actually a much more complicated process involving aesthetics, attention to detail, communication skills, and problem-solving.

In the following section, you will find a collection of recording best practices that will help you in capturing the perfect take, every time.

Recording best practices

Recording is by far the most complicated, difficult, and stressful part of the entire music production process. This is because several different and conflicting dynamics are at work during a recording session: artistic desire for creativity, technical urge to focus on details, pressure to finish the project on time, personal insecurities about the quality of performance, and so on. If you're recording yourself, all these conflicting dynamics will take place inside your head. If you're working as part of a team, they will surface on an interpersonal level. Regardless of how they manifest themselves, these conflicting factors will challenge the success of every recording session.

Here are some recording best practices that will assist in turning your next recording session into a smooth sailing experience:

- The ultimate goal of a recording session is to capture the best performance possible. Make sure that the person being recorded is feeling relaxed and stress-free.
- If you're recording someone else, go easy on your feedback. Saying "*There are some out-of-tune notes, let's try that again*" will not fix the problem. Be diplomatic (for example, you can play the recording back to your singer and let them spot the out-of-tune notes themselves).

- If you're recording yourself, don't let the technical side of your brain intimidate the creative side.
- If there are out-of-tune notes, ask your singer to put a headphone on one ear only and leave the other ear open.
- Do not stop a recording for minor mistakes. Keep going. Remember that you can use the **Auto Punch** feature to fix them in a subsequent pass. Many types of mistakes can also be corrected in post-production.
- Ask your singer/performer to do some ad-libs and record them. Sprinkle these bits on various parts of the song later to add color.
- I have cautioned against using effects in the **Inserts** section of the input channels; however, now comes the exception – apply a limiter on the input channel that you're recording from. This is an effect plug-in that allows signals below a specified level (set by the **Ceiling** parameter) to pass unaffected and lowers the signals that exceed the **Ceiling** level. Set the **Ceiling** value to -1 dB, like so:

Figure 5.13: Limiter inserted on Input L, with the Ceiling control set to -1 dB

This will act like a safety fuse and will protect your recording from accidentally clipping. Sometimes a singer may get carried away and, in the heat of performance, they may move closer to the microphone or sing louder than they did in the rehearsal. We don't want to lose an otherwise perfect performance because of a few clippings here and there. Remember that this is just a safety precaution. It should not be used as a substitute for setting correct levels, as we discussed earlier in this chapter.

- Divide long, challenging phrases and record them in smaller, more manageable chunks. If you do this, though, make sure that the tone and energy of the performance remain consistent from one take to the next.

- Do not obsess over one aspect of the recording and let other problems fly by. As the person doing the recording, it is your responsibility to capture the perfect take, so be on the lookout for all technical issues as well as performance issues.

- Stay positive. Embrace the recording session as the biggest opportunity to bring your song to life.

Observing these best practices will help you run a smooth, enjoyable, and effective recording session and capture the best possible performance.

Summary

In this chapter, you learned how to prepare your hardware for recording. You created your first audio track and configured Studio One to capture audio from a variety of sources. You then learned about the different recording modes and how each can be used to facilitate the recording experience. Finally, we discussed several recording best practices to help you capture the best performance possible.

In the next chapter, we will take a deep dive into recording and programming MIDI with Studio One.

6
Adding Virtual Instruments and Recording MIDI

Virtual instruments have been an integral part of music production for decades, and MIDI is the universal language that allows us to work with them. One of the most important duties of all DAWs is to take our creative ideas and convert them into **Musical Instrument Digital Interface** (**MIDI**) data that virtual instruments can process.

MIDI is an archaic and cumbersome language by today's standards, so this translation is by no means an easy one, but Studio One does an amazing job with it. Whether you're a total beginner or a seasoned expert, you will find plenty of alternative methods to channel your ideas into concrete musical productions in no time.

This chapter will start with a brief introduction to MIDI for the complete beginner, and then we will proceed to examine Studio One's several methods for recording and inputting MIDI. By the end of this chapter, you will have a solid understanding of how to translate your musical ideas into MIDI data and how to work with Studio One's virtual instruments to bring your ideas to life.

We will cover the following topics:

- Introducing MIDI
- Adding and configuring MIDI instruments
- Inputting and recording MIDI
- Using Melodyne to convert audio to MIDI

Technical requirements

To follow along with this chapter, you will need to have Studio One activated on your computer. A MIDI keyboard is not required but will help implement some of the recording techniques.

If you're interested in converting audio material to MIDI, you'll need to have Melodyne installed and activated on your computer. Melodyne comes bundled with Studio One Pro.

Introducing MIDI

MIDI is a communications protocol that allows electronic musical instruments to talk to one another. It was introduced as a technical standard in the 80s to make life easier for electronic musicians with lots of gear. A keyboard player in a rock band would be able to go on stage with just one keyboard and use it to play several devices tucked away on a rack at the back of the stage.

As computers became more and more common, it didn't take long for people to realize that since the signal going from the keyboard to the devices at the back of the stage was purely digital, it could be easily stored and processed on a computer. This was ground-breaking: people could now perform their musical ideas on a keyboard, record those performances on a computer, and then go back and edit them just like editing text with a word processor. Not only could they fix their mistakes after the performance, but they could embellish their ideas and do things that were not humanly possible, such as programming a drum part that a real drummer could never play. MIDI opened the gate to a whole new level of music production, and the rest is history.

Despite its revolutionary impact on music production, MIDI is actually based on a very simple principle. There are two components in a MIDI setup:

- A **MIDI controller** is a physical interface that translates your musical performance to MIDI data. This is most commonly found in the form of a music keyboard, but several different controller types have emerged over time, including drum pads, wind controllers, and MIDI guitars. You play a MIDI keyboard just as you would play a piano keyboard. Instead of creating sounds, though, the MIDI keyboard generates MIDI data based on your performance. This data contains information such as which note you played, how hard you played that note, and so on.

- The data generated by the MIDI controller is sent to a **MIDI device**. This device is responsible for converting MIDI data into actual sounds. It interprets data coming from the MIDI controller and synthesizes or triggers sounds depending on how it's programmed. A MIDI device can be in hardware form (a hardware synthesizer, for example) or software form. Software instruments are also referred to as virtual instruments. We'll use both terms interchangeably.

These two components are commonly connected by standard USB ports and USB cables in the present day, but if you have some older gear, you may find that they have five-pin inputs and outputs like so:

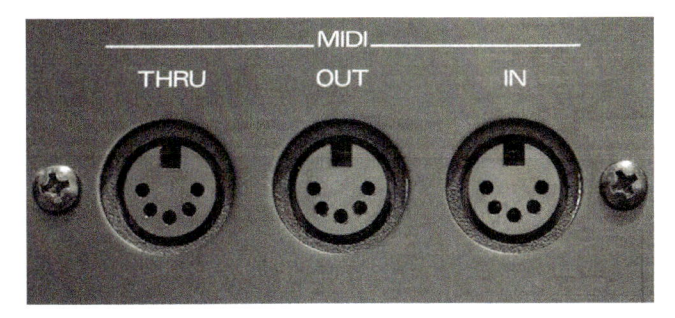

Figure 6.1: A MIDI device with five-pin connectors

Don't worry if you need to connect these devices to newer devices that have only USB ports, though, as USB-to-MIDI converters are readily available at a very low cost.

Connecting devices to Studio One

Studio One refers to MIDI controllers as **keyboards** and MIDI devices as **instruments**. We talked about how to connect and configure these in *Chapter 2*. Studio One does not impose a limit on the number of keyboards and instruments that you can add. You will, however, run into a practical limit if you want to connect several devices and your computer does not have enough USB ports available. If that happens, feel free to add a USB hub and connect all your devices to it; MIDI has a very low bandwidth and a standard USB hub will be able to handle several devices easily.

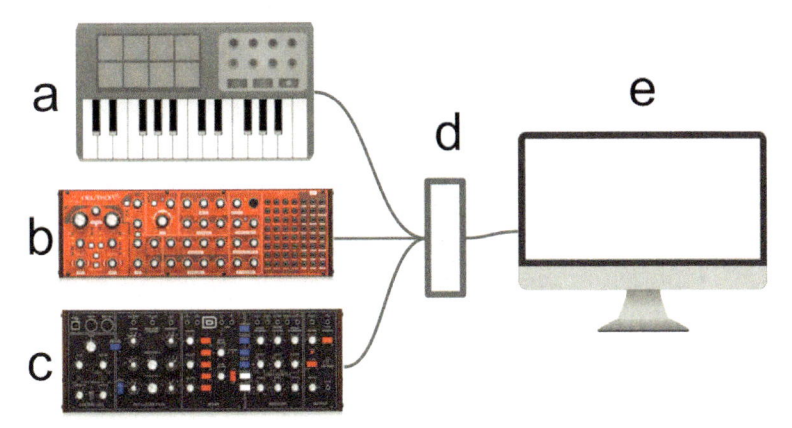

Figure 6.2: A typical home studio setup including (a) a MIDI keyboard, (b) a synthesizer, (c) another synthesizer, (d) a USB hub, and (e) a computer

It bears repeating here that if you have a combo device (also known as a MIDI workstation) comprising both a MIDI keyboard and a synthesizer, you will need to add it separately as a keyboard and as an instrument in the **Add Device** window.

Now, let's head over to a new Song in Studio One and put all this theory into action.

Adding and configuring MIDI instruments

Whether you're using a hardware MIDI device or a software instrument, Studio One makes it very easy to initiate recording with a simplified, drag-and-drop workflow. Let's take a look at each scenario.

Adding a software instrument

Preparing a virtual instrument for recording could not be any easier. If you'll only be using virtual instruments, simply follow the steps in this section and then skip over to the next section, *Inputting and recording MIDI*.

So, to add an instrument, follow these steps:

1. Create a new Song.
2. Open the **Browse** window.
3. Select the **Instruments** tab. Here, you will see a list of all virtual instruments installed on your computer.
4. On this list, find the virtual instrument you want to use. Then, drag it and drop it anywhere on the arrangement window.
5. Studio One will launch the selected instrument and create a new Instrument Track for it:

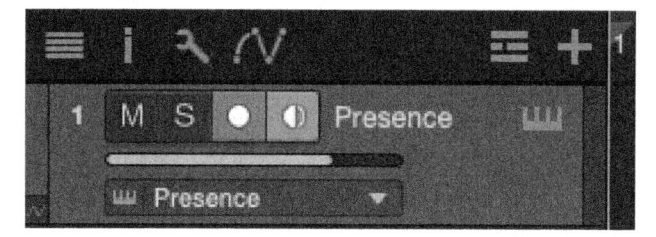

Figure 6.3: An Instrument Track

6. Load a sound into your instrument. The virtual instruments that come with Studio One all have several sound presets that you can use as starting points. You can find them under the **Preset** drop-down menu.

    Here's **Presence**, a virtual instrument that comes with Studio One, proudly displaying its preset options:

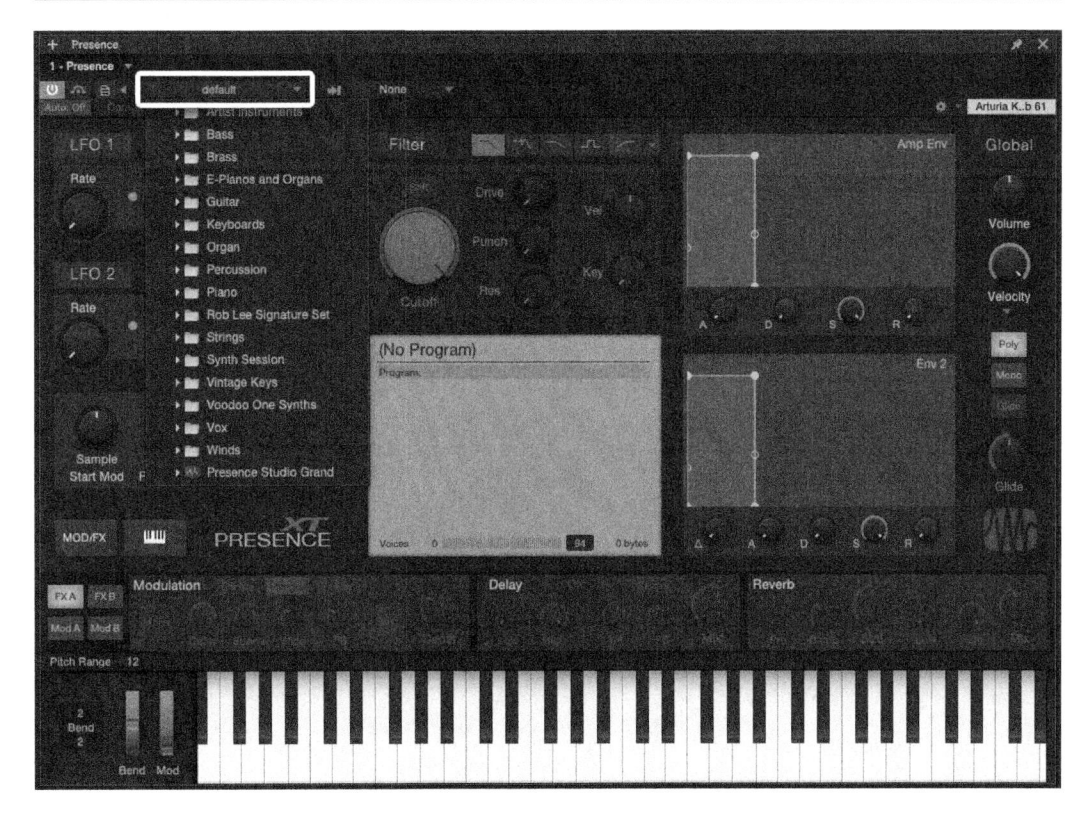

Figure 6.4: The preset drop-down menu in Presence

That's it! You are now ready to work with your virtual instrument.

Adding a hardware Instrument

Adding a hardware instrument to a song is a bit more complicated, but the good news is that you will only need to do this once for each instrument. In your next projects, you will just be able to drag and drop them like virtual instruments. Let's begin:

1. Create a new Song.
2. Open the **Mix** window and click **External** from the left-hand column. This will open the **External Devices** panel:

94   Adding Virtual Instruments and Recording MIDI

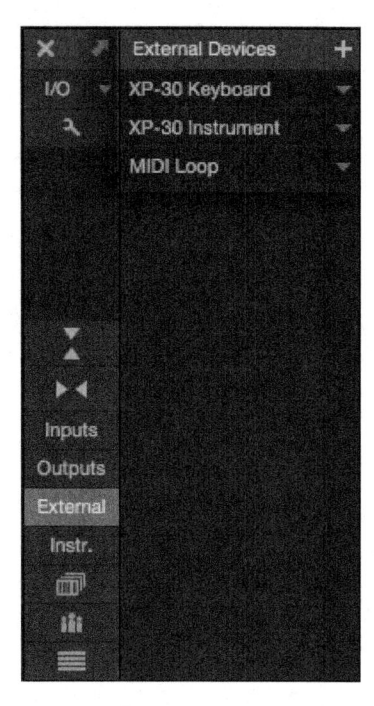

Figure 6.5: The External Devices panel

3. This panel will list all the MIDI devices connected to your computer. Locate the one you'd like to use. You will notice in *Figure 6.5* that my trusty Roland XP-30 appears twice in this list – first as a keyboard and then as an instrument. If that's the case with the device you're adding, apply the following steps on the instrument, and not the keyboard.

4. Now, click on the downward arrow to the right of the chosen instrument's name. Select **Edit…**, which will open an editor window for your device:

Figure 6.6: The External Devices editor window

5. Click the **Outputs** button on this window (highlighted in *Figure 6.6*).
6. From the new submenu, select **Add Aux Channel** (*Aux* stands for *auxiliary*). This will create a new channel strip on the mixing console that we will use to monitor the audio coming from this device. Click the input section of this newly created aux channel.
7. Here, select the inputs on your audio device that this instrument is connected to. *Figure 6.7* shows the options available for a typical audio device with two inputs, labeled **Left** and **Right**. Selecting **Input L+R - Front Left + Right** allows this channel to receive audio coming from both of these inputs.

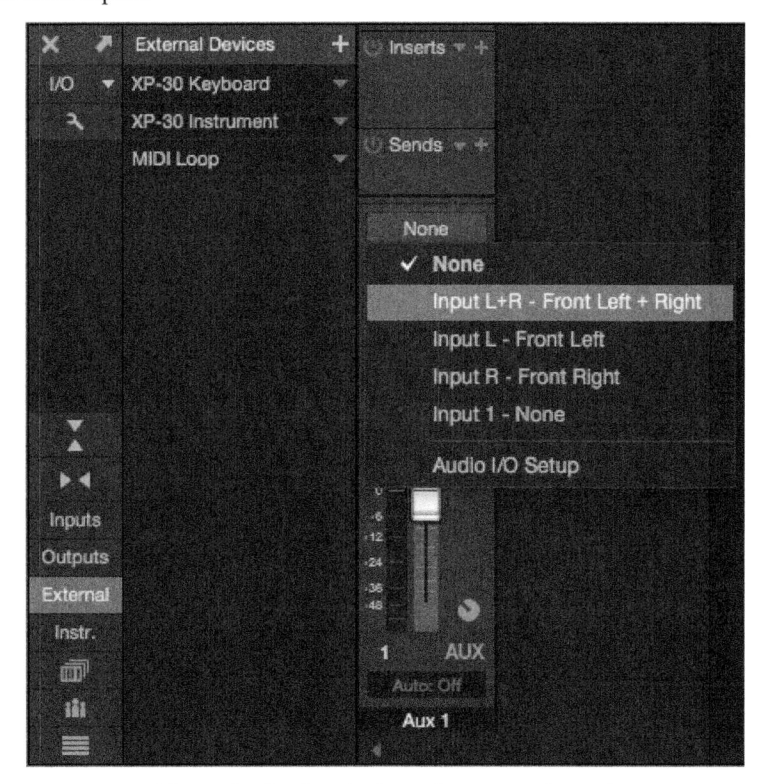

Figure 6.7: Setting the input for an aux channel

8. Go back to the **Output** button on the **External Devices** editor window and click **Save Default**.

That's it! From now on, adding this instrument to a project will be as easy as adding a virtual instrument. On the **Instruments** tab of the **Browse** window, this instrument will now be listed under **External Instruments**:

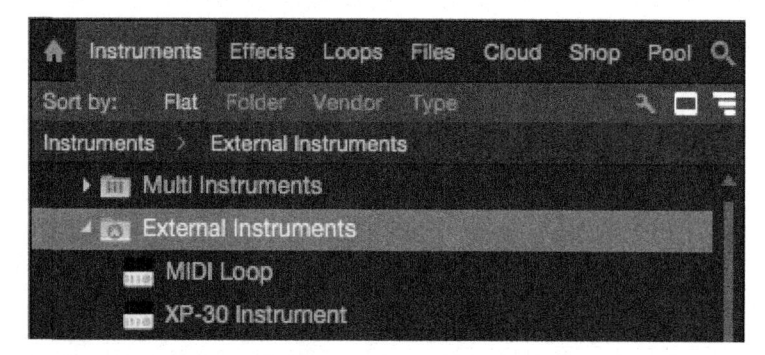

Figure 6.8: The External Instruments section in the Browse window

Simply drag the instrument and drop it anywhere on the **Arrangement** window. Your external instrument is ready for recording!

Inputting and recording MIDI

There are several methods for inputting and recording MIDI data in Studio One, each optimized for a different purpose. You can play everything live, input notes with a mouse, use a sequencer, or even create MIDI data from audio recordings. In this section, we will cover all of these methods in detail.

Let's start with the most basic one: capturing a live performance.

Recording a live performance with MIDI

If you can play the keyboard, even at a beginner level, the best way to pour your ideas into your project is the old-fashioned way – hitting the record button and playing it live. Once you're done recording, you'll be able to edit your performance to perfection. This takes the stress factor out of the equation and makes the whole process a breeze. Generally speaking, recording a live performance is much more practical compared to manually inputting notes.

This is all very well, but what if you don't have a MIDI keyboard?

Using your computer keyboard to record MIDI

Studio One allows you to use your computer keyboard just like a musical keyboard. All you need to do to activate this feature is to press *Caps Lock*. This will open the **Qwerty Keyboard** window:

Figure 6.9: The Qwerty Keyboard window ready to generate MIDI data

On a standard QWERTY keyboard, the first row of letters (from Q to P) will correspond to the *white* keys on a musical keyboard, and the number keys (from 2 to 0) will correspond to the *black* keys. So, for example, Q on your keyboard will give you the C note on the third octave, 2 will give you C# on the same octave, and so on.

If you live in a country with a different keyboard layout, just use the same physical keys, even if their labels are different. For example, if you use a Turkish-F keyboard, use F instead of Q.

You can use the left and right arrow keys to switch octaves and use *Tab* just like a sustain pedal. It takes a while to get used to, but it's a great alternative if you don't have a MIDI keyboard or if you just want to try out new ideas while waiting at the airport.

Keep in mind that keyboard shortcuts associated with these keys will not work as long as this feature is active.

Live recording walk-through

Now, let's pick up from where we left off in the *Adding and configuring MIDI instruments* section. So far, you've created a new Song and added an instrument. Studio One created an Instrument Track for you to work on:

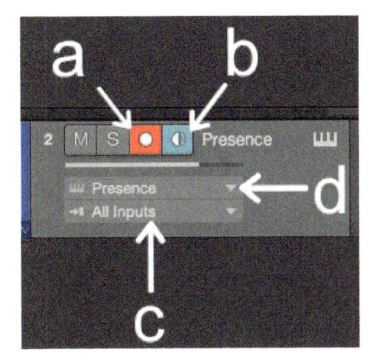

Figure 6.10: Controls on an Instrument Track

Follow these steps to record on this track:

1. The Record button (*a* in *Figure 6.10*) arms a track for recording. Make sure that this is enabled (red). You will need to deactivate this once you are happy with your recording and are ready to move on to another track.

2. The Monitor button (*b* in *Figure 6.10*) acts like a toggle switch that selects the input source for the instrument associated with this track. When it's active (blue), the instrument will respond to your MIDI keyboard. When it's inactive (gray), you will hear what is recorded on the track itself. We have nothing recorded yet, so leave it active.

3. Now, try playing a few notes on your MIDI keyboard or QWERTY keyboard. You should be able to hear a sound from your instrument.

4. If you don't hear anything, make sure that the input selector (*c* in *Figure 6.10*) points to the keyboard you're using and that the output selector (*d* in *Figure 6.10*) points to the instrument associated with this track.

5. Recording with a metronome will make your life much easier when you want to add other instruments or edit your recording. Activate the metronome's click sound by pressing C on your keyboard. If you need Studio One to count in before starting to record, set the **Metronome**, **Preroll**, and **Precount** options as described in *Chapter 5*.

6. Activate recording by clicking the Record button or by pressing * on your numeric keypad.

7. When you're done, click the stop button or press the spacebar.

If you're happy with your recording but there is a spot that you'd like to record again, you can re-record that part only, while leaving everything else intact, by using the Auto Punch feature described in *Chapter 5*.

This is all you need to do to record a live performance with a MIDI or QWERTY keyboard. Don't worry if there are a few mistakes in the performance that need to be fixed; you will be able to edit your performance to perfection using Studio One's powerful editing tools, which we will cover in *Chapter 7*.

Loop recording

Loop recording is a convenient feature that lets you loop a section of your song and allows Studio One to record on that section indefinitely until you hit stop. This saves you from constantly having to manually start recording, stopping, rewinding, and start recording again. It also allows you to focus on singing or playing your instrument.

There are two different loop recording modes when working with MIDI instruments, and they are designed for two distinct purposes: **Record Takes** and **Record Mix**.

Go to **View** on the top menu and select **Record Panel** to access these modes:

Figure 6.11: The instrument loop record panel

With **Record Takes** enabled, every time the timeline reaches the end of the loop, it will jump back to the beginning. Studio One will create a new layer inside the same track and record your performance as a new take on that layer. By the time you hit the stop button, you will end up with as many takes as you allowed the timeline to loop within the section.

This is excellent for trying out new ideas. When you're done recording, you can pick your favorite parts from all the different takes and create a perfectly edited composite take. You can also use this feature to focus on playing a difficult passage until you nail it.

With **Record Mix**, instead of creating a new layer, Studio One will keep recording on the same layer until you hit stop. This is useful when you want to build a track gradually. For example, when creating a drum groove, you may want to play the kick drum and snare in the first cycle of the loop, then add hi-hat in the second cycle, additional percussion elements in subsequent cycles, and so on. If you play something you don't like, hit stop, click **Undo Last Loop** (also shown in *Figure 6.11*), and start again.

Once you've selected the loop recording mode you'd like to use, follow these steps to start recording:

1. Set the left and right locators to the beginning and end of the section of your song that you'd like to work on.
2. Click the **Loop** button to enable looping.
3. Set **Metronome**, **Preroll**, and **Precount** (see *Chapter 5*).
4. Activate recording by clicking the Record button or pressing * on your numeric keypad.
5. When you're done, click the stop button or press the spacebar.

So far in this section, we have covered the methods you can use to record a live performance using a MIDI or QWERTY keyboard. Now, let's take a look at other methods of inputting MIDI data to use with virtual instruments.

Inputting MIDI notes manually

One of the coolest things about MIDI is that it allows you to program a performance as opposed to actually playing it. This opens the door to an amazing range of possibilities. You can use MIDI programming for something as ambitious as constructing an entire orchestral performance using nothing but a mouse, or something as simple as performing a musical idea that is beyond your keyboard-playing skills.

Studio One offers a MIDI programming method to fit every scenario. You can draw MIDI notes using a mouse, play them as slowly as you want without having to chase a metronome, or use a sequencer to craft detailed patterns that can be used over and over in a song. In this section, we will cover each of these in detail.

Drawing notes with the Paint tool

The simplest way of inputting MIDI notes is to use your mouse or touchpad. Once you've created a new Song and added an instrument, follow these steps to enter notes with this basic method:

1. Double-click on the track lane of the Instrument Track in the **Arrangement** window. This will create an empty instrument part:

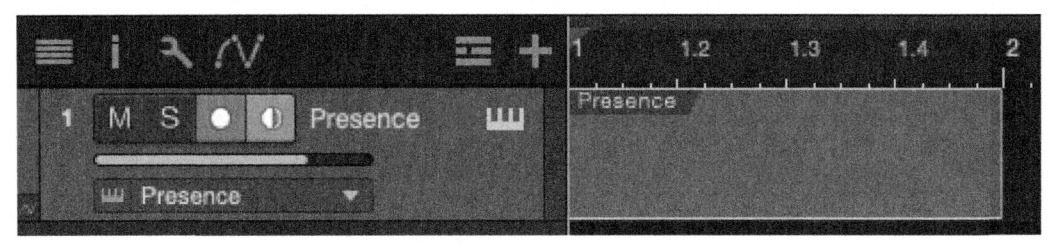

Figure 6.12: An empty instrument part next to the Instrument Track

2. Now, double-click on this new instrument part. It will open in the edit window.
3. The **Edit** window has three different view options:

   - The Piano view lets you view MIDI data on a conventional, piano-roll-style display, much like you would find on any other DAW program. This is the view that we will be focusing on, as it offers more options for programming and editing.

   - The **Drum** view is optimized for programming drum parts. It displays only the starting points of MIDI notes, and for each MIDI note, it displays the name of the corresponding part of a drum kit, such as kick, snare, hi-hat, and so on. This is an archaic way of working with MIDI, and I would advise against using this view. We will talk about a much more efficient and fun way of drum programming in the *Creating patterns* section.

   - The **Score** view allows you to input notes using musical notation, laid out on a music staff.

These three views are essentially three different ways of looking at the same MIDI data. Go ahead and select the view that fits your workflow. The steps we cover in this section will work equally on all three of them:

Figure 6.13: The view selector in the Edit window

Inputting and recording MIDI   101

4. With the **Edit** window in focus (you'll know it's in focus when there's a blue frame around it), press 3 on your keyboard to select the Paint tool. You can also activate it with your mouse if you like, but using keyboard shortcuts will let you work much faster.

Figure 6.14: The tool selector in the Edit window with the Paint tool selected

5. Make sure that the Snap function is active (highlighted in *Figure 6.15*). This will ensure that the MIDI notes you will be entering conform to the musical time base of your project. Disable Snap only if you're working on a song with a free tempo or if you intentionally want to place some notes outside of the musical grid.

6. Now, open the **Quantize** pull-down menu, also shown in *Figure 6.15*. This menu lists the most common note lengths used in music notation (**T** in this menu indicates triplet notes and **sw** indicates notes with swing). Select the length for the notes that you will be entering. For example, if you select sixteenth notes here, every note you enter using the Paint tool will snap to the nearest sixteenth note slot on the **Edit** window grid and the length of each note will be confined to a sixteenth note.

Figure 6.15: The Quantize pull-down menu with the Snap button highlighted

7. In the Piano view, you can also set the scale or mode for your song. When you do that, the Paint tool will not allow you to input any notes outside of that mode or scale:

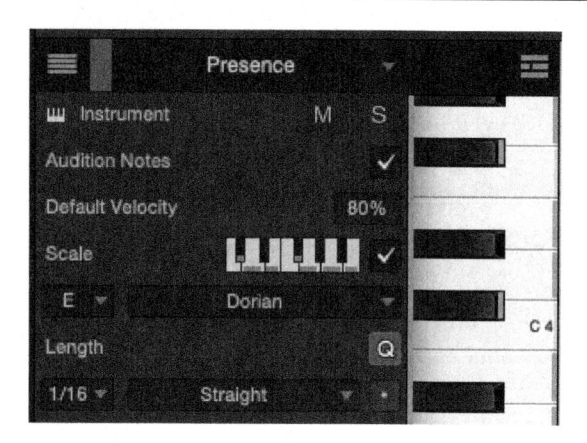

102 Adding Virtual Instruments and Recording MIDI

Figure 6.16: The scale Quantize menu in the Piano view, set to the E Dorian mode

8. Now, you can start inputting notes in the **Edit** window using the Paint tool. Click once to enter a note with the duration you set in the **Quantize** panel. Click and drag to enter longer or shorter notes.

9. To see the name of each note you enter, use the zoom slider located on the lower-right side of the **Edit** window.

Drawing notes with a mouse is the most basic way of entering MIDI data. Depending on your music style, this could be all you need, but if you're planning to do dense arrangements, you will find that this method is very time-consuming. Next, we will cover some more advanced techniques.

Step recording

Normally, when you record a live performance, the timeline keeps going in time with your project's tempo and you have to follow it precisely. If you're trying to play a difficult musical phrase and you just can't keep up, you have to try again and again until you get it right.

With **step recording**, you turn the tables. Now, the timeline waits for you until you are ready to play your next note. This is very handy for playing complex musical passages. Here's how it works:

1. Double-click on the track lane of the Instrument Track in the **Arrangement** window. This will create an empty instrument part (see *Figure 6.12*).

2. Double-click on this new instrument part. It will open in the **Edit** window.

3. Click the Step Record button (highlighted in *Figure 6.17*):

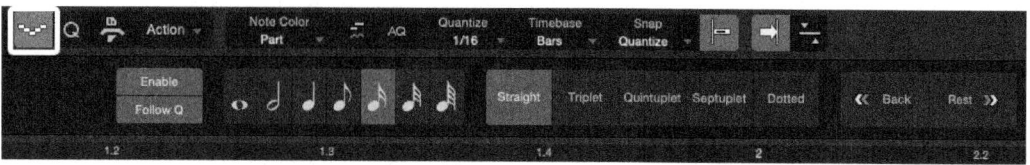

Figure 6.17: The Step Record panel

4. This will open the Step Record panel. Here, select the length of notes that you'd like to enter.
5. Place the timeline where you want to start inputting notes by clicking on the appropriate bar number on the timeline ruler.
6. Using your MIDI keyboard, play the notes one at a time. Every time you play a note, the timeline will advance by one step, corresponding to the note duration you selected on the Step Input panel.

    If you don't have a MIDI keyboard, you can also use your computer keyboard for step recording. Press *Caps Lock* to activate it.
7. You are not only confined to playing single notes; you can play chords (multiple notes) as well.
8. Change note duration as needed by using the note length selector on the Step Input panel.
9. Use the **Back** and **Rest** buttons on the **Step Record** panel to move the timeline one step back (to add a note) or forward (to insert a rest).
10. When you're done, don't forget to click **Enable** on the Step Record panel to deactivate the step recording. Otherwise, everything you play on your keyboard will continue to be added to the instrument part.

Step recording is an excellent tool that takes the stress out of recording complex or difficult musical passages. Up next, we will cover another MIDI programming method that really shines for repeating parts, especially drum grooves.

Creating patterns

Pattern sequencers allow you to create short, repeating patterns that can be used throughout a song. Although this method of programming a performance is even older than MIDI itself, it has aged really well and continues to be the current method of choice for programming drum grooves and melodic arpeggios.

Studio One makes pattern programming a breeze. Let's go:

1. Add the instrument that you'd like to create patterns for. Here, we will add Impact, Studio One's drum instrument, since the most common use for this method is for programming drum grooves. To add Impact, locate it in the **Instruments** tab of the **Browse** window, then drag and drop it anywhere on the **Arrangement** window.
2. Load a drum kit into Impact (or load a sound into any other instrument you've added) using its **Preset** menu (*Figure 6.4*).
3. On Studio One's top menu, go to **Event** and click **Insert Pattern**. This will insert an empty pattern on your instrument's track.

4. Double-click on the newly created pattern. This will open the Pattern Editor in the **Edit** window:

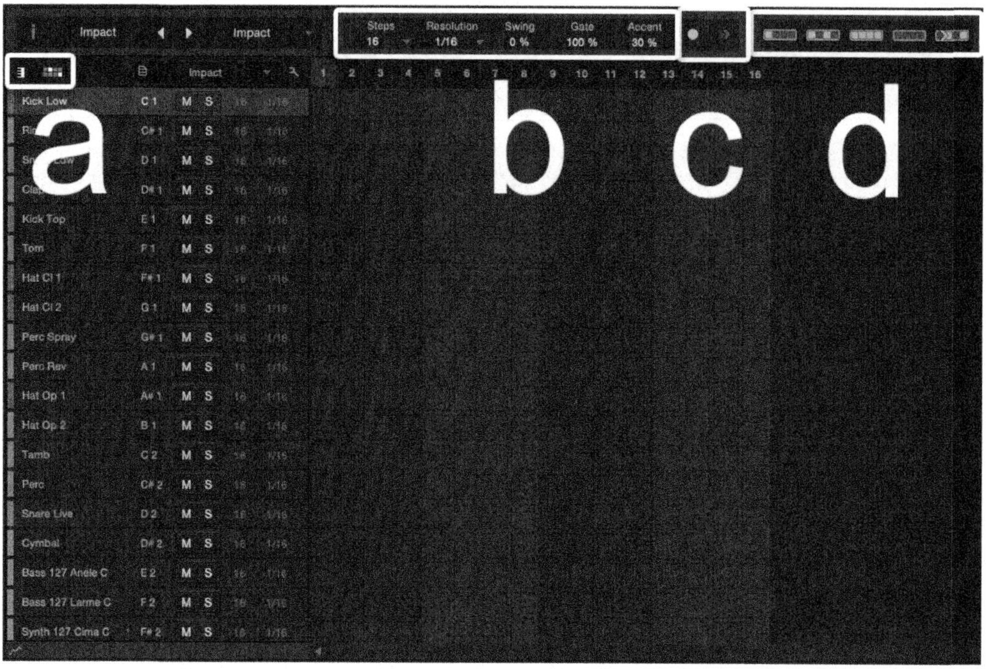

Figure 6.18: The Pattern Editor

The Pattern Editor has two viewing modes:

- **Melodic Mode** is suitable for programming arpeggiator-type sequences
- **Drum Mode** is designed for programming drum grooves

The editor displays the correct mode based on the instrument you're using, but if you want to switch to a different viewing mode, you can do so with the **Mode View** button (*a* in *Figure 6.18*).

> **Important note**
> Since Impact is a native instrument that comes with Studio One, it's tightly integrated with the Pattern Editor, and the name of each sound loaded into Impact is displayed on a separate line in the editor's interface. If you use the Pattern Editor with instruments from third-party vendors, it will not be able to display names like this, but other than that, the system will work just fine.

The Pattern Editor is essentially a matrix. Each note on your instrument is displayed in a row, and every 16th note in a bar is represented in a column. So, to trigger a note at a specific point in the bar, all you need to do is find the intersection of the row representing that note and the point where you want it to play and click on it. If you don't like it, click on the same point once again to remove it.

This is an intuitive method that lets you build a groove with instant feedback. Just loop the pattern and then add or remove notes until you're happy. Here's how:

1. Select the pattern in the **Arrangement** window.
2. Press *P* to set the left and right locators around the pattern.
3. Press / on your numeric keypad or click the **Loop** button.
4. Hit the spacebar or click play.
5. Add and remove notes on the Pattern Editor until you're happy with the pattern.
6. To fill an entire row with 8th or 16th notes, use the shortcuts provided (*d* in *Figure 6.18*).

> Tip
>
> You can also use step recording in the Pattern Editor. Activate it by clicking the Step Record button (*c* in *Figure 6.18*) and proceed as we discussed in the previous section.

Hi-hat rolls and **snare rolls** are fast repetitions of individual drum sounds and are found commonly in a wide variety of musical genres. They are cumbersome to execute on pattern sequencers, but Studio One's Pattern Editor makes implementing rolls easy:

1. Right-click on the lane in which you want to implement the roll.

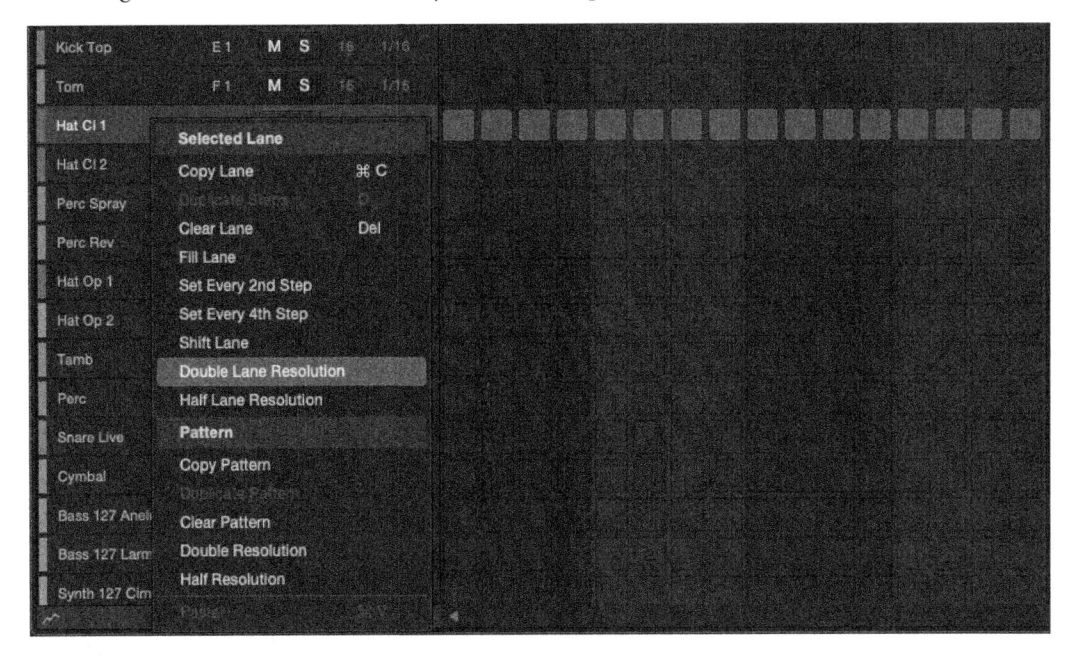

Figure 6.19: Increasing lane resolution on the Pattern Editor

2. From the menu, click **Double Lane Resolution**.

By default, a bar is divided into 16 steps for each lane. Once you click this command, that lane's resolution will be doubled, giving you 32 steps to work with. You can repeat this command if you want to execute an even faster roll, yielding 64 steps.

3. Drag the cursor across the areas where you want the roll to happen.

Use the global pattern parameters (*b* in *Figure 6.18*) to fine-tune the feel of your groove:

- **Steps** allows you to set the length of the pattern. You can use this to program complex rhythmic patterns with odd time signatures, such as 13/8.
- **Resolution** sets the length of each step, in standard note lengths. Options for triplet notes and dotted notes are available.
- **Swing** defines the time relationship between pairs of steps. When it's at 0, its default setting, each step in a pair is of equal duration. As you increase the swing value, the first note in a pair will become longer and the second will become shorter, resulting in a "swing" feel.
- **Gate** sets the length of each step. At its default value of 100%, every step is played at its full length. Reducing this value will make the notes shorter and increasing it will make them longer.
- **Accent** sets how much emphasis is placed on accented notes. You can set any note as an accented note by pressing *Ctrl* (Windows) or *Cmd* (Mac) and clicking on it.

You've created the perfect pattern, but using it over and over through the entire song will become monotonous. You need a way to create variations of your pattern and sprinkle them throughout your song to make it dynamic and exciting. Let's do it:

1. Click the Pattern Inspector button on the top-left corner of the **Edit** window. This will open the Pattern Inspector panel:

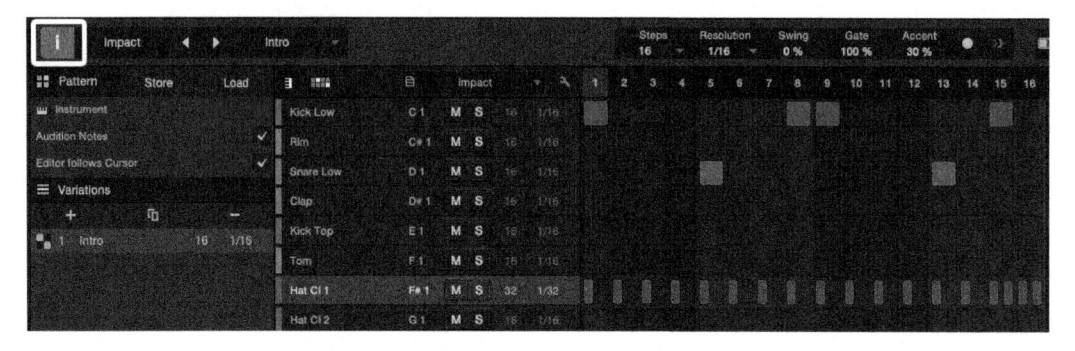

Figure 6.20: The Pattern Inspector panel with the Panel Inspector button highlighted

2. The pattern you're currently working on is listed here with the default name **Intro**.

3. Click the plus-shaped New Variation button to create an empty pattern or the Duplicate Variation button to create a duplicate copy of your existing pattern.

4. Select the newly created pattern by clicking on it. The Pattern Editor will now display whatever is inside the new pattern.

5. Work on the new pattern to create a variation to be used in a different section of the song.

6. Create as many variations as you need.

7. Double-click on the names of these variations to give them descriptive names.

8. Once you've created your arsenal of patterns, you can drag them from the Pattern Inspector panel and drop them directly on the **Arrangement** window.

This wraps up our coverage of Studio One's extensive MIDI inputting methods. Up next, we will take a look at a much more sophisticated way of creating MIDI data: converting audio recordings to MIDI.

Using Melodyne to convert audio to MIDI

Until recently, converting audio recordings to MIDI data was pure science fiction. But today, any DAW software worthy of its name boasts this function in its feature list. Studio One comes bundled with **Melodyne**, the industry standard in audio pitch detection and correction, so it has the upper hand compared to its competitors. Be warned, though, that this technology is still in its infancy. The success of conversion depends, to a large extent, on the source material.

Let's take a look at the things you can do to get the best results possible.

Choosing the right type of audio material

The first and most critical step in audio-to-MIDI conversion is to identify the pitches or notes in an audio recording. This task is performed by a pitch detection algorithm. The success of this algorithm depends heavily on two factors:

- Pitch detection works best with monophonic material. The term *monophonic* has different meanings in different contexts, so let's clarify: **Monophonic** audio material comprises one single melodic line only (that means no chords or any harmonic material, nor any accompaniments). So, for example, a guitar playing single notes is a monophonic source, but a guitar playing chords is not.

- Pitch detection algorithms yield the best results with material that allows them to clearly establish where a note begins. In practical terms, this means that legato material, where notes are connected, is more challenging compared to staccato material, where notes are detached. Also, if the performance in the audio recording has lots of sliding in and out of notes (glissandos), the algorithm will have a hard time determining the pitches and starting points of notes.

Even if your audio material does not meet the preceding criteria, there are a few tricks you can try to get mileage out of it. We'll cover those in the next section.

Audio-to-MIDI-conversion walkthrough

Once you have created a new Song, follow these steps to convert an audio recording to MIDI data:

1. Add the virtual instrument you'd like to use.
2. Next, load a sound into this instrument using its **Preset** menu.
3. Locate the audio file you'd like to convert to MIDI. Drag it from **Explorer** (Windows) or **Finder** (Mac) and drop it into the Song. Studio One will create an audio track and place the audio recording as an audio event inside the track.
4. Right-click on this audio event. From this menu, go to **Audio**, and then click on **Edit with Melodyne**. This will send the audio material to Melodyne, which will open in the **Edit** window:

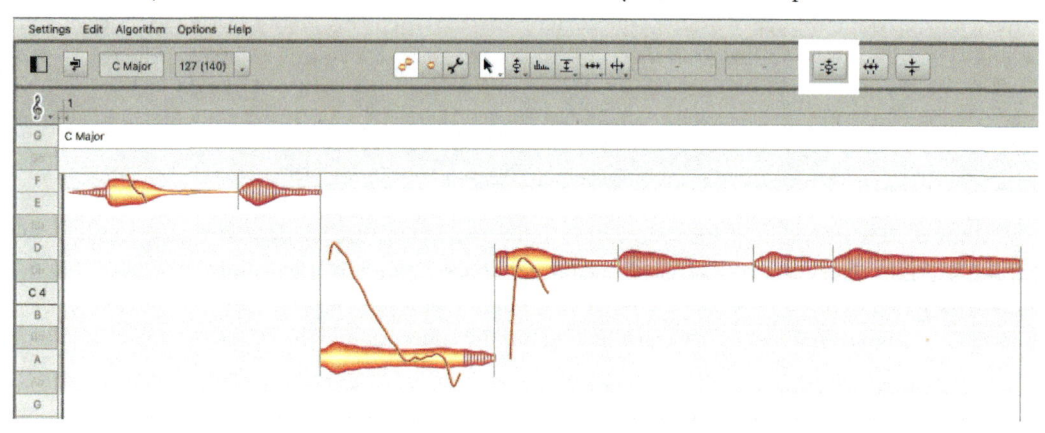

Figure 6.21: Melodyne with the Correct Pitch Macro button highlighted

Note that Melodyne has detected all the pitches in the audio recording and it's displaying them in a layout that resembles Studio One's Piano view, which we talked about earlier in this chapter. We will take an in-depth look at Melodyne in *Chapter 8*. For now, we will only perform a simple operation to make sure that there are no out-of-tune notes that may confuse the pitch detection algorithm.

5. Press *Ctrl + A* (Windows) or *Cmd + A* (Mac) to select all the notes.
6. Click the Correct Pitch Macro button. This will open a small dialog box:

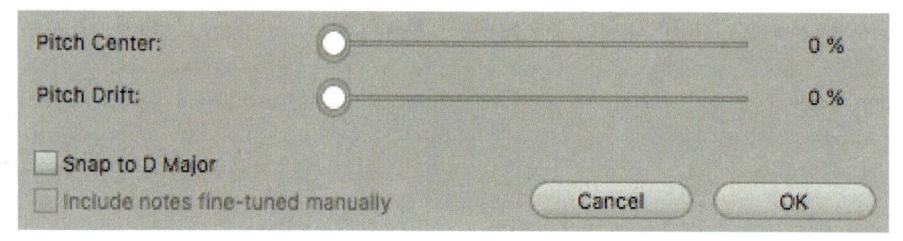

Figure 6.22: Melodyne's Correct Pitch Macro dialog box

7. Pull the **Pitch Center** and **Pitch Drift** sliders on this dialog box all the way up to `100` `%`. Click **OK**.

    This is a rather crude way of fixing out-of-tune notes, but it's perfectly adequate for our purpose here.

8. Close the **Edit** window. Back on the **Arrangement** window, you will see that the audio event now has some colorful dots overlaid on top of the audio waveform. These are the MIDI notes that have just been created.

9. You can now drag the audio event and drop it directly on the track you created for your virtual instrument. Studio One will copy the MIDI data over to the Instrument Track.

10. Play the project and see how the conversion went. Some manual tweaking will most likely be necessary. Refer to *Chapter 9* to edit the converted notes to perfection.

Converting audio to MIDI is an exciting feature that opens unlimited possibilities. You can, for example, use this procedure to convert a percussion recording to create your own rhythmic groove. It will only get better as algorithms improve.

Summary

In this chapter, we took an in-depth look at Studio One's several methods for recording and inputting MIDI data for use with virtual instruments. We covered a variety of music production scenarios and discussed which method would be the best choice for a given workflow, including recording notes live, painting them with a mouse, or programming them with a sequencer.

So far, we focused on creating and pouring our musical ideas into our projects. In the next part of this book, we will talk about how to rework and improve those ideas by using Studio One's excellent editing tools. We will start by taking an in-depth look at the global editing tools in the next chapter and lay the groundwork for the editing best practices that we will be using throughout this book.

Part 3: Editing in Studio One

In this part, you will learn all there is to know about editing your recordings on par with professional standards. We will explore Studio One's editing tools for both audio and MIDI tracks and see how you can use these tools for creative and corrective purposes. We will finish by covering Studio One's global tracks, which allow you to make changes to your Song on a global level.

This part includes the following chapters:

- *Chapter 7, Editing and Rearranging Your Song*
- *Chapter 8, Editing Audio*
- *Chapter 9, Editing MIDI*
- *Chapter 10, Using Global Tracks*

7
Editing and Rearranging Your Song

In music production, **editing** is the process of taking a rough musical recording and crafting it to perfection. This covers a wide range of applications, ranging from mundane to highly creative. Today's music producers spend more time on editing than any other phase of the production workflow, and becoming proficient in editing is essential. In this part of the book, we will take an in-depth look at Studio One's editing tools and how you can use them to take your projects to a whole new level.

In this chapter, we will talk about the editing tools and modes, and how you can use them to process material in the **Arrangement** window. Then, we will explore Studio One's **Arranger Track** and use it to edit your project at the Song level, to easily perform complicated tasks, such as rearranging the sections of your song.

In this chapter, we will cover the following topics:

- Exploring the editing tools
- Understanding Snap and various Snap modes
- Using the Arranger Track to edit a song
- Using the Launcher to try out new ideas

Technical requirements

To follow this chapter, you will need to have Studio One activated on your computer.

Exploring the editing tools

Studio One has eight editing tools, and they can be found at the top of the **Arrangement** window:

Figure 7.1: Editing tools from left to right – Arrow, Range, Split, Eraser, Paint, Mute, Bend, and Listen

You can activate these tools by simply clicking on them, but you'll increase the speed of your editing workflow if you learn the following keyboard shortcuts to switch between them:

- *1* activates the **Arrow** tool
- *2* activates the **Range** tool
- *3* activates the **Split** tool
- *4* activates the **Eraser** tool
- *5* activates the **Paint** tool
- *6* activates the **Mute** tool
- *7* activates the **Bend** tool
- *8* activates the **Listen** tool

Now, let's take an in-depth look at each of these tools.

Arrow tool

The **Arrow** tool is by far the most commonly used editing tool in Studio One, and for good reason: It can be used for a wide variety of tasks, whereas the other tools serve very specific purposes.

Here is a list of the basic operations you can perform with the **Arrow** tool, which can be activated by pressing *1* on your keyboard:

- Clicking on an event in the **Arrangement** window selects it. You can select multiple events by holding down the *Ctrl/Cmd* key while clicking on them. When you have several events in the **Arrangement** window and run a command from the top menu, Studio One will apply the command only to the selected events.
- Double-clicking on an event opens it in the **Edit** window.
- Right-clicking on an event opens a contextual menu that lists all available parameters and settings that pertain to that specific event.

- Clicking and dragging an event moves it.
- Clicking and dragging an event while holding down the *Alt* (Windows) or *Option* (Mac) key makes a copy of it.

However, there's a lot more to the **Arrow** tool than these basic functions; let's look at the more advanced tasks that it can perform.

Sizing events

An **event** in the **Arrangement** window is a visual representation of an audio or MIDI recording. Normally, it extends from the beginning to the end of the recording:

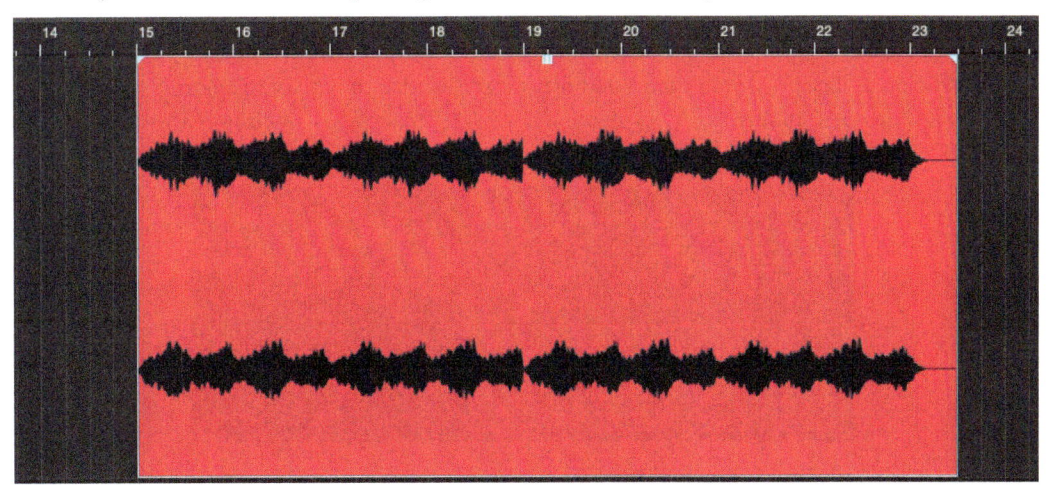

Figure 7.2: An audio event

The event in *Figure 7.2* represents an audio recording that starts at the beginning of bar 15 and ends in the middle of bar 23, as indicated by the ruler on the top. Let's say you want to trim this event so that it only plays between bars 17 and 21. Here's how you can do it easily with the **Arrow** tool:

1. Hover your mouse on the left edge of the event. The cursor will turn into a double-headed arrow.
2. Click and drag the edge of the event to the right until it reaches the beginning of bar 17.
3. Now, hover your mouse on the right edge.
4. Click and drag to the left until you reach the beginning of bar 21.

Sizing an event with this method is non-destructive; it does not delete your recording. It only tells Studio One to ignore the parts that are trimmed out. If you change your mind later, you can always use the **Arrow** tool to expand the event back to its original size, or anywhere in between.

> **Tip**
> Sizing works the same way for MIDI events.

Looping events

You can set any audio or MIDI event to loop throughout the entirety of your Song, and then use the **Arrow** tool to fine-tune the looping behavior (i.e., set which part of the event will be looped and for how long). Here's how to do it:

1. Right-click on the event that you'd like to loop.
2. On the contextual menu for the event, click the **Loop** checkbox. The event will be looped all the way to the end of your Song.
3. Now, go to the end of your Song and hover your mouse at the end of the loop. The **Arrow** tool will shape-shift momentarily, as seen in *Figure 7.3*. This hidden function of the **Arrow** tool is referred to as the **Looping tool**.

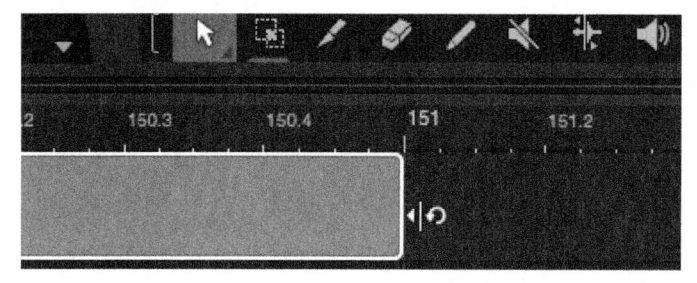

Figure 7.3: The Looping tool

4. Use the **Looping** tool to drag the end of the loop to where you want it to end.

There is a far more exciting functionality to the **Looping** tool: You can use it to adjust the length of a looping segment to try out different, creative possibilities. For example, if your song is in 4/4 time and you have a rhythm pattern that lasts for a bar, you can use the **Looping** tool to trim the pattern to a shorter value (e.g., three beats only) or extend it to a longer value (e.g., six beats). This will make the loop repeat at different periods compared to the rest of the elements in your song, resulting in a more interesting, polyrhythmic structure. To do this, hover your mouse at the lower end of the first segment of a loop. Once the arrow turns into the **Looping** tool, resize the segment to your heart's content.

Time stretching

Imagine that you are producing music for a commercial. The advertisement agency informed you that there would be a voiceover announcement at the beginning of the commercial, so you prepared a music bed with a quiet part at the beginning to accommodate the announcement. Then, you received the recording for the voiceover and found that it's a bit too long:

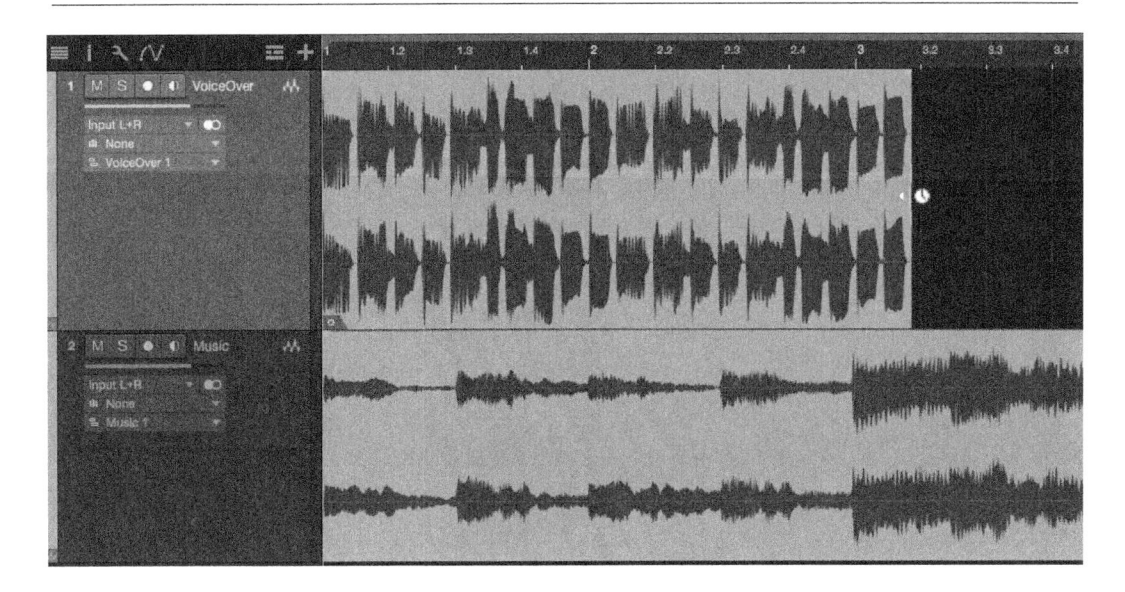

Figure 7.4: The voiceover recording (the track at the top) extends beyond
the quiet part of the music bed (the track at the bottom)

Resizing the voiceover recording as discussed in the preceding section will not work here, because it will trim out the last bit of the announcement. We want to be able to shrink the entire recording to fit in the desired space. This can be achieved by time stretching, and it's very easy to implement. Here's how to proceed with the **Arrow** tool:

1. Hover your mouse over the right edge of the event to which you'd like to apply time stretching. In our example, this will be the voiceover recording.
2. Hold down the *Alt* (Windows) or *Option* (Mac) key. The cursor will turn into an arrow with a clock icon, as seen in *Figure 7.4*.
3. Without letting go of the key, drag the edge of the event to the left to shrink it or to the right to expand it.

That's it! If you shrink an event, it will play faster. If you expand it, it will play slower. This method of time stretching does not change the pitch of the recording, so your voiceover artist will not end up sounding like a chipmunk or Darth Vader.

Time-stretching algorithms have improved massively over the past few years, but keep in mind that if you apply one in radical amounts (e.g., beyond 20 percent of the event's original size), noticeable artifacts will begin to appear.

Applying fades

Applying fades to audio events is one of the most common tasks in music production. A **fade-in** is a gradual increase in volume at the beginning of an event. You can use it to ease into the event by smoothing out any abrupt sounds that may be present at its beginning. A **fade-out** is a gradual decrease in volume at the end of an event. It is usually applied to end an event smoothly.

Applying fades is simple. Grab the **Arrow** tool and follow these steps:

1. Hover your mouse over the event that you'd like to apply fades to. You will see two tiny white triangles appear in its top-left and right corners (which can be seen in *Figure 7.2*).
2. To apply a fade-in, click on the triangle on the left and drag it to the right.
3. To apply a fade-out, click on the triangle on the right and drag it to the left.
4. As you drag the triangles, the resulting change in volume will be shown with a diagonal line drawn across the beginning or end of the event. You will notice a small white square appearing on this line, as can be seen in *Figure 7.5*. You can move this square up or down to change the line to a curve and experiment with the timing of the fade.

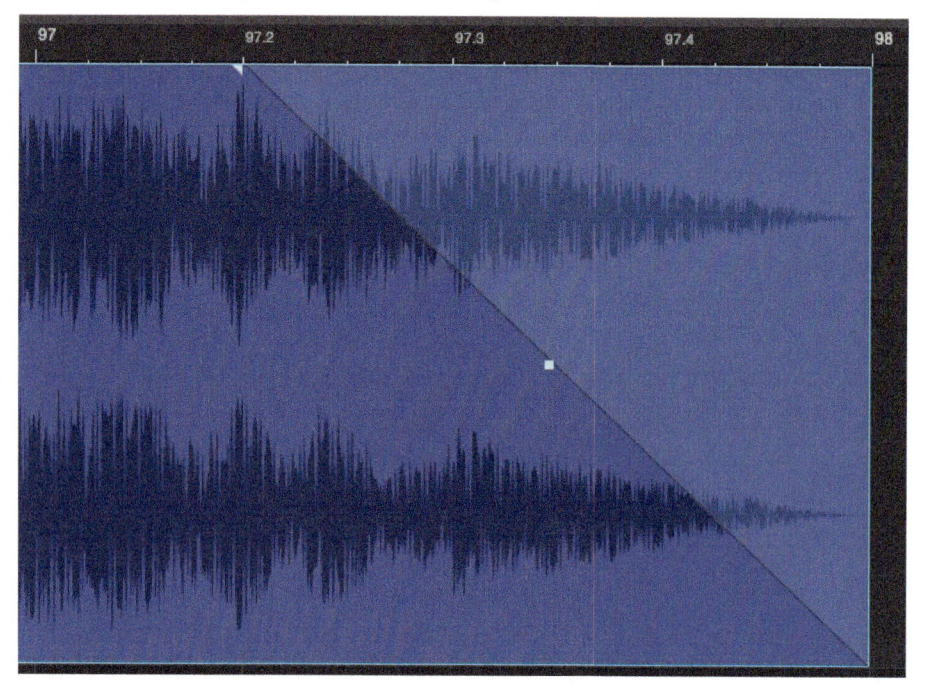

Figure 7.5: The small square on the fade line allows you to experiment with different fade alternatives

Adjusting gain

You can adjust the gain levels of individual audio events. This is useful for balancing the level of an inconsistent audio recording, as we will see in *Chapter 8*. It is also an essential part of mixing music, which we will talk about in *Chapter 11*. Here's how you can adjust the gain with the **Arrow** tool:

1. Hover your mouse over the event that you'd like to change the gain of. A small square will appear on its upper edge (which can be seen in *Figure 7.2*).
2. Drag this square up to increase the gain, and drag it down to decrease it.
3. As you drag the square, Studio One will display the amount of the resulting gain change in decibels. A value of zero indicates that no change has been made, a positive value indicates that the gain is being increased, and a negative value shows that it's being decreased.
4. If you want to make a finer adjustment, hold down the *Shift* key while dragging.

If you have fades on an event and then decide to change its gain, Studio One will automatically scale the fades to match the new gain value.

> **Tip**
> Although the terms *gain* and *volume* are often used interchangeably, there is an important difference. **Gain** refers to the level of a signal at the input of an audio device – in this case, an audio track. Changing the gain alters the level being fed into all the effects plug-ins on the audio track, and will affect how they process the sound. **Volume**, on the other hand, is the level of a signal at the output of the audio track. Changing the volume will simply change the loudness of the signal, without affecting its tonal character.

Slip editing

Slip editing preserves the length of an audio event while allowing you to move its contents forward or backward in time. It's usually used in conjunction with other editing methods, such as resizing and time stretching. To slip-edit an audio recording, follow these steps:

1. While holding your mouse on the lower half of the audio event, hold down the *Ctrl + Alt* (Windows) or *Cmd + Option* (Mac) keys. The cursor will turn into a double-headed arrow.
2. Without letting go of the keys, drag the contents of the audio event to the left or right.

Note that you can slip an audio event only as far as the length of the actual recording that it contains.

Selecting an alternative tool

Sometimes, you may find yourself constantly going back and forth between the **Arrow** tool and another tool. In such a case, click on the **Arrow** tool icon to open the **Alternative Tool** menu:

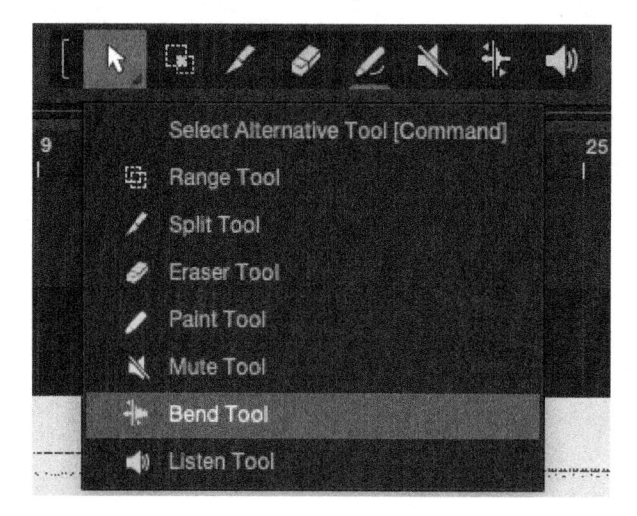

Figure 7.6: The Alternative Tool menu

Here, select the other tool that you are using frequently. Now, when you want to switch to the alternative tool, simply press *Ctrl* (Windows) or *Cmd* (Mac) on your keyboard.

So far, we have talked about the tasks you can perform with the Arrow tool. Now, let's continue with our tour of the other editing tools, which will allow you to directly interact with events in the **Arrangement** window by using a mouse. All actions you perform with these tools are non-destructive and can be undone, so feel free to experiment and explore!

Range tool

So far, we have worked with the **Arrow** tool, which lets you manipulate entire events. But what if you want to work on just a small part of an event? That's where the **Range** tool comes in. This tool lets you select a specific area inside an audio or MIDI event. That selected area is then treated as a separate event in and of itself. This is useful for applying a command only to a specific part of an event or for dissecting an event for further editing.

To use the **Range** tool, simply select it by pressing *2* on your keyboard and then drag over the area you wish to select. You can make multiple selections by holding down the *Shift* key. You can also drag vertically to select the same area on multiple events located across multiple tracks.

When you select an area with the **Range** tool and double-click on it, Studio One will create a new event covering that area, eliminating the need to use the **Split** tool. This is a major time-saver in situations where you'd like to select and delete several portions of a recording.

The **Range** tool can be linked with the **Arrow** tool, creating a tool with superpowers. To do this, click on the bracket on the left side of the **Editing Tools** menu (*Figure 7.1*). Now, when you bring your cursor to the lower half of an event, you'll get the **Arrow** tool, and on the upper half of the event, you'll have the **Range** tool. That way, you can select an area and then move, duplicate, or resize it as if it were a separate event.

Split tool

The **Split** tool splits events into multiple events. Activate it by pressing *3* on your keyboard. Now, when you move your mouse on the **Arrangement** window, a vertical line will follow your cursor, allowing you to use the ruler as a reference to pinpoint the exact location where you want to split an event.

If you select multiple events across multiple tracks, clicking with the **Split** tool on any one of them will split all selected events at the same time.

Eraser tool

The **Eraser** tool deletes events in the **Arrangement** window. Simply activate it by pressing *4* on your keyboard and then click on any event you wish to delete. You can also drag across several events to delete them in one go. If multiple events are selected, clicking on any one of them will result in all of them being deleted.

Paint tool

The **Paint** tool has several different functions in the **Arrangement** window:

- It creates an empty event on an instrument track by clicking and dragging on an empty space in the lane for that track.
- It creates song sections for the Arranger Track, as we will discuss later in this chapter under the section *Using the Arranger Track to edit a Song*.
- It creates chord symbols for the Chord Track, as we will discuss in *Chapter 9*.
- It modifies automation data, as we will see in *Chapter 13*.

- It modifies **gain envelopes** for audio events. Gain envelopes allow you to precisely change the gain levels throughout events in order to emphasize or conceal parts of an audio recording as necessary. In order to view the gain envelope for an event, right-click on it and check the **Gain Envelope** box:

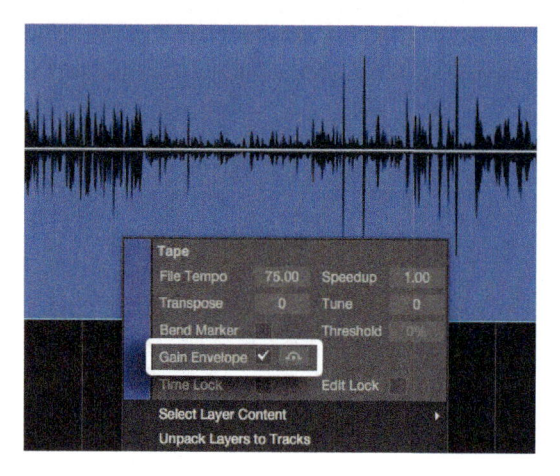

Figure 7.7: The Gain Envelope checkbox

A white line will appear inside the event. You can now use the **Paint** tool to add points to this line where you want to change the gain level. You can then move these points up or down to increase or decrease the gain as necessary.

Now, let's take a closer look at *Figure 7.7*. The white line that crosses the middle of the audio event represents the gain value for the event. Initially, it's a straight line, meaning that the event plays back with the same level of gain from start to finish. Note that there is a relatively quieter section in the middle of the event, represented by smaller waveforms. By using the **Paint** tool, you can redraw the white line to increase the gain in that part, like so:

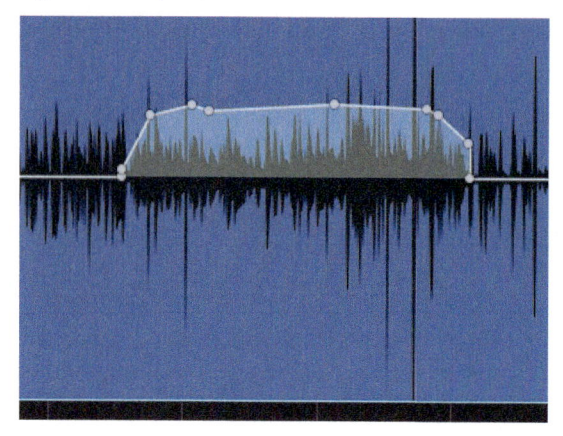

Figure 7.8: Using the Paint tool to redraw a gain envelope

When you use the **Paint** tool to modify a line in this way, you may find that it's rather jerky. Thankfully, the **Paint** tool comes with a selection of several alternative drawing shapes that offer more precise, smooth control to help you get the perfect result. Click and hold the **Paint** tool icon to access these shapes:

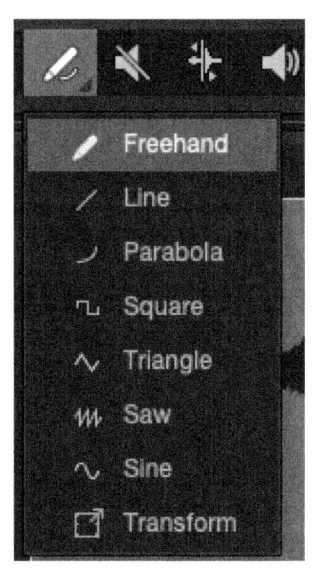

Figure 7.9: Shape options for the Paint tool

The **Freehand** option, selected by default, allows you to draw freely but may yield a bumpy result, as seen in *Figure 7.8*. For a smoother result, try the **Line**, **Parabola**, and **Transform** options. The **Square**, **Triangle**, **Saw**, and **Sine** options are perfect when you want to create an automation curve or gain envelope that changes periodically.

Mute tool

The **Mute** tool mutes an audio or MIDI event that you click on. You can also drag across several events to mute them at once. If multiple events are selected, clicking on any one of them will result in all of them being muted.

Bend tool

The **Bend** tool is used for time-stretching parts of an audio event by adding, manipulating, and removing **bend markers**. To understand what bend markers are and how they work, let's take a look at this drum recording:

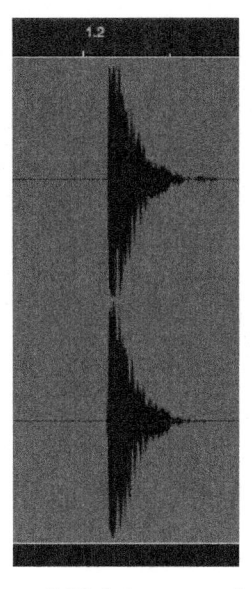

Figure 7.10: A drum recording

The spike in the waveform in *Figure 7.10* is a snare drum hit. It was supposed to be exactly on the second beat of the first measure (represented by **1.2** on the ruler), but the drummer was a bit late. Fortunately, we can easily fix this by using bend markers. Here's how:

1. Right-click on the event and check the **Bend Marker** checkbox:

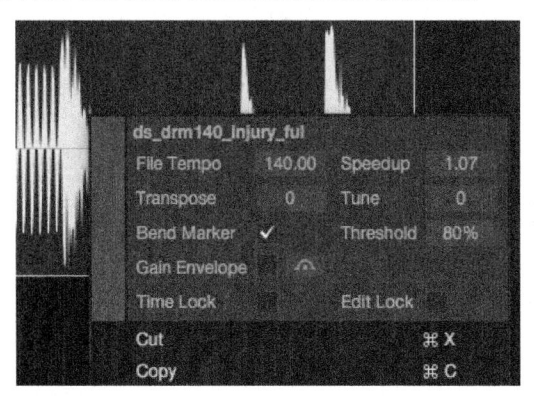

Figure 7.11: The Bend Marker checkbox

2. Activate the **Bend** tool by pressing *7* on your keyboard.

3. Now, add three bend markers by clicking on the event: one in the empty space before the snare hit, one in the empty space after the snare hit, and one exactly at the beginning of the hit, like this:

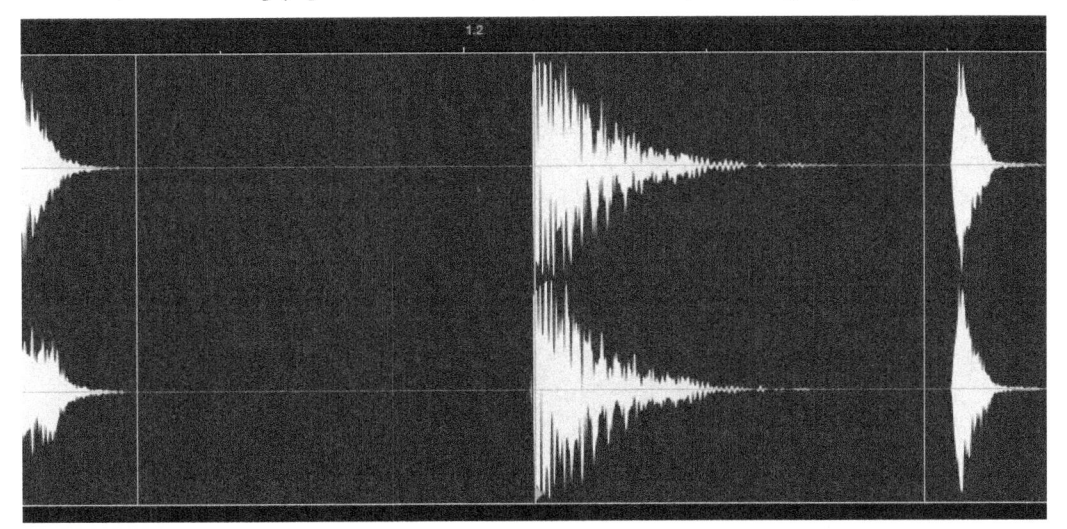

Figure 7.12: Bend markers inserted at and around a drum hit

4. You can now drag the bend marker at the beginning of the snare hit to move it into position. The reason we added markers in the empty spaces before and after the hit is that we don't want to move anything else in the event. Any time stretching is applied here, it will be limited to the area between those extra bend markers.

We will talk about audio bending in great detail in *Chapter 8*.

The Listen tool

The **Listen** tool lets you hear a specific part of a single audio or MIDI event. Activate it by pressing *8* on your keyboard and then click and hold on to the event. Studio One will solo the track associated with that event and start playback from the position you clicked. Playback will continue for as long as you hold down the mouse button. This tool is practical for instantly auditioning the content of events, especially in large projects.

This completes our tour of Studio One's editing tools. Up next, we will discuss snap, a vital feature that must be set up correctly in order to get the best results when editing a song.

Understanding Snap and various Snap modes

Editing music is a painstaking process that requires precision. We cannot just drag an event and hope that it falls into the right place. Studio One assists us in overcoming this issue by using **Snap**, an automatic alignment feature that ensures that any editing operation we perform is perfectly lined up with either a musical grid or with other events.

Snap affects the behavior of all the editing tools we discussed in the preceding section. So, when you move an event with the **Arrow** tool, select an area with the **Range** tool, or cut an event with the **Split** tool, **Snap** will align these actions automatically.

Snap is active by default, and you'll want to leave it like that most of the time. If you need to do some minor surgical editing that does not need to align with anything, such as removing a breath noise, Snap can be turned off by pressing *N* on your keyboard or by using the **Snap** toggle button:

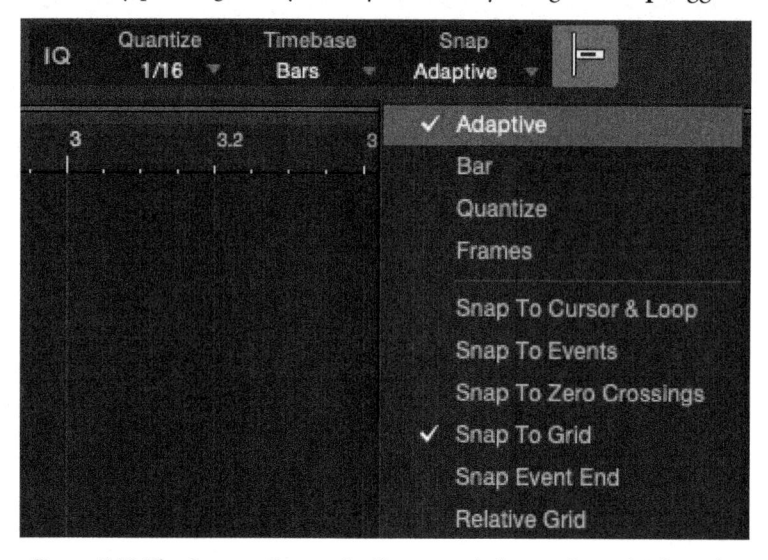

Figure 7.13: The Snap options – the Snap toggle button is on the far right

There are several modes for the Snap feature, accommodating various usage scenarios. These modes can be accessed and selected by the **Snap** drop-down menu in *Figure 7.13*. Now, let's take a close look at each of these modes.

Snap To Grid

In a typical music production workflow, you want all your editing actions to line up with musically meaningful points in time: bars, beats, or various note lengths. The **Snap To Grid** option does exactly that: it overlays a grid on the **Arrangement** window and ensures that any editing action you perform snaps to that grid precisely.

To work in this mode, open the **Snap** drop-down menu in *Figure 7.13* and select **Snap To Grid**. On the same menu, use the following options to set the sensitivity of the grid:

- **Adaptive** dynamically changes the resolution of the grid based on your zoom level. If you're zoomed all the way out, you will only be able to snap to the beginning of the bars. As you zoom in, you will be able to snap to beats within bars, and then to 8th notes, 16th notes, and so on.
- **Bar** limits the grid to the beginning of bars only. Select this option if you want to zoom in closely but restrain editing operations so that they snap only to the beginning of bars.
- **Quantize** allows you to set a specific note length value for the Snap grid regardless of your zoom level. For example, if you want everything to snap to 8th notes, select the **Quantize** option here, and then select **1/8** in the **Quantize** drop-down menu in *Figure 7.13*.

Next, let's take a look at a variation of **Snap to Grid** – **Relative Grid**.

Relative Grid

Relative Grid is a variation of **Snap To Grid** with a more specific field of application. Let's say you have an event that starts before the beginning of a bar:

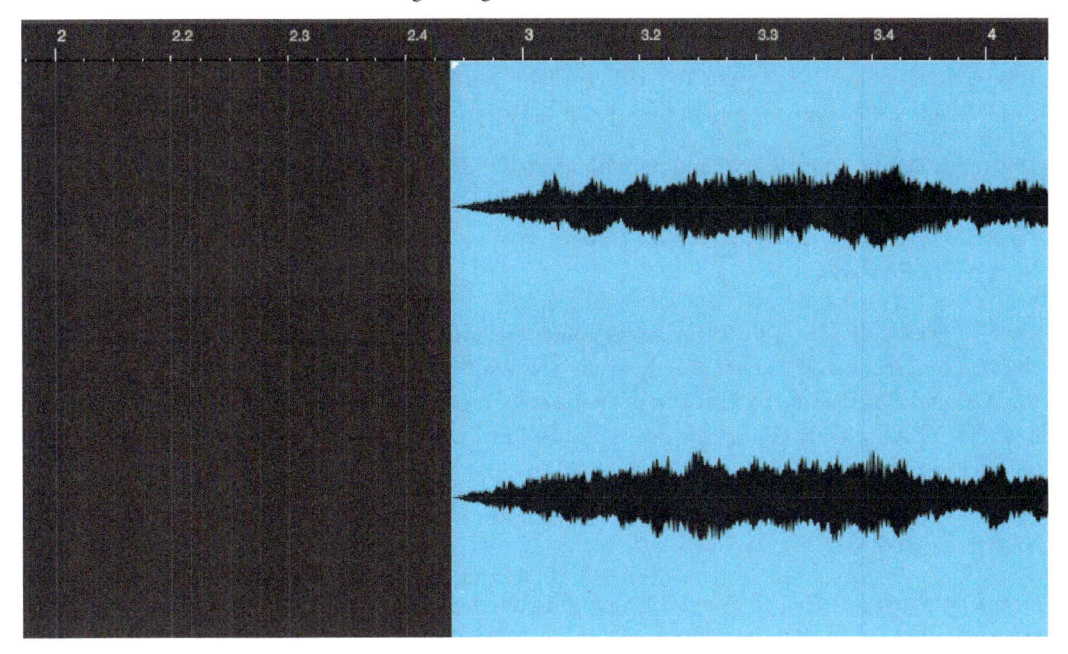

Figure 7.14: An event that starts before the beginning of a bar

The event in *Figure 7.14* starts slightly before bar 3. It does not align visually, but sometimes it makes musical sense, and you may want to keep it like this. Now, let's say you decided to add a new section to the beginning of your song. In order to make room for that section, you want to move everything forward in time by four bars. That would mean moving this event to bar 7. If **Snap To Grid** is selected, when you move this event, it will snap to the beginning of bar 7, which is not what we want. We want it to start slightly before bar 7, just like it did with bar 3. In other words, we want to move the event while preserving its position relative to the beginning of the bar grid. To do that, simply select **Relative Grid** and drag it to bar 7. It will snap to the exact relative position respective to this new bar.

Snapping events to a musical grid is all that you will need for most music production work, but a musical grid becomes irrelevant for other fields of audio post-production, such as editing dialog or working with sound effects. Fortunately, the **Snap** feature has a host of other modes that make life easier by assisting us in those fields as well.

Snap To Cursor & Loop

With **Snap To Cursor & Loop** selected, the cursor on the timeline and the loop indicators on the ruler will become magnetic. Any operation you perform in their vicinity will snap to them. This is useful for working at a specific point in your project: just select this mode, place the cursor at that point, and then edit to your heart's content, safe in the knowledge that everything will align to that point perfectly.

This mode is not as rigid as **Snap To Grid**. It will let you drag or split objects at other points as well. You will notice the magnetic pull of the cursor and loop locators only if you work close to them.

This mode can be activated in tandem with **Snap To Grid** or **Relative Grid** modes, so be sure to unselect those if you're working on a non-musical project.

Snap To Events

Snap To Events allows events on the **Arrangement** window to snap to each other. Let's say you have an event on Track 1 and it starts exactly where you want it to. Now, you add another event on Track 2 and want this new event to start at exactly the same moment as the one on Track 1. With **Snap To Events** selected, when you drag the new event on Track 2, it will snap precisely to the beginning of the event on Track 1.

Snap Event End

Normally, when you drag an event, the **Snap** function will align its beginning to the point dictated by the selected mode. With this option enabled, you can also snap the end of an event to an available snap location as well.

Snap To Zero Crossings

If you double-click on an audio event to open it in the **Edit** window and then zoom in real close, you will see that it oscillates around a horizontal line:

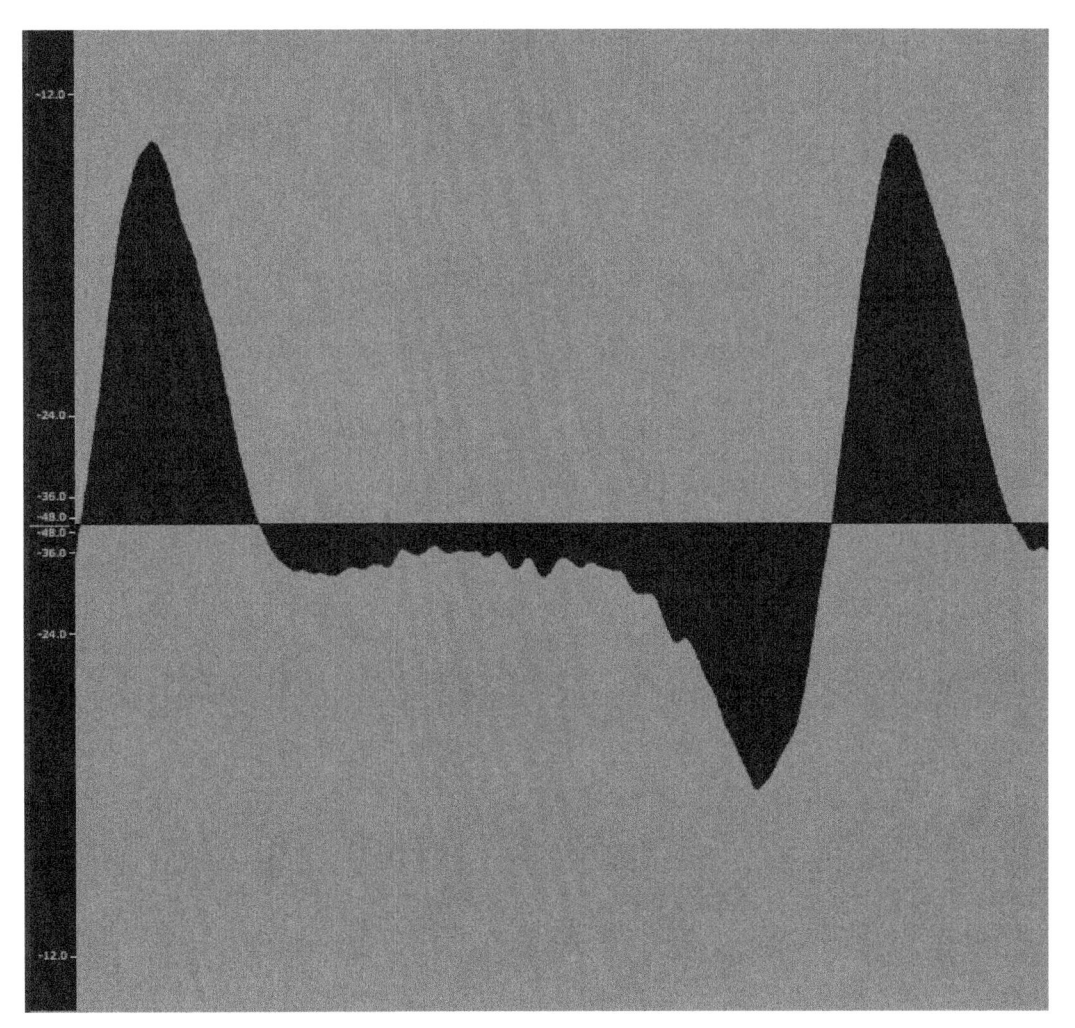

Figure 7.15: Close view of an audio waveform

This is basically a visual representation of how a speaker cone would move when playing back this audio material. Think of the horizontal line as the cone's resting position. Anything above the line would mean that the cone is moving forward, and anything below the line would indicate that it's pulling backward.

If you cut this waveform at a random point by using the **Split** tool or by trimming it with the **Arrow** tool, this would interrupt the smooth movement of the speaker cone and would result in an audible artifact, referred to as a click. Enabling **Snap To Zero Crossings** ensures that any editing you perform will snap to the nearest point at which the waveform crosses the horizontal line. These points are called **zero crossings**. At those points, the speaker cone will be at its resting position and there will be no clicks.

Leave this option enabled at all times. It will cause a slight shift in the placement of your edits but this will only be in the frame of milliseconds and will not be noticeable.

So far in this chapter, we have covered Studio One's editing tools and **Snap** options. Armed with this information, you are now ready to tackle any editing task in the **Arrangement** window. However, as your projects grow, working with a large number of events located across several tracks may become overwhelming and some extra assistance may become necessary. Thankfully, Studio One has a tool designed just for that purpose, and we are going to learn how to use it in the next section.

Using the Arranger Track to edit a song

A musical piece usually comprises several sections. Depending on the genre, a section could be a movement in a symphony, the head of a jazz arrangement, the chorus of a pop song, or a drop in an EDM track.

When creating a musical piece, we hardly ever know in advance how many sections it will contain, and in which order. As the song grows and these sections develop, we may be tempted to experiment with the form of the song by shuffling the order of its sections. Sometimes, this becomes a matter of necessity; a client may ask us to deliver several versions of a song – a short, radio-friendly version, a longer album version, and an even longer club version, for example.

All these scenarios require lots of audio and MIDI events to be shuffled within the project. It's a potentially messy task with lots of room for error. Studio One's **Arranger Track** is a feature designed to move, copy, delete, or otherwise manipulate entire sections of a song easily and non-destructively, and can be a lifesaver, especially when dealing with larger projects.

To work with the Arranger Track, follow these steps:

1. Click the **Global Track Visibility** button and select **Arranger**. This will make the Arranger Track visible.
2. Select the **Paint** tool by pressing 5 on your keyboard.
3. If Snap is not already active, enable it by pressing N on your keyboard.

4. Click and drag the **Paint** tool across the Arranger Track to cover each area you wish to define as a section. Add as many sections as you need. Here's an example project with several sections created on the Arranger Track:

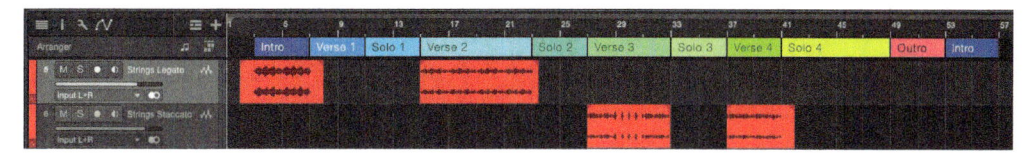

Figure 7.16: Several sections of a song marked on an Arranger Track

5. As you add new sections, Studio One will name and color them automatically. Right-click on a section to change its name and color as necessary.

6. You can now use the **Arrow** tool to move or copy the sections on the Arranger Track. All the events contained in those sections will follow along. Remember that the shortcut for copying an event is to drag it while holding down the *Alt/Option* key.

7. To remove a section from your song, along with all the events that are contained in it, right-click on it and select **Delete Range** in the popup menu.

Note that when you make copies of sections using the Arranger Track, these copies become independent entities, so you may work on each and every one of them separately to create variations from the original material.

Using the Launcher to try out new ideas

The **Launcher** is a companion to the **Arrange** window. It allows you to try out different ideas and shape your music without messing up your existing arrangement. If you're coming from Ableton Live, another fine DAW software, you can think of the Launcher as the **Session** view. For everyone else, this will be a total paradigm shift, so let's jump right in.

Once you've worked on your song for a while and you have the basic elements in place, you will typically start thinking about how to combine these elements – start with an intro, where you will have tracks A, B, and C, and then get to the verse, where you will add tracks D, E, and F, and so on. Normally, we arrange these tracks in a linear fashion in the **Arrange** window, with the beginning of the song on the left and the end of the song on the right. The Launcher, on the other hand, allows you to combine these tracks any way you want. Here's how:

1. Open the **Launcher** by clicking on its icon (*a* in *Figure 7.17*):

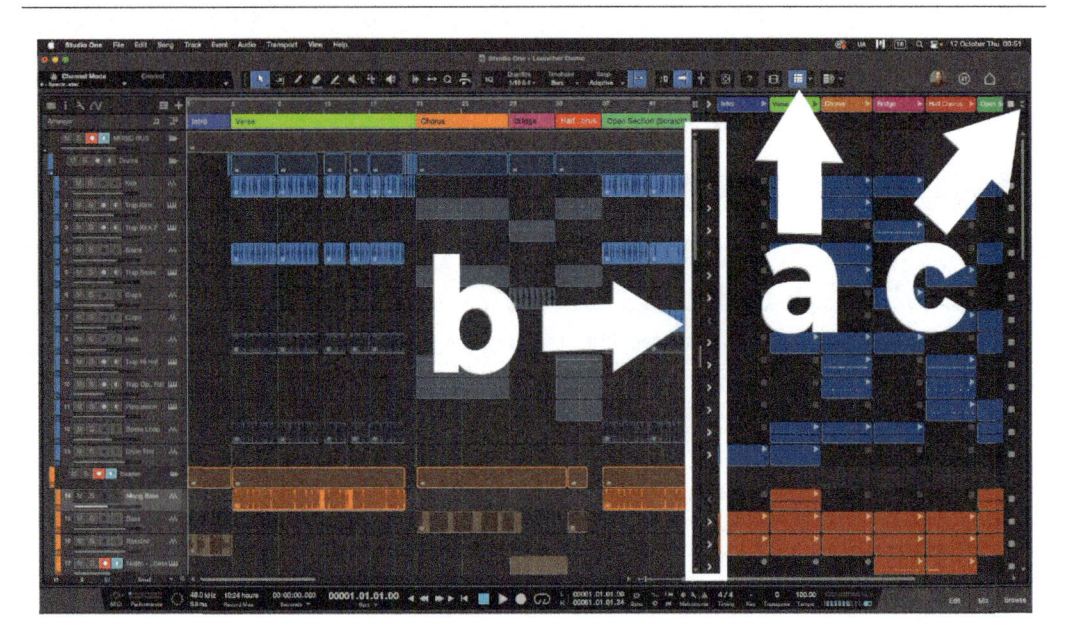

Figure 7.17: The Launcher

2. Now, you can drag any element from the **Arrange** window and drop it into the Launcher. If you've already marked sections of your Song on the Arranger Track, as we discussed in the preceding section, you can simply drag and drop those sections as well.

3. Here comes the fun part: You can shuffle the elements in the Launcher without changing anything in the **Arrange** window. This allows you to try out totally different combinations within your Song, while your original arrangement remains intact.

4. The arrows on the border separating the Launcher from the **Arrange** window (*b* in *Figure 7.17*) select what happens when you hit the play button. If the arrow for a track is pointing to the left, that track will play whatever is on the **Arrange** window. If the arrow is pointing right, it will play from the Launcher. This allows you to combine ideas from both windows.

5. The fun doesn't end here! The Launcher has its own **Playlist**, which can be accessed by clicking on the icon in its upper-right corner (*c* in *Figure 7.17*).

6. Once you open the **Playlist** window, you will see that the sections of your Song that you've been working on so far are listed as **Scenes** (*a* in *Figure 7.18*). Drag these Scenes and drop them on the upper half of this window, titled **Playlist 1**. Here, you can shuffle the order of the sections of your Song simply by changing their orders on the playlist. Much easier than copying and pasting things on the **Arrange** window, right?

Using the Launcher to try out new ideas   133

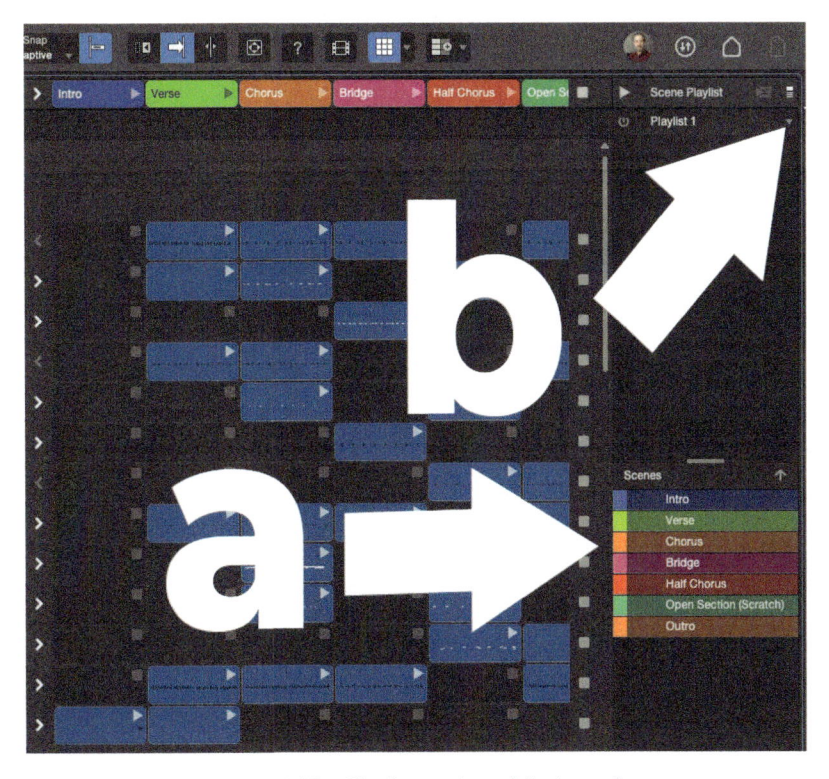

Figure 7.18: The Playlist section of the Launcher

7. Once you're happy with your new arrangement, click on the small downward arrow on the **Playlist** window (*b* in *Figure 7.18*).

8. Click on **Insert Playlist into Song**. This will open a dialog box (*Figure 7.19*).

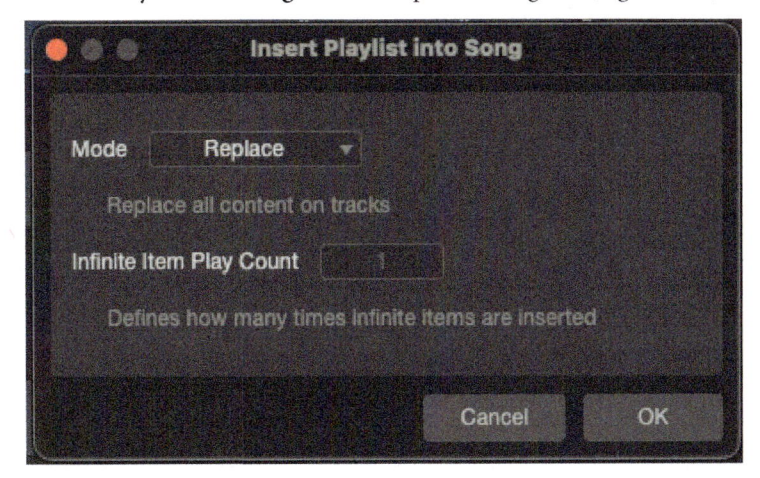

Figure 7.19: The Insert Playlist into Song dialog box

9. Here, select the **Replace** option in the **Mode** drop-down menu to insert whatever you have in the Launcher into the **Arrangement** window. If you still want to preserve your original arrangement, go to **File** in the upper menu, select **Save As**, and give this Song a different name.

This method allows you to create as many different versions of your Song as you want – create an album version, a shorter radio-friendly version, an extended club version, whatever you like.

In this section, we learned how to harness the power of the Launcher, a new feature in Studio One, to change the arrangement of your Songs easily. This concludes our tour of Studio One's editing tools.

Summary

In this chapter, we took an in-depth look at Studio One's editing tools and learned how to use them in the **Arrangement** window. We also discussed Snap and the Arranger Track, two vital features that work in tandem with these tools and make editing much easier.

In the next chapter, we will take a deep dive into audio editing and learn how to correct timing problems, fix out-of-tune vocals, and even create harmony vocals from existing takes.

8
Editing Audio

These are exciting times for music production. Today, in a modest home studio, we can do things that the biggest producers of previous decades could only dream about.

Vocals out of tune? Sloppy timing on a drum track? The neighbor decided to mow the lawn during a guitar solo? No problem! These can all be fixed in a matter of seconds, without any significant artifacts. The ability to fix errors in a recording is a game-changer in and of itself, but it's only the beginning. The ability to manipulate audio recordings opens the door for endless creativity – changing the groove of an existing drum track, creating background harmony vocals from a single vocal take, or creating an ensemble of instruments from a single instrument. The only limit is your imagination.

In this chapter, we will take a deep dive into Studio One's impressive audio editing features and learn how to use them to fix errors and for creative purposes. We will cover the following topics:

- Mastering the audio editing tools
- Fixing and enhancing the timing of audio recordings
- Using Melodyne to fix and enhance vocal recordings
- Using stem separation to isolate audio events

Technical requirements

To follow along with this chapter, you will need to have Studio One activated on your computer.

If you're interested in fixing out-of-tune material or creating harmony parts, you'll need to have **Melodyne** installed and activated on your computer as well. Melodyne Essential comes bundled with Studio One. You simply need to install and activate it using the license key on the **Products** tab at `my.presonus.com`, which we discussed in *Chapter 2*.

Mastering the audio editing tools

Studio One has an impressive list of audio editing tools, and the sheer number of available options may appear intimidating at first. However, these tools are powered by just two algorithms. The **pitch detection algorithm** tells Studio One which notes are played in an audio recording, and the **transient detection algorithm** tells it when those notes are played. Editing tools use these algorithms to make informed decisions on the audio material and perform automated tasks with precision.

In this section, we will cover the most commonly used editing tools. These are the tools that you will need in almost every project where audio is involved. Then, we will talk about how you can harness the power of other less common but equally exciting tools so that you can integrate them into your workflow as well.

Transposing and tuning audio events

Transposing and **tuning** allow you to alter the pitch of an audio event without changing its timing.

Transposing an audio event will change its pitch in semitones. For example, if you have a guitar loop in the key of C major but your song is in the key of D major, you can transpose the loop up by two semitones to bring it to your song's key.

Tuning an audio event, on the other hand, will change its pitch in cents. One hundred cents equals one semitone, so tuning is a much more subtle method of altering pitch. For example, if you have a recording of an instrument that is slightly out of tune and plays flat, you can use this feature to raise its pitch until you get it just right.

Now, let's take a look at how you can transpose or tune an audio event. Right-click on the audio event that you'd like to transpose or tune:

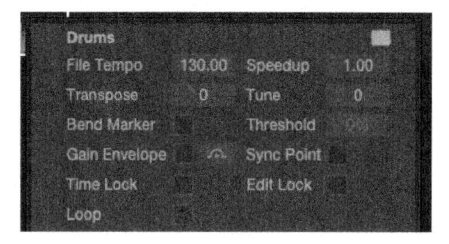

Figure 8.1: The Transpose and Tune fields on the audio event contextual menu

Among the various fields on the contextual menu, you need to work with the **Transpose** and **Tune** fields:

- The **Transpose** field accepts values between -24 and +24 semitones, allowing you to transpose up or down by as many as two octaves. Although pitch-shifting algorithms have developed immensely in the past few years, they still have their limitations. Transposing anything up or down by more than five semitones is best reserved for experimental and creative purposes.
- The **Tune** field accepts values between -100 to +100 cents.

Transpose and **Tune** are non-destructive operations. You can come back to this menu at any time and switch these values back to zero. The recording will play back in its original pitch.

The **Transpose** and **Tune** commands can also be applied to several audio events simultaneously. Just select the events that you'd like to tune or transpose and right-click on any one of them. The value you enter in the **Transpose** or **Tune** field will be applied to all selected events.

Strip Silence

Typically, an audio recording will contain gaps of silence between musical phrases. However, since most of us operate in less-than-ideal environments, these gaps may not contain real silence – they could be filled with sounds leaking from headphones, fan noises from computers, or other background sounds finding their way into the microphone.

Even if these unwanted sounds are relatively harmless, they pile up as you record take after take and result in what mixing engineers refer to as **mud** in a mix. Therefore, it's common practice to remove these gaps in order to clean up audio tracks.

We can certainly grab the Split tool, cut out these gaps, and delete them manually, but it will take forever on a large project with several busy tracks, and we have much better things to do. Thankfully, there's a fast and efficient way of cleaning up audio tracks or events automatically.

The **Strip Silence** command analyzes selected audio events and automatically removes gaps of silence. Executing the command is as easy as right-clicking on the events and selecting **Strip Silence** on the pop-up menu. Some fine-tuning, however, is often necessary to get the best results. Here's how to proceed:

1. Click on the **Strip Silence** button. This will open the **Strip Silence** menu:

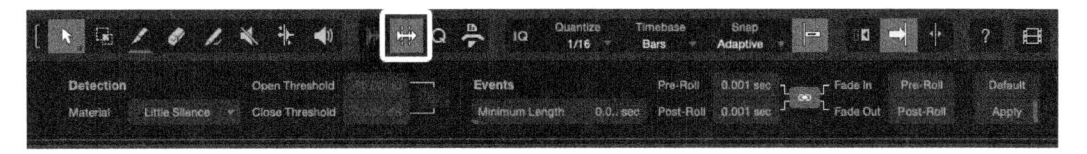

Figure 8.2: The Strip Silence button and menu

2. Using the **Detection** drop-down menu, tell the algorithm about your recorded material so that it sets the best parameters automatically:

   - Select **Lots of Silence** if the recording contains clear, well-defined sound elements (such as drum hits) surrounded by areas of silence.

   - Select **Little Silence** if the material is relatively busy but still contains some areas of silence.

   - Select **Noise Floor** if there is no real silence in the recording and you want to get rid of the background noise.

The options listed here are by no means clear-cut, so feel free to select one of the options and see how it works out. This operation is non-destructive, and if you're not happy with the result, it can be undone using the undo command by typing *Ctrl + Z* (Windows) or *Cmd + Z* (Mac).

3. If the previously listed options do not work, select **Manual** in the **Detection** drop-down menu. This will activate the **Open Threshold** setting, allowing you to manually set a silence threshold in decibels. All areas of the recording that are below this threshold will be considered silent and edited out.

4. Some recorded materials, such as drum hits, fade out very quickly and will fall below the threshold in a matter of milliseconds. This will result in the tail of the sound being chopped off, as you can see in this snare drum hit:

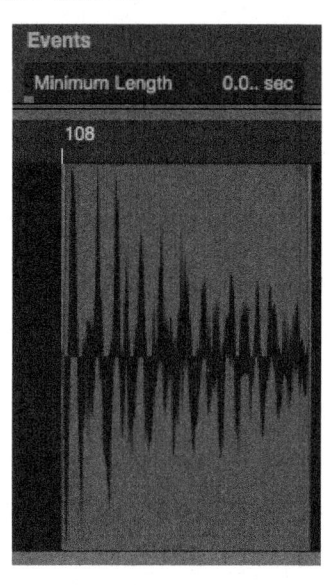

Figure 8.3: A snare drum hit chopped off by the Strip Silence command

When this happens, use the **Minimum Length** slider to set a longer duration for edited parts. This overrides the threshold setting, so even if the material falls below the threshold during the length of time you set here, it will not be edited out.

5. Normally, the Strip Silence command trims as tightly as possible, editing in as soon as the material goes above the threshold and then editing out as soon as it drops below the threshold. If you want to have some extra space before and after the edits, use the **Pre-Roll** and **Post-Roll** settings respectively.

6. If you hear any clicks or other artifacts introduced after executing the Strip Silence command, click on the chain icon to the right of the **Pre-Roll** and **Post-Roll** fields, as seen in *Figure 8.2*. This will activate the **Fade In** and **Fade Out** options. Here, you can manually set time values (in milliseconds) to add fades to each event created by the Strip Silence function.

7. Once done, click the **Apply** button to execute the Strip Silence command with the settings you just made.

Next, we will learn how to use an audio editing feature that will truly take your performances to the next level.

Creating the perfect take from several layers

In *Chapter 5*, we talked about loop recording and said that it was a great tool to create a perfect composite performance by selecting the best parts from several different takes. Armed with an in-depth knowledge of the audio editing tools at our disposal, we are now ready to tackle this task. Note that this process is sometimes referred to as **comping**, short for compositing.

Once you've performed a loop recording, as described in *Chapter 5*, the track heading for that recording will display an icon with three lines stacked on top of each other, as highlighted in *Figure 8.4*. Click that, and the track will expand to reveal the takes you've recorded.

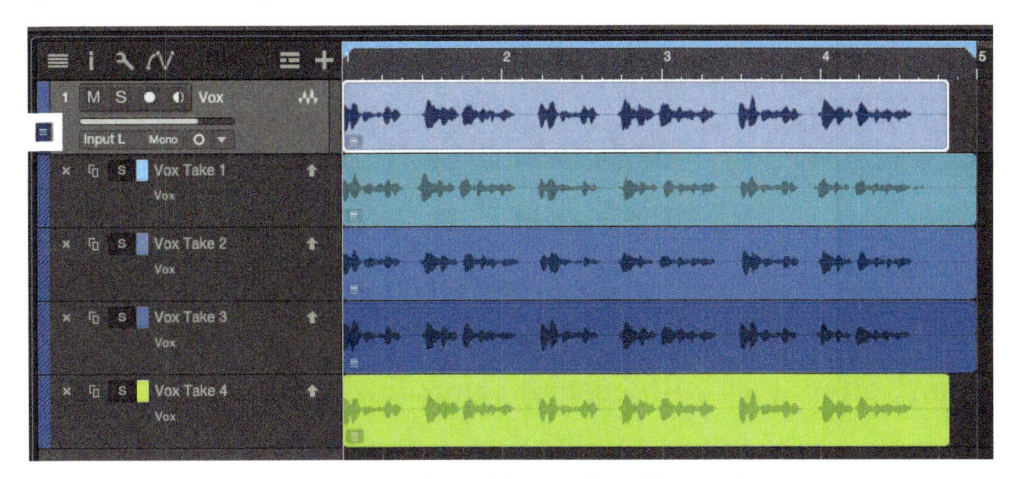

Figure 8.4: An audio track hosting four different takes

Figure 8.4 shows four different takes of a vocal recording. With Studio One in loop recording mode, the singer was asked to sing the same line of the song repeatedly. I stopped the recording after four takes. These takes are now displayed under the track heading, labeled **Take 1**, **Take 2**, and so on.

Comping the perfect performance from these takes is as simple as it gets. Let's do it:

1. Grab the **Listen** tool by pressing *8* on your keyboard. Use it to compare the same phrase across different takes.
2. Once you've selected your favorite phrase, press *1* on your keyboard. You'll notice that instead of the usual **Arrow** tool, the cursor turns into a bracket known as the **Comping** tool.

3. Drag the **Comping** tool across your favorite phrase. The area you selected will be **promoted** to the top, next to the track header. That's what you will hear next time you play back your Song.

4. Repeat steps 1 through 3 to promote all your favorite phrases to the top.

Figure 8.5 shows the same recording as *Figure 8.4* after I've selected and promoted each of my favorite phrases across different takes.

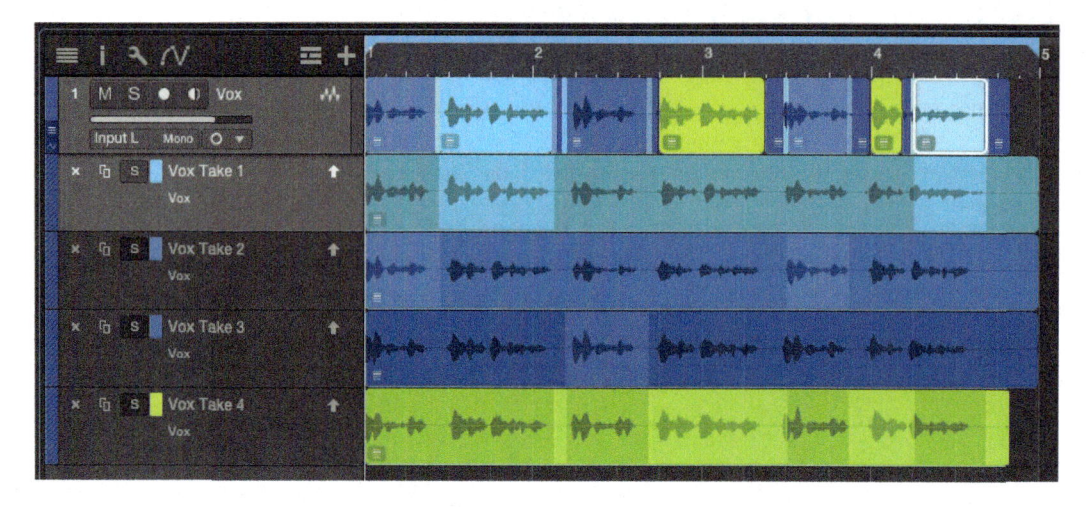

Figure 8.5: An audio track hosting several comped takes

That's it! You have just created the perfect performance from several different takes. Now, let's move on to other audio editing tools and see how you can harness their power effectively.

Working effectively with editing commands

Studio One has a plethora of editing commands on the contextual menu, which can be accessed by right-clicking on an audio event. When you explore this menu, you may be dazzled by the sheer number of available commands and find yourself wondering how you will ever learn how to use all of them.

This menu becomes much less intimidating when you start to look at it as a list of options and commands at your disposal. It shows you all the actions you can perform on an audio event. Depending on your production style and workflow, you will end up using some of these commands several times during a session, some of them not so much, and some of them not at all.

Let's consider the **Fade In to Cursor** command as an example:

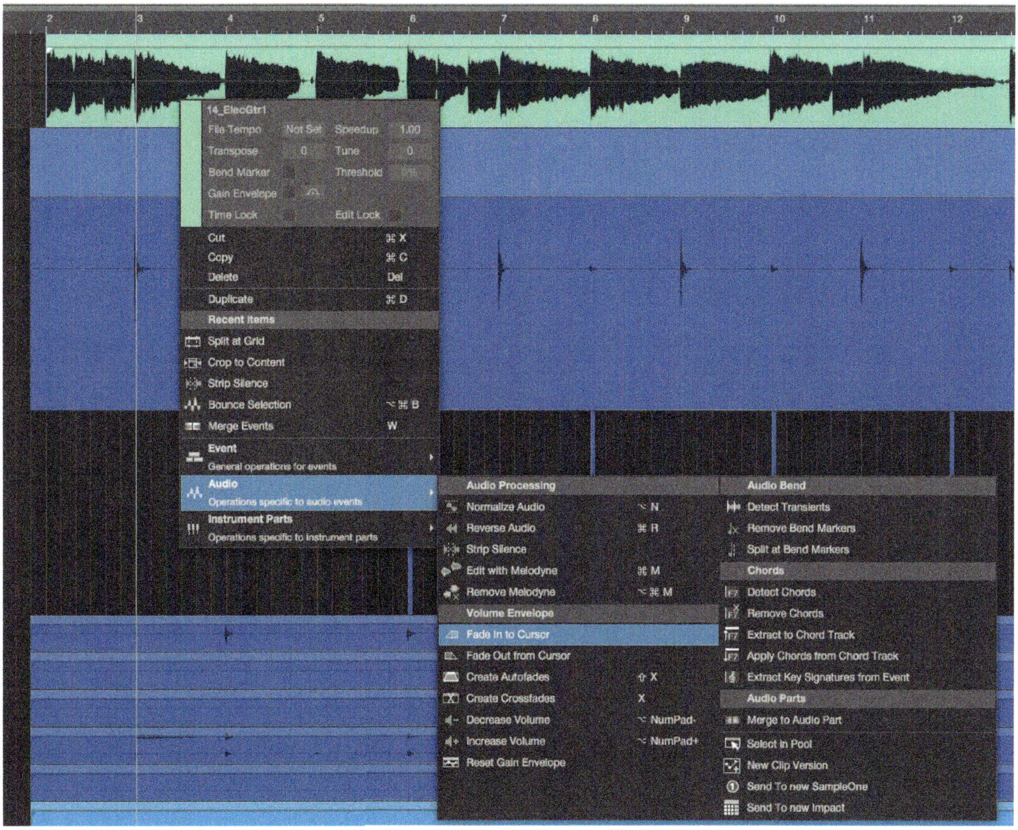

Figure 8.6: The contextual menu for audio events

The title of this command is self-explanatory. It creates a fade-in from the start of an event to the cursor's current position. In *Figure 8.4*, my audio event starts on bar 2. My cursor is on bar 3. So, when I initiate this command, I will get a fade-in that starts on bar 2 and ends on bar 3.

But why would you go to the trouble of searching this deep inside a menu to perform a simple fade-in? As we saw in *Chapter 7*, all you need to do to create a fade is click on the small triangle in the top-left corner of the event and drag it to the right.

However, if you're doing audio post-production work and need to do lots of fade-ins during each and every session, you can save a lot of time by assigning a keyboard shortcut to this command, selecting several events, and applying a fade-in to all of them by hitting just one key on your keyboard. That's when the **Fade In to Cursor** command will really shine.

The same holds true for all the commands available in the contextual menu. If you find a command that you will use frequently, assign a keyboard shortcut to it as follows:

1. On the top menu, go to **Studio One** and then **Keyboard Shortcuts**. This will open the **Keyboard Shortcuts** tab of the **Preferences** window:

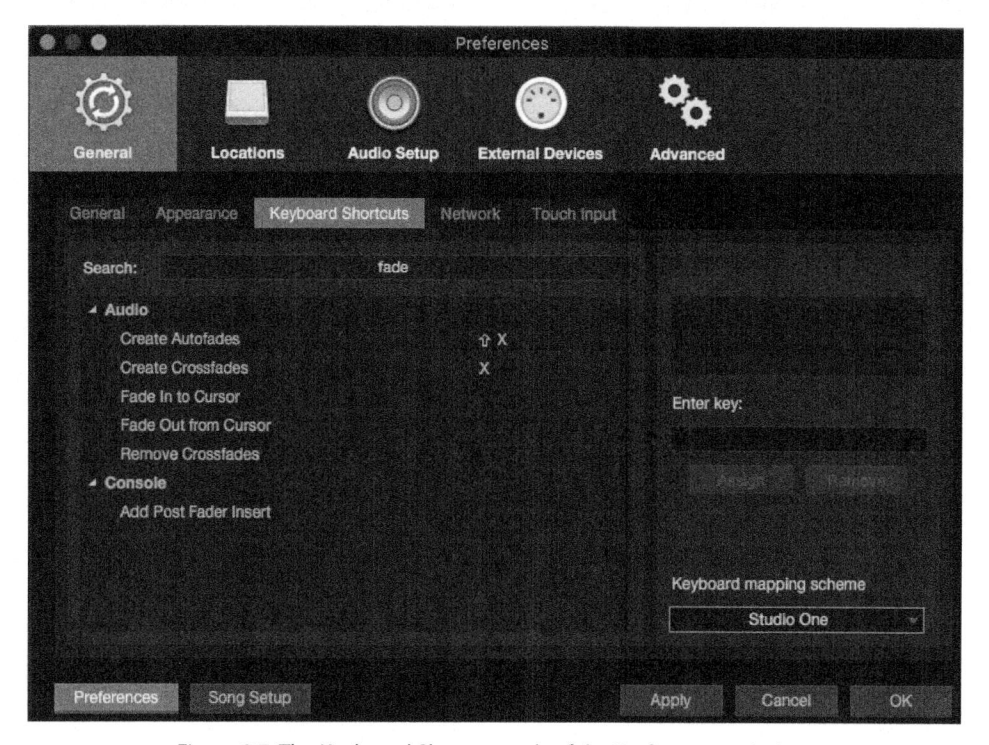

Figure 8.7: The Keyboard Shortcuts tab of the Preferences window

2. In the **Search** box, start typing the name of the command you wish to assign a shortcut for.
3. Select the command in the list of commands.
4. Click inside the **Enter Key** field and type the letter you wish to use as a shortcut for this command. You can use numbers and letters, and also add modifier keys, such as *Shift*, *Ctrl/Cmd*, and *Alt/Option*.
5. If the keys you typed in are being used as a shortcut for another command, Studio One will warn you about this. Then, try a different key combination.
6. Click **Assign**, and then **OK**.

Selecting commands that you are likely to use often and binding them with keyboard shortcuts this way will speed up your workflow, helping you to work much more effectively with your favorite tools. With the basic audio editing tools out of the way, we are now ready to tackle the more advanced methods and tools for manipulating audio.

Fixing and enhancing the timing of audio recordings

You recorded an amazing vocal performance, but the singer was late when singing a few of the words. You know that you can use the punch in recording mode to record just those words once again, but the singer slipped out of the mood and just cannot deliver the same magical performance. Alternatively, maybe you borrowed a friend's ukulele and came up with a great idea while noodling on it. You definitely want to record and use the idea, but you know that your timing will be shaky because you're new to the instrument.

In music production, there will always be cases like these where you'll need to fix the timing of an audio recording. Studio One makes this task incredibly easy to implement. In this section, we will take an in-depth look at the technology behind this functionality and how you can use it to correct timing errors and harness its power for creative purposes.

Understanding transients

Let's say that we have a drum recording with some timing errors. In order to fix these errors, we have to figure out a way to know when the drummer hit the drum kit. This is actually not as hard as it sounds. Take a look at these two audio events:

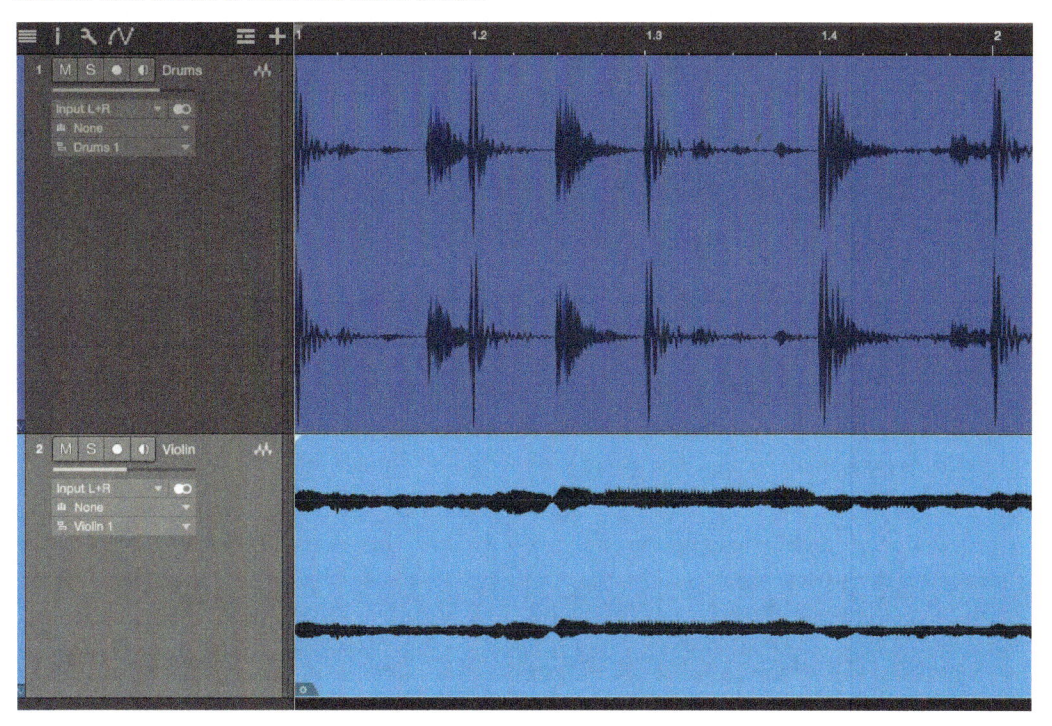

Figure 8.8: A project with a drum track (top) and a violin track (bottom)

In *Figure 8.8*, the track on top is a drum recording. Each drum hit is clearly visible as a sudden spike in the waveform. These spikes are called **transients**. Studio One has a transient detection algorithm that analyses an audio event and places **bend markers** at points where it has detected transients. You can then drag these markers to manually move the drum hits in time, or even tell Studio One to fix them automatically. Since Studio One knows where each hit should land (as represented by the timeline ruler at the top of *Figure 8.8*), correcting the positions of these hits is not as hard as it sounds either. It's just a matter of aligning bend markers with the grid laid out on the ruler. We'll see how to do this later, in the *Quantizing audio to fix timing errors automatically* section.

This sounds like magic, and it's certainly a blessing that saves tracks with timing errors. However, here's the flip side of the coin – the track at the bottom half of *Figure 8.8* is a recording of a violin played legato style – that is, by connecting several notes with a single movement of the bow. With such material, it is much harder for the transient detection algorithm to figure out when a note ends and another note begins. The same applies to vocal recordings with long, sustained notes. In such cases, even if you place markers manually, bending audio will not work as intended, and audible artifacts may be introduced.

The takeaway from this is that the success of transient detection and audio bending depends, to a large extent, on the material. Audio recordings with clear, distinct transients will yield much better results. With this in mind, we can now take a closer look at how to use this technology in our projects.

Using the Audio Bend tool to fix errors manually

Audio Bend is the algorithm used to detect and manipulate transients in Studio One. We interact with Audio Bend using the **Bend** tool. The best way to learn how this tool works is by using it manually to fix a timing error. Find an audio recording that contains a timing mistake, such as the one we saw back in *Figure 7.9*.

It's a good idea to start with a recording with clear and distinct transients, such as drums or percussion. Then, follow these steps:

1. On the **Arrangement** window, double-click on the audio event that you want to work on. This will open the event in the **Edit** window. This window has the same tools and buttons as the **Arrangement** window but allows you to focus on a single event. It's like placing the event under a microscope.

2. Click on the **Audio Bend** button on the **Edit** window. This will open the Audio Bend menu:

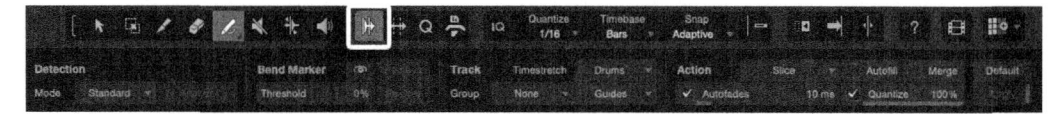

Figure 8.9: The Audio Bend button and Audio Bend menu

3. Click the Analyze button. Studio One will analyze the recording and place bend markers where it detects transients.

4. Look carefully at the waveform in the **Edit** window. Are there bend markers on all transients? Did the algorithm miss some of them? Did it place markers where it shouldn't have? Generally, the algorithm does a good job of automatically placing markers, but if you find that there are too few or too many markers, use the **Threshold** slider to adjust detection sensitivity. Increasing the threshold makes the algorithm more sensitive, resulting in more markers. Lowering the threshold results in fewer markers. Adjust the threshold until all transients are marked and there are no unnecessary markers. Use the following example as a reference:

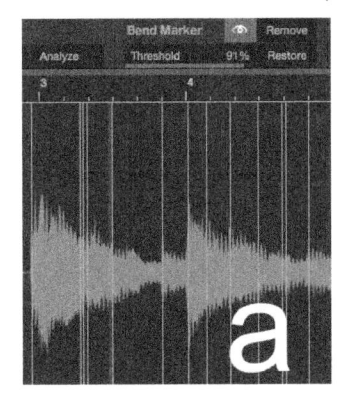

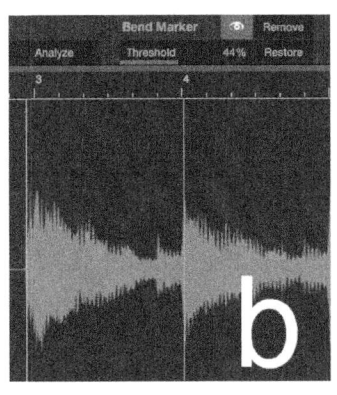

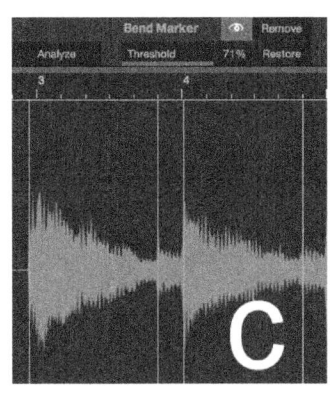

Figure 8.10: A comparison of various threshold settings

Figure 8.10 shows a side-by-side comparison of different **Threshold** settings applied to the same audio recording:

- In *a*, the threshold is set too high, making the algorithm extremely sensitive. This results in too many unnecessary bend markers.
- In *b*, the threshold is set too low. This causes the algorithm to miss smaller transients that should have been marked.
- However, *c* is the ideal setting for this material; all the transients are detected and there are no unnecessary markers.

5. Select the **Bend** tool by pressing *7* on your keyboard.
6. If the algorithm did not detect the transient you want to work on, you can add a bend marker manually by clicking at the beginning of the transient with the **Bend** tool.
7. Then, using the Bend tool, drag the transient to where you want it to be.
8. Note that the **Bend** tool's behavior is affected by **Snap**. If **Snap** is active, the transient you drag will snap to the nearest available location on the timeline grid. This is helpful to correctly align a drum hit, for example. You can turn Snap on and off by pressing *N* on your keyboard.
9. If you just want to correct the position of a single transient without affecting anything else on a recording, click on the empty space just before and after the transient to add bend markers before and after it. That way, any action you take with the **Bend** tool will be constrained between these two markers and the rest of the performance will remain unaffected.

10. Actions you perform with the **Bend** tool are non-destructive. If, at any time, you want to go back to the original recording, grab the **Arrow** tool by pressing *1* on your keyboard, select the audio event by clicking on it, and then click **Remove** in the **Audio Bend** menu. This will remove all the bend markers and restore the audio to its original state.

This method of fixing timing errors manually is very effective when there are just a few mistakes to correct. However, if there are too many mistakes or a recording is very busy, we need a way to fix errors automatically, and that's what we will do in the next section.

Quantizing audio to fix timing errors automatically

In music production, **quantization** is the process of automatically adjusting the timing of events or objects to align with a predetermined grid or beat. This makes it very easy to fix timing errors or create a more consistent rhythm.

If you have an audio recording with timing problems, it's very simple to fix in Studio One. Just select the event that contains the recording and press Q on your keyboard to quantize it. This will initiate a series of operations. The Audio Bend algorithm will analyze the event and place bend markers where it detects transients. It will then align these bend markers to the current quantize grid.

In most cases, this simple command will fix timing issues effectively. Do not lose hope if you do not get a perfect result on your first attempt, though. The outcome of quantization can be remarkably improved by some manual tweaking. The success of audio quantization depends on these three factors:

- **The type of material being quantized**: As we saw in the previous section, recordings with clear, distinct transients can be marked much more accurately and will yield better results. If you try to quantize a recording with indistinct transients, such as the one at the bottom of *Figure 8.8*, you can help the algorithm by manually adding bend markers or correcting the position of existing ones.

- **The Threshold setting in the bend marker menu**: Carefully review the bend markers in the **Edit** window and adjust the **Threshold** slider to make sure that all the transients that need to be quantized have been marked. If there are too many or too few markers, the algorithm will end up aligning the wrong markers with the quantize grid, yielding imperfect results.

- **Quantization settings**: These settings tell Studio One about your song's rhythmic structure and allow it to use the correct quantize grid. While default settings will work for most material, some tweaking may become necessary for others.

Quantization settings are based on musical note values, so you will get results much faster if you have basic knowledge of music notation. If you don't, there's nothing to worry about – quantization is non-destructive, and you can undo it if you're not happy with the result. Feel free to experiment to find the right setting.

Follow these steps to adjust the quantization settings:

1. Click the Quantize button to open the **Quantize** menu:

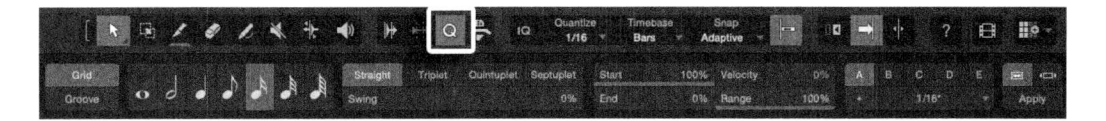

Figure 8.11: The Quantize button and Quantize menu

2. Select the desired quantization grid by using the note values on the left side of the menu. For best results, select the smallest note value used in your recording. For example, if you want to quantize a drum recording with a 16th note hi-hat pattern, select 16th notes.
3. The **Start** slider determines how closely the audio will follow the quantization grid. If you leave it at its default setting of 100%, audio will be precisely aligned with the grid, known as **hard quantizing**. While this is desirable in some genres of music, it is considered too mechanical in others. Lower this value if you want more of a loose, *human* feel.
4. Click **Apply**.

This method works perfectly to quantize audio to a grid, but not all music genres conform to a symmetrically organized rhythmic structure. In the next section, you will learn how to create custom grids for music with a unique rhythmic feel.

Extracting and quantizing to custom grooves

In music, **groove** refers to the rhythmic feel and characteristic pulse that gives a piece of music its rhythmic flavor and helps to define its style. The groove of a piece is created by the interaction between the timings of different instruments. In electronic music, rhythm is generally created on computers and drum machines and tends to be precise and predictable. Many other genres, on the other hand, contain variations in timing and phrasing as played by humans, and this gives them a unique character.

These types of music do not yield themselves to the grid quantization we discussed in the preceding section. If you try to quantize the recording of a Latin percussion ensemble to a grid, it will lose its *organic* feel.

So, what do you do if you're working on a song with a unique groove and still want to be able to fix timing problems? Studio One has a feature titled **groove quantization**, which is designed to replace grid quantize in such situations. Groove quantization allows you to apply the rhythmic feel of a reference audio or MIDI event to other audio or MIDI events. That way, you can maintain a consistent groove across multiple tracks.

Let's say you have a drum track with a groove that you'd like to use. You also have a bass guitar track, with a totally different groove, that you want to conform to the drum track. Follow these steps to do this using groove quantization:

1. On the **Arrangement** window, click the Quantize button to open the Quantize menu (*Figure 8.11*).
2. In this menu, click the **Groove** button on the left to switch to Groove Quantize mode.
3. Now, drag the drum recording and drop it into the **Groove** panel (*a* in *Figure 8.12*):

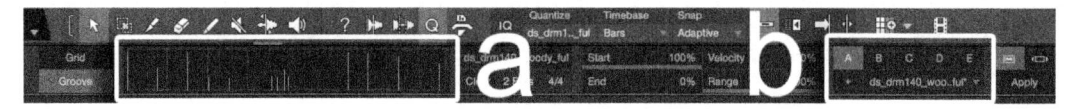

Figure 8.12: (a) The Groove panel and (b) the Groove Preset window

You have extracted the groove from the drum track.

4. On the **Arrangement** window, click to select the event that contains the bass guitar recording.
5. Press Q on your keyboard to quantize the bass guitar to the groove of the drums.
6. If you want to be able to use this groove in your future projects as well, click the plus sign on the Groove Preset window (*b* in *Figure 8.12*).
7. Type a name for this groove, and click **OK**.

Groove quantization generally works best when it's applied to all the tracks in a project. If some instruments are quantized to a groove whereas others are quantized to the grid, their rhythms will be inconsistent. In order to maintain a coherent arrangement, make sure to stick to either one of the grid or groove quantization methods.

In this section, we took an in-depth look at several methods to fix timing errors in audio recordings. Now, we are ready to tackle a slightly more complicated task – working with Melodyne to enhance vocal recordings.

Using Melodyne to fix and enhance vocal recordings

Melodyne is an industry-leading software tool that allows you to manipulate the pitch and timing of individual notes in an audio recording. Melodyne is developed by **Celemony**. Although Celemony is not affiliated with PreSonus, they have worked in close cooperation for more than a decade now to forge an unmatched level of integration between Melodyne and Studio One. **Melodyne Essential**, the most lightweight version of the software, is bundled with Studio One. The capabilities provided by Melodyne Essential are sufficient for the needs of most day-to-day music production.

The same holds true for all the commands available in the contextual menu. If you find a command that you will use frequently, assign a keyboard shortcut to it as follows:

1. On the top menu, go to **Studio One** and then **Keyboard Shortcuts**. This will open the **Keyboard Shortcuts** tab of the **Preferences** window:

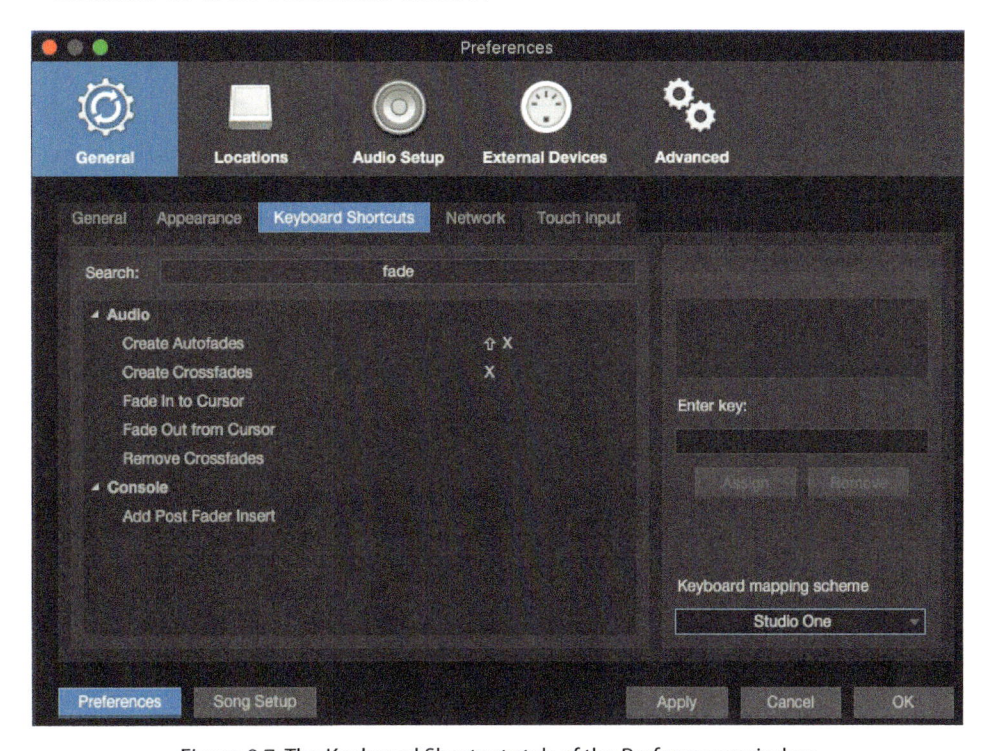

Figure 8.7: The Keyboard Shortcuts tab of the Preferences window

2. In the **Search** box, start typing the name of the command you wish to assign a shortcut for.
3. Select the command in the list of commands.
4. Click inside the **Enter Key** field and type the letter you wish to use as a shortcut for this command. You can use numbers and letters, and also add modifier keys, such as *Shift*, *Ctrl/Cmd*, and *Alt/Option*.
5. If the keys you typed in are being used as a shortcut for another command, Studio One will warn you about this. Then, try a different key combination.
6. Click **Assign**, and then **OK**.

Selecting commands that you are likely to use often and binding them with keyboard shortcuts this way will speed up your workflow, helping you to work much more effectively with your favorite tools. With the basic audio editing tools out of the way, we are now ready to tackle the more advanced methods and tools for manipulating audio.

Fixing and enhancing the timing of audio recordings

You recorded an amazing vocal performance, but the singer was late when singing a few of the words. You know that you can use the punch in recording mode to record just those words once again, but the singer slipped out of the mood and just cannot deliver the same magical performance. Alternatively, maybe you borrowed a friend's ukulele and came up with a great idea while noodling on it. You definitely want to record and use the idea, but you know that your timing will be shaky because you're new to the instrument.

In music production, there will always be cases like these where you'll need to fix the timing of an audio recording. Studio One makes this task incredibly easy to implement. In this section, we will take an in-depth look at the technology behind this functionality and how you can use it to correct timing errors and harness its power for creative purposes.

Understanding transients

Let's say that we have a drum recording with some timing errors. In order to fix these errors, we have to figure out a way to know when the drummer hit the drum kit. This is actually not as hard as it sounds. Take a look at these two audio events:

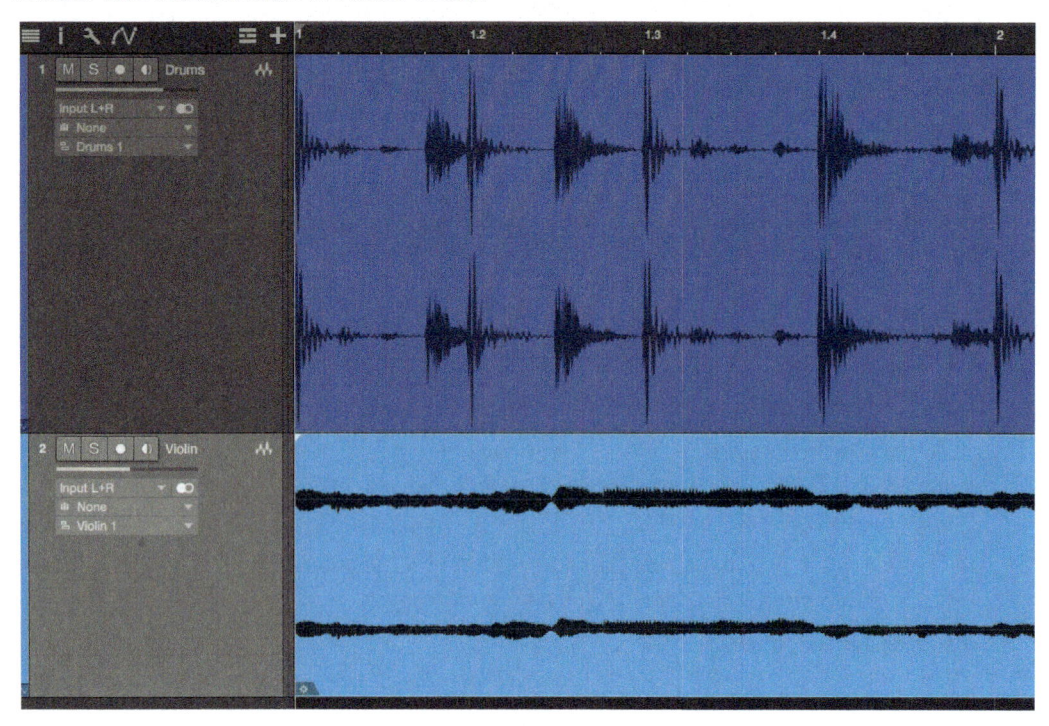

Figure 8.8: A project with a drum track (top) and a violin track (bottom)

In *Figure 8.8*, the track on top is a drum recording. Each drum hit is clearly visible as a sudden spike in the waveform. These spikes are called **transients**. Studio One has a transient detection algorithm that analyses an audio event and places **bend markers** at points where it has detected transients. You can then drag these markers to manually move the drum hits in time, or even tell Studio One to fix them automatically. Since Studio One knows where each hit should land (as represented by the timeline ruler at the top of *Figure 8.8*), correcting the positions of these hits is not as hard as it sounds either. It's just a matter of aligning bend markers with the grid laid out on the ruler. We'll see how to do this later, in the *Quantizing audio to fix timing errors automatically* section.

This sounds like magic, and it's certainly a blessing that saves tracks with timing errors. However, here's the flip side of the coin – the track at the bottom half of *Figure 8.8* is a recording of a violin played legato style – that is, by connecting several notes with a single movement of the bow. With such material, it is much harder for the transient detection algorithm to figure out when a note ends and another note begins. The same applies to vocal recordings with long, sustained notes. In such cases, even if you place markers manually, bending audio will not work as intended, and audible artifacts may be introduced.

The takeaway from this is that the success of transient detection and audio bending depends, to a large extent, on the material. Audio recordings with clear, distinct transients will yield much better results. With this in mind, we can now take a closer look at how to use this technology in our projects.

Using the Audio Bend tool to fix errors manually

Audio Bend is the algorithm used to detect and manipulate transients in Studio One. We interact with Audio Bend using the **Bend** tool. The best way to learn how this tool works is by using it manually to fix a timing error. Find an audio recording that contains a timing mistake, such as the one we saw back in *Figure 7.9*.

It's a good idea to start with a recording with clear and distinct transients, such as drums or percussion. Then, follow these steps:

1. On the **Arrangement** window, double-click on the audio event that you want to work on. This will open the event in the **Edit** window. This window has the same tools and buttons as the **Arrangement** window but allows you to focus on a single event. It's like placing the event under a microscope.

2. Click on the **Audio Bend** button on the **Edit** window. This will open the Audio Bend menu:

Figure 8.9: The Audio Bend button and Audio Bend menu

3. Click the Analyze button. Studio One will analyze the recording and place bend markers where it detects transients.

4. Look carefully at the waveform in the **Edit** window. Are there bend markers on all transients? Did the algorithm miss some of them? Did it place markers where it shouldn't have? Generally, the algorithm does a good job of automatically placing markers, but if you find that there are too few or too many markers, use the **Threshold** slider to adjust detection sensitivity. Increasing the threshold makes the algorithm more sensitive, resulting in more markers. Lowering the threshold results in fewer markers. Adjust the threshold until all transients are marked and there are no unnecessary markers. Use the following example as a reference:

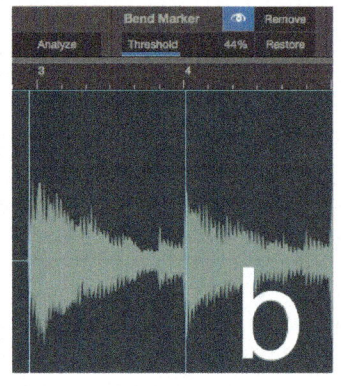

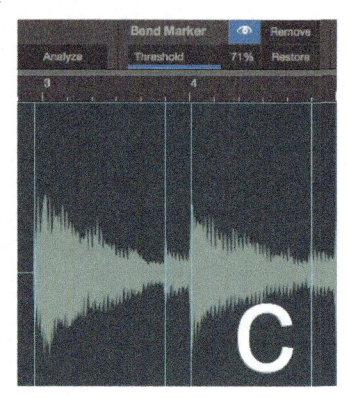

Figure 8.10: A comparison of various threshold settings

Figure 8.10 shows a side-by-side comparison of different **Threshold** settings applied to the same audio recording:

- In *a*, the threshold is set too high, making the algorithm extremely sensitive. This results in too many unnecessary bend markers.

- In *b*, the threshold is set too low. This causes the algorithm to miss smaller transients that should have been marked.

- However, *c* is the ideal setting for this material; all the transients are detected and there are no unnecessary markers.

5. Select the **Bend** tool by pressing 7 on your keyboard.

6. If the algorithm did not detect the transient you want to work on, you can add a bend marker manually by clicking at the beginning of the transient with the **Bend** tool.

7. Then, using the Bend tool, drag the transient to where you want it to be.

8. Note that the **Bend** tool's behavior is affected by **Snap**. If **Snap** is active, the transient you drag will snap to the nearest available location on the timeline grid. This is helpful to correctly align a drum hit, for example. You can turn Snap on and off by pressing *N* on your keyboard.

9. If you just want to correct the position of a single transient without affecting anything else on a recording, click on the empty space just before and after the transient to add bend markers before and after it. That way, any action you take with the **Bend** tool will be constrained between these two markers and the rest of the performance will remain unaffected.

So far, we have talked about using Melodyne for corrective purposes. Up next, we will explore a more creative method of working with Melodyne to enhance your projects.

Using Melodyne to create background harmony vocals

Background harmony vocals definitely take a song to the next level. However, creating and singing harmony vocals takes a lot of experience and requires at least a basic knowledge of music theory, so it may not be possible to record them live. Using Melodyne, we can create harmony vocals from a singer's original performance. Here's how:

1. During your recording session, record a few extra takes of your singer's performance. Keep the best take for the lead vocal. We will use the other takes to create background harmony vocals.
2. Right-click on one of these extra takes and select **Edit with Melodyne**.
3. In Melodyne's window, click on the **Chord Track Visibility** button:

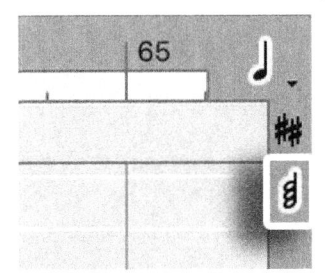

Figure 8.18: The Chord Track Visibility button in the Melodyne window

4. Type in the chords of your song on the chord track.
5. On Melodyne's own top menu, go to **Options | Pitch Grid | Pitch Background**, and select **Chord**. Now, the background of the Melodyne window will display the notes of the chords in white and all other notes in gray.
6. Again, on Melodyne's own top menu, go to **Options | Pitch Grid**, and select **Chord Snap**. Now, the blobs can only be moved to the notes of the chords used in your song.
7. Drag the blobs to these notes to create harmonious vocals. Since the blobs snap to your chord tones only, there is no chance of coming up with a wrong note. Feel free to experiment.
8. Repeat the previous steps to create as many harmony vocal tracks as you want.

Remember that Melodyne can be used with instruments as well, so you can use this method to create a violin section from a single violin performance, for example. The only limit is your imagination!

This concludes our guided tour of corrective and creative ways to use Melodyne in your projects.

Using stem separation to isolate audio events

Stem separation refers to the process of isolating different elements or **stems** of a mixed audio file, such as vocals, drums, bass, and other instruments, into individual audio tracks. This allows for more possibilities in remixing, re-arranging, or enhancing the components of the original mix, offering creative flexibility.

Stem separation has been available for quite some time now, but it was commonly found on websites operated by third-party vendors, and the typical workflow for extracting stems involved uploading the original file, paying and waiting for the extraction, and then downloading the extracted files.

As of version 7, Studio One has stem separation capability built right into its feature set. Here's how it works:

1. Drag the audio file you'd like to extract stems from and drop it into your Studio One Song.
2. Select the audio file by clicking on it with the **Arrow** tool.
3. Press *Cmd + U* (Mac) or *Ctrl + U* (Windows) to open the **Separate Stems** dialog box (*Figure 8.19*).

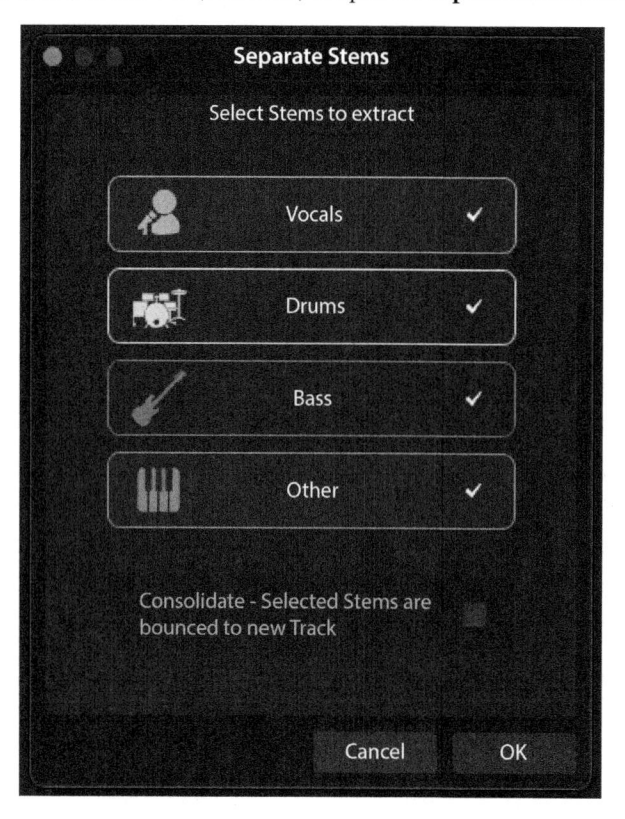

Figure 8.19: The Separate Stems dialog box

4. Here, select the audio material that you'd like to extract from the original recording. You can select **Vocals**, **Drums**, and **Bass**, which are self-explanatory, and **Other**, which is basically every other instrument that does not fall under the first three categories.

5. Click *OK*.

Studio One will use its AI magic to analyze the recording and extract the stems you have selected into separate, individual tracks. From there, you can work with these stems to sample, remix, and rearrange music to your heart's content. If you're planning to release the fruit of this labor on digital platforms, though, make sure that you are not violating any copyright regulations!

Summary

In this chapter, we explored Studio One's audio editing tools and discussed several different methods to use these tools in your projects. We started with common editing tasks, such as cleaning up an audio track, and then moved on to more complex tasks, such as conforming one track to the groove of another. We continued with an in-depth discussion of how you can incorporate Melodyne into your projects to enhance vocal performances. We concluded by exploring how to use stem separation technology to extract material from already mixed music files.

In the next chapter, we will explore Studio One's MIDI editing tools and discover how they can help bring your virtual instruments to life.

9
Editing MIDI

Working with MIDI is like playing an instrument. It's a mixture of art and science, and you cannot just focus on one while ignoring the other. Just like playing an instrument, working with MIDI requires practice. Whether you're new to music production or a seasoned pro who's switched to Studio One, this new instrument will offer powerful tools to create and shape your musical ideas while retaining a friendly learning curve.

In this chapter, we will cover Studio One's extensive set of MIDI editing tools using a step-by-step approach, starting with the basic ones and proceeding to the more advanced ones. By the end of this chapter, you will be able to use these tools confidently to adjust the pitch, timing, and dynamics of MIDI performances. This will allow you to achieve a wide range of musical results, from correcting simple mistakes to creating complex and layered musical arrangements.

We will cover the following topics:

- Using basic editing tools and quantization
- Adjusting MIDI data to enhance a performance
- Working in the Pattern Editor
- Using Note FX to spark creativity

Technical requirements

To follow along with this chapter, you need to have Studio One installed and activated on your computer.

Using basic editing tools and quantization

In *Chapter 6*, we covered several different methods of recording and programming a MIDI performance. While a MIDI performance is an excellent starting point to present musical ideas, it's hardly ever used in its original form. It is meant to be processed and refined, just like a precious metal ore.

In this section, we will explore Studio One's basic MIDI editing tools and then take a deep dive into MIDI quantization. All the tools and methods discussed in this section will be based on the **Edit** window, which can be easily accessed by double-clicking on the MIDI event that you'd like to work on.

As we noted in *Chapter 6*, the **Edit** window itself has three viewing options – the Piano view, Drum view, and Score view (see *Figure 6.13*). Unless otherwise noted, we will use the Piano view throughout this section, as it offers the maximum number of editing tools and options. Any action you perform in this viewing mode will be reflected in the other modes instantly.

Now, we're ready to start exploring the editing tools. Find a MIDI performance that you want to fix, improve, or enhance, and let's get our hands dirty.

Using the Arrow tool to perform basic editing tasks

When working with MIDI, the most capable tool in our arsenal is the good old **Arrow** tool. Let's take a quick look at the things you can accomplish with it:

1. In the **Arrangement** window, double-click on the MIDI event that you want to work on. This will open the event in the **Edit** window.

2. Grab the **Arrow** tool by pressing *1* on your keyboard.

3. To change the timing or position of a MIDI note, drag it to the left or right. If **Snap** is active, you will only be able to drop it at a position that corresponds to the timeline grid. This allows you to align notes precisely. Press *N* on your keyboard to toggle the Snap function.

4. To change the pitch of a MIDI note, drag it up or down. Studio One will give you aural feedback to help you find the correct note value.

5. As an alternative, click on a note to select it, and then use the up or down arrow keys on your keyboard to change its pitch. Hold down the *Shift* key while pressing the up or down keys to move the note up or down by an octave.

6. To adjust the length of a note, hover the **Arrow** tool at the beginning or end of a note. It will turn into a double-headed arrow. Use this to resize the note. Note that this action is controlled by the Snap feature as well.

7. To copy a note, hold down the *Alt/Option* key while dragging it.

8. To change the velocity of a note, drag its velocity indicator at the bottom of the **Edit** window (we will talk about velocity in detail later, in the *Adjusting velocity* section).

> **Tip**
> Note that the **Arrangement** window and **Edit** window have their own independent tool menus. For example, if you select the **Listen** tool in the **Arrangement** window and the **Arrow** tool in the **Edit** window, the tool at your disposal will change accordingly as you move your mouse across the two windows.

All the actions we have discussed so far can be applied to several notes at once. Select all notes in a MIDI event by typing *Ctrl + A* (Windows) or *Cmd + A* (Mac). Select a group of notes by drawing a marquee around them with the **Arrow** tool. If you want finer control over which notes to select, use the **Select Notes** window, which we will cover in the next section.

Using the Select Notes window to make a precise selection

Selecting MIDI notes with a mouse is fine for most purposes, but sometimes, you'll need to select notes that only meet certain criteria. Doing that with a mouse on busy MIDI events extending across several tracks is a tedious task.

The **Select Notes** window allows you to quickly select notes that meet specific criteria. You can then issue commands that you want to apply to these notes only. To open this window, click the **Action** button on the **Edit** window and then click **Select Notes…**:

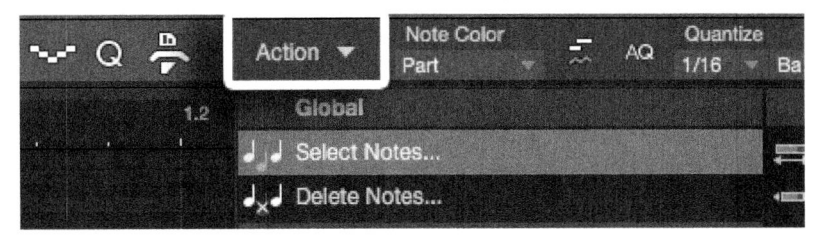

Figure 9.1: Opening the Select Notes window

This will open the **Select Notes** window:

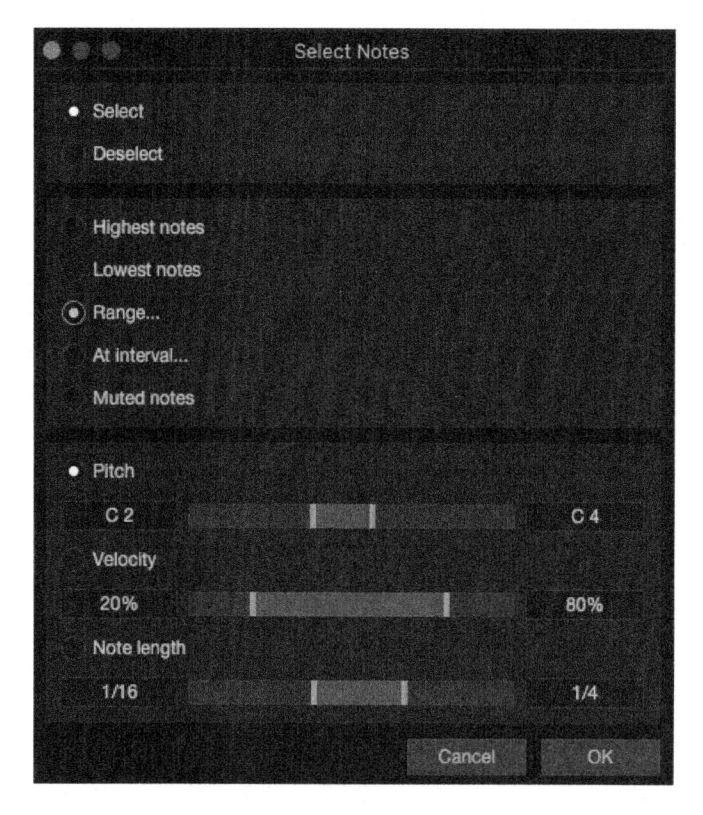

Figure 9.2: The Select Notes window

This window has two modes of operation, displayed at the top:

- The **Select** mode selects notes that meet your criteria, such as selecting all notes that are between notes C3 and C4.
- The **Deselect** mode selects all notes except those that meet your criteria, such as selecting all notes except for those that are between C3 and C4.

In the center of the window, you can set the parameters based on how you want the selection to be made:

- **Highest notes** selects the highest notes available at any time within an event.
- **Lowest notes** selects the lowest notes available at any time within an event.
- **Range…** allows you to select notes that fall within a specific range of **Pitch**, **Velocity**, or **Note Length** values. When you click this option, the window will expand to reveal sliders where you can set these parameters, as shown at the bottom of *Figure 9.2*.

- **At interval…** allows you to select notes based on their position on the timeline grid, or based on numeric relationships between notes. This option has two operation modes:

  - **Beat** selects notes based on their position relative to the grid. You can set the sensitivity of the grid using the **Beat grid** parameter.

  - **Event count** selects notes based on their distance from each other. For example, if you have a series of notes and you want to select every third note, set the **Select at every n-th position** setting here to 3.

- **Muted notes** selects all the muted notes within an event.

Now that we know exactly how to target specific notes, we are ready to tackle more advanced editing operations.

Quantizing MIDI notes to change the timing of a performance

In *Chapter 8*, we described quantization as the process of automatically adjusting the timing of events or objects to align with a predetermined grid or beat. We then cautioned against using quantization beyond a reasonable limit because audio quantization entails time stretching, and it will degrade sound quality if used excessively.

Now is the time for some good news – quantizing MIDI does not affect sound quality at all, so you can be as bold and creative as you like. A MIDI note is just an instruction that tells a MIDI instrument to start producing a sound. When you quantize a MIDI note, you're only changing the time at which the instruction gets sent to the instrument, with absolutely no effect on sound quality. This allows you to try out creative ideas without any limitations.

Quantizing MIDI notes is easy: just select the notes you want to quantize and press Q on your keyboard. This will quantize the selected notes with your current quantization settings. To review and change those settings, click the Quantize button to open the Quantize menu (*Figure 8.9* in *Chapter 8*).

We explored the Quantize menu in *Chapter 8*. The grid quantize and groove quantize methods we covered there can be used for MIDI notes as well, following the exact same steps. There are, however, two settings in this menu that we have not talked about so far:

- In general, when we talk about quantizing a MIDI note, we refer to aligning its beginning to a grid on the timeline. However, sometimes, you may wish to align the end of a MIDI note precisely to a grid as well. This especially makes sense for arpeggiated synth lines, sustained pads, string sounds, or any other scenario where you want to precisely control the point at which a note ends. The **End** slider allows you to set how much you want to quantize the ends of MIDI notes. Leave this at 0% (default setting) if you don't need to quantize note ends; set it to 100% to hard-quantize them. Any value between 0% and 100% will apply gradually increasing levels of quantization to the ends of MIDI notes.

- The **Range** slider allows you to set a time range around grid lines. When you issue a quantize command, any note within this range gets quantized, and any note outside this range remains unaffected. By default, this slider has a value of `100%`, which means that every note, no matter how far from the grid, will be quantized. If you set it to `0%`, the other extreme, none of the notes will be quantized. You can adjust this setting to taste to tighten the timing of some elements in a performance while maintaining the loose quality of others.

Now, let's talk about more advanced quantization features that are specific to MIDI events only.

Humanizing stiff performances

While quantization is indispensable for many music genres, there are many other genres where it's not equally welcome. A heavily quantized performance that feels right at home on an EDM track may be considered as stiff and mechanic on a rock track. In such cases, it's possible to add some artificial realism (yes, we also have our share of oxymorons in music production) to disguise quantization.

The **Humanize** function aims to make a heavily quantized performance sound more organic by injecting random variations to the velocities and starting positions of MIDI notes. To access this function, click the **Action** button on the **Edit** menu, and select **Humanize**. This will open the **Humanize** window:

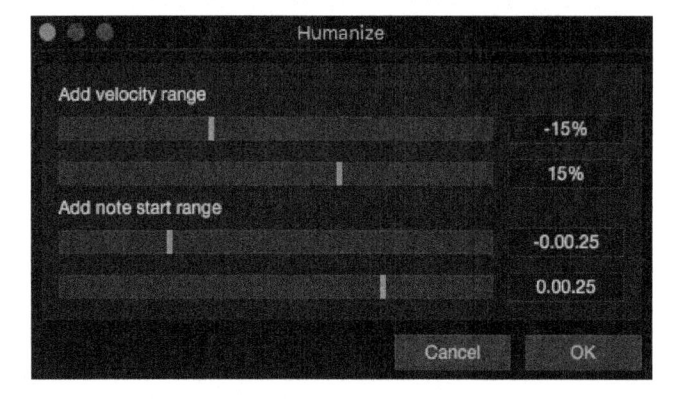

Figure 9.3: The Humanize window

Here, set ranges within which you wish to allow random variations in velocities and starting points of notes. When you click **OK**, Studio One will generate random values within these ranges and commit them to the MIDI notes.

Used in conjunction with the **Select Notes** window, as discussed earlier, the **Humanize** command can become a powerful tool. For example, you can selectively target and humanize certain elements of a rhythm loop while leaving the kick drum and snare hard quantized.

Restoring and freezing quantization

When you quantize or humanize notes in a MIDI performance, Studio One still keeps a record of their original positions. This allows you to restore a MIDI performance back to its original state, even if you save and close the project and come back to it at a later time. To restore a performance back to its original state, click **Action** on the **Edit** window, and select **Restore Timing**.

This is certainly a helpful feature that allows you to change your mind down the line, but it can sometimes become a hindrance. For example, let's imagine that you quantized an event while working on a project yesterday. Today, you open the project again. You're happy with your quantization idea but just want to quantize a bit more to tighten up things. In this case, when you initiate the quantize command, Studio One will take into consideration the original positions of the notes, not the positions you quantized them to yesterday. The solution is to freeze the quantization you made yesterday, replacing the original positions of the notes. To do that, click **Action** on the **Edit** window, and select **Freeze Quantize**.

This concludes our coverage of Studio One's MIDI quantization options. Up next, we will start exploring the in-depth editing features.

Adjusting note lengths and applying half-time or double-time

Being able to control the length of notes precisely is an important factor in the MIDI editing skillset. You can take short notes written for a piano and convert them into long, sustained notes for string instruments. Conversely, you can take long notes and chop them into arpeggios that a synth can play. Transforming notes in this way opens the door to endless possibilities.

Studio One allows you to precisely control the length of MIDI notes using the **Length** command. To use this command, click the **Action** button on the **Edit** window, and select **Length**. This will open the **Length** window:

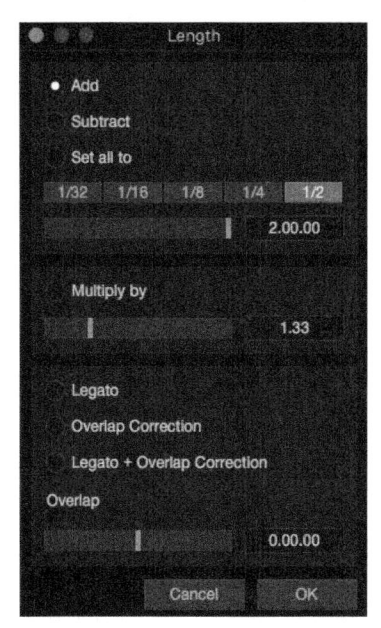

Figure 9.4: The Length window

Let's review the options:

- Select **Add** or **Subtract**, and use the slider below to set how much to add to or subtract from the existing length of selected notes.
- **Set all to** allows you to set the duration of all selected notes to standard note length values (eighth note, quarter note, etc.).
- Use **Multiply by** to modify the length of selected notes by a common multiplier. Entering a value smaller than the one here will effectively shrink the selected notes.
- Select **Legato** to connect the end of each note to the beginning of the next one. This is very useful to create sustained passages from short, unconnected notes.
- Sometimes, a MIDI performance may contain notes that overlap each other – one note continues to sound after a second note has started. Normally, this is not an issue, but some monophonic synths and sample library patches act abnormally when they receive overlapping notes. Use the **Overlap Correction** option to fix this automatically:

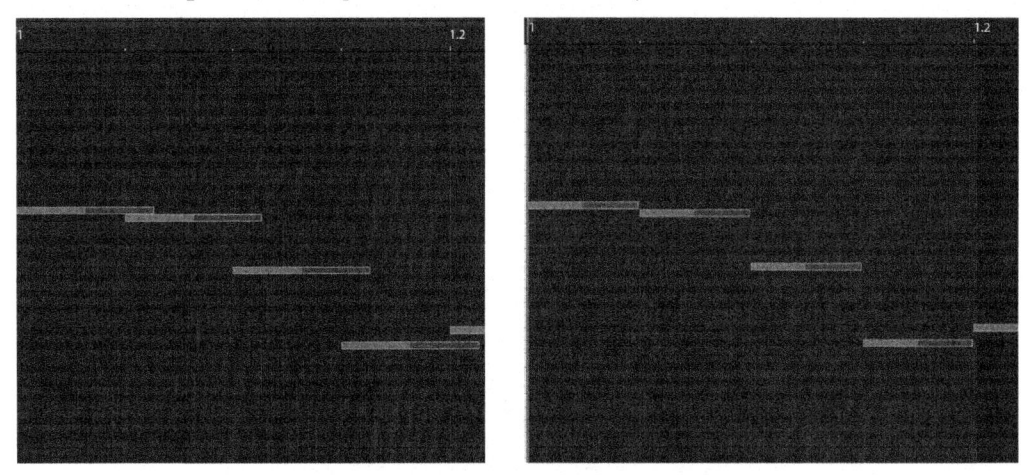

Figure 9.5: Overlapping notes (left) corrected with Overlap Correction (right)

Sometimes, it's just the opposite – some string library patches yield a much more realistic legato performance when consecutive notes slightly overlap. If you're going for a smooth legato transition between notes, select **Overlap Correction** again, but this time, dial in a small amount of overlap using the slider at the bottom of this window – somewhere around 0:00:25 should do (the sliders in this window use an ancient MIDI measurement unit called the **pulses per quarter** (**PPQ**) note).

You can also dial in a negative value with the overlap slider. This will result in each note cutting off just before the next note starts.

- Use the **Legato + Overlap Correction** option to automatically tie disconnected notes and apply whatever legato correction level is set in the slider, as described previously.

> **Tip**
> Combine the **Length** tool with the **Select Notes** window to perform complicated editing tasks easily. For example, select only the middle voices in a densely orchestrated MIDI event and turn them into legato parts for a string arrangement.

By default, Studio One automatically adjusts all MIDI events to match a project's tempo. Sometimes, you may want to override this feature and have precise control over how time-stretching is applied to a MIDI event. A typical scenario where you may want this is when applying a double tempo or half tempo feel to your project, where some elements in a song play twice as fast or slow compared to the rest of the instruments. This requires manually shrinking or stretching everything in a MIDI event by a certain amount, and this can be achieved with the **Stretch** command, as follows:

1. Click the **Action** button in the **Edit** window, and select **Stretch**. This will open the **Stretch** window:

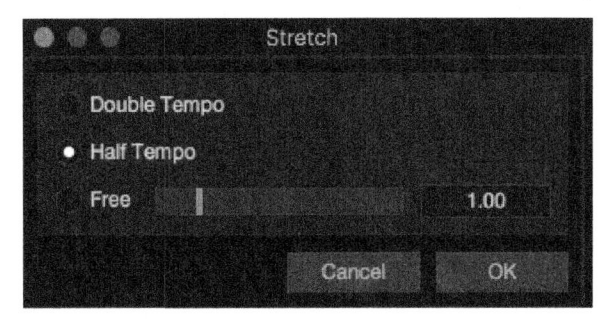

Figure 9.6: The Stretch window

2. In this window, select how much you want to shrink or stretch the MIDI event:

   - **Double Tempo** shrinks the contents of the MIDI event to half of its original size; therefore, it will end up playing twice as fast.

   - **Half Tempo** stretches the contents of the MIDI event to twice its original size; therefore, it will end up playing twice as slow.

   - Use the **Free** option to stretch the MIDI event by any value. Entering a number smaller than one shrinks the event. Entering a number larger than one stretches the event.

3. Click **OK**.

Note that if you use this command to stretch MIDI notes, Studio One will not automatically extend the boundaries of the MIDI event containing the notes. You will need to go to the **Arrangement** window and resize the event using the **Arrow** tool.

So far, we have covered the essential tools to edit a MIDI performance. In the next section, we will take a deep dive into more advanced editing features that will assist you in bringing your musical ideas to life by adjusting the pitches of the notes, conforming them to different keys, and refining other MIDI parameters in order to change the timbre of your sounds.

Adjusting MIDI data to enhance a performance

Although MIDI has been with us for almost half a century, it is still regarded by some music producers as artificial and sterile. Some music genres, such as pop, EDM, and hip-hop, have embraced this quality, whereas other genres, such as rock and jazz, treat it as a necessary evil, an unfortunate side effect of technology that must be handled with care.

It is possible to inject realism and emotion into a MIDI performance, and Studio One has several tools to help you with this. In this section, we will cover several MIDI editing techniques that will bring your MIDI tracks to life.

Transposing notes

Being able to transpose notes easily and without sacrificing sound quality has been one of the strengths of MIDI. Transposing allows you to change the key of your song without rerecording anything. This is useful to find the best key for your vocal range, match your song to an existing set of tracks, or try out different keys to find which one sounds best for your song. However, that's only the tip of the iceberg. Transposing opens the door for creative possibilities that are often overlooked – you can transpose your song to a different scale (e.g., from major to minor) and create harmonies for an existing melody.

There are a couple of methods to transpose notes. Let's start with the most basic:

1. Double-click on the MIDI event that contains the notes you want to transpose.
2. With the **Edit** window now open, make sure Snap is enabled.
3. Grab the **Arrow** tool by pressing *1* on your keyboard.
4. Select all the MIDI notes by typing *Ctrl + A* (Windows) or *Cmd + A* (Mac).
5. Using the **Arrow** tool, drag the notes up or down to the desired note.
6. You can also use the up and down arrow keys on your keyboard to move the notes vertically. Press *Shift* and the up or down keys to transpose the notes by an octave.

Here's a faster method to transpose notes:

1. Click the **Action** button on the **Edit** window and select **Transpose**. This will open the **Transpose** window:

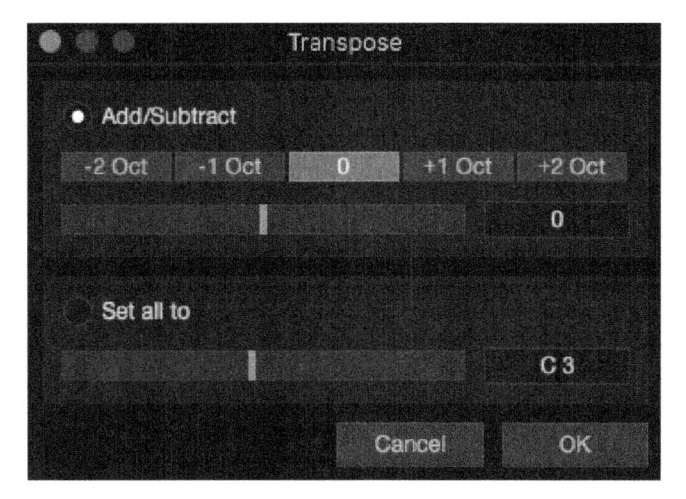

Figure 9.7: The Transpose window

2. Use the slider in the **Add/Subtract** section of this window to set the amount of transposition in semitones. Enter a negative value here to transpose notes down, and a positive value to transpose them up.
3. If you only want to transpose by octaves, you can use the shortcut keys labeled **-2 Oct** through to **+2 Oct**.
4. Use the **Set all to** option to reduce all the notes to just a single note. This can be useful to create a rhythmic part from a melodic part. For example, if you have a bass pattern and you want a kick drum to play at exactly the same time as the bass, use this option to set all bass notes to **C 1** and trigger the kick drum.
5. Click **OK**.

Now, we've come to the fun part – we will have Studio One transpose a melody to a totally different scale or mode. By using this technique, you can completely alter the feel of the melody and present it in a totally different mood. Here's how to do it:

1. On the left side of the **Edit** window, find the section titled **Scale**.

2. Here, use the dropdown on the left to select the key and the dropdown on the right to select the scale or mode that you want to use:

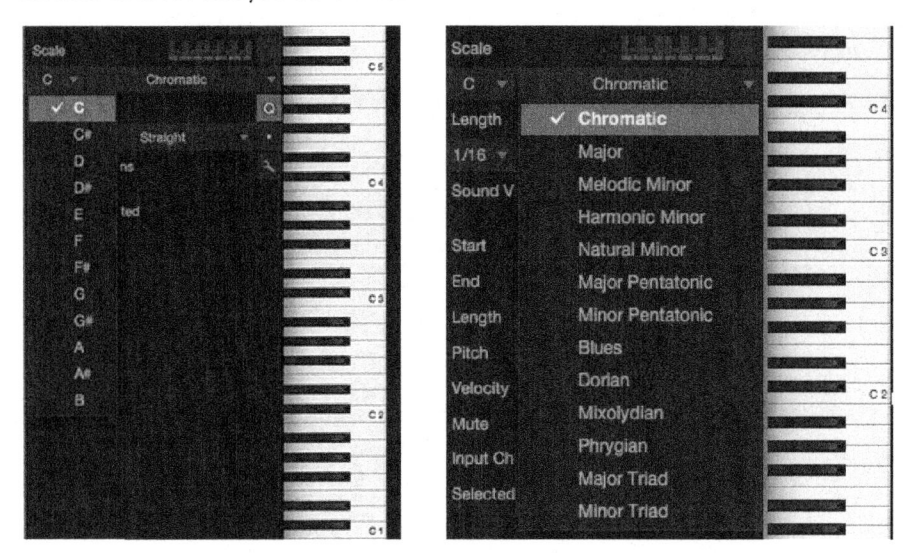

Figure 9.8: Selecting a key (left) and a scale or mode (right)

3. Click the **Action** button and select **Apply Scale**. Studio One will transpose the MIDI notes to the scale or mode you just selected.

Go ahead and try all the different scales in the drop-down list. Once you find a scale you like, repeat the preceding steps for all MIDI events in your song to transpose them to that scale. Although this would normally require a solid knowledge of music theory, it's a breeze to accomplish in Studio One.

Adjusting velocity

In MIDI, **velocity** is a value that accompanies every single note and indicates how hard that note was played. This information is used by synthesizers and other MIDI-controlled devices to determine the volume, timbre, and other characteristics of the resulting sound.

When you record a piece of music with your MIDI keyboard, the velocity value corresponding to each note is recorded as well. You can then edit these values to fine-tune the dynamics of your performance. Here's how to do it:

1. Double-click on the event you'd like to edit. This will open the event in the **Edit** window. The velocity value for each note will be displayed as a column on the **Automation Lane** at the bottom of the window. The Automation Lane allows you to control a specific parameter of a track over time, creating dynamic changes during the course of the song.

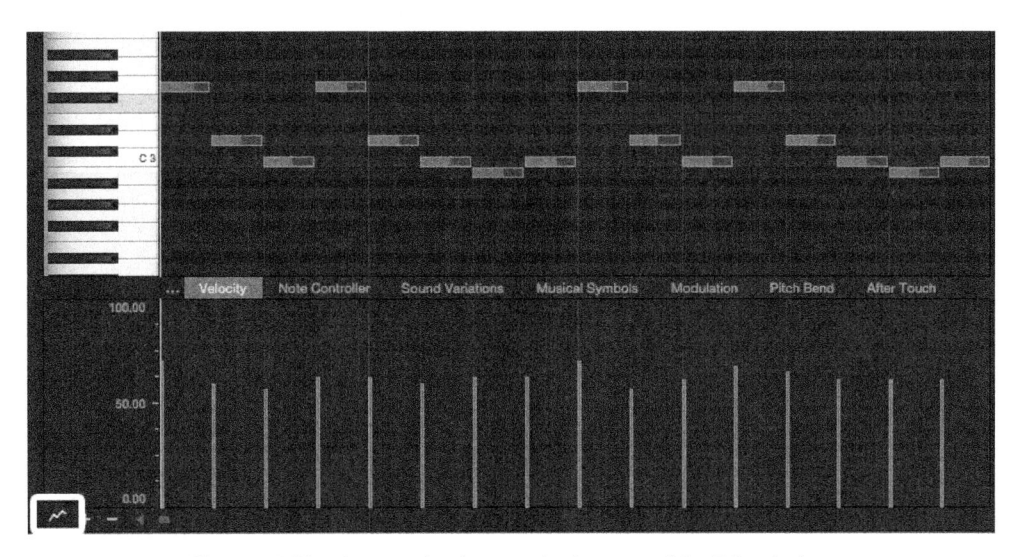

Figure 9.9: The Automation Lane at the bottom of the Edit window

If you don't see the Automation Lane, click the **Show/Hide Automation Lanes** button (the wavy button in the bottom-left corner in *Figure 9.9*) and select the **Velocity** tab.

2. Each column in this lane represents how hard or soft the corresponding note was played, on a scale from 0 to 100. Grab the **Arrow** tool and drag a column up or down to change a note's velocity. Studio One will play the note repeatedly to let you hear how changing the velocity changes the resulting sound.

3. To change the velocity of a group of notes, select the notes and then drag the velocity column corresponding to any one of them. Velocity values for all selected notes will be modified by the same amount.

That method is fine for adjusting the velocities of a small number of notes, but sometimes, you want to adjust velocity on a larger scale. Imagine you have a series of notes and want to apply a crescendo to them so that they will gradually sound louder and brighter. This is how you can do it:

1. Double-click on the event you want to edit.
2. On the **Edit** window's toolbar, click on the **Paint** tool:

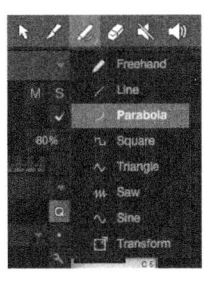

Figure 9.10: Options for the Paint tool

3. From the list of options, select **Parabola**.

4. Now, head over to the Automation Lane at the bottom of the **Edit** window and draw a parabola (i.e., a curve). You will end up with something like this:

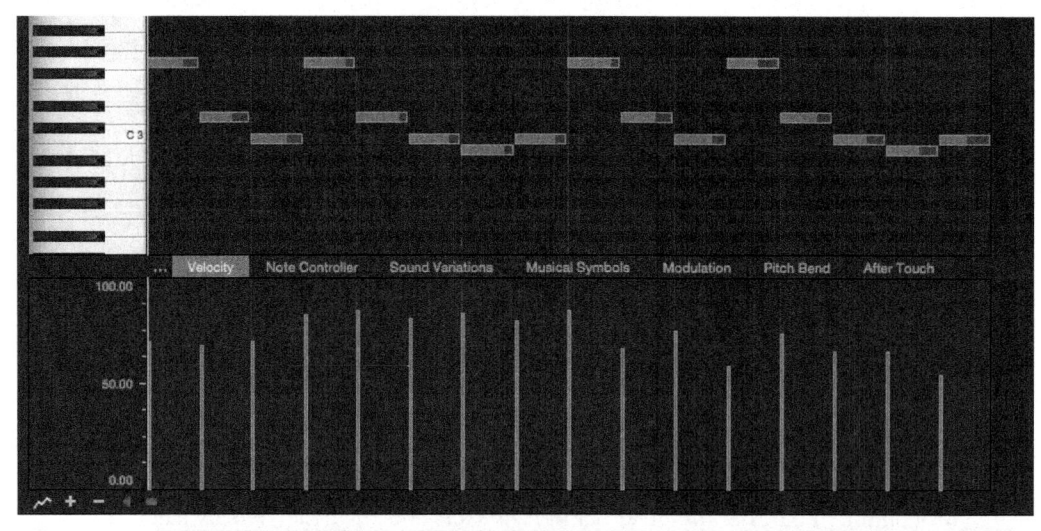

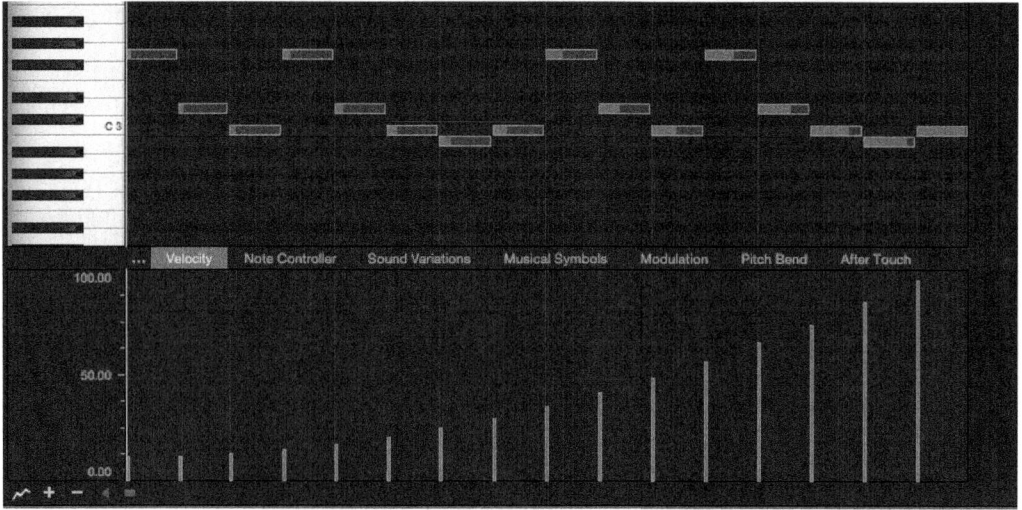

Figure 9.11: A series of MIDI notes (top) and the same notes with a parabola applied to their velocities (bottom)

5. Note that some MIDI devices are very responsive to changes in velocity and others not so much, so the curve in *Figure 9.11* may yield anything from a dramatic crescendo to a barely noticeable change in timbre, depending on the device you work with. Experimentation is key. If you think the result could be better, undo your last move by typing *Ctrl + Z* (Windows) or *Cmd + Z* (Mac) and try again.

Some MIDI devices require velocity to be at a specific value, or within a limited range of values. For example, some sound libraries with sampled violin sounds will play a certain articulation only if the velocity is between `0` and `10`. If you're working with such an instrument, you need to be able to set precise values for velocity. Proceed as follows:

1. Click the **Action** button in the **Edit** window, and select **Velocity**. This will open the **Velocity** window:

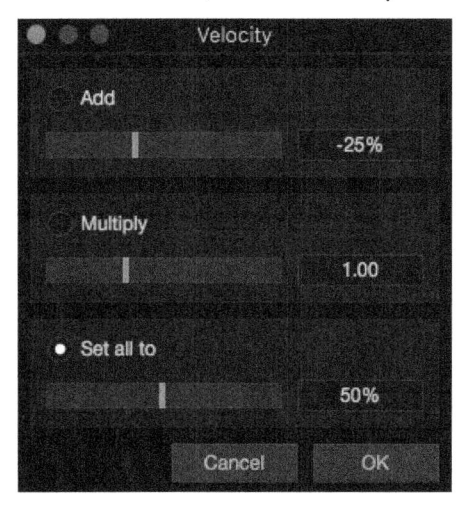

Figure 9.12: The Velocity window

2. To increase or decrease the velocities of all the notes by the same amount, click the **Add** option and select the value you want to add to or subtract from their current velocities.
3. To multiply all velocities by the same amount, click **Multiply** and select the value you want to multiply with.
4. To set all velocities to the same value, click **Set all to** and select the value that you want all notes to have. Remember that in Studio One, velocity can have a value between `0%` and `100%`.

Finally, there may be times when you have a MIDI performance that sounds robotic because all notes have exactly the same velocity value. This happens when you enter notes with your mouse using the **Paint** tool or the QWERTY keyboard, as we discussed in *Chapter 6*. In such cases, it's a good idea to inject realism and dynamism into the performance by adding some variation to note velocities. Here's an easy way to do it:

1. Click the **Action** button in the **Edit** window, and select **Humanize**.
2. In the **Humanize** window, use the **Add velocity range** sliders to set a range within which velocity values should vary.
3. Set the **Add note start range** sliders to `0` so as not to shift the positions of the notes.
4. Click **OK**.

This concludes our tour of MIDI velocity and several different methods of working with it. Now, let's move on to modulation and other MIDI parameters, seeing how we can work with them to adjust a sound during the course of a song.

Adjusting modulation and other parameters

Velocity is effective in measuring how hard you hit a key, but it does not convey any information about what happens after that initial hit. If you hold down a note for a long time, you will need another method to add expression and variety to it.

The smart people who created the MIDI protocol back in the 1980s were aware of this problem, so they added several parameters called **continuous controller messages** (**CCMs**). These allow you to use knobs and faders on a MIDI device to continuously control certain aspects of notes, regardless of their length. For example, you can use CCMs to gradually increase the volume of a single note or add vibrato just when the note is about to end.

Just like velocity, CCMs can be recorded during a performance and edited afterward, which will be our topic in this section. Studio One handles all CCMs in the same manner, so once you learn how to work with one CCM, you can use the same method to record and modify any other CCM that you need to work with.

To see how CCMs are handled in Studio One, we will work with **modulation**, the most popular CCM. In fact, modulation is so popular that most MIDI keyboards come with a dedicated hardware control called a **modulation wheel**, which allows you to manipulate modulation data in real time. Modulation is often used to add vibrato to a sound or open up a filter so that the sound gets gradually brighter, but again, every manufacturer's approach is different.

Now, let's explore how to create and edit modulation data.

Recording modulation data

Recording modulation data during a performance allows you to hear exactly how much expression you add and lets you adjust the modulation level on the fly. There are several ways of doing this, so let's explore them one by one:

- If your MIDI keyboard has a modulation wheel, simply start recording on a MIDI track, as we discussed in *Chapter 6*. As you play the notes, use the modulation wheel to add expression to them. Modulation data will be recorded on a separate lane inside the same track.

- If you use both hands for your performance or find it impractical to manipulate the wheel as you play, don't worry. Just record the notes first. Then, hit record again, and this time, work the modulation wheel. Since modulation data goes on a separate lane, this will not erase the notes.

- If your keyboard does not have a modulation wheel, or if you don't have a keyboard, you can still record modulation data. Remember the onscreen QWERTY keyboard? It has a virtual modulation wheel on the left-hand side, labeled **Mod** (*Figure 6.9*). Hit record and use that to add expression to your performance.

Once you've recorded your modulation data, it's time to edit it to perfection, and that's what we're going to do next.

Editing modulation data

Modulation data is stored and displayed in the **Track Automation Lane**. Follow these steps to reveal this lane and start tweaking:

1. Double-click on the event you want to edit. This will open the event in the **Edit** window.
2. If you don't see the Automation Lane, click the **Show/Hide Automation Lanes** button and select the **Modulation** tab. The modulation data you recorded will be displayed in the form of a continuous graph under the notes:

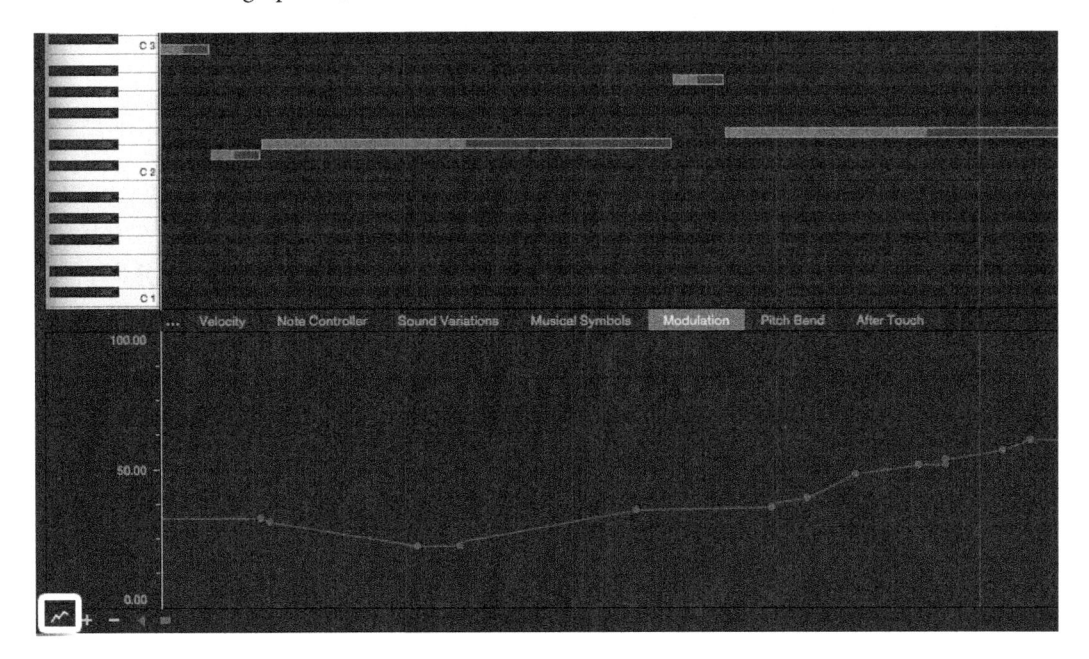

Figure 9.13: The Automation Lane displaying modulation data

3. Click on the **Paint** tool in the **Edit** window, select one of the options from *Figure 9.10*, and tweak this graph to your heart's content. Use a line or parabola to get a smooth change, or try a periodic option, such as **Sine** or **Triangle**, for a creative effect. There is no standard measure for this (or any other CCM) parameter, so experimentation is key.

One important thing to note is that while CCM data is recorded alongside notes, it is not directly linked to them. This means that if you move the notes, modulation data will remain in its original position and become out of sync with the notes. Take a look at these two screenshots:

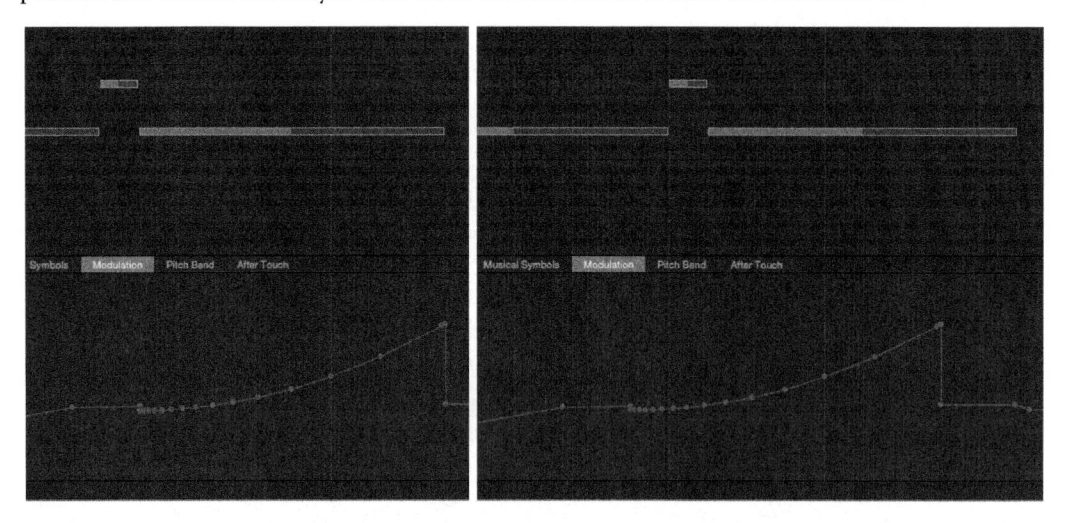

Figure 9.14: Modulation data does not follow notes

On the left in *Figure 9.14*, we can see a nice smooth curve that has been edited to align perfectly with the long note on top. Now, if we decide to move the notes to a different position, the modulation curve will stay put, and any expression added by modulation will become out of sync with that note, as shown on the right. To fix this, enable the **Select Part Automation with Notes** option:

Figure 9.15: The Select Part Automation with Notes toggle button

Now, when you select a note or a group of notes in the **Edit** window, all modulation data underneath those notes will be selected as well, so you will be able to move them together.

This concludes our coverage of Studio One's general MIDI editing options. Up next, we will take a look at the Pattern Editor and talk about the editing features unique to that window.

Working in the Pattern Editor

As we saw in *Chapter 6*, the **Pattern Editor** is a perfect tool for creating musical ideas that are meant to be repeated. While its strictly grid-based design lacks the **Edit** window's what-you-see-is-what-you-get approach, the Pattern Editor offers some unique features that are not available anywhere else in Studio One. So, let's take a look at each of these.

To start using the Pattern Editor, double-click on the pattern you want to edit. This will open the **Pattern Editor** window. Just like the regular **Edit** window, this window has an Automation Lane in its lower section but with a different set of options:

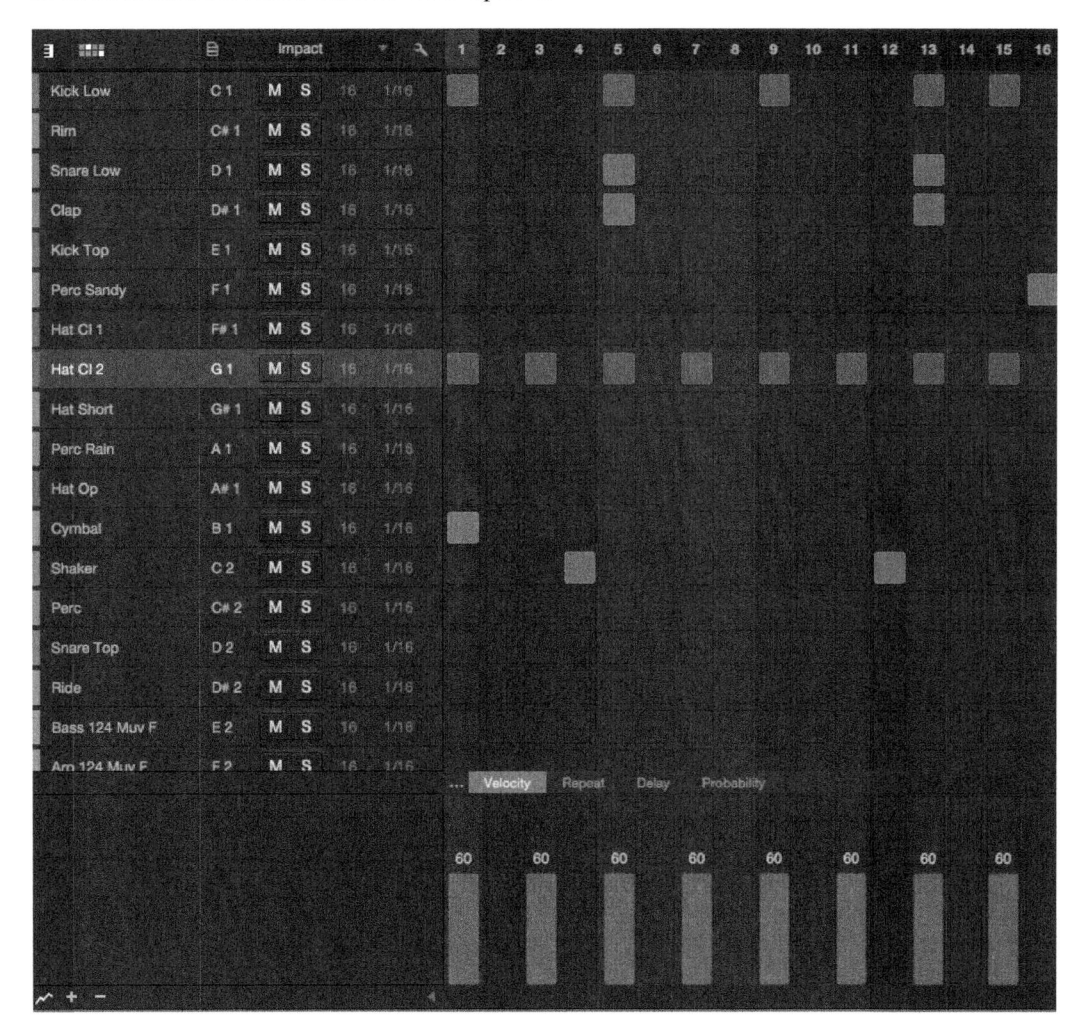

Figure 9.16: The Automation Lane of the Pattern Editor

Now, let's go over these options one by one:

- **Velocity** allows you to set the velocity value for a note, on a scale from 0 to 100. Note that in this window, you cannot select a note by clicking on it; this will delete the note. Instead, click on the lane that contains the note, and its velocity value will be displayed on the Automation Lane.

- **Repeat** lets you quickly add a flam or roll (as in a drum roll) to a note. This is equivalent to adding a roll using the Double Lane Resolution method we discussed in *Chapter 6*. Normally, the **Repeat** value is at 0, meaning there will be zero repeats, but you can increase this value to add as many repeats as you wish.

- Using the **Delay** value, you can set a note to be played sooner or later than its position on the grid. By default, this setting is at 0. Enter a positive value to delay the note, resulting in a laid-back feel. For example, if you program a drum groove and you have a snare drum and a clap hitting simultaneously on beats 2 and 4, delaying the claps slightly while keeping the snare in place will yield a tasty, humanized feel, as if the drummer is playing right on the beat and the people clapping are coming in a bit later, which usually is the case in real life. If you enter a negative value on the delay slider, the corresponding note will be played before its position on the grid, resulting in a rushed feel. This can be useful to inject excitement and anticipation into a drum groove, especially at higher tempos.

- **Probability** is a unique feature that sets the likelihood that a specific note will be played. This allows you to add a random element to your pattern to make it more interesting and less repetitive. By default, this is set to 100%, meaning that the corresponding note will always be played. By decreasing this value, you decrease its chances of being played. This is useful for creating realistic MIDI performances and adding humanized variations and imperfections to your patterns.

Taking command of these editing features will help you create much more dynamic elements with the Pattern Editor and get past most of the limitations that have plagued pattern sequencers in the past. We are now ready to move on to the last step on our tour of the MIDI editing tools – Note FX.

Using Note FX to spark creativity

Note FX plug-ins are effects processors that modify notes in real time as they are sent to a MIDI instrument. This allows you to try creative ideas on the processor's interface, without actually changing or editing the original performance.

There are four Note FX plug-ins in Studio One:

- Arpeggiator
- Chorder
- Repeater
- Input Filter

We will explore each of these processors, but first, let's take a look at how you can load them onto a MIDI track.

Loading Note FX plug-ins

FX plug-ins can be initiated in two ways. Here's the first method:

1. Open the **Browse** panel and go to the **Instruments** tab.
2. In the list of instruments, find **Note FX**, and click the small triangle next to it. This will reveal the Note FX plug-ins installed on your system:

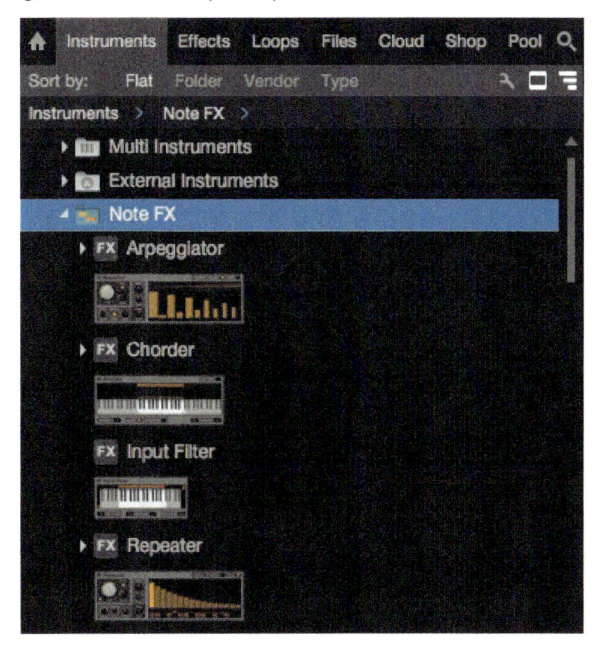

Figure 9.17: The Note FX plug-ins listed on the Browse panel

3. Drag the processor you want to use and drop it onto a MIDI track.

Here's the second method:

1. Open the **Inspector** panel of the track that you want to add a Note FX processor to.

2. Find the **Note FX** box. If you work on a small screen, this panel may get crammed, so you may have to dig for it by resizing other boxes:

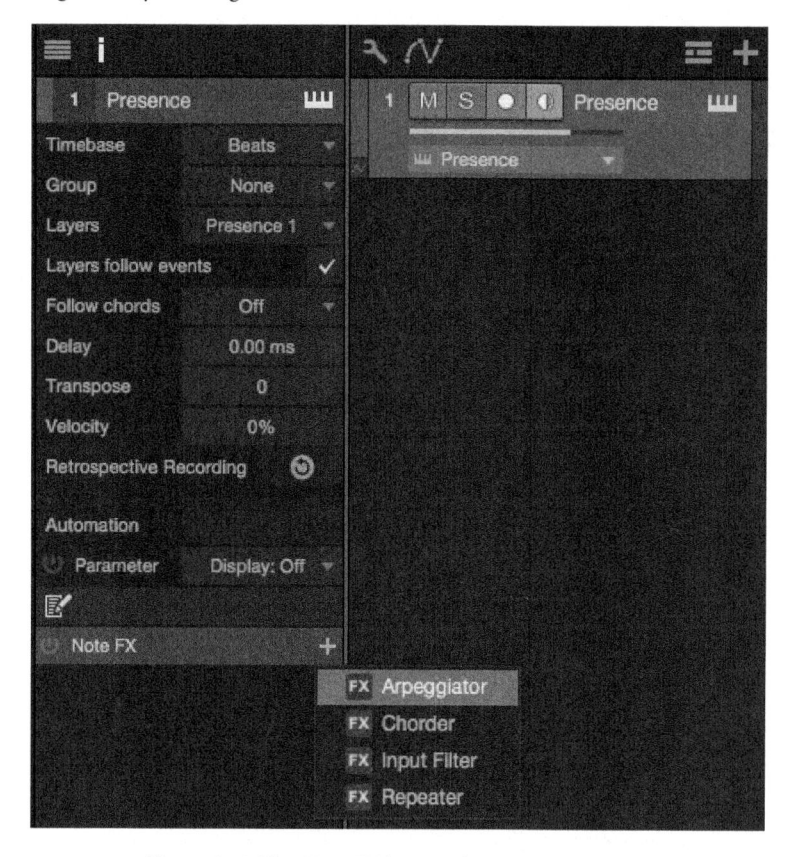

Figure 9.18: The Note FX box on the Inspector panel

3. Click the plus sign next to **Note FX**. This will display a list of the Note FX plug-ins installed on your system.
4. Select the plug-in you want to use.

Once you load a Note FX plug-in onto a MIDI track, you can open its interface by clicking on the Note FX editor icon located on the track:

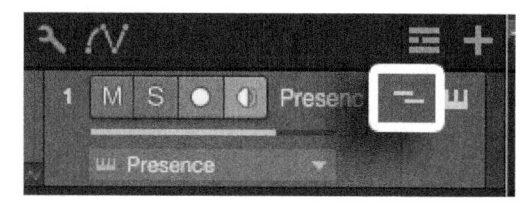

Figure 9.19: The Note FX editor button

Now, let's explore each Note FX plug-in one by one.

Arpeggiator

Arpeggiator generates a complex, rhythmic pattern based on a chord or a single note coming from a MIDI track, or played live on a keyboard. This pattern is synced to the project's tempo, so it will stay in time with the rest of the music. This makes Arpeggiator a perfect tool to add movement and interest to MIDI tracks, as well as to create intricate, evolving patterns.

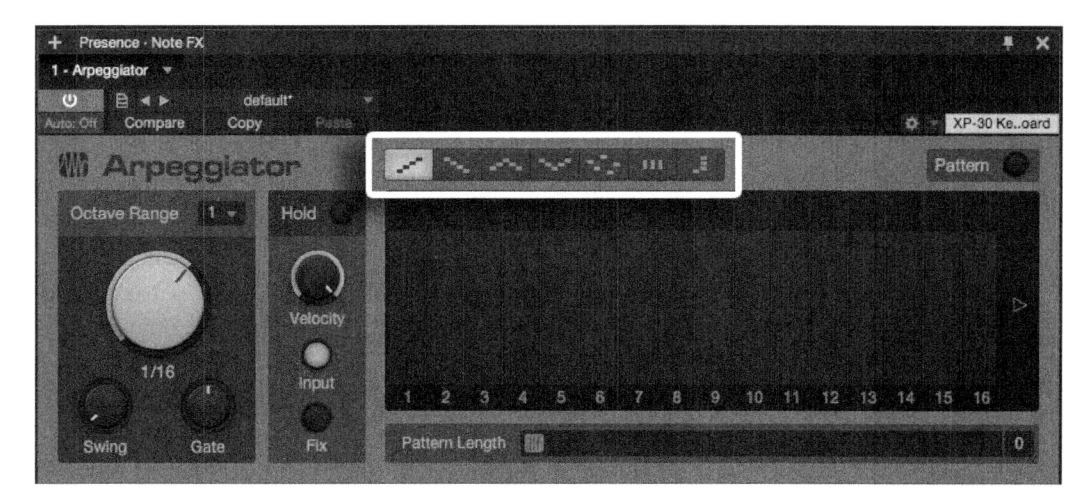

Figure 9.20: Arpeggiator

Let's dissect Arpeggiator's interface to see how it works:

- The buttons highlighted in *Figure 9.20* are called direction selectors. When you play a chord, these select the direction in which the notes of that chord will be arpeggiated. Let's assume that you're playing a C major chord, consisting of the notes C, E, and G. This is how each direction selector will arpeggiate those notes:

  - If you select Up, the first option, notes will be arpeggiated as C, E, and G. When G is reached, the pattern will start over.
  - If you select Down, the notes will be arpeggiated as G, E, and C.
  - Up and Down will yield C, E, G, E, C.
  - Down and Up will yield G, E, C, E, G.
  - Random will arpeggiate the notes in a random order.
  - From Input will arpeggiate the notes in the order in which you played them.
  - Chord Mode will repeat the entire chord instead of arpeggiating it.

- The **Octave Range** selector refers to the range of octaves over which Arpeggiator will play the generated notes. If this is set to 1, its default value, arpeggiated notes will remain in the same octave as the original notes that you play. If you set it to 2, the arpeggio will cover a span of two octaves. This can be set to a maximum value of 4, yielding a range of four octaves in total.
- The big untitled knob on the left is actually called the **Rate** setting. This lets you select a rhythmic value for each arpeggio step. It accepts all note length values from a whole note to a 64th note, including all dotted and triplet varieties.
- **Swing** lets you add a swing feel to the arpeggio (we talked about swing in *Chapter 6*).
- **Gate** determines the length of arpeggiated notes. As you turn this setting down, notes will become shorter. As you turn it up, notes will become longer, overlapping each other.
- The **Hold** button tells Arpeggiator to keep going even if you release the notes on your keyboard. When you play new notes, these will replace the previous notes.
- The **Velocity**, **Input**, and **Fix** settings determine how velocity values will be set for the arpeggiated notes. Select **Input** if you want Arpeggiator to follow the velocities of notes as you play them. Select **Fix** if you want to fix the velocities of arpeggiated notes and dial in the desired value using the **Velocity** knob.

The repetitive patterns created by arpeggiators have become a trademark in some music genres, but for other types of music, you may want the ability to customize these patterns for a more intricate, complex arrangement. Studio One's Arpeggiator has a feature that allows you to do just that, and that's what we are going to explore next.

Using Arpeggiator's Pattern Sequencer

Arpeggiator has a **Pattern Sequencer**, which can be used to program detailed rhythmic patterns. This works in conjunction with all the settings just described and adds an extra layer of control. You can use the Pattern Sequencer to specify velocity and gate values for every arpeggiated note.

To start using the Pattern Sequencer, click the **Pattern** button in the top-right corner of Arpeggiator. Eight columns will appear in the **Pattern Editor** window:

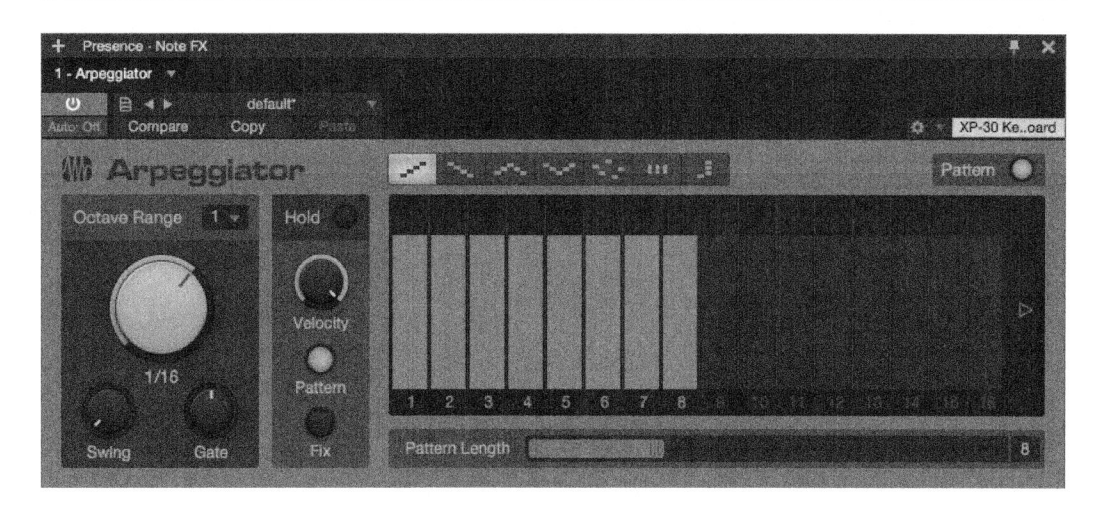

Figure 9.21: The Pattern Sequencer inside Arpeggiator

These columns represent the steps triggered by Arpeggiator. Drag a column up or down to adjust its velocity. Drag a column left or right to adjust its width (acting as a gate setting for individual notes).

Drag the **Pattern Length** slider at the bottom if you want to program a pattern with more than eight steps. The maximum number of available steps is 32.

Using Arpeggiator in this manner opens the door to many creative possibilities, but this is just the tip of the iceberg. You can automate every parameter on Arpeggiator to change your patterns dynamically throughout a project. You can even assign several arpeggiators on a track and go back and forth between them using automation. We will talk about automation in *Chapter 13*.

Chorder

Chorder is an intelligent chord generator that lets you trigger chords by playing single notes. This allows you to play complex chords easily even if you have limited keyboard skills.

Chorder's interface consists of two rows of piano keys:

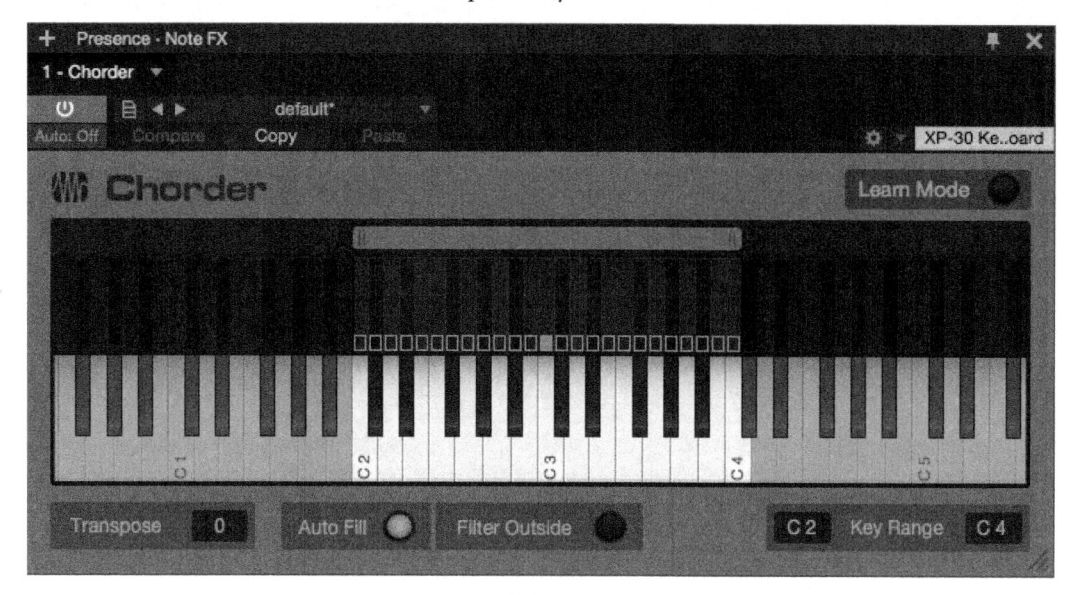

Figure 9.22: Chorder

The keyboard at the bottom shows the note that you play on your keyboard. The keyboard at the top shows the notes that will be triggered when you play that note. The slider above the keyboards sets the range within which Chorder will operate. If you play any note outside of this range, Chorder will ignore it.

If you're new to music theory and don't know how to construct chords, you can still get a lot of mileage out of Chorder. In the **Preset** menu, you'll find a good collection of chord combinations optimized for various music genres. Open the **Preset** drop-down menu (at the top of the interface, look for the field labeled **default**), select a chord combination that matches your style, and you're good to go. However, if you want to program your own chords to use in Chorder, then read on.

Programming Chorder to use custom chords

You can teach Chorder to trigger as many custom chords as you want. As an example, we will program it to trigger a C Maj7 chord when we play the C2 note on our MIDI keyboard. To do so, follow these steps:

1. Click the **Learn Mode** button.
2. On the lower keyboard, click on the note that you want to use as a trigger. In our example, that will be C2.
3. On the upper keyboard, click the notes that you want Chorder to trigger when you play C2. In our example, these will be C, E, G, and B. Feel free to arrange these notes any way you like to create different chord voicings, add tension notes such as D, F#, and A, and use different octaves. You can use any note in any octave on the upper keyboard.

4. Instead of clicking with your mouse on the upper keyboard, you can add notes by playing them on your MIDI keyboard as well. Chorder will register them in the same manner.
5. If you add a wrong note, click on it or play it on your keyboard again to remove it.
6. To enter another chord, repeat *steps 2* to *4* as many times as necessary.
7. Click the **Learn Mode** button again to exit Learn Mode.

Now, you only need to record the trigger notes on the track. When you play back the recording, Chorder will automatically generate the chords that you have programmed.

Repeater

Repeater is a simplified version of Arpeggiator. Instead of arpeggiating the notes that it receives, it simply repeats them at predetermined intervals. This is useful for creating rhythmic sequences from long, static notes.

Most of the settings on Repeater's interface are identical to those on Arpeggiator:

Figure 9.23: Repeater

To avoid repetition (no pun intended), we will cover only the settings unique to Repeater here.

Steps determines how many times the original note will be repeated. The default is 8, but it can go as high as 32. Once this number of repetitions is completed, Repeater will stop.

The **Scale** settings for **Velocity**, **Gate**, and **Pitch** allow you to change these values gradually. For example, by adjusting the **Scale** setting for **Velocity**, you can tell Repeater to increase or decrease the velocity of each subsequent step compared to the previous one.

The velocities and lengths of all steps are controlled globally by the **Velocity** and **Gate** settings, respectively. You can override these settings and set specific velocity and length values for individual steps by activating the individual **Velocity** and **Pitch** buttons in the top-right corner. When these are active, you will be able to drag the columns in the sequencer window to adjust their length and velocity, just like in Arpeggiator.

Input Filter

Input Filter is a utility plug-in that lets you filter out unwanted notes before they reach your MIDI device. This is useful in situations where you want an instrument to respond to only specific notes, leading to some creative applications.

Let's take a look at how Input Filter works. The interface is simple:

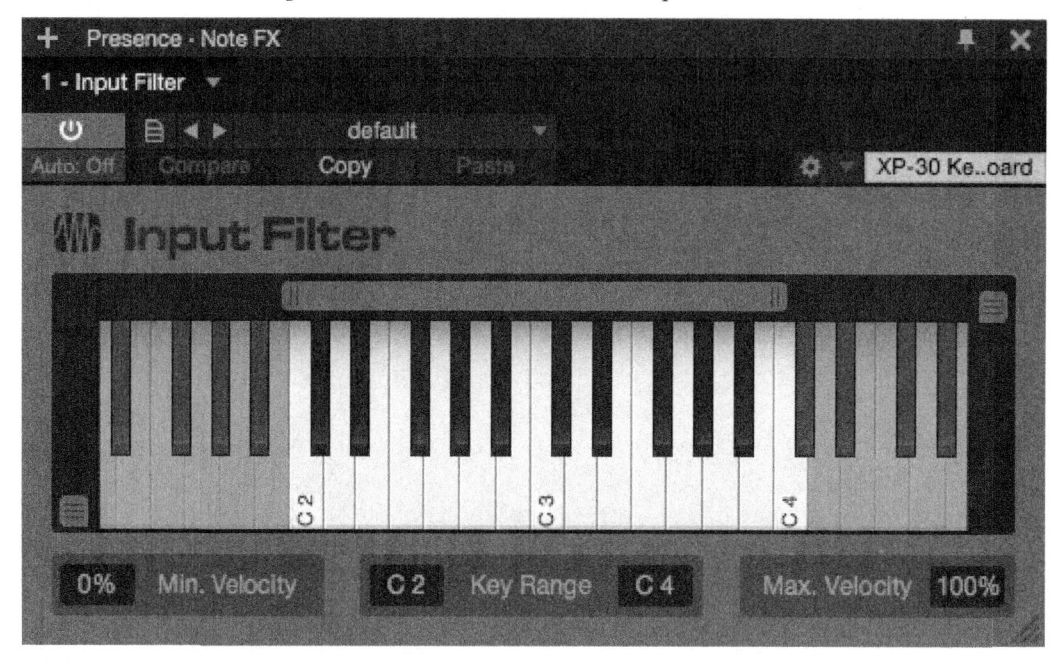

Figure 9.24: Input Filter

The notes within the key range will be allowed to pass, and notes outside the range will be stopped. Input Filter, as shown in *Figure 9.24*, is set to pass all notes between C2 and C4, stopping all other notes. You can edit this range by typing in note names directly inside the boxes on both sides of the **Key Range** field, or by using the slider above the keyboard.

Input Filter also allows you to set a velocity range for notes that will be allowed to pass. Remember that in Studio One, MIDI notes can have a velocity value between `0%` and `100%`. You can set a lower and upper threshold for velocity using the **Min. Velocity** and **Max. Velocity** fields respectively. Any notes above or below these thresholds will be stopped.

Now, let's think of a couple of scenarios where these features would be useful. For example, let's say you want to split your keyboard between two instruments so that when you play in lower octaves, instrument A will respond with a bass guitar sound, and when you play in higher octaves, instrument B will respond with a piano sound. You can do this as follows:

1. Create two Instrument Tracks, one for instrument A and one for instrument B.
2. Select the same MIDI keyboard as the input source for both tracks.
3. Load an Input Filter on both tracks.
4. On the Input Filter for the instrument A track (bass guitar), set the allowed range of notes between `C0` and `C2`.
5. On the Input Filter for the instrument B track (piano), set the allowed range of notes between `C2` and `C8`.

Here's another scenario. Let's say you're working on an orchestral arrangement. Instrument A gives you the sounds of a string section, and you want instrument B to come in and play timpani sounds only when you play hard to accent certain notes. Here's how to set it up:

1. Create two Instrument Tracks, one for instrument A and one for instrument B.
2. Select the same MIDI keyboard as the input source for both tracks.
3. Load an Input Filter on both tracks.
4. On the Input Filter for the instrument A track (strings), set the allowed range of velocity between `0%` and `100%`.
5. On the Input Filter for the instrument B track (timpani), set the minimum velocity threshold to `75%`.

Now, you will hear the timpani only if you play at a velocity higher than `75%`.

Each Note FX plug-in offers an exciting opportunity for creative experimentation, but when you start cascading them so that one triggers the other, the possibilities become mind-boggling. Try inserting a Chorder, and then a Repeater, and two arpeggiators on the same track. Set arpeggiators to wildly different time values, and you will be in uncharted territory – an instant way to fuel your inspiration and spark creativity!

In this section, we explored Note FX plug-ins, which provide a wide range of tools and effects that can be used to manipulate and transform MIDI data in a variety of ways, allowing you to create new and unique musical ideas.

Summary

In this chapter, we took an in-depth look at Studio One's extensive list of MIDI editing features and discussed several methods to manipulate MIDI data for corrective and creative purposes. You learned how to adjust the pitch, timing, and other parameters of a performance to achieve a wide range of musical results. You also gained a deeper understanding of what Note FX plug-ins are and how you can use them to create complex arrangements from simple ideas.

Having command of these MIDI editing features will allow you to explore new possibilities and take your music in new directions.

In the next chapter, we will talk about Studio One's global tracks. You will learn how to add chords to your project for all instruments to follow, how to work with video, and how to add lyrics and markers to facilitate navigation. Taking command of global tracks will be the next step in taking your projects to the next level.

10
Using Global Tracks

Global tracks in Studio One allow users to control parameters that affect an entire project, rather than just a specific track or region. These tracks can be used to dynamically change the overall attributes of a song, such as its key, tempo, or harmonic structure. As a creative tool, they allow you to quickly try out new ideas, explore various possibilities, and easily commit to them once you're happy. Global tracks also allow you to include additional content in a project, such as a video or lyrics.

In this chapter, we will take an in-depth look at Studio One's global tracks and learn how to harness their power to gain more control over your projects. We will cover the following topics:

- Using the Chord Track to control the harmonic content of a song
- Using the Ruler, Marker, and Lyric Tracks to work more efficiently on a project
- Using the Video Track to add sound and music to a video

Technical requirements

To follow along with this chapter, you will need to have Studio One activated on your computer.

Using the Chord Track to control the harmonic content of a song

The **Chord Track** provides a powerful and intuitive way to create and manipulate chord progressions and control the notes played by MIDI instruments. This gives you the opportunity to try out new harmonic ideas and construct sophisticated chord progressions in real time.

Even if you're totally new to music theory and have limited knowledge of how chords work, you will still find the Chord Track highly useful. This is because the Chord Track works in conjunction with Studio One's built-in chord detection algorithm, which can automatically identify and transcribe chords from audio recordings. This opens the door to a wide range of possibilities. For example, if you like the chord progression of an existing song, you can use this feature to extract its chords and use those chords as a template to compose your own songs.

Chord progressions are not considered intellectual property and are not protected by any form of copyright, so feel free to use this technique to spice up the harmonic content of your compositions.

Now, let's take a look at how you can use the Chord Track in your projects.

Getting started with the Chord Track

By default, the Chord Track is hidden from view. To make it visible, click on the **Global Track Visibility** button and select **Chords** from the list of global tracks:

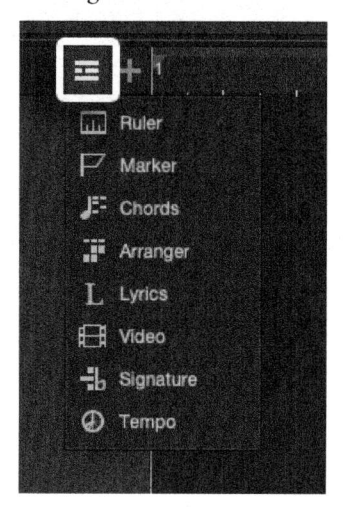

Figure 10.1: The Global Track Visibility button and a list of global tracks

> **Tip**
> We already covered three of these global tracks in previous chapters. We explored the **Tempo Track** and **Signature Track** in *Chapter 4*, and the **Arranger Track** in *Chapter 7*.

An empty Chord Track will now be displayed at the top of the **Arrange** window, ready to be populated with the chords of your song. If you already have an audio or MIDI recording inside your project, Studio One can analyze this recording, detect the chords in it, and automatically extract those chords to the Chord Track. If you don't have a recording yet, you can enter the chords manually. We'll cover both of these methods next.

Detecting and extracting chords automatically

Studio One has a powerful chord detection algorithm that can accurately detect chords in an audio or MIDI recording. If you have a recording that you want to use as a harmonic template for your song, you can use this feature to automatically populate the chords on your project's Chord Track.

To extract chords from an audio recording, proceed as follows:

1. Right-click on the event that contains the audio recording. This will open a pop-up menu:

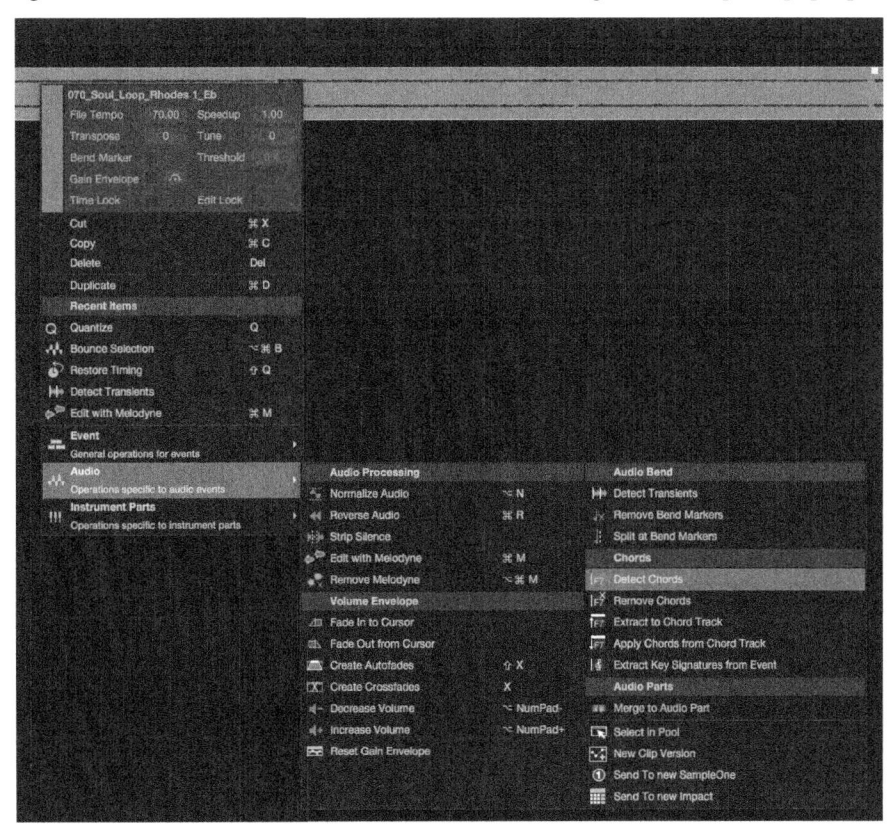

Figure 10.2: Detecting chords in an audio recording

2. On this menu, go to **Audio** and select **Detect Chords**. Studio One will analyze the recording, identify the chords in it, and display these chords on the lower half of the audio event.
3. Then, right-click on the audio event once again, go to **Audio**, and this time, select **Extract to Chord Track**. Studio One will populate the Chord Track with the chords it has just detected.

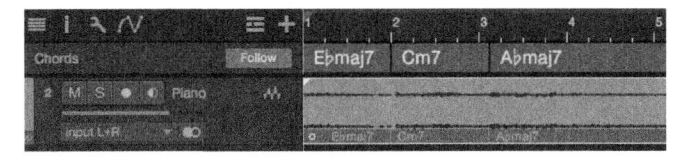

Figure 10.3: The Chord Track (top) displaying chords extracted from an audio event (bottom)

Extracting chords from a MIDI event is even easier – just drag the event to the Chord Track. That's it!

Alternatively, right-click on the event, and on the pop-up menu, go to **Instrument Parts**, and then select **Extract to Chord Track**. Let's take a look at the second method now.

Entering chord information manually

If you know the chords that you'll be using in your song, you can add them to the Chord Track manually. Here's how to do it:

1. Grab the **Paint** tool by pressing *5* on your keyboard.

2. Click on the bar in which you want to enter a new chord. This will add a tentative C major chord (notated as **C** in *Figure 10.4*) that lasts for the entire duration of that bar:

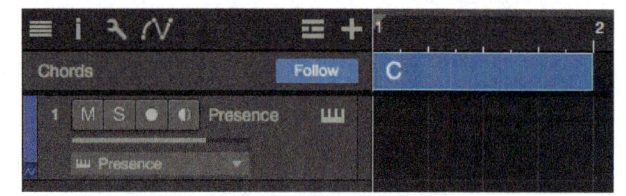

Figure 10.4: Adding chords manually to the Chord Track

3. Select the **Arrow** tool by pressing *1* on your keyboard.

4. If you want this chord to last longer or shorter than a bar, bring the **Arrow** tool to the right edge of the chord event and drag it left or right to resize it as necessary.

5. Double-click on the name of the chord on the Chord Track. This will open the **Chord Selector** window:

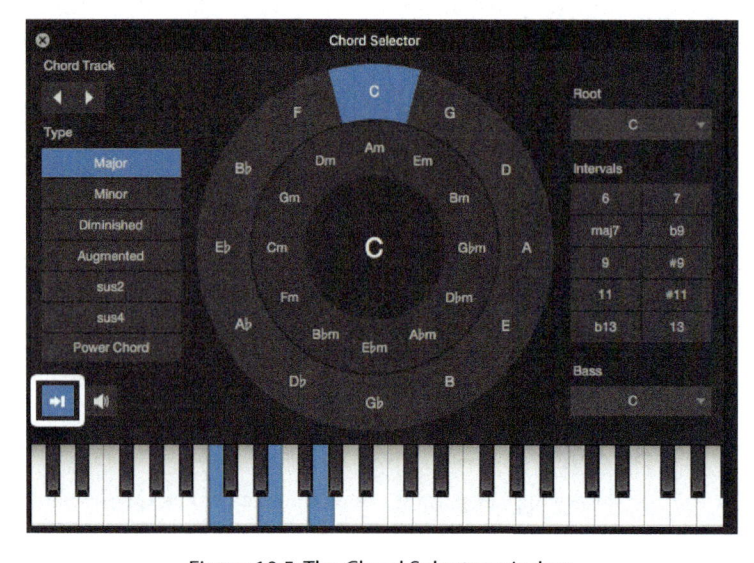

Figure 10.5: The Chord Selector window

6. Use the circle-of-fifths wheel at the center of this window to select your chord.
7. To choose a chord type beyond basic **Major** and **Minor** chords, use the **Type** selector on the left.
8. Use the **Intervals** section on the right if you want to add upper chord tones, also known as tensions.
9. By default, the Chord Track uses root position to order notes within a chord. Root position refers to a chord where the root note, the note that gives the chord its name, is the lowest-sounding note. Sometimes, you may want to have a note other than the chord's root note in the bass to create chords with different colors, referred to as inversions or slash chords. In such cases, use the **Bass** section on the right to select the note that should be used in the bass. When you're done naming a chord, use the arrow keys in the top-left corner of the **Chord Selector** window to move on to the next chord.
10. Repeat *steps 1* to *9* to add as many chords as you need.
11. You can move, duplicate, and copy chords on the Chord Track just like other events in the **Arrange** window, using the **Arrow** tool's standard editing options.

As an alternative to *steps 6* to *9*, you can play chords directly from your MIDI keyboard and have Studio One name these chords automatically. To do this, enable the **Instrument Input** button (highlighted in *Figure 10.5*). Now, when you play a chord on your keyboard, Studio One will identify it and place it on the Chord Track automatically.

Now that you have populated the Chord Track, the next step is to tell the MIDI instruments in your project to follow these chords, which is what we're going to cover next.

Setting Instrument Tracks to follow the Chord Track

By default, Instrument Tracks in your project are not affected by the Chord Track. This means that the chords you enter on the Chord Track will not change the way MIDI events are played – well, not just yet. There are two methods you can use to make sure that MIDI events in Instrument Tracks follow the chords on the Chord Track. Let's start with the simple method.

Adding chords by drag and drop

Once you have the chords of your song laid out on the Chord Track, you can simply drag these chords and drop them on any Instrument Track. Studio One will automatically create MIDI notes that correspond to each chord, with the same duration as the chord event on the Chord Track:

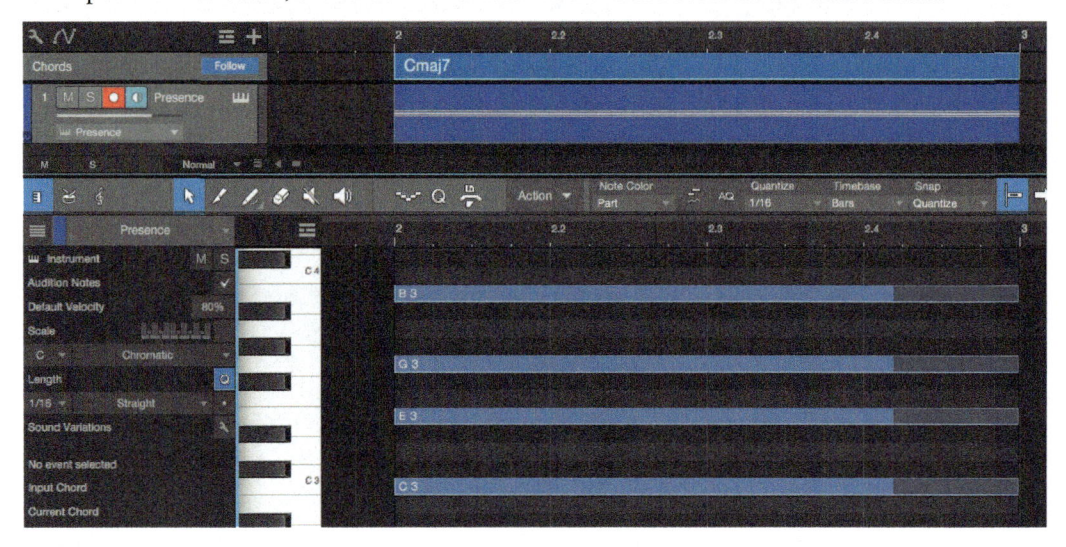

Figure 10.6: Drag a chord to an Instrument Track to automatically create notes corresponding to that chord

If you're new to music theory and don't know how to construct chords yet, this can be a lifesaver. Just add **Arpeggiator** to this Instrument Track and turn these long, static notes into much more interesting patterns!

If you applied chord detection to an audio event, as shown in *Figure 10.2*, you can directly drag that audio event and drop it on an Instrument Track as well. Studio One will automatically create MIDI notes corresponding to each detected chord.

This drag and drop method is fast and simple, but its downside is that the Instrument Track and Chord Track are still not connected. So, if you decide to try out a new chord on the Chord Track, the Instrument Track will still play the original chord. The next method will solve this issue by linking the two tracks.

Setting the Follow Chord parameter

The biggest strength of the Chord Track is its ability to let you easily try out new harmonic ideas. Just change a chord in the Chord Track and all the tracks in your project will be automatically modified to conform to the new chord. In order for this to work, we need to set the tracks in your project to follow the Chord Track. Here's how to do it:

1. Select a track that should follow the Chord Track, and click on the **Inspector** button to open the **Inspector** window.

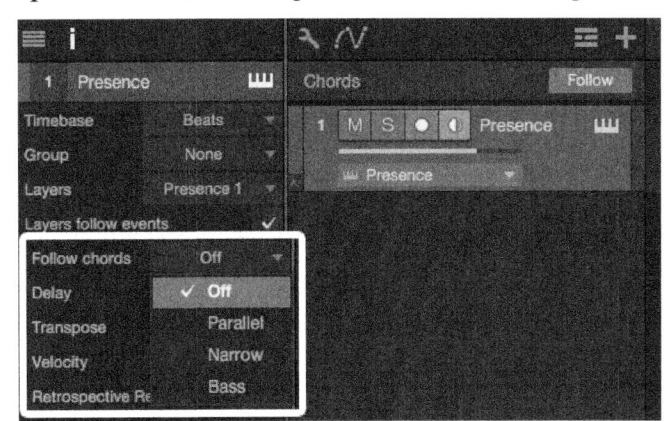

2. From the **Inspector** window, click to open the **Follow chords** drop-down menu:

Figure 10.7: The Follow chords drop-down menu

3. In this drop-down menu, select how you want the notes on this track to be modified when you change a chord on the Chord Track. Here are the available options:

- **Off**: This is the default mode. The Instrument Track does not follow the Chord Track.
- **Parallel**: With this option selected, when you change a chord on the Chord Track, notes on the Instrument Track will be transposed in parallel to the original chord structure, maintaining the same intervals between notes. To illustrate, take a look at the example in *Figure 10.8*. I started with three identical C major 7 chords. I kept the first one (left) as is. Then, using the Chord Track, I changed the second one (center) to F major 7 and the third one (right) to A minor 7. This is how they ended up being transposed with the **Parallel** setting:

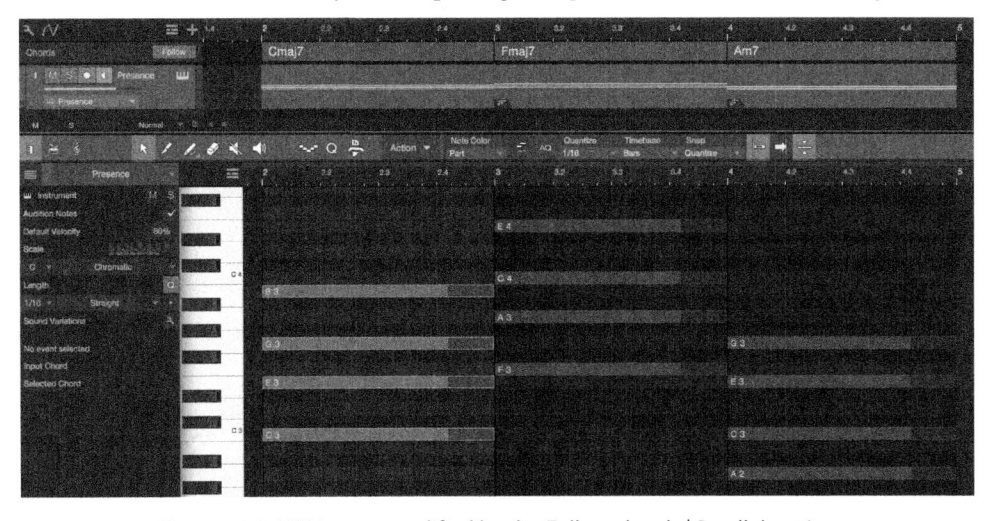

Figure 10.8: MIDI notes modified by the Follow chords | Parallel setting

This results in large leaps between chords, which is not desirable from an orchestration point of view, but it may be useful if you want to maintain the same voicing and texture in all your chords.

- **Narrow**: In this mode, notes are shifted to the nearest note available for the new chord. This results in a smoother transition from one chord to the next, mimicking an orchestration technique known as voice leading. Here are the same chords in *Figure 10.8*, this time modified with the **Narrow** setting:

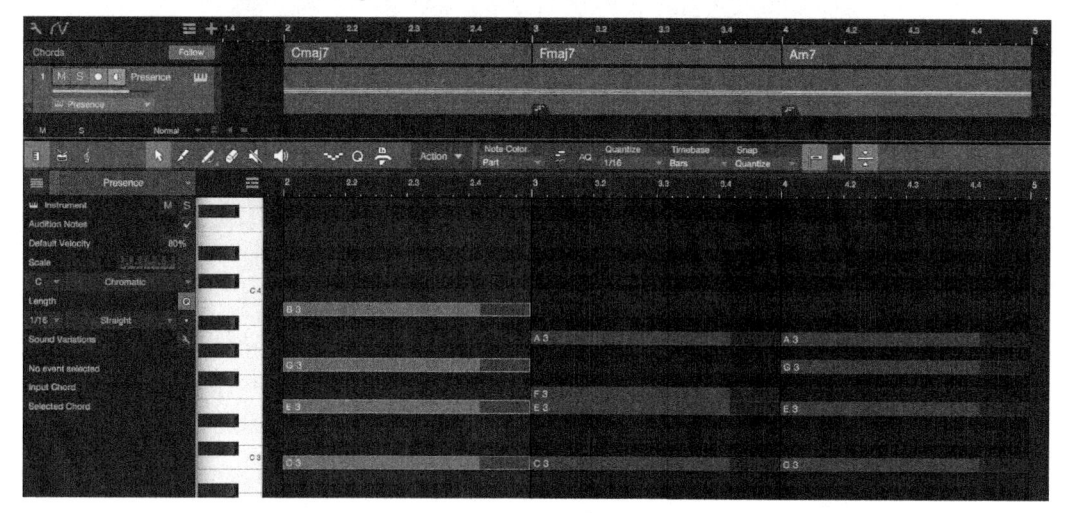

Figure 10.9: MIDI notes modified by the Follow chords | Narrow setting

- **Bass**: This option is used for bass instruments. It assigns the chord's root note or bass note to the lowest note in the chord. The best way to use this mode is to delete all the notes in a chord except the lowest note and then transpose that note to the first octave (the octave between C1 and C2).

4. Double-click on a chord on the Chord Track. This will open the **Chord Selector** window (*Figure 10.5*). Change the chord as necessary.

Now, when you change a chord on the Chord Track, all the Instrument Tracks will be modified accordingly. Audio Tracks can be set to follow the Chord Track as well, but they have some limitations, and there are some extra steps involved. We will talk about these next.

Setting Audio Tracks to follow the Chord Track

Detecting chords and shifting notes is fairly straightforward for MIDI material, but the process becomes much more complicated when working with audio. Although detection and pitch-shifting algorithms for audio material have developed immensely in the past few years, they are still not perfectly accurate and may also produce noticeable artifacts in sound quality. Being aware of these limitations will help you to get better results. In this section, we will cover issues specific to audio material and discuss several workarounds.

What to do when chord detection fails

Detecting chords on an audio recording is no easy task. When you drop an MP3 file of a pop song into Studio One and tell it to detect the chords in it, most of the time you will be impressed with the accuracy of the result. However, there will be times when the detection is not so accurate, which is understandable – there's so much going on in a typical pop song that could confuse the algorithm. The biggest challenge for the algorithm here is to only focus on the sounds that make sense in the harmonic context of the song and filter out everything else. If it fails, chord detection will yield incorrect results.

If you already know the chords to your song, you may think that this is not a big deal – you just enter the chords manually on the Chord Track and you're good to go. However, Studio One has to know which chords are being played on an Audio Track to be able to transpose them correctly when following the Chord Track.

If you have an audio track that's not following the Chord Track properly, follow these steps to fix this problem:

1. Right-click on the audio event. This will open the pop-up menu shown in *Figure 10.2*.
2. Go to **Audio** and select **Apply Chords from Chord Track**. This will override any chord detection that was performed on the audio event and, instead, populate it with the chords on the Chord Track.

Now, when you make a change to the Chord Track, the audio event will be transposed accurately.

Options specific to audio material

When you transpose a MIDI note, you're basically telling a MIDI instrument to trigger the same sound at a different pitch. While this may change the timbre of the sound, it will not degrade sound quality. On the other hand, transposing an audio event is a much more complex operation that requires altering the frequencies of intertwined waveforms contained in an audio recording. This operation is known as **pitch-shifting**.

Pitch-shifting algorithms have developed remarkably in the past few years, to the point where transposing an audio recording by a couple of semitones will not result in any noticeable side effects. However, when you work with the Chord Track, you will end up transposing audio recordings by much larger intervals, and this will inevitably result in a loss of sound quality. Therefore, let's explore a couple of methods built into Studio One to alleviate this issue.

In the previous section, we covered the standard options under the **Follow Chord** menu (*Figure 10.7*). This menu offers two additional options when you work on an audio track. If you're not happy with the options we covered in the previous section, give these extra options a spin:

- **Scale**: This mode uses a very smart algorithm. First, it constructs a musical scale based on the original audio recording. Then, it transposes the notes of that scale to follow the Chord Track. It's pretty advanced stuff, but with one caveat – in order for this to work correctly, the algorithm first has to be able to correctly detect the chords in the original recording. If that detection is not accurate, the transposition will not work correctly either. If so, try the method we discussed in the *What to do when chord detection fails* section, or move on to the next option.

- **Universal**: In this mode, the algorithm will just detect the notes in the audio recording and then transpose them to the notes of the chord you select on the Chord Track. This eliminates the prerequisite of having to correctly detect chords and will generally yield a safe result.

In addition to the **Follow Chord** options discussed, every Audio Track has a **Tune Mode** selector that helps you to optimize the pitch-shifting algorithm for the type of audio material contained in that track:

Figure 10.10: The Tune Mode selector

Use this selector to tell the algorithm what type of material it's dealing with, but don't take these option names too literally. Depending on the timbre of the instrument, the **Guitar** option may yield a better result on a piano recording, for example. So, go ahead and try different options until you get the best result. As always, experimentation is key.

Despite its amazing performance, pitch-shifting technology is not perfect yet. This may change in a few years, but today, it's still not a good idea to pitch-shift audio material anywhere beyond a couple of semitones, especially if the material will be prominent in the song. As far as audio tracks are concerned, your best bet is to use the Chord Track just to try out new chords and harmonic ideas. Once you find a chord progression that you're happy with, rerecord the audio tracks to match those new chords. That way, your project will be free from any sound degradation caused by pitch shifting.

In this section, we explored the Chord Track and discussed the best practices for using it to spice up the harmonic content of your projects. Next, we will cover three global tracks designed to help you navigate much more effectively inside your projects.

Using the Ruler, Marker, and Lyric Tracks to work more efficiently on a project

As your projects grow, it will become harder to find your way inside them. Trying to locate a certain point in a project by constantly having to scroll through the timeline as you zoom in and out is time-consuming and distracting. The global tracks we will cover in this section are designed to help you navigate smoothly and locate important points precisely in any project. While they are not the most exciting features in Studio One, they will definitely make life easier and allow you to remain focused on your work.

Being able to mark and locate important points in a project becomes even more important when you work as part of a team and start sharing files among collaborators, as it allows every contributor to hit the ground running as soon as they open a project.

Let's start by exploring the Ruler Track, the simplest member of the global track family.

Keeping track of different time units with the Ruler Track

The **Ruler** at the top of the **Arrange** window displays time in a musical format – bars, beats, quarter notes, and so on. This makes perfect sense when you're working on a music project but becomes totally irrelevant for any other application. For example, if you edit a podcast, you may be asked to "*remove the cough at 8 minutes and 23 seconds.*" If you're doing sound design for a film, your task could be to "*add a sound effect for the explosion on frame 00:02:26:18.*"

As a solution, you can change the time unit displayed on the Ruler. To do this, open the **Timebase** drop-down menu on the upper panel. Here, you can set the Ruler to display time in seconds or frames:

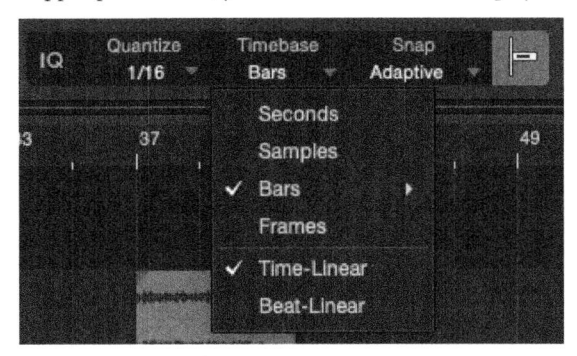

Figure 10.11: The Timebase drop-down menu

However, what if you need to see time both in frames and musical units? This is very common in film scoring, where you may be asked to *"write a 16-bar action cue that ends precisely at the explosion on frame 00:02:26:18."* That's where the Ruler Track comes in.

The **Ruler Track** adds an additional ruler below the **Arrange** window's default ruler and allows you to display time in a secondary format. That way, you can have two separate rulers at the top of the **Arrange** window, displaying different time units for different purposes.

Make the Ruler Track visible by clicking on the **Global Track Visibility** button (*Figure 10.1*). Then, use its drop-down menu to select the time unit you want to see:

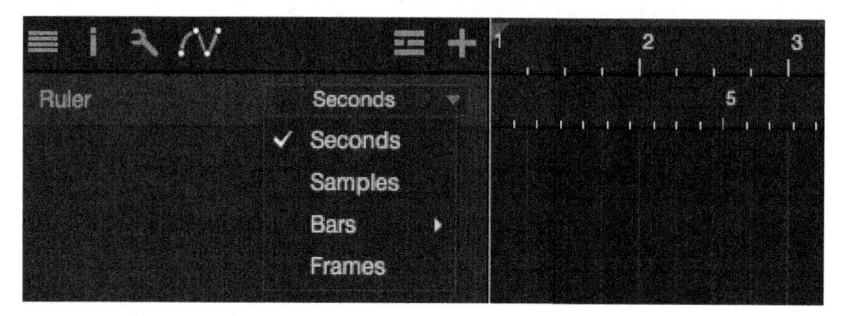

Figure 10.12: The Ruler Track

Note that in *Figure 10.12*, the **Arrange** window's native Ruler (top) displays time in a musical format, while the Ruler Track (bottom) is set to display time in seconds.

The Ruler Track is for visual reference only. It will have no effect on the behavior of the **Snap to Grid** function. Events in the **Arrange** window will snap to whatever time unit is selected on the top Ruler.

Now that we know how to display the correct time unit, the next step is to jump to any point in time. That's what we're going to do with our next global track.

Using the Marker Track for easy navigation

The Marker Track allows you to easily navigate your project by placing markers at key points in the timeline, such as the start and end of sections, or the location of specific events. You can add descriptive labels to your markers, making it easy to keep track of what's happening in your project and stay on top of your work.

The **Marker Track** can be used to help manage and organize your project, especially if it's a large and complex production. If you're working with other people, the Marker Track can be a valuable tool for communication and collaboration.

To add markers to your project, proceed as follows:

1. Click the **Global Track Visibility** button and select **Marker**. This will reveal the Marker Track.
2. Click on the Ruler to place the timeline at the point where you want to add a marker. If you know the exact position where the marker should be (e.g., you have been given a specific timecode by the production team), you can type it directly into the time indicators on the lower panel:

Figure 10.13: Time indicators on the lower panel

3. Now, go to the Marker Track and click on the + sign. This will add a new marker.
4. Double-click on the marker and give it a descriptive name, such as Verse, Chorus, and so on.
5. Repeat *steps 2* to *4* to add as many markers as you need:

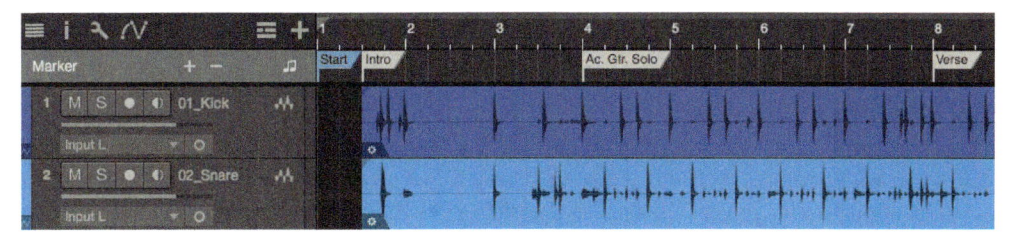

Figure 10.14: Adding markers on the Marker Track

6. Delete markers by selecting them and clicking on the - sign on the Marker Track.

Once you've added your markers, you can use them to navigate easily within your project. For example, if you work in the middle of a section inside your project and want to jump to the beginning or end of that section, type *Shift + N* to jump to the next marker or *Shift + B* to jump to the previous one.

You can also jump to markers directly by using the number keys on your numeric keypad. Here's how markers are numbered – when you first create a song, Studio One creates two markers, labeled **Start** and **End**, and places them at the beginning and end of the timeline. These markers are assigned numbers *1* and *2*, respectively. The names and numbers for these markers cannot be changed. Then, every marker you add using the Marker Track is numbered sequentially, starting with *3*. You can jump to any marker by pressing the corresponding number on the numeric keypad. If you have markers with two-digit numbers, type *Ctrl + Alt + M* (Windows) or *Cmd + Option + M* (Mac), and then type the number in the pop-up dialog box.

To see a list of all markers and their corresponding numbers, select the Marker Track and open the **Inspector** window:

Figure 10.15: Markers listed in the Inspector window

Markers are effective for organization and navigation, but Studio One has a feature that takes this functionality to a whole different level – the Lyric Track. That's what we'll explore next.

Using the Lyric Track

The **Lyric Track** provides a convenient way to display the lyrics of a song onscreen in real time while you record or play back a project. This makes it easier to stay on track during production. If you record yourself while singing, this saves you the burden of having to write down the lyrics and track them on paper. If you record somebody else's song, it will help you find your way inside the song much more easily. If you're working with other musicians or producers, the Lyric Track can be a valuable tool for communication and collaboration. When you share your project with other members of your team, they will be able to see the lyrics as well, allowing everyone to stay on the same page and understand the song's structure.

The Lyric Track provides a user-friendly interface to enter and edit lyrics, making it easy to adjust the timing and placement of the lyrics to match the music. To get started with using the Lyric Track, follow these steps:

1. Click the **Global Track Visibility** button and select **Lyrics**. This will reveal the Lyric Track.
2. To start adding lyrics, simply double-click on the desired location on the Lyric Track and begin typing:

Figure 10.16: Typing lyrics on the Lyric Track

3. To start a new line and advance to the next bar, press *Enter*.
4. To advance to the next bar without starting a new line, press *Tab*.

Once you've entered the lyrics, you can use the **Arrow** tool to edit them just like other events in the **Arrange** window. Drag to move them in order to fine-tune their position, copy a group of lyric events to repeat them in the next chorus, and arrange them to fit the song's structure.

To view the lyrics on the same page, click on the **L** button on the Lyric Track. This will open the Lyrics Display:

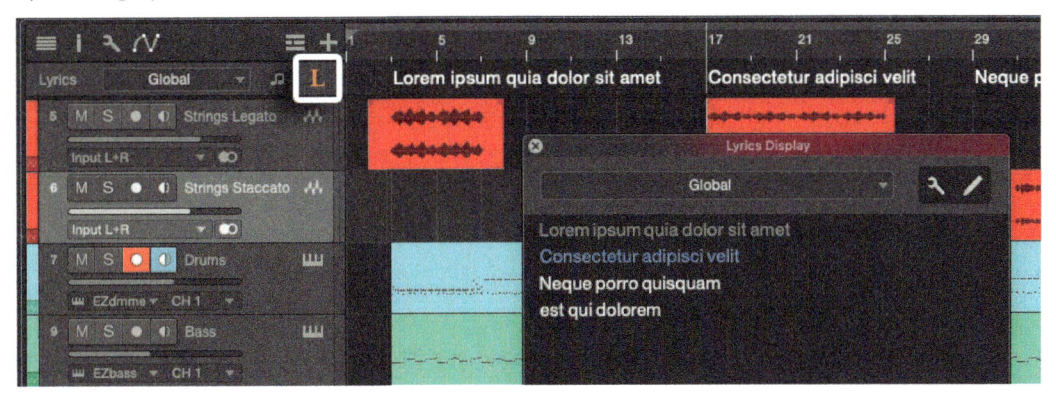

Figure 10.17: The Lyrics Display

The Lyrics Display will show the lyrics of a song in sync with the timeline, karaoke style. Lyrics will auto-scroll as the project plays. The line that's sung currently will be displayed in blue. The lines before that will be gray, and the lines after that will be white. You can also click on a line on the Lyrics Display to jump to that specific point in the song.

Here are two useful tips when working with the Lyrics Display:

- When recording vocals, you may want the lyrics to be displayed slightly ahead of time so that the singer knows what's coming. To do this, click on the wrench icon on the Lyrics Display, go to **Settings**, and select **Ahead**. This will let you set a time offset for the displayed lyrics.
- If you're reading lyrics from the screen while recording and your microphone is at a distance from the screen, you may want to increase the font size for the Lyric Display. Click on the wrench icon, go to **Settings**, and select **Font Size**.

In this section, we explored three global track types in Studio One that are designed to help you gain better control of your project. Next, we will take an in-depth look at the Video Track and see how you can integrate video files into your projects to score music or create sound design for film or multimedia productions.

Using the Video Track to add sound and music to a video

The **Video Track** allows you to add one or more video files to a project. You can then use Audio Tracks and Instrument Tracks to create dialogue, sound effects, and music for the video.

The Video Track provides a powerful and intuitive way to add perfectly synchronized audio to film, video, and other multimedia projects, even with limited experience in video post-production. To get started with the Video Track, we will first explore how to add video files to a project.

Importing video files

To import a video file, simply drag it from File Explorer (Windows) or Finder (Mac) and drop it into your project. MPEG and M4V files are supported on both operating systems; on Mac computers, it is possible to import QuickTime files as well.

You can import as many video files into the same project as you wish, but make sure that these have the same file format and frame rate. If you import files with mixed file types and frame rates, Studio One will do its best to accommodate them, but you may experience system instability and even crashes.

If you're new to working with video files and don't know about file types and frame rates, don't worry. Just install **Handbrake**, a free open source tool, to convert video files, and it will transcode all your video files to the same file type and frame rate for you. Get your copy here: `https://handbrake.fr`.

> **Tip**
> Playing back a video file at high resolution is a demanding task for most computers. If the video you work on has a high resolution (usually marked as 4K or Ultra HD), use Handbrake to create a low-resolution version of it and import that into your project. That way, you'll be able to free up your computer's resources and allocate more horsepower to audio production.

Navigating the Video Track and Video Player

When you import a video file, Studio One will automatically create a Video Track and place the file in it. It will then take a moment to scan through the video, create thumbnails, and place them across the **Arrange** window:

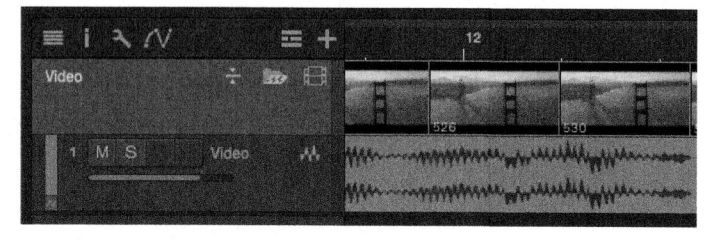

Figure 10.18: The Video Track (top) and the Audio Sub-Track (bottom)

If the video file already has audio in it, this audio will be extracted to a special track right below the thumbnails, referred to as the **Audio Sub-Track**.

Thumbnails displayed on the Video Track are great for visually locating specific scenes or frames on the timeline, but they are not useful for actually viewing the video. That's where the Video Player comes in. The **Video Player** is a floating window that plays back the video in sync with the timeline's position in the **Arrange** window:

Figure 10.19: The Video Player

You can resize and place this window anywhere you want. To toggle its visibility, go to **View** on the top menu and select **Video Player**.

Now that we have imported a video file and explored the basic interface, we are ready to start working with video.

Editing video

Before we begin to talk about audio production for video projects, it is worth noting that Studio One can perform basic editing functions on a video file as well. You can line up several video files on the Video Track and split, move, copy, and resize them just like other events in the **Arrange** window. You can then export the resulting montage as a new video file, complete with all the audio production elements you created for it.

While Studio One is not likely to replace full-fledged video editing programs anytime soon, it's good to have this extra capability to try out different ideas or deliver rough sketches to a client.

By default, when you edit a video, its corresponding audio material on the Audio Sub-Track will be edited as well. If you want to edit audio on this track independently, click on the **Link Audio Track Editing** button, located right on the Video Track.

Synchronizing audio and MIDI events with video

For all audio production programs, including Studio One, the whole purpose of importing video inside a project is to be able to synchronize and match audio to specific points in the video. In this section, we will discuss two methods to achieve that goal.

As an example, we will assume that you work as a sound designer on a short 3D video, in which a ball hits several blocks stacked together. The director asked you to place a sound effect at the precise moment when the ball hits the blocks:

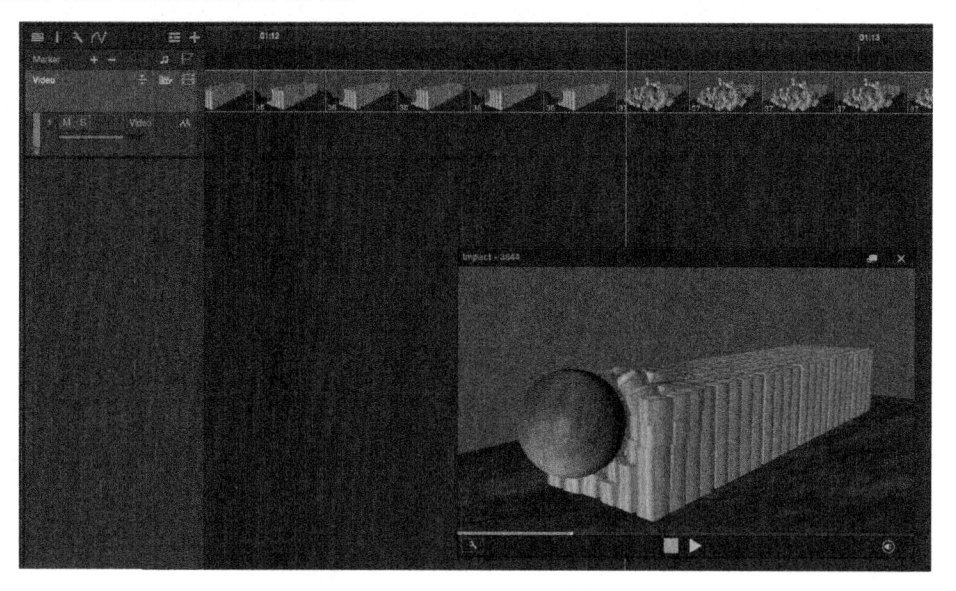

Figure 10.20: The Video Display showing the exact frame to which a sound effect is to be added

Once you find or create a sound effect that works for this context, follow the steps below to synchronize it perfectly to the action on the video:

1. Zoom in really close to the beginning of the audio event and make sure that there is no gap of silence before the sound starts. Then, using the **Arrow** tool, trim the beginning of the event so that the sound effect starts immediately at the beginning of the event. Be surgical.

2. Next, zoom in really close to the Video Track and locate the exact frame where you want the sound effect to begin. Click the ruler to place your cursor there. If the production team sent you a timecode for the exact spot, type it in the **Time Indicator** window (*Figure 10.13*).

3. Open the Marker Track and click the + plus sign. This will add a new marker at that point in time.

4. Enable **Snap** if it's not already activated.
5. Open the **Snap** drop-down menu, select **Snap to Events**, and deselect **Snap to Grid**:

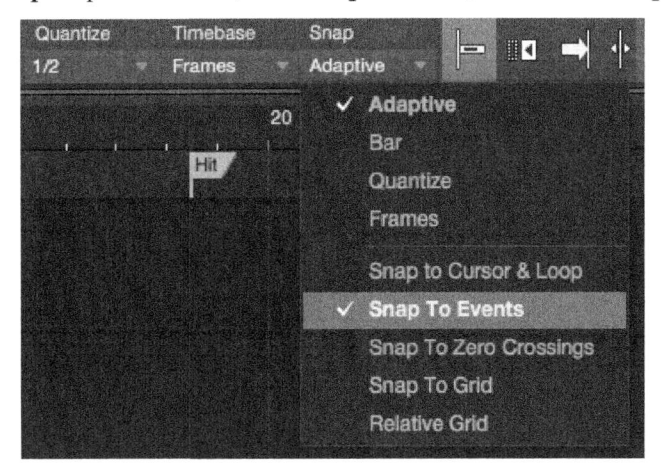

Figure 10.21: Snap settings to align an event to a marker

6. Using the **Arrow** tool, drag the audio event containing the sound effect. It will snap perfectly to the marker you created in *step 3*:

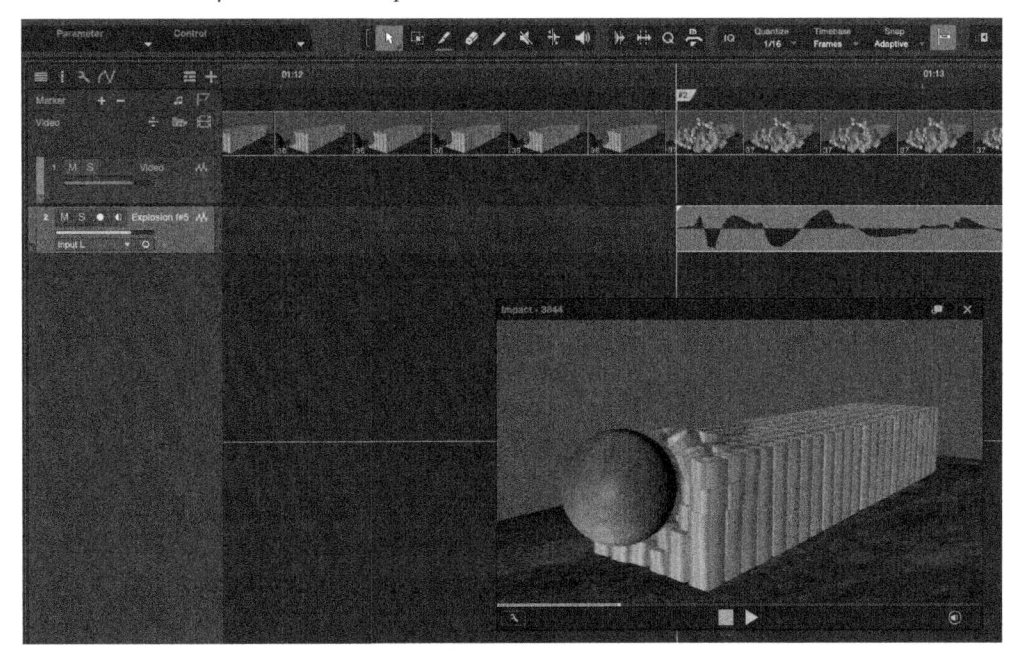

Figure 10.22: The audio event snaps to a marker

The method we just discussed allows you to align events with absolute precision relative to specific frames in a video. However, such a level of precision is not required for every project or every sound element. For example, if you add an ambient sound effect to a video, such as the sound of rain, you can save time by using the following quick-and-dirty method:

1. As with the previous method, zoom in really close to the beginning of the audio event and make sure that there is no gap of silence before the sound starts.
2. Click the **Cursor Follows Edit Position** button to activate it:

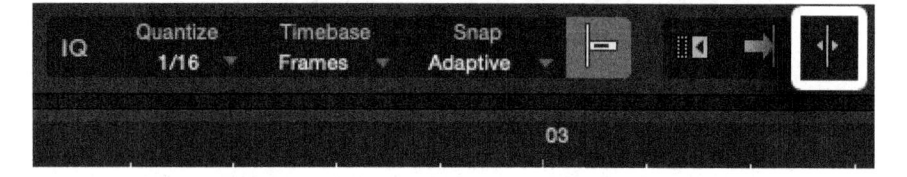

Figure 10.23: The Cursor Follows Edit Position button

3. Now, using the **Arrow** tool, click on the audio event containing the sound effect and start dragging it across the timeline. You'll notice that the timeline cursor will snap to the beginning of the event. As you drag the event along the timeline, Video Player will jog through the video rapidly to match the cursor's position.
4. Once you find the spot where you want the sound effect to be heard, let go of the event.

You will find that nudging sound effects forward or backward even by a few frames will significantly affect their impact and realism. In the preceding example, placing the sound effect on the exact frame when the ball hits the blocks will probably not sound realistic. This is because light travels faster than sound; we see the ball hit the cubes before we can hear it. Try moving the sound effect a couple of frames to the right. Experiment till you get it perfect.

Understanding Timebase

You're doing sound design for a video. You already have dialogue and sound effects, all perfectly synchronized, laid out on several tracks across the project. Now, it's time to start working on the music.

You want to try a musical idea that starts at a slow tempo and then gradually accelerates to highlight a climactic point in the video. Tempo changes are the bread and butter of film scores. What better way to convey a gradual build-up of excitement, right?

So, you open the Tempo Track and draw a nice curve to increase tempo gradually. Your musical idea works perfectly, but now all the dialogue and sound effects are in the wrong places. Changing the tempo shifted them all over the place. What's going on, and how can you fix it?

Here's a concept that becomes essential to understand once you start working with video. In audio production, we work with two different versions of time – absolute and relative. At first glance, this may look like a topic for Einsteinian physics, but it's actually very simple. Let's take a look at both versions of time to clarify:

- Absolute time assigns the position of events on the timeline to absolute values. A dog barking at 4 minutes and 38 seconds in a podcast is an absolute value. A sound effect starting at frame 00:19:08:03 is an absolute value.

- Relative time assigns the position of events on a timeline to musical bars and beats. If you have a piano chord playing on bar 5, that makes perfect musical sense, but it tells us nothing about when that chord will play in absolute time. That's because the temporal length of a musical bar changes depending on tempo. If the tempo of the piece is set to 60 BPM, the piano chord on bar 5 will play at an absolute value of 16 seconds. If the tempo is set to 120 BPM, the same chord will play at 8 seconds. That's what makes musical time relative.

Figure 10.24 illustrates this with a side-by-side comparison. In both images, the top ruler shows relative time in bars and beats, and the bottom ruler shows absolute time in seconds. Note that the audio event is aligned with bar 5 on both images. For the image at the top, the tempo is set to 60 bpm, so bar 5 corresponds to 16 seconds on the second ruler. For the image at the bottom, the tempo is set to 120 bpm, so bar 5 corresponds to 8 seconds on the second ruler.

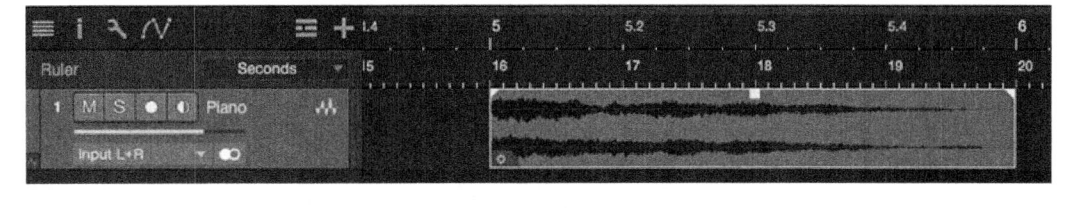

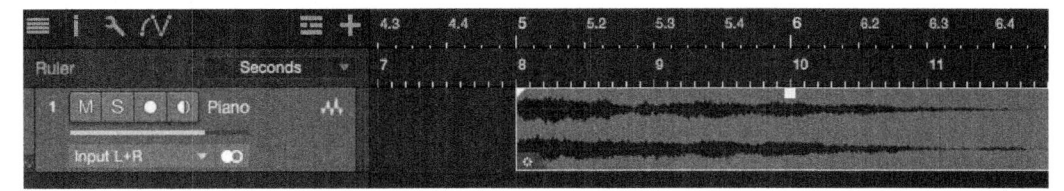

Figure 10.24: Musical time shifts relative to absolute time

By default, all tracks in Studio One use musical time. Changing tempo will shift the position of everything, even markers, on the absolute time scale.

You can override this behavior on a track-by-track basis. If you want the events on a track to remain locked to their absolute time positions when the tempo changes, follow these steps:

1. Click on the track header to select the track.
2. Open the **Inspector** panel.

3. Click on the **Tempo** drop-down menu and select **Don't follow**:

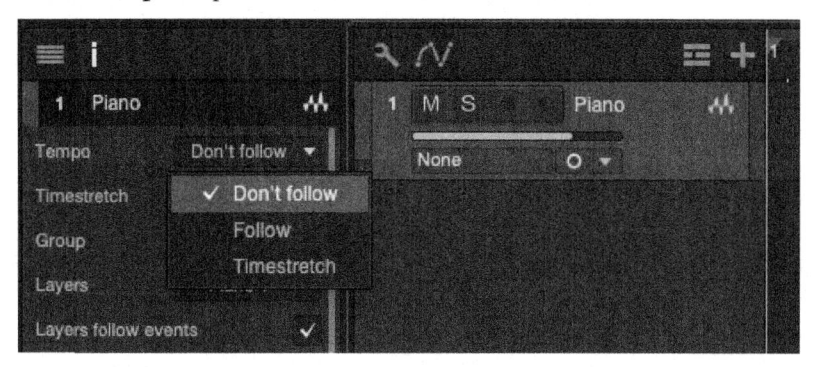

Figure 10.25: The Tempo drop-down menu

Now, the events on this track will remain in their absolute positions no matter how much the tempo changes.

By default, the Marker Track follows tempo changes as well. To lock markers to their positions in absolute time, click on the musical note icon on the Marker Track:

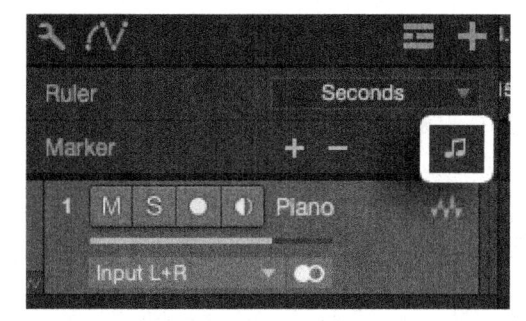

Figure 10.26: The Timebase selector for the Marker Track

As a rule, set all tracks containing dialogue, foley, sound effects, and ambient effects to use absolute time. Set all musical tracks to use musical time.

Exporting video

Studio One has the capability to export a video file right out of the **Song** page, complete with all the audio you added to it. This is not a feature you will use if you work at a professional level. Production houses will ask you to deliver high-quality audio files and take care of joining these files to video using dedicated software. However, having this option might come in handy if you only need to create a simple video or share a rough sketch of an idea with a collaborator.

To export a video from your project, proceed as follows:

1. Go to **Song** on the top menu and select **Export Video**. This will open the **Export Video** window:

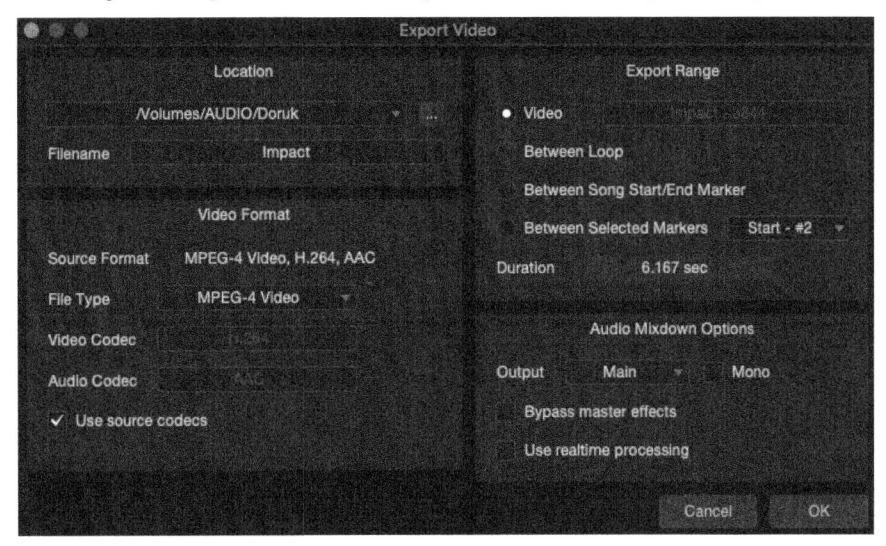

Figure 10.27: The Export Video window

2. Under **Location**, select a folder and filename for the video file you're about to create.
3. Under **Video Format**, select a video format for the video file. The options you see here will vary, depending on your operating system and the codecs installed on your computer. MPEG-4 is a good choice; it provides good quality and can be viewed on any computer or device.
4. Under **Export Range**, select what part of the project you want to export as a video file. Selecting **Video** here will export the entire video. You can also use the other options to export only a part of the project.
5. Click **OK**.

In this section, we took an in-depth look at how to work with video in Studio One. We started by adding a video file to a project, explored the video editing interface, and then took a deep dive into synchronizing audio and MIDI events with key moments in a video. We concluded by exporting our final project as a complete video file. Armed with this knowledge, you are now ready to take on sound design for video and multimedia projects.

Summary

In this chapter, we covered Studio One's global tracks. We started with the Chord Track, which allows you to control the harmonic structure of a song with a few clicks. Then, we explored the Ruler, Marker, and Lyric tracks, which help you and your collaborators to navigate smoothly even in the most complex projects. Finally, we covered the Video Track and learned how to add perfectly synchronized sound elements to a video.

This concludes our coverage of Studio One's extensive editing features. In the next part of the book, we will focus on mixing, the next big step in music production. We will start by discussing how to prepare a project for mixing, ensuring that all your mixing sessions go smoothly and deliver the best results possible.

Part 4: Mixing and Mastering

In this part, we will lay out an efficient workflow that will allow you to finalize your projects on a professional level. First, we will take an in-depth look at the various stages of mixing. We will explore Studio One's immersive audio capabilities and see how you can create three-dimensional experiences for movies, games, and interactive media. Then, we will take a look at Studio One's unique Project page and learn how to create final masters of your Songs. We will finish with a bonus chapter that explores three additional features of Studio One: the Show page, Score Editor, and Sample One XT.

This part includes the following chapters:

- *Chapter 11, Preparing for the Mix*
- *Chapter 12, Working with Effects Plug-Ins to Craft a Mix*
- *Chapter 13, Optimizing Signal Flow and Elevating Your Mix*
- *Chapter 14, Working with Spatial Audio*
- *Chapter 15, Navigating the Project Page and Producing Final Masters*
- *Chapter 16, Using Additional Studio One Features*
- *Appendix, Customizing Studio One and Following Best Practices*

11
Preparing for the Mix

Mixing is a critical step in music production. When it's done correctly, it takes your music to a whole new level. When it's executed poorly, even the best song can turn into a painful listening experience.

Many people are intimidated by the process of mixing. There is so much to consider during a mix session, both at an artistic and technical level, that being able to maintain a sharp focus throughout the session may become overwhelming.

I've been teaching music technology for more than 20 years now, and I've observed on countless occasions that people mostly struggle with their mixes due to a lack of preparation – they get lost inside an endless maze of unorganized musical material and lose their ability to focus. Once we sort everything out by organizing a project, a mix session becomes much more manageable, allowing you to focus on what really matters and present your music in the best light possible. It brings an element of Tao into music production: you're not just organizing tracks and events in a project, you're streamlining your own approach as to how you'll mix the song.

In this chapter, we will explore several steps you can take to make sure that your mixing sessions run smoothly. This will help you craft the best possible mixes from your projects. We will cover the following topics:

- Preparing a Song for the mix session
- Organizing tracks for better control
- Setting levels, panning, and automation

Technical requirements

To follow along with this chapter, you will need to have Studio One activated on your computer.

Preparing a Song for the mix session

Let's start by talking about the preparation steps you will need to take at the Song level. Following these steps will help your mixing sessions run smoothly.

Optimizing hardware and software for the mix

Mixing is a resource-intensive task for most computers, so before starting a session, it's a good idea to give Studio One as much horsepower as your computer can provide. Use these techniques to optimize your system for a mix session:

- The first thing you can do is increase **Dropout Protection**. We talked about **Dropout Protection** in *Chapter 2*, and so far, we had this set to **Minimum** because we wanted to minimize latency when recording audio or playing virtual instruments. Minimizing latency comes at a price, though: it forces your computer to perform its tasks within a very short period of time. This is fine for recording and editing tasks, which do not require too much processing power, but when you start mixing, you will add more and more effects plug-ins, which will place a heavy load on the system.

  With **Dropout Protection** set to **Minimum**, you will soon start to hear clicks and dropouts in audio, and may even experience system crashes. So, go ahead and set this to **Maximum** so that your computer can take its time to perform the calculations required during the mix. The added latency will not be a problem in a mix session; we don't mind waiting for an extra 50 milliseconds when we hit the *spacebar* to play back the project.

- As the Song plays, keep an eye on the **Performance** indicator on the lower panel:

  Figure 11.1: Performance indicator

  The top bar in this indicator shows CPU performance and the bottom bar shows disk performance. If you have a large project with lots of tracks, the disk on your computer may struggle to read audio data from all those tracks at once. In such a case, you'll see sudden spikes on the disk performance section as the Song plays back, and the audio may stutter. If that happens, move the entire project folder to a fast disk (ideally, an internal SSD) to fix this.

- A mix session requires an uninterrupted flow of a large stream of audio data, as well as uninterrupted processing power to process that data. Quit all other applications and disable background processes such as antivirus programs and firewalls to allow your computer to allocate all its resources to Studio One.

Following these points will improve your computer's performance significantly, but there's another dimension to improving a computer's performance, which is the subject of an age-old debate.

Should I convert instrument tracks to audio?

If we were to compile a list of frequently asked questions for music production, this would easily make it to the top. Your project has instrument tracks containing MIDI data. Is it worth the extra effort to convert them to audio before starting a mix session or can you just treat them like audio tracks?

There is no definitive answer to this question. Many people find it unnecessary to convert instrument tracks to audio because of the following:

- It adds an extra step to the workflow.
- Audio data takes up space on a disk, whereas MIDI's footprint is negligible.
- You can keep tweaking the virtual instrument until the end of the mix session.

These are all valid points. However, I convert all instrument tracks to audio tracks, and suggest that you do the same, for the following reasons:

- Once you render instrument tracks to audio, you can disable the virtual instruments on the instrument tracks, freeing up computer resources for the mix session.
- It will be much easier to apply gain staging. We will talk about gain staging in the next section, titled (surprise!) *Gain staging*.
- Your project will become portable. You can send the audio files to your collaborators and they can work on the song, even if they don't have any of the virtual instruments you used in the project.
- Your project will become future-proof. If you need to revise a project in the future, you may not be able to work with an instrument track if you no longer have that virtual instrument installed on your computer. By converting the track to audio, you will have access to the original sounds in that track forever.

There are several methods to convert an instrument track to an audio track. Here's the most practical one:

1. Pick the **Arrow** tool by pressing *1* on your keyboard.
2. Select all the MIDI events on an instrument track.
3. Click the right edge of one of those MIDI events and drag it to the right to create an extra bar of silence at the end:

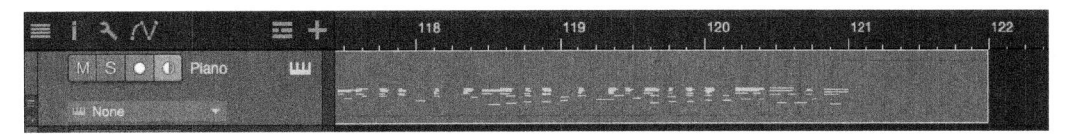

Figure 11.2: A bar of silence at the end of a MIDI event

This will prevent the tail of the sound from being chopped off when you convert the event to audio.

4. Now, right-click on the event, then on the pop-up menu, go to **Event** and select **Bounce Selection**. This is a smart command that will perform several tasks while you take a sip of coffee – it will bounce the MIDI event to audio, create a new audio track with the same name as the instrument track, place the audio in the new audio track, and mute the MIDI event:

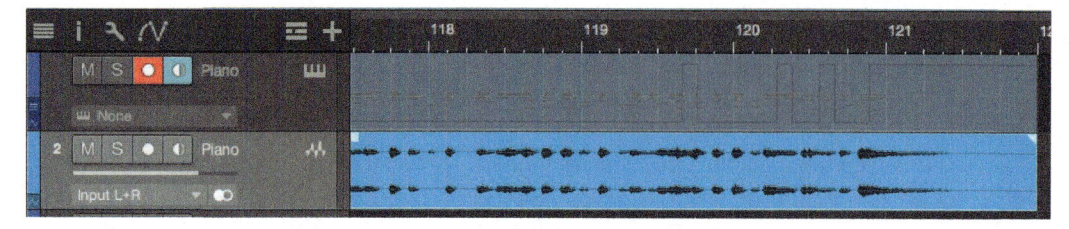

Figure 11.3: Audio bounced from an instrument track

5. You can now safely disable the virtual instrument to free up your computer's resources. To do this, use the power button on the virtual instrument's window:

Figure 11.4: Disabling a virtual instrument

6. You can now also retire the instrument track to reduce clutter on your screen; right-click on the instrument track's track header and select **Hide Track**. If you ever need to revise this project, you can bring the track back using the **Track List** button (*Figure 3.4*).

Converting all your instrument tracks to audio tracks using this method takes only a couple of minutes and is well worth the extra storage space required for audio, considering all the advantages we have discussed.

Editing for perfection

Before you start a mix session, make sure that all your tracks are edited perfectly and are free from timing and intonation problems. This is the single most important prerequisite for achieving clarity and consistency in a mix. Listen to each track carefully, and if you spot any problems, fix them using the editing methods we discussed in *Chapters 7* and *8*.

Vocal tracks require special care, as we are naturally tuned to pay more attention to the human voice. Take your time and work with the editing tools until your vocal tracks are perfect. The time you spend at this point will be well worth your effort.

If a track has severe inconsistencies in volume, chop it into smaller events using the **Split** tool and adjust the gain of each event, as we discussed in *Chapter 7*. To illustrate, take a look at *Figure 11.5*. The track on top is the recording of a singer who was moving excessively during a performance. The volume of the recording changed drastically as they moved closer to and away from the microphone. The track at the bottom is the same recording after I chopped it into pieces and adjusted the gain individually for each piece. You can see that it's now much more consistent.

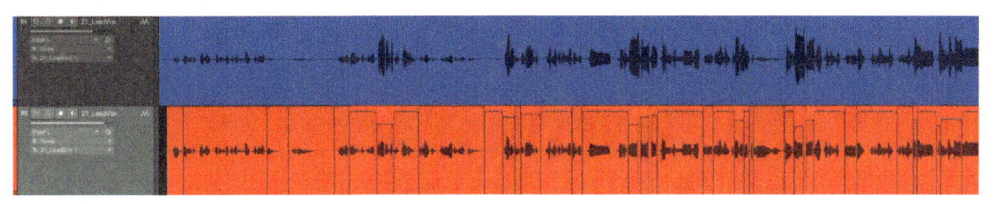

Figure 11.5: Manually adjusting the gain of an audio event

We could use a compressor plug-in to level the gain automatically, but this method is much more transparent and predictable and gives you much greater control. It's well worth the extra effort and time.

Gain staging

In audio, **gain** refers to the increase in signal level or amplitude of an audio signal, measured in **decibels** (**dB**). Gain can be applied at different stages of the audio signal chain, such as the microphone, preamp, or mixer, and can be used to boost the level of a low-level signal, compensate for a weak signal source, or create a desired tonal or dynamic effect.

Gain staging refers to the process of setting the level or gain at each stage of an audio signal chain to ensure that the signal remains at the optimal level throughout the entire process, from input to output.

The goal of gain staging is to achieve the best possible signal-to-noise ratio, meaning that the signal should be as strong as possible in relation to any background noise that may be present. If the signal is too weak, it will be drowned out by the noise. If it's too strong, it may cause distortion and clipping, which degrades the quality of the audio.

In practical terms, gain staging is achieved by using a combination of volume controls on different devices, such as the effects plug-ins and the mix console.

In a mix session, we're essentially taking several different tracks and summing them into a single stereo track. Even if there is no distortion or clipping on the individual tracks, clipping may occur on the main output of the mix console during this summing process.

To see whether there's any clipping on the main output, open the **Mix** window, play back the project, and keep an eye on the peak level meter for the **Main** output. It's on the right edge of the window:

Figure 11.6: Main output channel (right) clipping terribly

The peak level meter displays the highest instantaneous level reached by an audio signal. This level is indicated in **decibels relative to full scale** (**dBFS**). This is a reference scale that defines the maximum possible level of a signal as **0** dBFS. All other levels are measured relative to this maximum, and they are typically negative values. Any signal that exceeds 0 dBFS will clip, resulting in distortion because digital systems cannot represent values above this point. In *Figure 11.6*, the dBFS values for both left and right channels, indicated on the top of the channel strip, are **6.00**. This is a positive value and indicates that the maximum level has been exceeded.

If there's clipping, the peak level meter will turn red to give you a heads-up. There will also be a number on top of the peak level meter indicating how many times the signal clipped. The signal in *Figure 11.6* has clipped 26 times.

Clipping results in a nasty type of distortion; fortunately, it's very easy to fix, but first, a word of warning about what you should not do to prevent clipping because I see people do this all the time: don't try to fix clipping by turning down the fader on the **Main** channel! This is misleading because it will clear the visual warnings, leading you to believe that you have taken care of the distortion, but the distortion will still be there. This is because distortion happens at the summing stage, the point in the signal chain where the mixer combines all the tracks in your project into a single stereo channel. The fader on the **Main** channel comes after the summing stage, so turning this fader down cannot prevent clipping; it only turns down a signal that's already been clipped.

> **Important note**
>
> Although the maximum possible level is **0** dBFS, it is common practice to leave some **headroom** between 0 dBFS and the actual levels of your mixes. The main reason for leaving this headroom is to leave room for any further processing that will be applied to your mixes during the mastering process. Aim for your final mixes to peak at -6 dBFS to -3 dBFS on the **Main** channel. This leaves sufficient headroom for mastering processing.

To fix clipping on the **Main** channel properly, proceed as follows:

1. Go to the **Arrange** window and press *Ctrl + A* or *Cmd + A* to select all the events.
2. Lower the gain on any one of the audio events. The gain values of all events will be lowered by the same amount.
3. On the **Mix** window, click on the VU meter for the **Main** channel to clear any clipping warnings.
4. Play back the project and make sure there's no more clipping. Repeat *steps 1* through *3* if necessary.

As you work on your mix and start adding effects plug-ins, it's a good idea to keep an eye on the **Main** channel's VU meter to see whether any of the plug-ins have introduced clipping. If so, simply repeat the steps listed.

So far, we have adjusted the buffer size to give your computer a performance boost, edited our tracks to make sure all your material is in top shape, and taken care of any distortion that may be caused by clipping. In the next section, we will start organizing the tracks so that you'll have a much better command of the project during a mix session.

Organizing tracks for better control

When the inspiration strikes and you start developing a musical idea, the last thing you'll want to think about is naming and organizing your tracks. It's okay, and actually desirable, to be messy during the process of creation. But if you start a mix session with that same messy project, you'll soon be lost in a maze of unorganized tracks and clips.

It only takes a couple of minutes to organize a project for a mix session, and you'll thank yourself for doing it. Not convinced? Start your stopwatch and follow these steps:

1. Start by ordering the tracks – you can do this by clicking on a track header and dragging it up or down. Most people start a mix session with the drum tracks, so it makes sense to place them on top. Then, maybe place your percussion tracks below the drums, and then all the instruments playing chords. There is no right or wrong way of doing this; just pick an order that makes sense to you and place your tracks accordingly. You will save yourself from having to scroll up and down the project looking for tracks.

2. During the process of creation, you may have let Studio One take care of naming the tracks automatically, but generic names such as `Audio_09` will not make much sense in a mix session. Double-click on those names and give short, descriptive names to your tracks. That way, you'll know what's in a track at a single glance. This will be even more helpful when you're working on the **Mix** window since, in that window, you will not be able to see the events on the tracks.

3. Colorize your tracks! Most people see this as eye candy, but it's a great way of finding your way in a project, especially if there are lots of tracks. To do this, click on the colored rectangle on the left side of a track header and pick a color from the color palette:

Figure 11.7: Track color palette

Use the same color for similar instruments; for example, use one color for drum tracks, another color for percussion tracks, and so on. That way, you'll easily be able to identify what's on a specific audio event, without even having to look at the track name.

4. If you have lots of tracks in your project, you can place them in folders. **Folders** in Studio One work very much like folders in your operating system. They store tracks neatly to minimize clutter on the **Arrange** window. To add folders to your project, follow these steps:

    I. Click the **Add Tracks** button, which will open the **Add Tracks** pop-up menu:

Figure 11.8: The Add Tracks pop-up menu

   II. In the **Name** field, type a descriptive name for the folder you're about to create, such as `Drums`, `Vocals`, `Percussion`, and so on.
  III. In the **Type** field, select **Folder**.
   IV. In the **Color** field, select a color for this folder.
    V. Click **OK**.

VI. Now, select all the tracks you want to place inside this folder by *Shift*-clicking them, and then drag and drop them into the folder. Tracks placed in a folder will appear slightly indented:

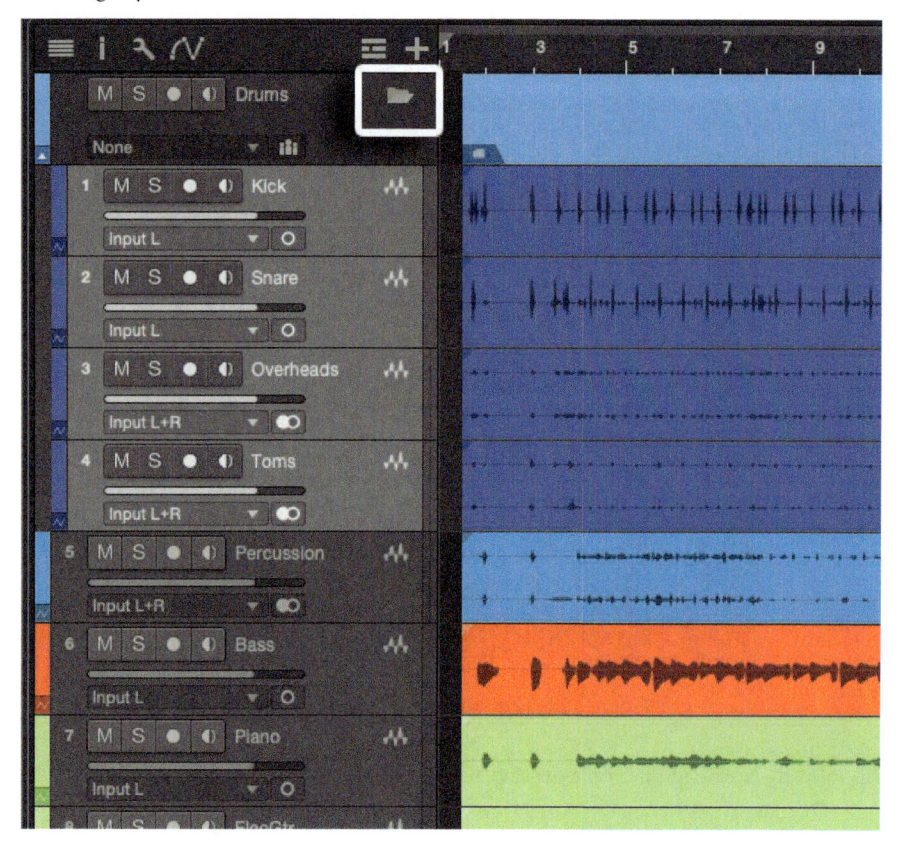

Figure 11.9: Tracks inside a folder appear slightly indented

VII. Clicking on the *folder* icon (highlighted in *Figure 11.9*) collapses the folder and allows you to focus on other tracks.
VIII. Feel free to add as many folders as you need.

That didn't take too long now, did it? And look how well-organized your project is. It will be a breeze to run a mix session when you know exactly where to find the material you need. In the next section, we will start working with the most basic parameters in a mix session to construct what is commonly referred to as a rough mix.

Setting levels, panning, and automation

Think about the Mona Lisa for a second – yes, I'm talking about the famous painting. It's actually quite a busy composition: in the frame, there is a young woman, as well as hills, trees, rivers, paths, clouds, and even a bridge. Yet Leonardo da Vinci arranged them in such a way that when you look at the painting, your eyes are immediately locked on the main subject of the composition.

This is what we strive for in a mix. You have several instruments and vocals laid out across several tracks in your project, and you must clearly and unmistakably direct the listener's attention to the most important element in the song, while also providing a fulfilling background.

There are several tools and methods for creating a sense of composition and perspective in a mix session. In this section, we'll cover two of these tools – volume and panning. Then, we will talk about how you can manipulate these tools dynamically throughout the course of your song using automation.

Setting levels

Adjusting the volume of a track makes perfect intuitive sense in terms of creating perspective. Increase the volume to bring an instrument forward in the mix, and decrease the volume to send it to the background. It's as simple as that.

However, there are several ways to set the level of a given track, and each will have a different effect on the resulting sound. Let's take a look at each of these:

- As we already know, each audio event in Studio One has a dedicated gain control. You can chop an event into smaller chunks and set gain levels independently for each of these, allowing you to control the volume on a granular level.

  The gain setting on an audio event is actually the first control on a track's signal chain. It changes the level of signal that is being sent to the effects plug-ins placed on that track and, therefore, affects the way these plug-ins respond to and colorize the sounds on that track. So, depending on the type of effects you are using, changing the gain level may affect the timbre and color of the sound, and not only its volume.

- A more common method of adjusting the volume of a track is to use that track's fader. A **fader** is a sliding control that moves up and down in a linear fashion, increasing or decreasing the volume of a track or channel. Faders are arranged in a horizontal row across the **Mix** window.

By default, they may appear tiny, but they are resizable. Click and drag at the top of the fader section of the **Mix** window to enlarge the faders. That way, you will have a better resolution to make fine adjustments:

Figure 11.10: Tiny faders (left) enlarged to provide better resolution (right)

Faders are the last elements on a track's signal chain, so they have no effect on how much signal is being sent to that track's effects plug-ins. They will only increase or decrease the volume transparently, without altering the timbre in any way.

One advantage of using faders is that you can change their position using automation, so you can dynamically control the volume of a track continuously throughout the song, as we will see later in this chapter, in the *Adding automation to create a dynamic mix* section.

- Another method of controlling the level of a track is to use the input and output level settings on individual effects plug-ins placed on that track. This allows for a more specific, granular control of volume and lets you specify how each plug-in responds to and colorizes the sound of that track. We'll cover effects plug-ins in detail in *Chapter 12*.

By using a combination of these tools and methods, you can control the volume of a track and bring it forward or send it backward in a mix with absolute precision.

Panning to create a stereo image

Panning refers to the placement of audio material within a stereo sound field. In a music mix, panning is used to determine the perceived location of each sound. For example, if a sound is panned to the left, the volume of the audio signal is adjusted to be louder in the left ear and softer in the right ear. This creates a sense that the sound is coming from the left.

The goal of panning is to create a clear and distinct stereo image, where each sound is easily identifiable and located in a specific place in the mix. Panning can also be used for creative effects by moving a sound source gradually from one speaker to the other.

In Studio One, panning is performed using pan controls located on the mix console:

Figure 11.11: Pan control on a track on the mix console

226   Preparing for the Mix

These pan controls have three different modes of operation, which can be selected by right-clicking on a pan control:

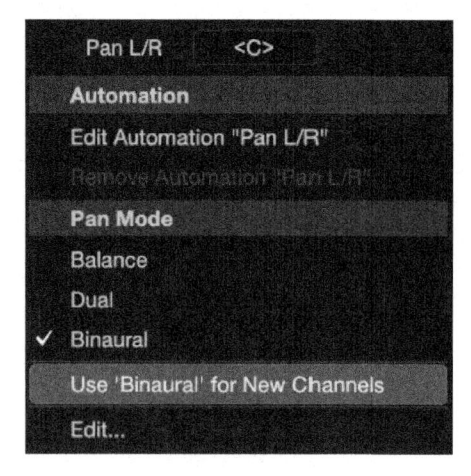

Figure 11.12: Panning modes

Now, let's take a look at each of these modes:

- **Balance**: This is the default mode. It allows you to position the signal on a track to the left, right, or anywhere in between. This is what you will be using most of the time; it's perfectly adequate for the basic placement of sounds on your stereo field.
- **Dual**: This option is available on stereo tracks only. It gives you two separate pan controls, one for the left channel of the track and one for the right channel:

Figure 11.13: Dual panner

Using these controls, you can pan the left and right channels on a track independently. This has more limited use compared to the **Balance** mode but can be a lifesaver in the right context.

Here's an example. Typically, piano sounds in sample libraries are panned from the player's perspective – keys on the left, representing the lower octaves, are panned to the left, and keys on the right are panned to the right. This is because the people who create those sample libraries want the piano to sound full and wide when heard as a solo instrument. But that's not how we hear a piano when we listen to it in a classical music concert, for example. It's usually placed somewhere to the left of the stage, and we hear it as a single sound source coming from slightly left in the stereo field.

To achieve that with a widely panned piano sample, select the **Dual** mode and bring the two pan controls closer together, effectively narrowing the stereo width of the piano. Then, click in the area in the middle of these pan controls and drag them slightly left to place the piano where you want it to be on your virtual sound stage, as shown in *Figure 11.13*.

- **Binaural**: This mode is also available on stereo tracks only. **Binaural panning** is a technique for simulating a three-dimensional sound image that can be used to create an immersive audio experience for the listener and is commonly used in virtual reality and gaming, as well as in music production. The **Binaural** panner in Studio One features a regular pan control and a stereo width control:

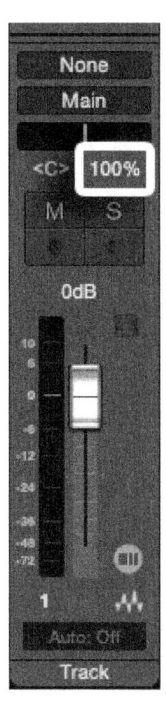

Figure 11.14: Binaural panner

The stereo width control uses a sophisticated technique referred to as mid-side processing to adjust the perceived width of a stereo signal. **Mid-side processing** manipulates the stereo image of an audio signal by splitting it into two components: the mid component, which represents the audio signal that is identical in both the left and right channels, and the side component, which contains the audio signal that is different between the left and right channels. By processing these components separately, it is possible to adjust the stereo image of the audio signal in a number of ways.

In Studio One's **Binaural** panner, this can be achieved by using the stereo width control. When this is set to **100%**, its default value, the stereo width of the signal on that track is not affected. Decreasing the value emphasizes the mid component of the signal, effectively turning it to mono at the lowest setting of **1%**. Increasing the value above **100%** emphasizes the side component of the signal, progressively widening the stereo image of the sound on that track. While this may instantly make your mix sound bigger, resist the temptation to crank the width up to its maximum level of **200%** since this may cause phase issues and make a mix unusable in certain contexts. We'll cover phase issues and how to spot them in *Chapter 15*, when we talk about mastering.

So far, we have discussed volume and panning, the two most important tools used for placing sounds on a virtual, three-dimensional sound stage in a mix. Setting these correctly is essential for crafting a coherent mix, but for most genres of music today, you will want these settings to change from one section of the song to the other, to create dynamism and contrast. That's achieved by using automation, and that will be our next topic.

Adding automation to create a dynamic mix

Automation is a powerful tool in music production that allows you to control various parameters of a mix, such as volume, panning, and effects, over time. Automation can be used in a variety of ways to create contrast between sections of a song and create interesting and dynamic effects.

Here are a few typical examples of where you could use automation:

- Bring background vocals up during the chorus of a song.
- Reduce the volume of a lead guitar during a quiet section.
- Increase the amount of reverb on the lead singer's voice in the bridge section.
- Emphasize a word sung by the lead singer that is masked by a cymbal hit on the drums.

Each and every parameter on the mix console and the effects plug-ins can be automated in Studio One, so the only limit is your imagination. Now, let's take a look at how you can work with automation.

Automation modes

Every track and channel on the **Mix** window has an **Automation Mode** selector at the bottom, and every plug-in window has the same selector in its upper-left corner:

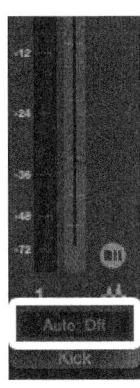

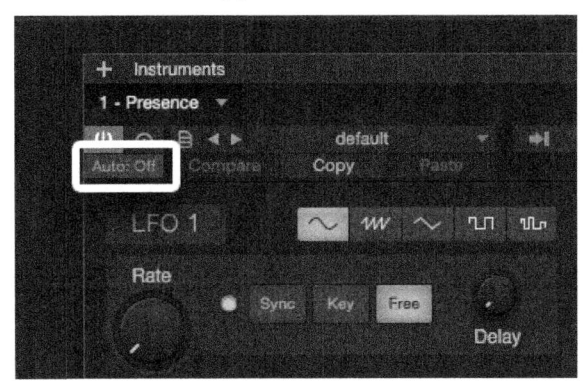

Figure 11.15: Automation Mode selector on a track (left) and on a plug-in window (right)

Clicking on this selector will reveal five options. Let's take a look at these options one by one:

- **Auto: Off**: This option disables automation for that track or plug-in. All parameters will remain locked in their current positions.
- **Read**: In this mode, Studio One will read and execute all existing automation data on that track.
- **Touch**: When you select this mode and press **Play**, new automation data will be created as soon as you touch a parameter on that track with your mouse or an external hardware controller. When you let go of your mouse or controller, Studio One will go back to reading and executing the existing data. This is an excellent method to make finer adjustments to an already existing automation.
- **Latch**: This mode is similar to the **Touch** mode except that when you touch a parameter in this mode, Studio One will continue to add automation data until you stop playback.
- **Write**: When you select this option and press **Play**, automation will be continuously written based on the current values of all parameters. If you already have automation data on that track, it will be overwritten. Use this method with caution to avoid accidentally overwriting your previous adjustments.

Now that you know about the automation modes, we can go ahead and start adding automation data.

Adding automation

Adding automation is fairly straightforward. To illustrate with an example, let's assume that you are mixing the song in *Figure 11.16* and you want to increase the volume of the first track (labeled **Synth**) gradually between bars **8** and **9**, in order to build some excitement in anticipation of the song's verse:

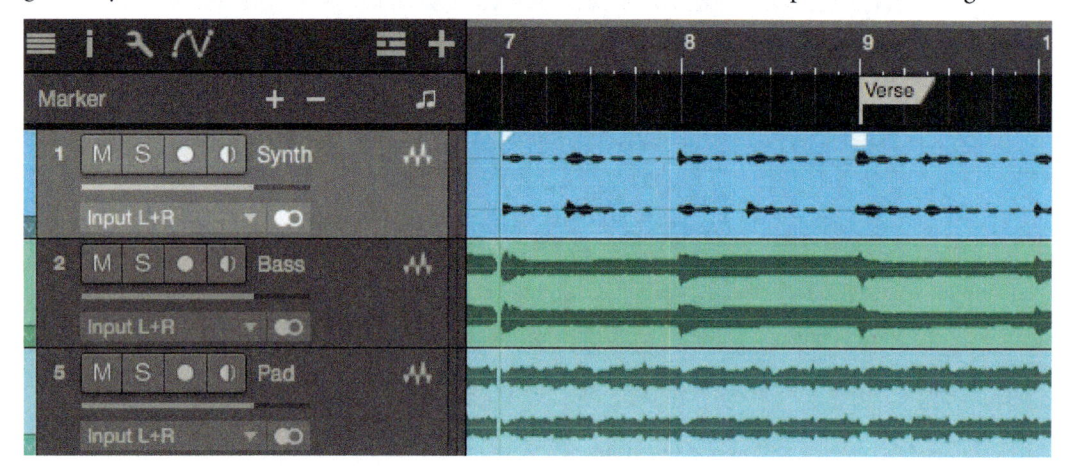

Figure 11.16: A track before adding automation

Here's how you can do it:

1. Open the **Mix** window and locate the fader for this track.
2. Click on the **Automation Mode** selector below the fader and select **Touch**.
3. Place the timeline to a point before bar **8** and press the *spacebar* to play back the project.
4. As the timeline reaches bar **8**, click on the fader for that track and drag it up. Don't worry if you don't get it perfect – we'll edit it in the next section, titled *Editing automation*.
5. Press the *spacebar* again to stop playback.
6. Click on the **Automation Mode** selector again and, this time, set it to **Read**. This will prevent you from accidentally adding or overwriting any automation data.

The changes you made to the fader are now written as automation data on that track. You can do another pass and, this time, add automation for another parameter. Automation data for each parameter is stored on separate lanes, which can be edited independently, as we are about to see.

Editing automation

All the automation data you add to a track is stored on individual automation lanes. To reveal these lanes, right-click on a track's header, and on the pop-up menu, select **Show/Hide Automation**. This will overlay a visual representation of all the automation data for a given parameter, referred to as an **automation envelope**. Here's the automation envelope for my attempt to raise the volume of the track in *Figure 11.16*:

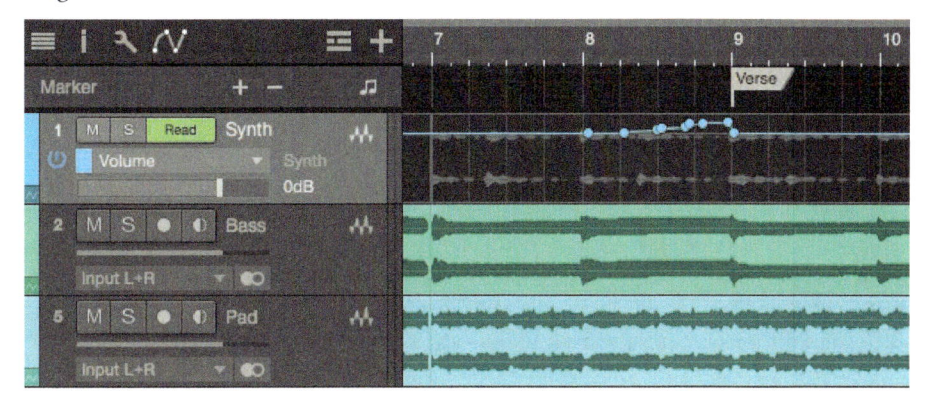

Figure 11.17: Automation envelope displayed on an automation lane

It doesn't look very smooth, but it's very easy to edit. Here's how:

1. Click on the bottom of that track's header and drag down to enlarge the track. This will give you more room to work with.
2. Click and hold the **Paint** tool to see its list of options. Select an option that serves your purpose (**Line** or **Parabola** would work perfectly for this example).
3. Click and drag at the beginning of bar **8** and let go at the beginning of bar **9** to create a smooth line or parabola:

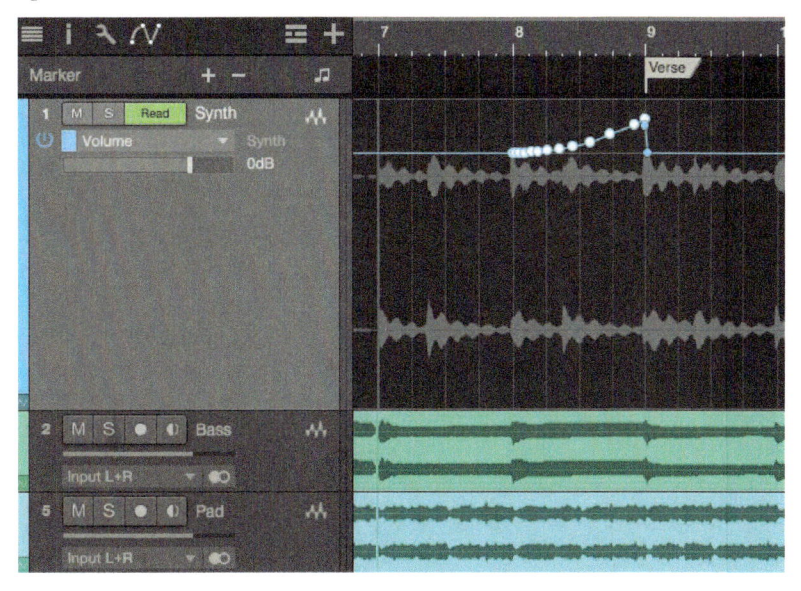

Figure 11.18: Automation envelope after editing

Other options for the **Paint** tool, such as **Sine** or **Square**, can be used to achieve more creative or experimental results with automation, such as continuously panning a sound between two speakers – definitely worth a try if your musical style has room for such experimentation.

This concludes our coverage of the two most basic and essential tools used in mixing: volume and panning. Armed with this knowledge, you can place the sounds inside a mix with pinpoint accuracy and even change their positions throughout the course of the song using automation.

Summary

In this chapter, we covered all the essential tools and methods you will need to prepare your song, and yourself, for a mix session. Then, we talked about how to set volume and pan controls for each track and how to change these settings dynamically throughout the song using automation.

Performing the steps we discussed in this chapter will lay down a strong foundation that will help you run a mix session much more smoothly, allowing you to focus on bringing out the best in your song.

In the next chapter, we will talk about effects plug-ins in Studio One and discuss the best methods of using them in order to craft the best mix possible.

12
Working with Effects Plug-Ins to Craft a Mix

Effects plug-ins are audio processing tools that allow you to modify the sound of an individual track or the overall mix. They can be used to create a wide range of different sounds and effects, making them a versatile tool for music production. Whether you need to add warmth to a vocal track, create a spacious reverb on a guitar, or add a gritty distortion to a bassline, there is always a plug-in that can achieve the effect you're looking for.

In this chapter, we'll take a tour of Studio One's **bundled plug-ins** (also known as **stock plug-ins**) to get you started with using them. As of writing, Studio One Pro comes bundled with more than 40 plug-ins, so we will not be able to cover each and every one of them in detail. Instead, we'll focus on the ones that you are most likely to use, and a few that merit special mention for their highly innovative features.

By the end of this chapter, you'll have a solid understanding of the plug-ins in your arsenal, and you will be able to confidently choose the right plug-in for any audio manipulation task.

We'll cover the following topics in this chapter:

- Controlling level and frequency with dynamics plug-ins and equalizer
- Adding depth and space with reverb and delay plug-ins
- Adding color and character with plug-ins
- Using special tools and analysis plug-ins

Technical requirements

To follow along with this chapter, you will need to have Studio One Pro activated on your computer.

Controlling level and frequency with dynamics plug-ins and equalizer

Dynamics processors refer to a type of audio processing tool used to modify the level of an audio signal over time. They control the dynamics of a sound source and achieve a more consistent and polished sound. Now, let's take a look at the dynamics processors that come bundled with Studio One Pro.

Compressor

A **compressor** is a dynamics processor that reduces the dynamic range of an audio signal by attenuating the level of loud sounds. It's commonly used to create a more consistent level for a vocal or instrument track, and can also be used to add sustain to guitar and bass sounds.

Studio One's **Compressor** plug-in looks and operates just like hardware compressors found in professional music studios. *Figure 12.1* shows Studio One's **Compressor** plug-in side by side with a coveted hardware compressor used in studios all around the world. Although the interfaces look different, note that both units have the same set of controls.

Figure 12.1: A well-known hardware compressor (left) and Studio One's Compressor plug-in (right)

Studio One's **Compressor** plug-in has some additional features, including internal and external sidechain capability and a **Mix** knob that allows you to apply parallel compression without the need for an FX track. If you're new to mixing and these words are foreign to you, don't worry – we'll cover all these techniques in *Chapter 13*.

Limiter²

A **limiter** is a type of compressor that is designed to prevent audio levels from exceeding a certain threshold. It is commonly used to prevent distortion or clipping in audio signals and is often used in the mastering phase to ensure that the final mix has a consistent level and avoids any clipping or distortion.

Limiters are, by definition, very simple devices, but Studio One's **Limiter**² plug-in has a somewhat unique operating principle that may be confusing for people coming from other platforms, so it's worth taking a closer look.

Let's imagine that you're driving on a highway where the speed limit is 100 km per hour. If your car allows you to set a maximum speed limit, you can set it to 99 km/h (leaving a small margin for error) and then step on the gas pedal without having to worry about speeding. This is exactly how **Limiter**² works: you set the maximum allowed level using the **Ceiling** knob and then increase the **Gain** value as much as you want, without the risk of clipping the audio signal.

Figure 12.2: Limiter²

It's the **Threshold** setting that makes this unit confusing for most people. To understand how it works, let's go back to our car analogy. Imagine that on top of the automatic speed limit we already talked about, you'd like your car to automatically adjust its speed so that it goes as fast as possible without exceeding the speed limit. This means that if you're traveling at, say, 60 km/h, the car will automatically accelerate until its speed reaches the maximum allowed speed. But having this automatic acceleration feature available at all times will be hazardous; you don't want it to be active when you're pulling out of your garage, for example. So, you set a minimum speed, in other words, a threshold, at which this automatic acceleration will kick in. This is exactly what the **Threshold** control on **Limiter**² does.

The **Threshold** setting works relative to **Ceiling** and allows you to set a range below the ceiling where automatic makeup gain begins to operate. As you set **Threshold** to lower values, automatic makeup gain will extend more and more into the quieter parts of the audio material, allowing those parts to become louder as well.

We'll talk more about the other parameters on **Limiter**[2] when we discuss mastering in *Chapter 15*.

Expander

Expansion is the opposite of compression, where the dynamic range of the signal is increased by attenuating the level of the lower parts of the signal. This can be useful for restoring the dynamic range of a compressed signal or eliminating background noise.

Studio One's **Expander** plug-in offers internal and external side-chain capability and a **Range** control that adjusts the maximum amount of attenuation applied to the signal.

Gate

A **gate** is a simple processor that cuts the sound completely when the sound falls below a certain threshold. It's often used to eliminate background noise or bleed from other sources.

Studio One's **Gate** plug-in is simple, effective, and handles the job perfectly.

De-Esser

A **de-esser** is used to reduce or remove harsh sibilance and other high-frequency noises in a vocal or other audio signal. **Sibilance** is a sharp hissing sound that is sometimes created when certain letters such as *s* and *sh* are pronounced and can be a problem when recording or mixing vocals.

A de-esser is basically a compressor that focuses only on the frequency range where sibilances occur. When the signal in that range exceeds a given threshold, the de-esser will attenuate the signal to tame the sibilance.

For most vocal sibilances, Studio One's **De-Esser** plug-in works perfectly with its default settings:

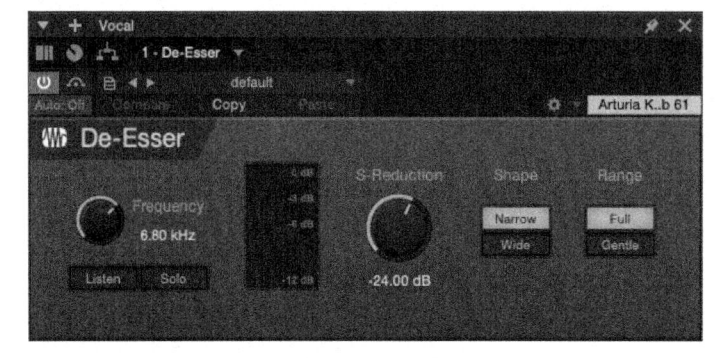

Figure 12.3: De-Esser

If you feel that it's not catching the sibilances in your material, you can tweak its settings as follows:

1. Click the **Listen** button. This will allow you to hear only the frequencies being targeted for reduction.
2. Adjust the **Frequency** knob to zero in on the sibilances.
3. Click the **Listen** button again to resume normal operation. **De-Esser** will now begin to target the frequency range you selected.
4. Adjust **S-Reduction** to set a threshold point at which **De-Esser** will begin to attenuate the selected frequency.

While de-essers are mostly used for vocal recordings, they can be used to tame harsh frequencies on other instruments as well, so feel free to experiment.

Multiband Dynamics

Multiband Dynamics is a plug-in that combines five independently adjustable compressor and expander units that work on dedicated frequency bands. This plug-in is often used in the mastering phase, and we will talk about it in detail in *Chapter 15*.

Tricomp

Tricomp is a less complicated alternative to **Multiband Dynamics**. It's a three-band compressor that does most of its chores automatically, almost in a set-it-and-forget-it kind of way, and it does a remarkable job of finalizing and adding punch to a mix. We will take a closer look at it when we talk about mastering in *Chapter 15*.

Pro EQ³

An **audio equalizer**, also known as **EQ**, is a device that allows you to adjust the balance of frequencies in an audio signal. The purpose of an equalizer is to make the audio sound more balanced and pleasing to the listener, by boosting or cutting certain frequency ranges.

Studio One comes bundled with **Pro EQ**³, a powerful equalizer plug-in that lets you adjust the frequency of an audio signal with eight separately adjustable bands. It has a spectrum display on top of its interface to help you visually pinpoint the frequencies that you'd like to target:

Figure 12.4: Pro EQ³

Pro EQ³ can be set to work as a dynamic equalizer as well. A **dynamic equalizer** adjusts the level of a frequency range dynamically as the incoming signal passes a certain threshold. To use this feature, proceed as follows:

1. Click the **Dynamics** button above the spectrum display to reveal the dynamics controls for all frequency bands.
2. You can then enable the dynamic EQ function on any individual band by clicking on its **D** button.
3. Use the **Thrs.** (threshold) setting on a band to determine the signal level at which that band will become active.
4. Use **Range** to set how much adjustment will be applied once the signal level passes the threshold.

Pro EQ³ is a very powerful tool that will meet all your tone-shaping needs. Unless you're going for a plug-in that emulates the analog sound of a vintage hardware unit, **Pro EQ**³ is a perfect all-round solution.

Dynamic processors and equalizers are essential tools that help you lay a solid foundation for your mixes. Next, we will start exploring the tools you can use to add an artistic, creative touch to bring your mixes to life.

Adding depth and space with reverb and delay plug-ins

Reverb and delay plug-ins give your mix a sense of space, depth, and three-dimensionality. Studio One covers all the bases in this category by offering plenty of solid options to choose from. Let's start by exploring the reverb plug-ins.

Reverb plug-ins

Reverb plug-ins are tools that are used to add artificial reverberation to audio recordings. **Reverberation** is the acoustic effect created when sound waves reflect off surfaces in an enclosed space, creating a complex series of echoes and reflections that can give a sense of space and depth to audio recordings.

Reverb plug-ins typically work by simulating the acoustic properties of different types of spaces, such as concert halls, recording studios, or small rooms. They can be used to add a sense of space to dry recordings or to adjust the amount and character of the existing reverberation in a recording.

Studio One Pro comes bundled with three reverb plug-ins, which we will see now.

Mixverb

Mixverb is simple to use and, contrary to most reverb plug-ins, very light on your computer's resources. You probably will not want to use it on your main vocal track, but it's perfectly fine for spicing up instruments in the background without taxing your computer's processor.

Room Reverb

Room Reverb is a versatile plug-in that lets you create virtual acoustic environments with incredible detail. It starts with the usual parameters such as room size and reverb time and then adds settings that I haven't seen in any other reverb plug-in on any other platform. You can determine how many people will be in your virtual room, set the height of the sound source relative to the audience, and even adjust the level of humidity of the air inside the room. And this is just scratching the surface!

Figure 12.5: Room Reverb

While this much detail is overkill for most audio production work, you'll find yourself using **Room Reverb** in all of your projects because it just sounds fantastic. If the abundance of options is overwhelming, just focus on these three parameters and you should be well on your way to creating the perfect acoustic environment for your mix:

- Use the **Type** buttons to select the size and characteristics of your virtual space. The options are small room, room, medium hall, and large hall.
- Use the **Size** knob to further refine the dimensions of the room.
- Use the **Length** setting to adjust how long the reverb will continue to be heard.

It is common practice to roll off the extreme high and low frequencies generated by a reverb plug-in because this creates a smoother reverb tail and helps achieve clarity in the mix. Some reverb plug-ins come with a built-in filter section for this purpose. **Room Reverb** does not have such a filter section, so it's a good idea to add an equalizer (such as **Pro EQ³**) after **Room Reverb** and use the equalizer's high-cut and low-cut filters to roll off the extremely high and low frequencies.

Open AIR

Open AIR is a high-end reverb plug-in that uses convolution reverb technology. **Convolution reverb** is a type of audio processing that uses impulse responses to simulate the acoustic properties of a real-world space, such as a concert hall, recording studio, or cathedral. An **impulse response** is a mathematical representation of the way that sound waves reflect and decay in a particular space, and can be captured by playing a short burst of sound (an "impulse") in the space and recording the resulting reflections (a "response").

Open AIR uses this technology to deliver very realistic reverberation based on the modeling of real spaces and vintage hardware reverb units. In order to get started using it, you must first load an **impulse response** (**IR**) file into it. Studio One Pro is bundled with several IR files. Here's how to download and use them:

1. Log in to your my.presonus.com account and go to the **Products** page.
2. Locate **Studio One Impulse Responses** in the list of bundled downloads:

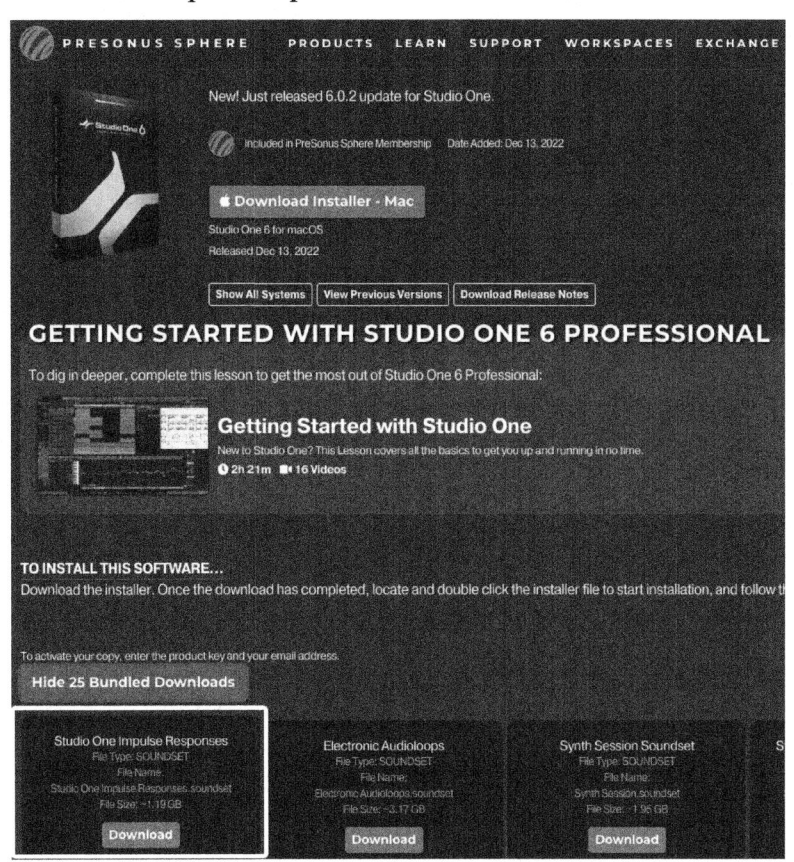

Figure 12.6: Downloading Impulse Responses

3. Click the **Download** button.
4. Once the download is completed, move this file from your computer's downloads folder to a more permanent location. We talked about file locations in *Chapter 2*.
5. Double-click on the file. This will register all the impulse responses contained within the file with **Open AIR**.
6. On **Open AIR**'s interface, click the preset drop-down menu and select an impulse response from the list:

Figure 12.7: Open AIR list of available impulse responses

Open AIR is state-of-the-art technology, but it also does an excellent job of modeling vintage reverb equipment with all their quirky tonal characteristics, so it's a great tool to add a lo-fi vibe to your tracks as well.

Delay plug-ins

Delay is an audio effect that creates an echo-like repetition of sound. Delay plug-ins are a type of audio processing tool that can be used to add this effect to an audio signal. These plug-ins can be used in a wide range of applications, from creating subtle spatial effects to adding complex rhythmic patterns to a mix. They are commonly used in electronic music, ambient music, and other genres where creating interesting and unique soundscapes is a key part of the production process.

Studio One comes bundled with three delay plug-ins, each specializing in a different flavor of delay suitable for a wide variety of scenarios. Let's take a look at each of them.

Analog Delay

Analog Delay simulates the tape-based analog delay units that were widely used in the 1960s and 70s. Its fun, simple interface allows you to dial in all the quirks and characteristics that made those units popular, making it an excellent tool for adding a vintage vibe to your tracks.

Use the controls in the **Color** section to give the delayed sound a warmer, more saturated character. Then, use the controls in the **Motor** section to add the idiosyncratic wobble created by an aging tape motor. You'll be able to create psychedelic, dub-style delay effects in no time!

Beat Delay

Beat Delay is a general-purpose delay unit that synchronizes to the tempo of your project and lets you create complex and interesting rhythmic patterns from existing music material. The **Ping-Pong** option in this plug-in bounces the delayed signal back and forth between the left and right channels, creating a stereo effect that adds movement and width to an otherwise static sound.

Groove Delay

Groove Delay belongs to the multi-tap delay family. A **multi-tap delay** combines several independently adjustable delay processors in one unit and can create intricate rhythmic patterns and complex delays. This type of delay is commonly used in dance and electronic music.

The interface may look intimidating at first, so let's break it down:

Figure 12.8: Groove Delay

Groove Delay comprises four independent delay units, called **taps**, arranged in columns across the interface and labeled **Tap 1** through **Tap 4**. Here is an overview of the controls available for each tap:

- The **Pos.** (position) knob adjusts the delay time for each tap. By default, it uses increments of an eighth note.
- The horizontal fader below the position knob allows you to offset the delay time. This could be useful if you want the tap to sound slightly before or after the beat. If you slide this control all the way to the right, this will be equivalent to the length of a dotted eighth note.
- The **FB** (feedback) setting determines how long the tap will be repeated. When this is at **0 %**, you will hear only one tap. This is sometimes referred to as a **slap-back delay**. When this is at **100 %**, the delays will continue indefinitely. This is sometimes referred to as **loop mode**, as it's used by musicians on stage to establish a rhythmic background on which they add other musical material.
- The **Level** and **Pan** knobs set the volume and stereo positioning of the tap, respectively.
- The **Filter** section at the bottom of each tap allows you to add high-cut, low-cut, and band-pass filters to color the sound of the tap. By automating these filter settings, you can achieve some really dynamic, evolving patterns from very simple rhythmic material. We'll talk about automating effects later in this chapter.

As with most plug-ins, the best way to get a sense of what **Groove Delay** can do is to explore the presets. Open the preset menu (labeled **Default**), browse through the presets, and be ready for some fun!

Reverb and delay plug-ins place your mix in a three-dimensional environment and bring it to life. The next set of plug-ins will add endless possibilities to your sonic palette and help you give your tracks a unique character. We're about to step into the most creative side of mixing!

Adding color and character with plug-ins

Today, almost every photo we see in a magazine or billboard ad is retouched extensively in Photoshop or similar software to enhance the image and reinforce its impact. The same is true for music tracks as well. Most of the material we hear on music platforms is augmented by special effects to make them sound bigger and more powerful. If you're thinking about releasing your songs on music platforms such as Apple Music or Spotify, you'll want to make sure that your tracks are as polished and compelling as all the others. Thankfully, Studio One offers plenty of tools to help you achieve the impact your tracks need. In this section, we'll take a close look at these tools.

Distortion plug-ins

Distortion effects are a common tool in music production used to add grit, warmth, and character to a sound. Distortion plug-ins come in many flavors with different names such as overdrive, fuzz, saturation, and bit reduction. These affect the sound on a very wide spectrum, ranging from hardly noticeable to total obliteration.

Studio One has three plug-ins in the distortion category. Let's learn about each of these plug-ins.

Ampire

Ampire is a versatile plug-in that emulates all the analog hardware equipment you would expect to find in a guitar player's rig: effects pedals, amplifiers, speaker cabinets, and microphones for recording those cabinets. It offers a wide range of tonal possibilities to shape a guitar sound – from a clean jazz tone to a highly saturated metal shred machine, and anything in between. While its primary target is electric guitars, it works wonders for adding punch and bite to other sounds as well. Try it on a lead synth sound to kick it up a notch, for example.

The interface is hefty and may not even fit on smaller screens. Let's take a look:

Figure 12.9: Ampire consists of three sections – stage (a), amp (b), and pedalboard (c)

The interface consists of three sections: stage, amp, and pedalboard. Use the button highlighted in *Figure 12.9* to toggle the visibility of these sections. Let's start exploring all the equipment that this amazing technology places at your fingertips:

1. Use the **Amp** and **Cabinet** selectors at the top of the window to select the amplifier and speaker cabinet you'd like to use. **Ampire** comes with a basic selection of amplifiers and cabinets, and you can download many more from the **Products** page on Presonus' website (`https://www.presonus.com/products`).

2. Once you've selected your amp, its controls will be laid out in the middle of the window. Tweak these controls just as you would tweak the physical amplifier (all controls are modeled after the real thing as well!).

3. Next, try adding some effects pedals to add more color to your sound. The virtual pedalboard at the bottom of the window has eight slots available for you to insert different pedals. You can add or remove pedals by simply clicking on the pedal selector at the very bottom of the window.

   Note that pedals are on bypass when you first insert them. You have to click on their virtual foot switches to activate them. Once active, their LEDs will turn red.

4. Just as with amplifiers, the controls on the foot pedals are modeled as well, so knobs and switches on these virtual foot pedals will behave just like the controls on their physical counterparts. Tweak them to your heart's content until you get just the right tone for your instrument.

5. You can drag pedals around the pedalboard to change their order in the signal chain.

Ampire is tons of fun, but it is one of the more CPU-hungry plug-ins in Studio One's arsenal. That's quite understandable, considering all the modeling technology under the hood. But you may want to keep an eye on the performance indicator if you have several guitar tracks with **Ampire** running on all of them. If you start hearing clicks and dropouts, increase the **Audio Dropout Protection** setting, as we discussed in *Chapter 11*.

Bitcrusher

Bitcrusher represents the extreme end of the distortion spectrum. It's the plug-in you'll reach out for when you want to obliterate your sound. With controls such as **Wreck**, which lets you specify how much you want to degrade the sound by reducing its bit depth, and **Dirt**, which introduces instability to higher frequencies to create an aggressive effect, you can be sure that this thing will not be gentle.

Red Light Distortion

Red Light Distortion is a very flexible plug-in that emulates analog distortion with a very wide range of flavors. Use the **Type** drop-down menu to select the distortion type and use the other settings to fine-tune the level of distortion. **Red Light Distortion** can be very gentle; use it to add sparkle to liven up a dull vocal recording. It can also be very bold; use it to make a sound appear as though it's coming from a broken radio. Feel free to experiment, but keep the volume down when experimenting. Distortion can suddenly make things very loud!

Modulation plug-ins

Modulation effects are a group of audio effects used in music production to create movement, depth, and interest in sound. These effects can be applied to a variety of elements in a mix, including instruments, vocals, and drums. Modulation effects help you to create unique and expressive sounds that make your music stand out.

Studio One Pro comes bundled with seven modulation effect plug-ins. Let's take a look at them one by one.

Autofilter

Autofilter has two independent frequency filters that can be controlled and programmed in a variety of ways. You can tweak the filters manually, control them with a built-in low-frequency oscillator, program them with a 16-step sequencer, or lock them to your project's tempo to create anything from DJ-style filter sweeps to complex rhythmic patterns.

It's a bit of a learning curve, but certainly worth the effort if you're producing EDM or similar genres.

Chorus

Chorus is an effect that creates a thick, rich sound by duplicating a signal and adding slight variations to its pitch and time. It can be used to add warmth and depth to a sound, as well as to create a sense of space and movement.

Studio One's **Chorus** plug-in has a retro-style interface, which reflects the fact that it actually models vintage analog chorus devices. It adds a warm analog color to the sound and lets you quickly dial in the rich chorus tones prized in many music genres.

Flanger

Flanger is a similar effect to chorus but with a more pronounced sweeping sound. Flangers create a swirling, jet-like sound by combining two identical signals that are slightly delayed and then modulated with a filter. Flanging is most commonly used on electric guitars but is equally at home on synth tracks as well.

Flangers are simple devices with just a few controls, and Studio One's **Flanger** plug-in is no exception. One feature worth noting is that it can be synchronized to your project's tempo, so you can set its dramatic sweeping sounds to make more rhythmic sense.

Phaser

A **phaser** creates a series of notches and peaks in a sound by splitting the signal into two paths, delaying one path, and modulating it with a filter. The result is a unique sound that creates a sense of movement and depth, which can be anywhere from subtle to psychedelic.

Studio One's **Phaser** plug-in is a very simple device that offers the capability to lock its sweeps to your project's tempo.

Rotor

Rotor emulates the sonic characteristics of rotating speaker cabinets. These cabinets are traditionally paired with Hammond organs and are responsible for that instrument's unique sound, but having this plug-in at your fingertips will allow you to try it on anything – it sounds great on electric guitars and synthesizers, for example.

248 Working with Effects Plug-Ins to Craft a Mix

This plug-in is an accurate model of the real thing, so much so that you can even see the virtual speakers rotating inside the cabinet, and their spinning speed changes based on your settings. Go ahead and play with this plug-in. It's tons of fun and sounds great.

Vocoder

A **vocoder** analyzes and synthesizes the spectral and temporal characteristics of human speech and applies them to another audio signal. Here's how it works: a vocoder takes a modulator signal (usually a human voice) and a carrier signal (usually a musical instrument) and combines them to create a unique, synthesized sound (which usually sounds like a singing robot). Vocoders are used in a wide variety of genres, from electronic to hip-hop to film music and sound design.

Studio One's **Vocoder** plug-in is a powerful tool that allows you to come up with some very creative sounds and textures. Setting up **Vocoder** is a bit different compared to the other effects plug-ins, so let's walk you through it:

1. Open the **Browse** panel and go to the **Effects** tab.
2. Find **Vocoder**, then drag and drop it on the track you'd like to process. The audio on this track will be **Vocoder**'s modulator signal. Here's what **Vocoder** looks like:

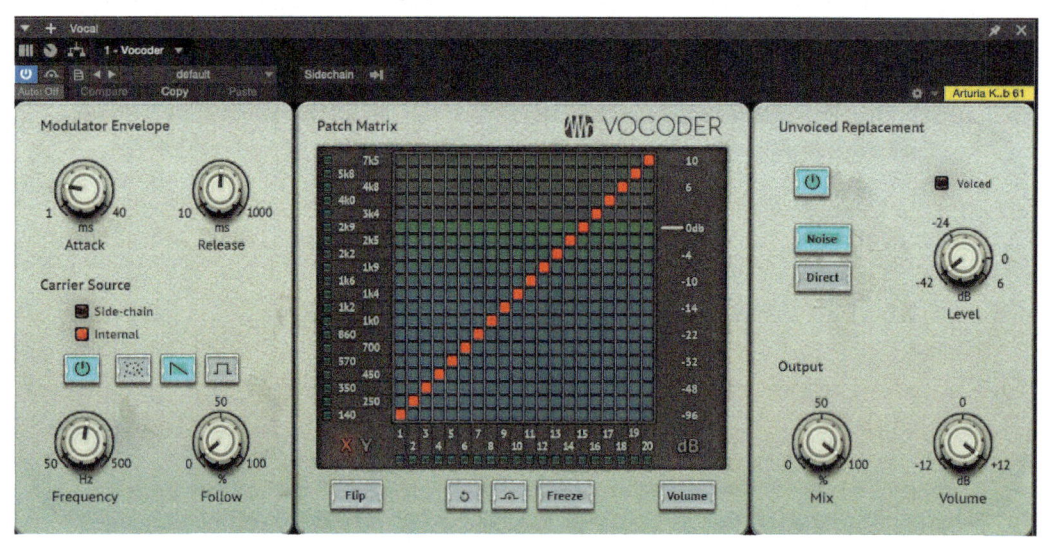

Figure 12.10: Vocoder

3. Now, let's take care of the carrier signal. **Vocoder** can use audio from another track as the carrier, or create a carrier signal using its own oscillator. If you'd like it to use audio from another track, click the **Sidechain** button on top of the **Vocoder** window, and click on the **Send** column corresponding to the track you'd like to use as the carrier signal:

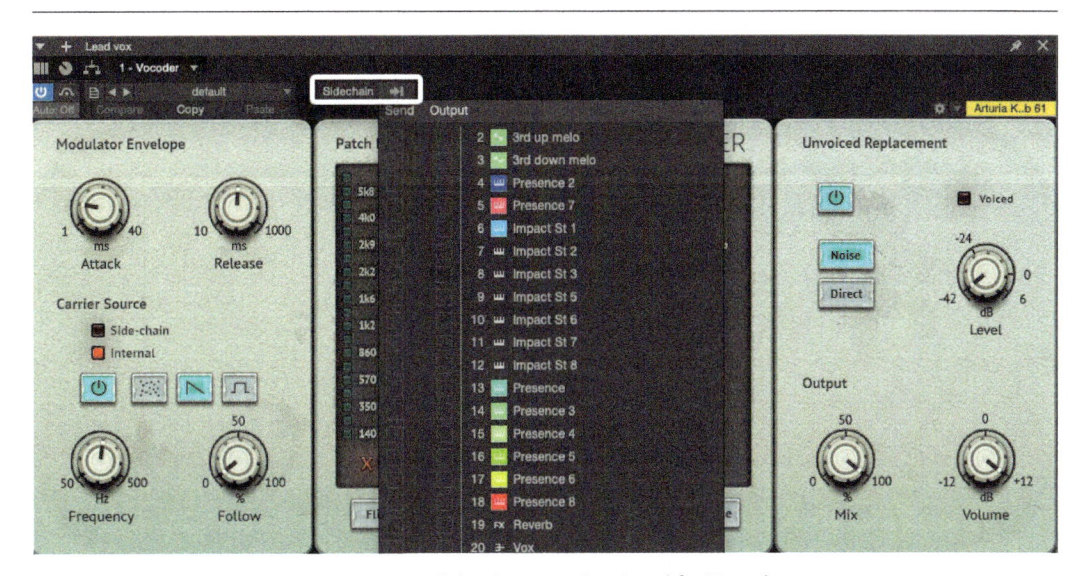

Figure 12.11: Selecting a carrier signal for Vocoder

4. If you'd like **Vocoder** to use its own oscillator as the carrier signal, use the internal carrier settings to set the oscillator to the desired waveform and frequency.

5. Now it's time to play! The **Patch Matrix** section in the middle of the **Vocoder** window sets how the **Vocoder** analyzer section is routed to its synthesizer section. This routing is displayed by the small red "pins" on the matrix. By default, these sections are matched sequentially, which results in the most intelligible vocoded voice, but you can change the position of the pins to modify the routing and come up with some otherworldly effects. You can nerd up on the science behind this, but it's much faster, and definitely more fun, to learn how it works by playing with it.

6. Vocoding works best with vowels. Consonants don't perform that well. The **Unvoiced Replacement** section on the right side of the window controls an algorithm that detects consonants in the modulator signal and replaces them with other signals to increase speech intelligibility. The success of this algorithm depends on source material, so there is no general recipe. As always, experimentation is key.

Of all the effects plug-ins, **Vocoder** is probably the most creative and fun. It allows you to morph two sounds into one, creating an instrument that seems to talk or a singer that seems to be controlled by a MIDI keyboard. There's a lot of creative potential waiting to happen, so it's definitely worth a serious look.

X-Trem

X-Trem is a tremolo effect. **Tremolo** creates a pulsating or rhythmic sound by modulating the volume of a signal. It can be used to add a sense of motion or rhythmic quality.

The **X-Trem** interface is as simple as it gets. One cool feature that may go unnoticed is hidden under the **Mode** button: When you select **Trem** mode, the plug-in will modulate the signal's volume, and when it's in **Pan** mode, it will modulate the signal's panning across the left and right channels.

Combined mix plug-ins

The plug-ins in this category are combinations of the effect types we discussed earlier. So why are they packaged as different plug-ins and why should we use them? Let's explore them one by one and find out.

Channel Strip

The large hardware mixing consoles in music studios appear intimidating at first sight. But on a closer look, it becomes obvious that a big part of these consoles actually consist of an identical set of knobs and buttons laid out across several identical strips. These are referred to as **channel strips**. Each channel strip contains all the controls and processing tools required to process a single audio channel. On a typical mixing console, these tools include a simple equalizer, a gate, and a simple compressor.

Studio One's **Channel Strip** plug-in is based on the same idea. When you add this plug-in to a track, you get a simple compressor, a simple EQ, and a gain control. Nothing fancy, but it does the job without taxing the computer's CPU like dedicated compressor and EQ plug-ins do. It is perfect for tracks that need just a few simple tweaks.

Fat Channel XT

Fat Channel XT is the opposite of **Channel Strip**. It's the plug-in to go to when simple compressor and EQ plug-ins won't cut it. **Fat Channel XT** provides accurate modeling of prized vintage hardware compressors and equalizers and allows you to add the sonic color of those devices to your signal flow.

Fat Channel XT comprises five sections:

- **HPF** (high pass filter)
- **Gate**
- **Compressor**
- **Equalizer**
- **Limiter**

If you can't see all these sections, toggle their visibility by clicking the **Stacked Mode** button:

Figure 12.12: Fat Channel XT

By default, all these sections are off. You need to switch them on by using their respective power buttons.

For the **Compressor** and **Equalizer** sections, you can choose between simulations of different vintage units. To do that, click on the **Compressor** and **Equalizer** drop-down menus next to the **Stacked Mode** button and select the devices you'd like to use.

Be aware that these modeled plug-ins consume more CPU power compared to Studio One's stock **Compressor** and **Pro EQ**[3] plug-ins, so it's a good idea to use **Fat Channel XT** only if you really need that analog color on a track.

Mix Engine FX

Mix Engine FX is a feature unique to Studio One and operates quite differently from all the other effects plug-ins. Rather than being added to an individual track, **Mix Engine FX** is added to the entire mix console. **Mix Engine FX** then applies modeling technology to replicate the sonic color and character of prized analog mixing consoles, including idiosyncratic traits such as crosstalk between channels, noise, and saturation. According to Studio One's user manual, "*It's as true to analog as digital can get.*"

To add **Mix Engine FX** to your project, open the **Mix** window and click the **Mix FX** button on top of the **Main** channel:

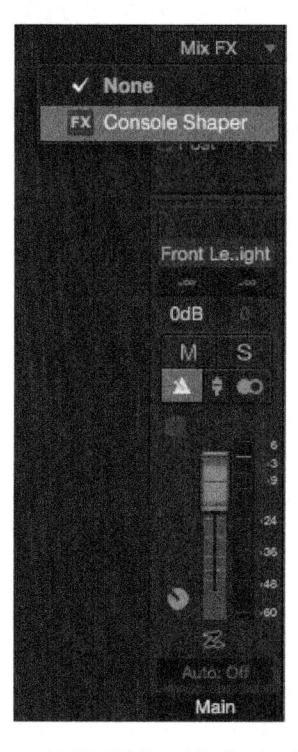

Figure 12.13: Adding Mix Engine FX

Once you add an effect, double-click on the **Mix FX** button again to open the effect's interface and reach its parameters. There are several **Mix Engine FX** options available on Presonus' website (just log in and visit the **Products** page), representing the modeling of different mixing consoles. If you're looking for a lo-fi, vintage vibe in your mixes, definitely give these effects a spin.

By now, we have covered all the tools available in Studio One that will help you control, polish, and enhance your tracks. To complete our tour of Studio One's plug-ins, we just need to visit a couple of utility tools that are designed to supplement the mixing process.

Using special tools and analysis plug-ins

The final set of plug-ins in Studio One's arsenal are designed to perform some specific, technical tasks and to provide visual feedback on the quality of your mix. In an age where music production has largely shifted from commercial studios to home studios, we are more and more concerned about the accuracy of our room acoustics and monitor speakers, so this visual feedback has become extremely valuable for ensuring that our mixes are in top shape.

Special tools

The plug-ins in this category are utility tools that are designed to help you perform specific tasks. With the exception of **Tuner**, there may be little use for them in a typical home studio workflow, but it's good to know they're there when the need arises. Let's take a quick look at what's in the toolbox.

Tuner

Studio One has a built-in tuner (**Tuner**) that you can use for tuning guitars, basses, or any other instrument that requires tuning. It's pretty fast and reliable, and the visual feedback is much better compared to tiny displays on pocket tuners. It has a **Strobe** mode, which is usually preferred by instrument technicians for improved accuracy, and you can also set the tuner to a reference frequency other than the international standard of 440 Hz.

Mixtool

Mixtool is a Swiss army knife: it can swap the left and right channels of a stereo track, invert the phase of left or right channels, encode or decode MS signals to and from stereo tracks, and block DC offset. If these terms are foreign to you, you can still find use for **Mixtool** because it has a **Gain** knob. This comes in handy for those occasions where you'd like to precisely control the signal level between two effect plug-ins that don't have gain controls (many of them don't). Just insert an instance of **Mixtool** between them and adjust gain as necessary.

Tone Generator

Tone Generator produces noise and basic waveform types. These are commonly used for testing and calibration purposes, but the **Modulation** and **Wobble** functions can actually turn this plug-in into a secret weapon for electronic music producers, opening the door to lush filter sweeps and sound effects.

IR Maker

IR Maker allows you to create your own impulse response files. You can then use these impulse responses in **Open AIR** or in the cabinet section of **Ampire**. It's a bit of a hassle to set up, but definitely worth it if you want to create your own customized, three-dimensional environments for sound design purposes. See Studio One's user manual for detailed instructions. To view the manual, go to **Help** on the top menu and select **Studio One Reference Manual**.

Analysis tools

Studio One offers four analysis tools that are available as plug-ins. These tools provide visual feedback on various aspects of audio and allow you to pinpoint problem areas even if you can't hear them due to your listening environment:

- **Phase Meter** is used to visualize the stereo width of an audio signal. It's a critical tool that helps us identify any phase correlation issues between left and right channels. This is important for us to ensure that the stereo image of the mix is consistent across different playback systems. We will talk about phase correlation in *Chapter 15*, where we will visit **Phase Meter** again.

- **Spectrum Meter** displays the frequency content of the audio signal. It helps you to visually pinpoint a problem area, such as an unwanted ringing sound. **Spectrum Meter** also allows you to compare and match the frequency content of your mix to that of a reference track, as we will see in the next chapter.

- **Level Meter** shows the amplitude of the audio signal and provides a numerical measurement of the signal's perceived loudness. This is useful for ensuring that our final mixes meet the loudness standards implemented by digital music platforms.

- **Scope** works like a hardware oscilloscope and is used for identifying audio issues that may not be apparent from simply listening to the signal. These issues may include crosstalk between channels, background noise, or clipping.

This concludes our tour of the effects plug-ins that come bundled with Studio One. Remember that there are several more available for download with a Pro+ membership. Although interfaces and tonal colors may differ, we have covered all major plug-in types and you can now confidently use this knowledge to determine which plug-in will work best to achieve the sound you're going after.

Summary

In this chapter, we took a deep dive into Studio One's impressive line-up of effects plug-ins and discussed the scenarios where each plug-in would become useful.

In the next chapter, we will put this knowledge into practical use by exploring several different methods of adding these plug-ins to a mix session.

13
Optimizing Signal Flow and Elevating Your Mix

Mixing is an intimidating task for most people, so the title of this chapter may seem a bit daunting. In fact, it's just another skill set that will take your music productions to the next level. While mixing is not something that should be taken lightly, today's technology makes the whole process much more accessible. And with Studio One's intuitive design, techniques that were once hard to understand and even harder to implement are now at your fingertips.

In this chapter, we will take an in-depth look at how signal processing works in Studio One and how you can harness the power of the Mix Console to present your songs in the best light. Then, we will discuss some expert-level practices to make your mixes sound much more polished and refined. Finally, we will talk about how to export stems and final mixes from your songs so that you can share them on music platforms.

We will cover the following topics:

- Understanding Studio One's signal flow
- Applying advanced techniques
- Exporting final mixes and stems

Technical requirements

To follow along with this chapter, you will need to have Studio One activated on your computer.

Understanding Studio One's signal flow

Signal flow refers to the path that audio signals take through the mixer and its components, including the plug-in effects we discussed in *Chapter 12*. Typical signal flow paths in today's music production programs are highly flexible, allowing producers to implement creative and innovative mixing techniques, but this also brings more complexity. It is important to understand the topography of signal flow in order to make the most of the potential presented by this versatile technology, and that's what we will cover in this section.

The anatomy of a mixer channel

Let's start by exploring a channel on the **Mix Console**. Every track in the **Arrange** window has a corresponding channel in the **Mix** window that looks like this:

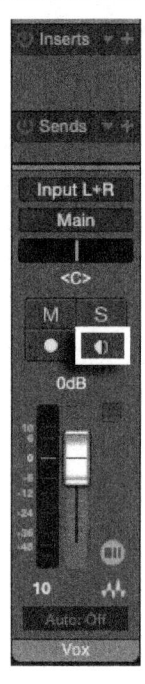

Figure 13.1: A channel on the Mix Console

Let's break it down:

- The top part of this channel hosts two sections titled **Inserts** and **Sends**. In Studio One, these two sections are collectively called **Device Racks**. We use these sections to add effect plug-ins.
- Right in the middle of the channel, we have the **Input** and **Output** selectors. We talked about the **Input** selector back in *Chapter 5*, when we used it to select the physical input(s) on our audio interface that we wanted to record from. But now, we're in the mixing stage, so we want this channel to listen to what's already recorded on the corresponding track. To do this, make sure that the **Monitor** button (highlighted in *Figure 13.1*) is disabled. When it's enabled (blue), this channel listens to the signal coming from your audio interface's physical inputs. When it's disabled (gray), the channel listens to the recording on the track, and that's what we want.

- By default, the output of every channel is routed to the **Main** output channel of the Mix Console. The **Main** output channel is where all channels on the Mix Console are combined. It's always located on the far-right side of the Mix Console.
- At the bottom of the channel, we have the fader, which controls the channel's volume.

Figure 13.2 shows the signal flow for the components we have discussed so far:

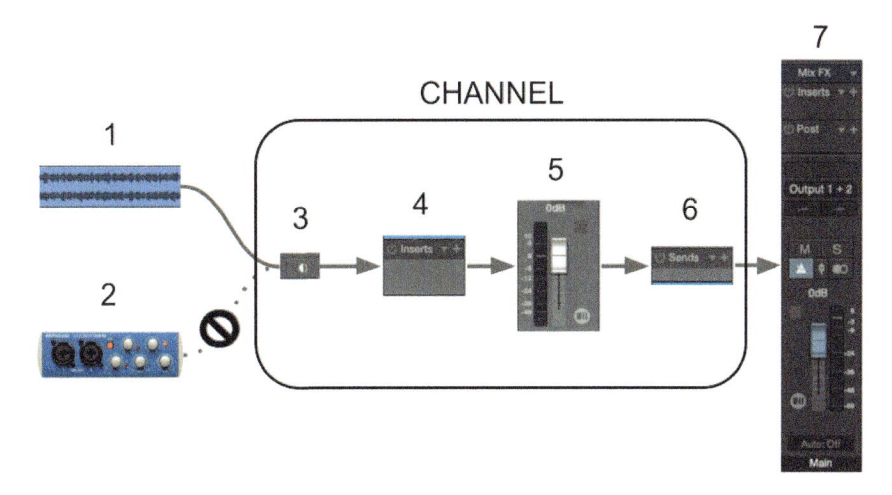

Figure 13.2: Signal flow on a mixer channel

Now, let's break down the components in *Figure 13.2*:

1. **Audio event**: This is the recording on your computer's hard disk. It is represented as an audio event on the corresponding track in the **Arrange** window. This recording will be our raw material for the mix session.
2. **Live input**: This is the signal coming from your audio interface. We used it to record the aforementioned audio event, but we have no more use for it during the mix session.
3. **The Monitor button**: This acts as a selector between the two aforementioned input sources, namely the audio event and live input. In its current state (gray), it's set to allow input from the audio event.
4. **The Inserts rack**: This is the section we will use to insert effects plug-ins to this channel.
5. **The fader**: We will use this to set the volume for this channel.
6. **The Sends rack**: We will use this section to send a signal from this channel to other channels.
7. **The Main channel**: This is the last element in the entire signal flow, where all channels on the mixer are combined into a single stereo output.

Everything inside the rectangle in *Figure 13.2* is a component of a channel. Now, let's take a closer look at these components to explore various methods of processing the audio passing through that channel.

Using the Inserts rack to add effects

The **Inserts** rack is a critical component in signal flow. It is the point where we add effects plug-ins to a channel to process the audio. The term **insert** refers to adding a plug-in directly into the signal flow of a chain to apply audio processing. To illustrate, let's assume that you have an electric guitar track and want to add some simulated amp distortion to it using **Ampire**. Here's how to do it:

1. Open the **Browse** window and go to the **Effects** tab. You will see a list of all the plug-ins installed on your system:

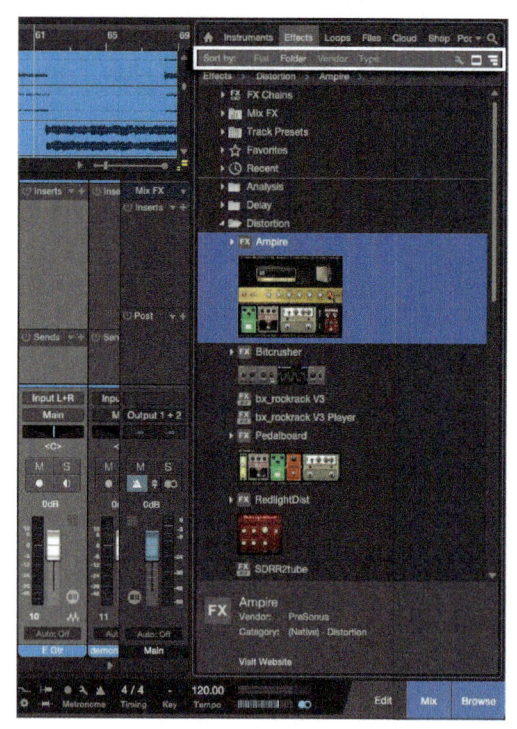

Figure 13.3: A list of effects plug-ins

2. If you know the name of the plug-in you're looking for, click the magnifier icon in the upper-right corner of the **Browse** window to open a search box, and type it in.

   If you don't remember the name of the plug-in, or if you want to see all available effects, use the sorting options (highlighted in *Figure 13.3*) to organize the list. **Folder** sorts all plug-ins based on effect type, similar to the categories we used when exploring effects in *Chapter 12*, while **Vendor** sorts them by manufacturer.

3. Open the **Mix** window if it's not open already. Locate the channel that you'd like to insert Ampire into.
4. Drag **Ampire** from the **Browse** window and drop it on the channel's **Insert** rack.

You can use this method to add as many plug-ins as you like. Here, I inserted **Ampire**, **Chorus**, and **Pro EQ** on a channel:

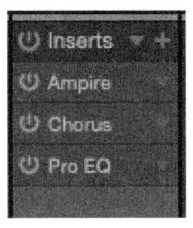

Figure 13.4: The Inserts rack holding multiple plug-ins

Beware that the order of these plug-ins is important. A signal travels from top to bottom in an **Inserts** rack – in this case, from **Ampire** to **Chorus**, and then to **Pro EQ**[3]. By arranging the plug-ins in this way, I'm adding distortion followed by a chorus effect. This will sound very different from a chorus effect followed by distortion. This quickly turns into a chicken-and-egg discussion among audio engineers, and your best bet is to try out different combinations and see which one you like best. You can easily change the order of plug-ins by clicking and dragging them inside the **Inserts** rack.

Now, let's update our signal flow diagram to include insert effects:

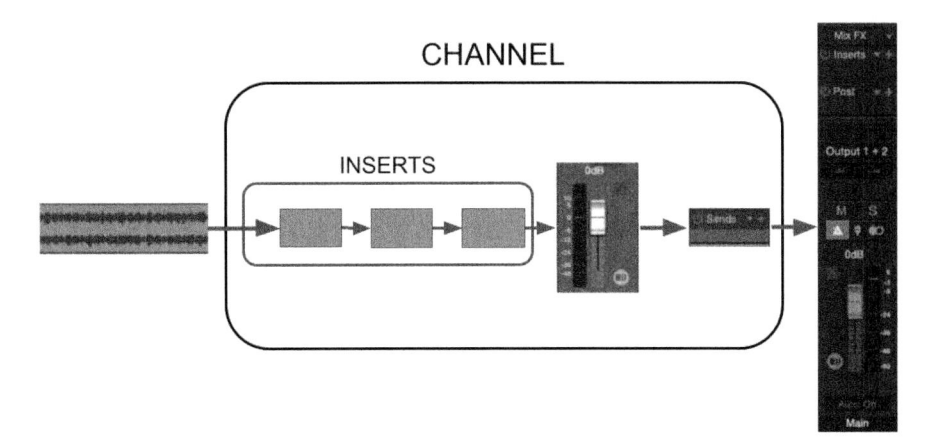

Figure 13.5: Signal flow with insert effects

Once you've inserted a plug-in, simply double-click on its name in the **Inserts** rack to open its interface and start tweaking. To remove it, right-click on its name and select **Remove** from the drop-down menu.

Using FX channels

Another way to add effects to a channel is to use an FX channel. Let's illustrate this with an example. Let's assume you have a drum recording on a track. It's a delicate performance with lots of nuances, but it tends to get lost among other instruments in the mix. In order to solve this, you think about compressing the signal because compressing adds punch to a recording and brings out details. However, at the same time, you don't want to compress the signal because compressing reduces the dynamic range, and it will take out all the excitement and expressiveness in the recording. What can you do?

The solution is to split the signal on the drum channel into two paths – one path goes to the **Main** output without any processing, therefore preserving the expressiveness of the original performance, and the second path is sent to a separate channel, called an FX channel, that has a compressor inserted on it, adding punch and detail. This scenario gives us the best of both worlds. *Figure 13.6* clarifies how this works:

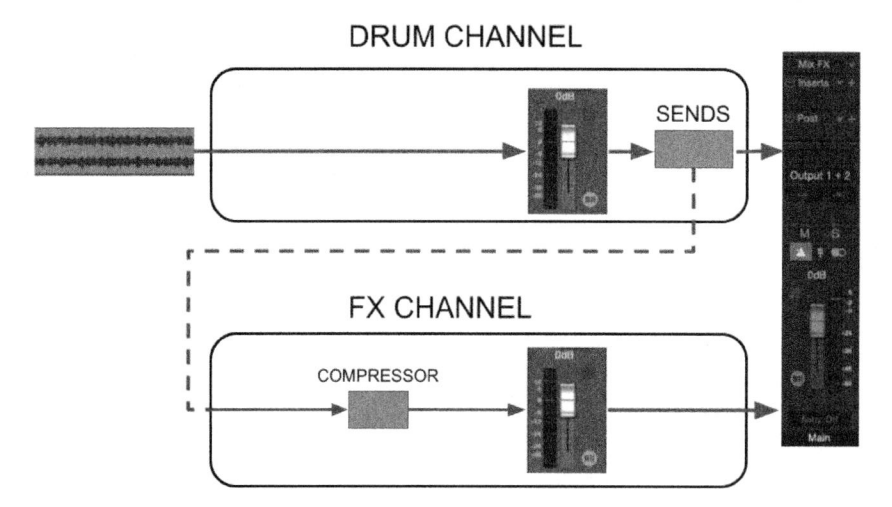

Figure 13.6: Signal flow for an FX channel

In *Figure 13.6*, the top channel is our drum channel. The **Sends** rack on this channel divides the signal into two paths. The first path continues to the **Main** channel of the Mix Console, carrying the dry, unaffected signal. The second path, represented by the dashed line, is sent to the FX channel, where it's processed by the compressor. The processed signal is then sent to the **Main** channel, where it's blended with all other channels in your project.

Now that we have discussed how an FX channel works, let's provide a definition as well – an **FX channel** is an independent channel that is not connected to any track as its input source. Instead, we send a signal to it using the **Sends** racks on other channels. The FX channel then processes these signals using the effects on its own **Inserts** rack.

Since this layout allows the same signal to flow in two parallel channels, it is sometimes referred to as **parallel processing**. The configuration we just described, with a compressor inserted on the FX channel, is such a commonly used technique that it even has its own name – **parallel compression** or **New York compression**. It's a great trick that's been used by mixing engineers to make drums louder and bigger in a mix, and it's very easy to implement thanks to Studio One's drag-and-drop interface.

Here's how you can add effects to a channel using the FX channel method. We will continue to use our scenario with the drum track as an example:

1. Open the **Browse** window and go to the **Effects** tab. You will see a list of all the plug-ins installed on your system. Then, locate the **Compressor** plug-in.
2. Open the **Mix** window if it's not open already and locate the drum channel.
3. Drag **Compressor** from the **Browse** window and drop it on the drum channel's **Sends** rack. Studio One will automatically do the following:
   - Create a new FX channel
   - Place the **Compressor** on the FX channel's **Insert** rack
   - Create a link to the FX channel on the drum track's **Sends** rack

   The end result will look like this:

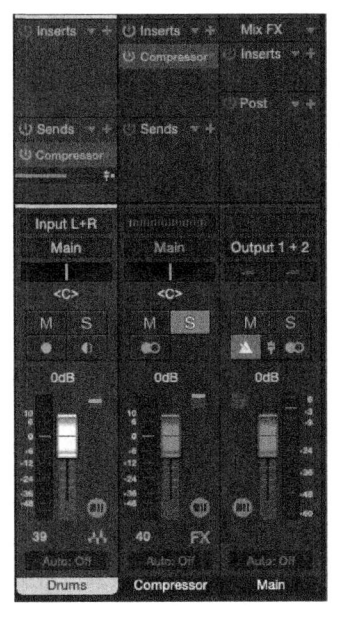

   Figure 13.7: A drum channel (left) sending a signal to an FX channel (center). Both are routed to the Main output (right)

4. Use the little blue horizontal slider in the drum channel's **Sends** rack to set how much signal you'd like to send to the FX channel. This effectively adjusts the balance between the original drum signal and the processed signal.

262   Optimizing Signal Flow and Elevating Your Mix

Note that *Figure 13.7* is exactly what *Figure 13.6* looks like in real life – the drum channel's **Sends** rack points to the FX channel, which has the **Compressor** plug-in on its **Inserts** rack. You can compare the two images to get a better sense of the signal flow.

One convenient thing about FX channels is that you can send a signal to them from as many channels as you want. So, if you have a large project with, say, 60 tracks, and you want to apply reverb on half of those tracks, you can create one FX channel with a reverb plug-in on it and send a signal to it from all those 30 tracks. This is much better than inserting reverb plug-ins on all those channels separately because of the following:

- It reduces the load on your computer's CPU. Reverb plug-ins are particularly resource hungry.
- It makes life easier for you. If, as your mix progresses, you find that you have too much or too little reverb, you can dial the right amount by tweaking just 1 plug-in, instead of 30.
- It makes more sense physically and acoustically. In the real world, all instruments in a musical performance are subject to the same reverberation, so you'll get a more realistic result by sending all your channels to the same reverb unit. Depending on your genre and production style, this level of realism may or may not be a goal, so feel free to disregard this point if it does not apply to your projects.

Once you've created an FX channel, it's easy to send signals to it from other channels. Just click the + button on the **Sends** rack of any channel that you'd like to send to the FX channel. Going back to our example in *Figure 13.7*, we will send a signal from the **E Gtr** channel to the FX channel:

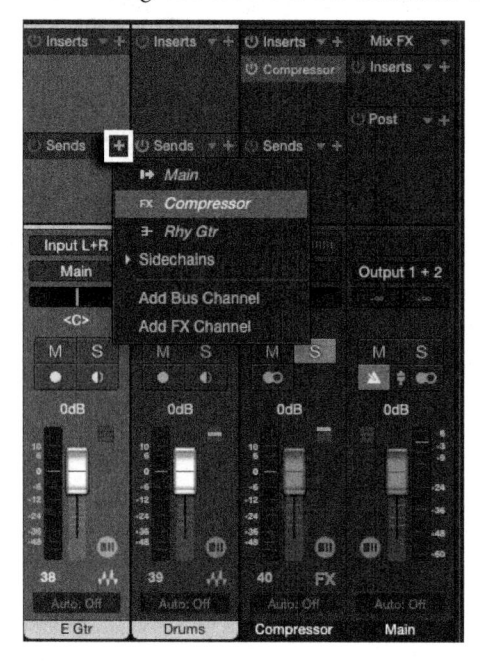

Figure 13.8: Sending a signal to an existing FX channel

You can create as many FX channels as you need within a Song. Since FX channels have their own **Sends** racks, you can send signals between FX channels as well, opening the door for some versatile signal routing possibilities with lots of creative potential.

Using buses to control several channels

A **bus** is a channel on the Mix Console that combines several other channels. For example, if you have several drum tracks in your song, you can route all of them to a bus channel. Then, you can use the bus channel's controls to process all the drum channels collectively. It's a great way of simplifying the mixing process.

Follow these steps to route multiple channels to a bus channel:

1. Open the **Mix** window.
2. Select the channels that you'd like to combine in a bus channel. You can select multiple channels by holding down *Ctrl* (Windows) or *Cmd* (Mac) and clicking on them.
3. Right-click on any one of the selected channels. On the pop-up menu, select **Add Bus for Selected Channels**. This will create a new bus channel, named **Bus 1**, right next to the **Main** output. All the selected channels will be automatically routed to this new bus channel:

Figure 13.9: Drum channels have been routed to a bus channel

4. Double-click on the name of the new bus channel and give it a descriptive name.

This is what the signal flow for this channel configuration will look like:

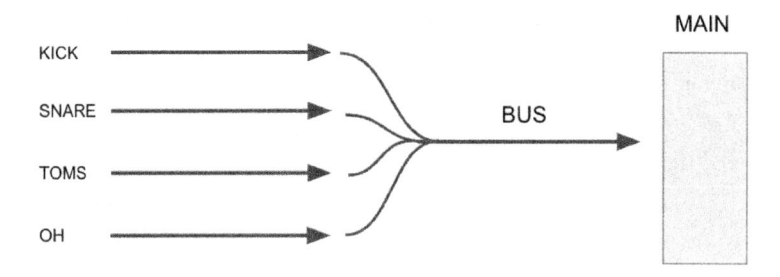

Figure 13.10: The signal flow for the channel configuration in Figure 13.9

You can now use this bus channel's fader to control the level of the entire drum kit and use its **Inserts** and **Sends** racks to apply effects to all drum channels collectively. Note that any settings or effects that you apply on individual drum channels are still active; the bus channel adds an additional layer of control on top of that.

> **Tip**
>
> On some hardware mix consoles, such as SSLs, and on some other music production programs, such as Cubase, buses are referred to as groups or group channels. If you're switching to Studio One from one of those programs, beware of this change in terminology, since *group* means something else in Studio One, as we will see in the *Using groups for a faster workflow* section.

Combining several channels within a single bus allows you to treat them as a single channel. For example, you can now use the bus we created to apply New York compression to all four drum tracks simultaneously. Just drag a compressor from the **Browse** window and drop it on the **Sends** rack of the bus. The end result will look like this:

Figure 13.11: Applying FX channel to a bus

And this is what the signal routing for the previous configuration will look like:

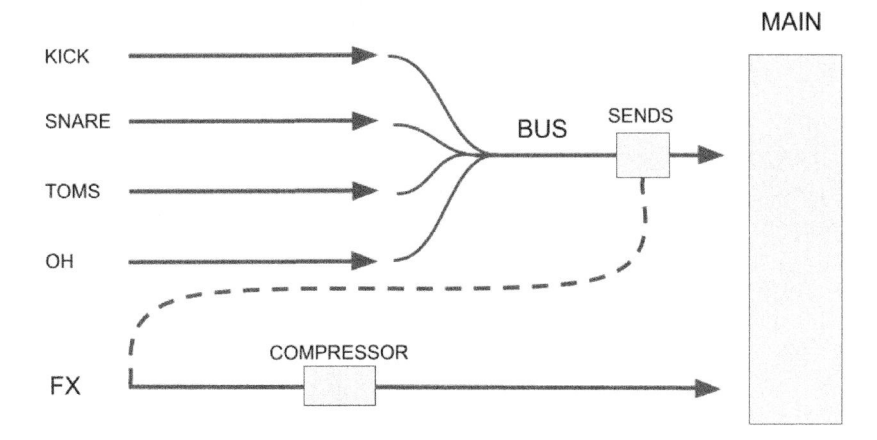

Figure 13.12: The signal flow for the channel configuration in Figure 13.11

You can create as many buses as you want and route buses into other buses. Once you get used to incorporating buses and FX channels into your mixes, the possibilities are endless, opening the door to some very creative and time-saving options.

Using VCA channels to control volume

Voltage-Controlled Amplifier (**VCA**) channels allow you to control the level of one or more channels. You can think of a VCA channel as a simplified version of a bus channel. Whereas a bus channel has **Inserts** and **Sends** racks as well as a fader, a VCA channel just has a fader.

To understand why VCA channels are a brilliant idea, let's go back to the four drum channels and the drum bus channel that we've been working on. Imagine that as you work on your mix, you add some intricate automation to the fader on the drum bus, adjusting the level of the entire drum kit to fit with the flow of the song. The next day, you listen to your mix with fresh ears and notice that the drums actually overpower the mix throughout the entire song. Due to this, you decide to turn the drums down by a couple of decibels.

Normally, that would mean editing the automation on the fader of the drum bus. While that's certainly feasible, it's not a practical or convenient method, especially if you want to actively adjust the level as you listen to your mix.

Here's where the VCA channel concept comes in – it adds a second fader on the signal path, which can be used to further adjust the level of the drum bus. That way, you can let the fader on the drum bus take care of the automation and use the fader on the VCA channel to fine-tune the drum kit's overall volume.

Here's how to add a VCA fader to a channel:

1. Select the channel(s) you want to control with a VCA fader. This could be any combination of channels – for example, if you want the volume of some percussion channels to change by the same amount as drum channels, select individual percussion channels and the drum bus at the same time.
2. Right-click on any one of the selected channels. From the pop-up menu, select **Add VCA for Selected Channels**. This will create a VCA channel and route the faders of the selected channels to the fader on the VCA channel. This routing will be indicated below the affected faders:

Figure 13.13: The fader on the bus is routed to VCA 1

You can now use the VCA channel's fader to control the level of all channels that have been routed to it. Note that you can even automate the fader on the VCA channel to add an extra layer of control.

Congratulations! You now have boss-level signal routing skills. This is as complicated as things will get for a typical music mix session, as far as signal flow is concerned. Armed with this knowledge, you are now ready to effectively address almost any signal processing challenge a project may throw at you. We will build upon this knowledge in the following section as we explore some more sophisticated mixing techniques.

Applying advanced techniques

In this section, we will cover some more innovative ways of manipulating sounds in a mix. Although these are generally regarded as advanced techniques, this does not mean they are hard to understand or execute. Rather, it implies that you will find them useful only after you have mastered the basic techniques we covered in the preceding section. Once you reach that point, the techniques we're about to discuss are fairly easy to implement.

Let's start with the most popular of all these advanced techniques.

Sidechain processing

Sidechain processing (or **sidechaining**) is a technique where the audio signal from one source is used to control the processing of another audio source. In other words, the sidechain signal is used to trigger a specific processing effect on a target audio signal.

Sidechaining can be used for an infinite number of purposes, ranging from the creative to the highly technical. Here are some possible scenarios where it can be used:

- In a live performance, apply half-playback so that when a singer sings into a microphone, we hear the actual performance, but when they stop singing, playback kicks in automatically.
- In electronic dance music production, create the hallmark pumping effect between kick and bass tracks.
- In a TV documentary, automatically duck the background music when the voice-over starts.
- In a pop song, make the kick cut through the mix by automatically lowering the volume of the bass track when the kick drum hits.

Although these are the most common scenarios, this is just scratching the surface of what sidechaining can be used for.

Now, let's see how you can implement this technique in your mixes. As an example, take a look at these kick drum and bass guitar tracks:

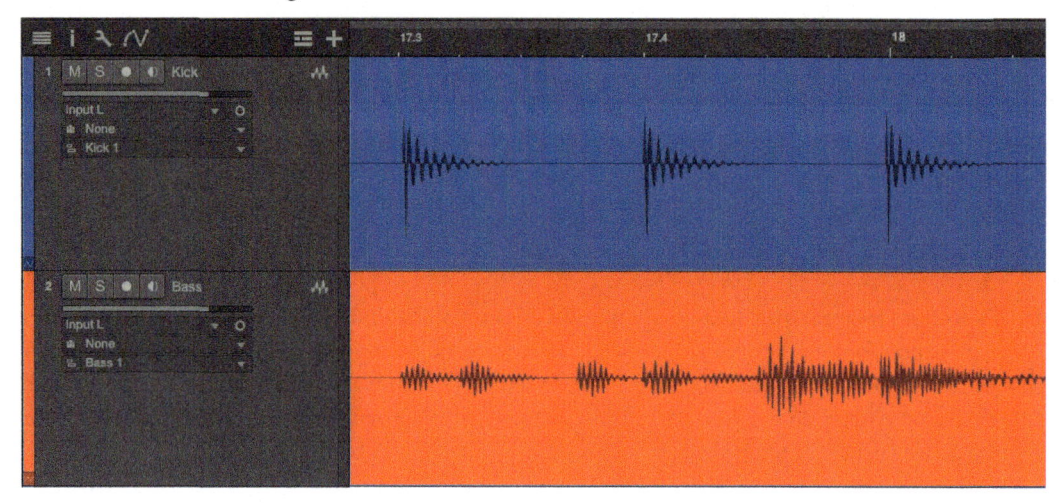

Figure 13.14: A kick drum track (top) and an electric bass track (bottom)

In most genres of popular music, kick drum and bass guitar play at the same time. In *Figure 13.14*, there is a bass note corresponding to every hit of the kick drum. This becomes a problem when mixing because we want both of these instruments to be loud and prominent in a typical pop mix, and in those instances where they play together, their combined energy becomes so loud that they take up most of the headroom available in the Main channel, leaving very little space available for other instruments. This may result in clipping on the Main channel, forcing you to turn down the volume of the entire mix.

If you take a closer look at *Figure 13.14*, you'll notice that the temporal characteristics of these two sounds are very different – the kick drum has a sharp attack, referred to as a transient, and fades out very quickly. Bass, on the other hand, has a much slower attack and sustains for quite a while. The problematic overlapping between these two instruments happens only during the attack phase of the kick sound, lasting for a very short time, within a range of milliseconds.

If we can find a way to turn the bass down for just those milliseconds, the problem will be solved. This can easily be achieved by a specific version of sidechaining, known as **sidechain compression**. Basically, we will insert a compressor on the bass track, but instead of listening to the bass track, this compressor will listen to the kick track and turn the bass down when it detects a signal on the kick track.

Here's how to implement sidechain compression based on our example of kick and bass tracks:

1. Open the **Mix** window if it's not open already.
2. Insert a compressor on the bass channel.

3. Click the **Sidechain** button on top of the compressor interface. This will open a pop-up menu containing the list of all channels active in the project:

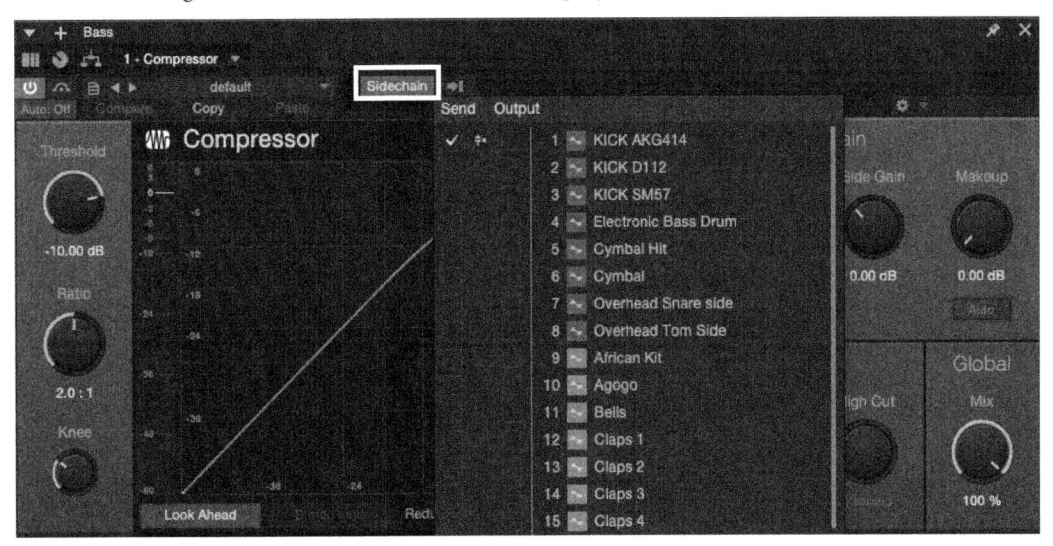

Figure 13.15: The sidechain options for a plug-in

4. From this list, click the **Send** checkbox corresponding to the kick channel.

5. We want the compressor to act as soon as it detects a hit on the kick channel, so next, we set the compressor's **Attack** parameter to a fairly low value: 4 or 5 milliseconds is a good average setting. Studio One's compressor can act much faster than that, but such extreme attack values may result in clicking sounds.

6. We also want the compressor to stop compressing as soon as the sharp attack of the kick drum has ended. Set the **Release** time to somewhere around 50 milliseconds, but you can try higher values if you want to create the landmark pumping bass sound used in electronic dance music. There is no clear-cut value here; it depends on the song's tempo and the temporal characteristics of the sounds, so experiment till you get it just right.

7. You can be a bit more aggressive with the compressor's **Ratio** and **Threshold** settings since this compression will take place within a time frame of milliseconds. The goal here is to turn the bass down momentarily as much as possible without causing a noticeable drop in its volume.

That's it! Now, although this compressor is inserted on the bass channel, it listens to the kick channel and responds to the hits of the kick drum. The signal flow looks like this:

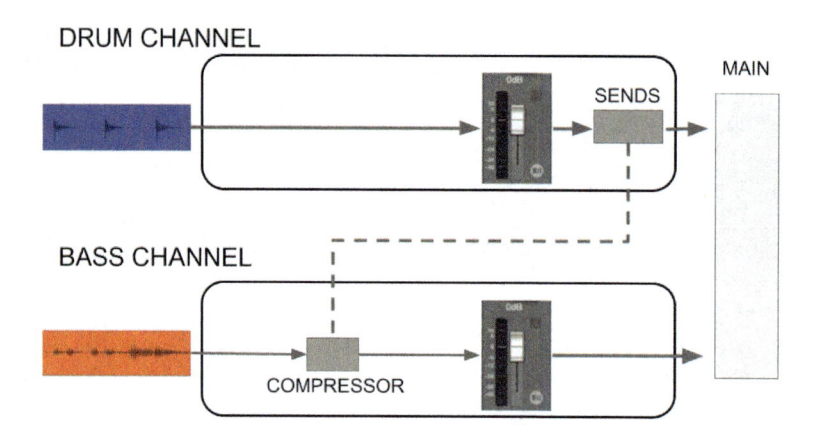

Figure 13.16: The signal flow for sidechain compression

This example is just one way of using sidechain processing in your projects. Sidechain capability is not available on all effects plug-ins, but it's being added to more plug-ins with each new version. Next time you open a plug-in, check whether it supports sidechaining and think about how you can use that capability to add creative, dynamic effects to your mix.

Using Splitter for precise targeting

Splitter is a utility plug-in that lets you split a signal into multiple paths. You can then process each of these paths separately, which opens the door to some versatile and powerful sound processing options. Here are some of the possibilities:

- Split a drum loop into two identical paths and compress one of them. This will effectively give you New York compression within a single channel.

- Split the low-frequency content of a sound into a separate path and convert it to mono. This technique is used to maximize mono compatibility of mixes and can normally be achieved only with high-end plug-ins called **multiband imagers**; however, by using Splitter, you can do this using nothing more than Studio One's stock plug-ins.

- Split the left and right channels of a stereo track and process them separately. This allows you to come up with some very creative sound design ideas that would not be possible when processing left and right channels with a single plug-in.

Whereas the plug-ins we've discussed so far modify the sound going through a channel, Splitter modifies the signal path itself, so using Splitter requires a different method compared to other plug-ins. Let's walk through the procedure step by step:

1. Drag **Splitter** from the **Browse** window and drop it on the **Inserts** rack of the channel you want to process. This will open the **Routing** window:

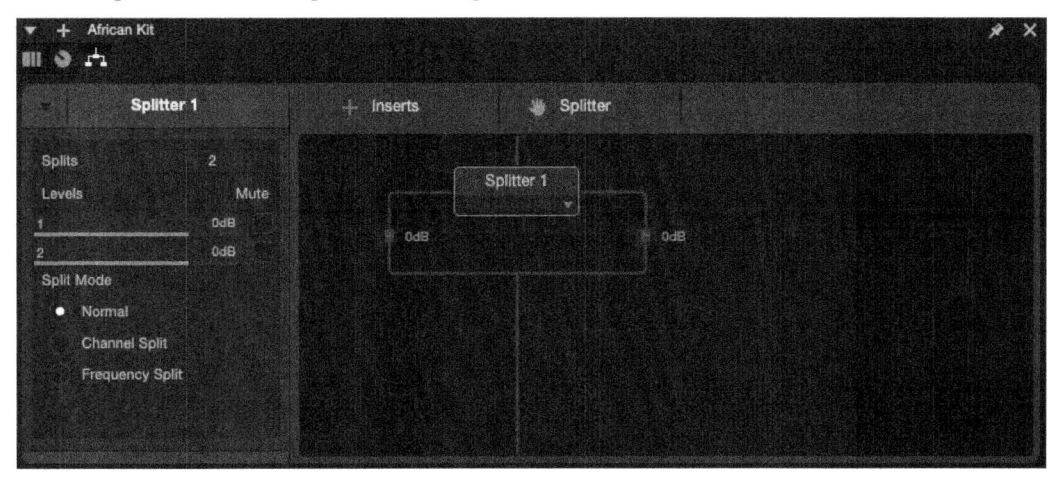

Figure 13.17: The Routing window with Splitter

2. The left side of the **Routing** window shows the settings for the Splitter we've just inserted. Use **Splits** to choose how many paths you'd like to split the signal into. For this example, we will have two paths.

3. Use **Levels** to set the volume for each path and **Mute** to mute paths temporarily.

4. **Split Mode** sets the criteria based on which the signal will be split. There are three options:

    - **Normal** splits the signal into two or more identical copies. This is useful for applying parallel processing within a single track.

    - **Channel Split** splits a stereo channel into pairs of mono signals, allowing you to process left and right channels separately.

    - **Frequency Split** splits the signal into frequency bands and places each band on a separate path. In *Figure 13.18*, I'm splitting the signal at 240 Hz. You can think of this as a crossover point; any frequency below 240 Hz will be routed to path one and any frequency above that will be routed to path two. If you need to divide frequencies into smaller bands, increase the **Splits** setting to create additional paths and adjust their respective crossover frequencies as needed.

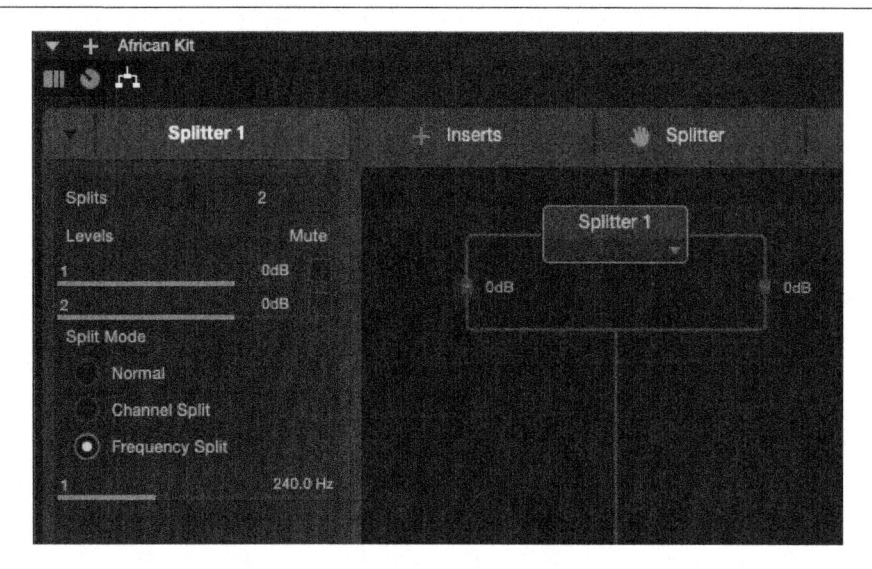

272　Optimizing Signal Flow and Elevating Your Mix

Figure 13.18: Frequency Split mode on a Splitter

5. Once you've split your channel, you can drag effects plug-ins from the **Browse** window and drop them on a path you want to process. In *Figure 13.19*, I have an **Autofilter** plug-in processing the left channel and **Beat Delay** processing the right channel.

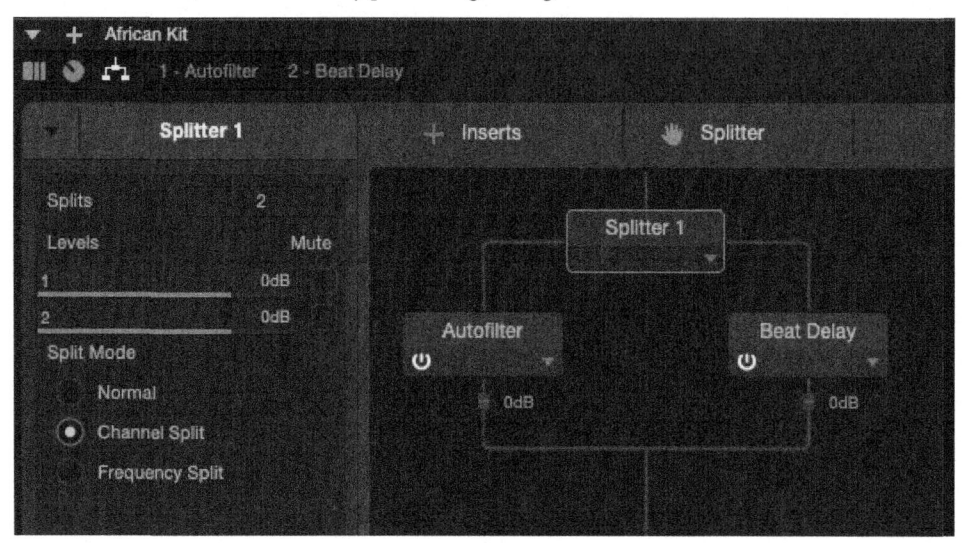

Figure 13.19: Adding plug-ins to Splitter's paths

You can add as many Splitters as you like, create as many Splits within each of them as you like, and insert as many plug-ins on each path as you like. You can also drag every item in the **Routing** window to change its position in the signal flow and create awesome effects chains that are unique to you. Splitter really is an audio engineer's playground!

Using groups for a faster workflow

If you have several channels that you want to process together, you can link their parameters using the **Group** function. Actions you perform on any channel within a group will be applied to the other channels as well. This is a great time-saving feature that will help streamline your workflow.

To place channels in a group, proceed as follows:

1. On the **Mix** window, select the channels that you want to group together and right-click on any one of them.
2. Select **Group Selected Tracks** in the pop-up menu. This will open a dialog box where you can name the group.
3. Give the group a short, descriptive name and click **OK**. This will help you identify groups easily when you're working on a large project.

   Channels in a group will be marked by a group icon on top of their faders:

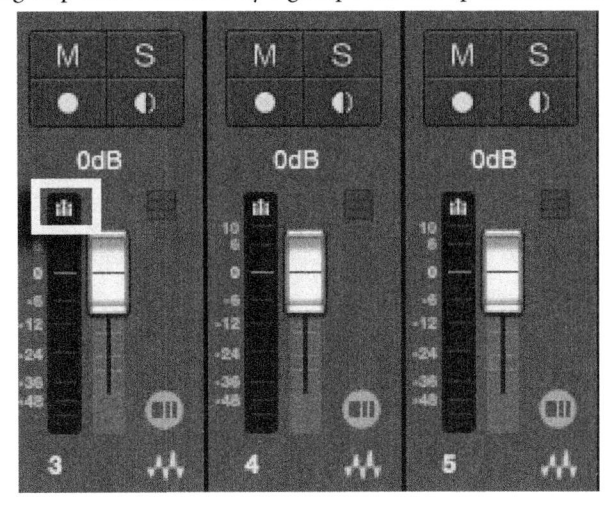

   Figure 13.20: Group icons indicating grouped channels

By default, placing channels in a group links their faders, pan controls, and solo, mute, record enable, and monitor buttons, as well as send routings. To exclude any of these parameters from the group, do the following:

1. Click the **Show Groups** button on the **Mix** window. This will open the **Group Panel**:

Figure 13.21: The Show Groups button and Groups panel of the Mix window

2. Right-click on the name of the group you'd like to modify.
3. In the pop-up menu, clear the checkboxes for the parameters that you want to exclude from the group behavior.

Sometimes, you may want to make minor adjustments to individual channels within a group. To do so without affecting the other channels, hold down the *Alt* (Windows) or *Option* (Mac) key while modifying a parameter so that other channels will remain unchanged.

If you no longer have use for a group, you can dissolve it by going to the pop-up menu in *Figure 13.21* and selecting **Dissolve Group**.

Customizing plug-ins

As we saw in *Chapter 12*, there is a huge selection of effects plug-ins, and there are infinite ways to use them, but as you develop your mixing abilities, you'll find yourself building a short list of tried and trusted plug-ins and using them more than the others. You will also find that you set those plug-ins pretty much the same way across your projects. This is not a bad thing; on the contrary, it's part of your unique production style.

Studio One makes it easy for you to arrange your favorite plug-ins and launch them in your projects just as you want to see them, saving you time and streamlining your workflow. Let's explore the features that make this possible.

Adding to Favorites

If you find yourself using a plug-in quite often, consider adding it to the **Favorites** category in the list of plug-ins:

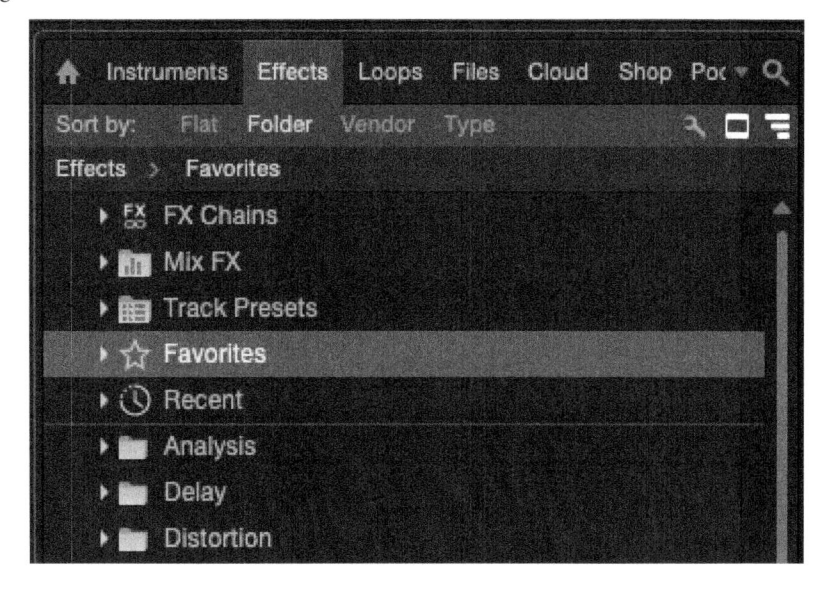

Figure 13.22: A list of plug-ins on the Browse panel

This will make the plug-in easy to find, especially if you have an extensive set of plug-ins. Here's how to do it:

1. Open the **Browse** panel and go to the **Effects** tab.
2. In the list of plug-ins, right-click on the plug-in you want to designate as a favorite.
3. On the pop-up menu, select **Favorite**.

Favorites will appear on the top of all the plug-in lists – on the **Inserts** racks of the **Mix** window, on the **Inspector** panel, and in the **Browse** window. Your favorite plug-ins will always be just a click away.

Creating FX chains

If you find yourself using the same plug-ins, with the same settings and arranged in the same order, you can save them in an FX chain and instantly recall them in your projects.

For example, I like using **Room Reverb**, but since it does not have a built-in equalizer section or filters, I add **ProEQ3** after the reverb to get rid of the extreme frequencies. Then, I add **Binaural Pan** to add some extra width to the reverb for a more three-dimensional mix. This has been my go-to reverb setup for quite some time now.

Instead of adding these plug-ins one by one and tweaking them from scratch on every project, I can create an FX chain for them and recall it in my future projects. Here's how to do it:

1. Arrange your plug-ins on a channel's **Inserts** rack.
2. Open each plug-in and tweak it just as you want to see it on your next project. Studio One will remember your settings for each plug-in as well.
3. Click the small triangle at the top of the **Inserts** rack. This will open the **FX Chain** menu:

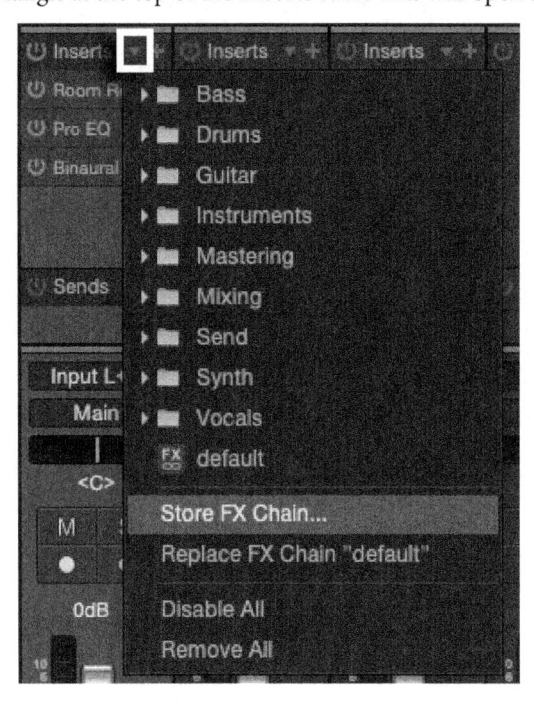

Figure 13.23: The FX Chain menu

4. On this menu, click **Store FX Chain**. This will open a dialog box, asking you to name your new FX chain.

5. Give a short, descriptive name to your FX chain (such as `main vocal reverb`) and click **OK**.

Next time you open the **FX Chain** menu from any channel on any project, this FX chain will be waiting for you to launch it with exactly the same settings. What a time saver!

Adding presets to plug-ins

If you frequently use the same settings on a plug-in, you can save yourself the trouble of adjusting them from scratch on every project by making them a preset. Follow these steps to do so:

1. Set all the parameters of the plug-in the way you want to store them in the preset.

2. Click the tiny page icon on the plug-in's interface to open its presets menu:

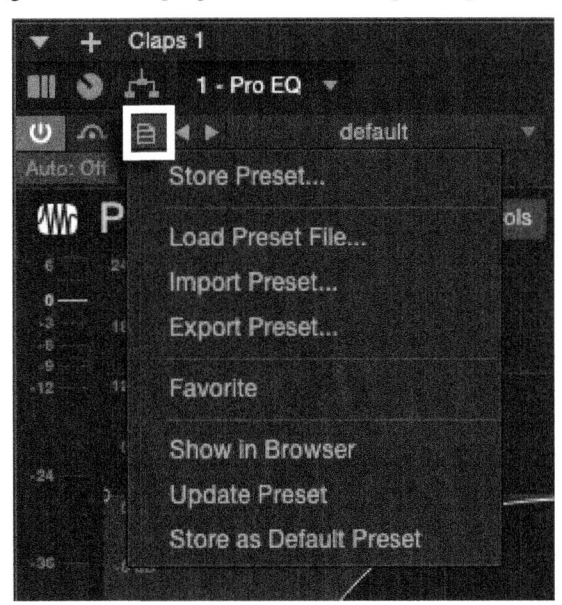

Figure 13.24: The plug-in preset menu

3. Click **Store Preset**, give a descriptive name to the preset (such as `lead guitar delay`), and click **OK**.

Now, this preset will be available every time you launch this plug-in on any channel and in every project.

This concludes our tour of advanced mixing techniques and workflow hacks within Studio One's Mix Console. Next, we will talk about how to export final mixes or stems from your Songs so that you can publish them or share them with collaborators.

Exporting final mixes and stems

Once you're happy with your mixes, you'll want to share them with the rest of the world. However, since the rest of the world cannot open our Studio One project files, you will first need to convert your mixes to a standard file format that everyone can open in their media players. This process is called **exporting**. When you export a Song in Studio One, the multitude of channels in your project will be bounced down to a single stereo channel, which will then be saved in a globally recognized audio file format.

There are two methods of exporting a Song from Studio One, which are used for different purposes. Let's start with the more commonly used method.

Exporting final mixes

Exporting a final mix from a Song means bouncing all the channels into one stereo channel and embedding that stereo channel in an audio file. It sounds complicated, but Studio One handles the task gracefully once you set a few parameters.

Follow these steps in order to export the final mix from your Song:

1. Set the left and right locators in the **Arrange** window to mark the beginning and end of the Song, respectively. By default, Studio One will export only the part of the timeline that falls between these two locators, so take your time and position them correctly.

> **Important note**
>
> It's a good idea to leave a tiny bit of silence at the beginning of a song (about half a second will do). This will prevent consumer-level media players from chopping off the beginning of the song.
>
> At the end of the song, make sure that all reverb tails have decayed completely before the right locator so that they don't cut off abruptly when played back.

2. Go to the top menu, click **Song**, and then **Export Mixdown**. This will open the **Export Mixdown** window:

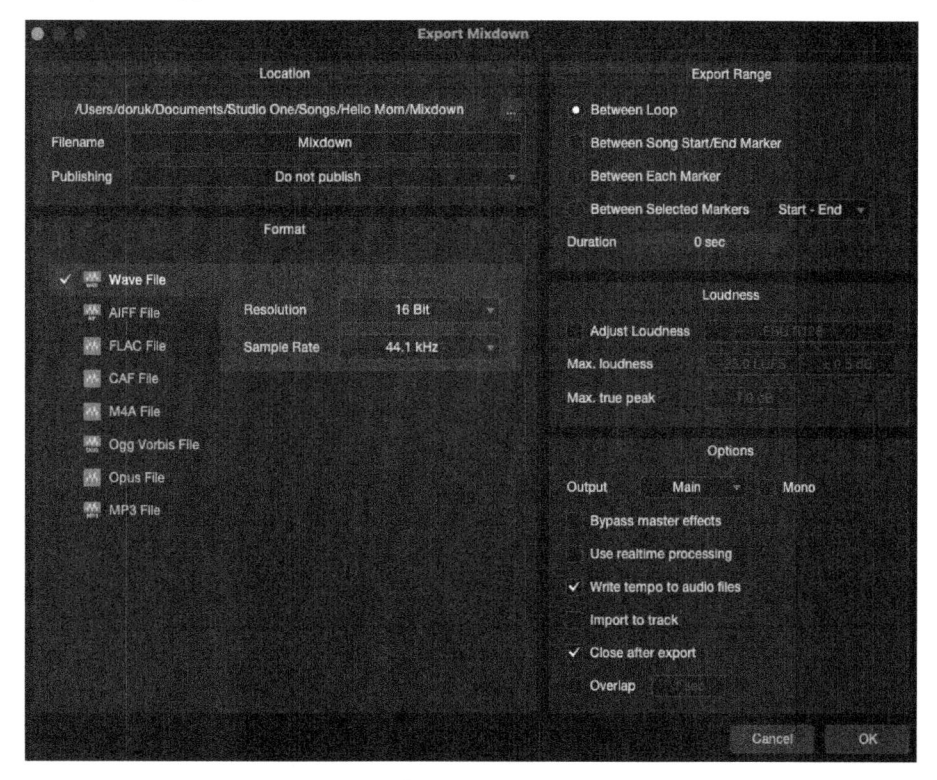

Figure 13.25: The Export Mixdown window

3. In the **Location** section of this window, select a folder and name for the audio file(s) that you're about to create.

4. In the **Format** section, select the format of the files you want to create. You can use the checkboxes to select multiple file types. Click on each file type to access its applicable parameters. While there are several file type choices, here are the two that you're likely to use the most:

   - **Wave File** is the industry standard and is also universally recognized by consumer-grade media players. Wave files offer high sound quality at the price of large file sizes. Use this format to deliver final mixes to distribution networks, clients, or mastering studios. Here are the two most common parameters for wave files:

     - If you export a song that will be distributed to music platforms such as Apple Music or Spotify, set **Resolution** to **16 Bit** and **Sample Rate** to **44.1 kHz**. This is known as the **CD standard**. It's been the standard format for music distribution since the 1980s and is still used by music-only platforms.

- If the exported wave file will be used in video production (as a music bed, sound effect, etc.) set **Resolution** to **24 Bit** and **Sample Rate** to **48 kHz**. This is the **DVD standard** that's been around since the 1990s and is still required by video platforms. It defines the parameters for the audio component of video files. Although video production programs can import audio files at almost any resolution and sample rate, delivering your files with the preceding parameters will provide the best sound quality.

- **MP3 File** is a compressed file format, offering much smaller file sizes at the price of reduced sound quality. Use this format to quickly share your mix with a friend in an email attachment to get a second opinion. The important setting for MP3 files is **Bitrate**, expressed in **kilobits per second** (**kbps**). Higher bitrates give better sound quality but result in larger file sizes; **192 kbps** is a good compromise.

5. The **Export Range** section of the window allows you to set which part of the timeline will be exported. We took care of this in *step 1*, so you can leave this at its default setting – **Between Loop**.

6. The **Loudness** section of the window activates an extremely useful feature that analyzes the level of your mix and automatically adjusts it to fit the loudness standards required by digital platforms. Click **Adjust Loudness** to activate a drop-down menu that allows you to adjust your song's loudness, conforming to standards implemented by any platform from the European Broadcasting Union to YouTube:

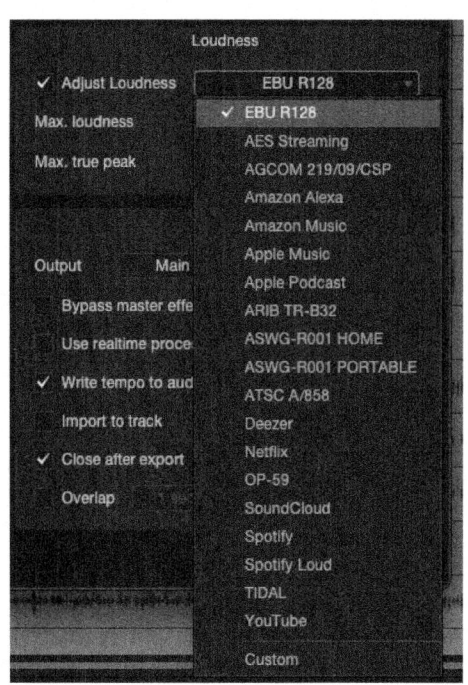

Figure 13.26: The Loudness setting on the Export Mixdown menu

7. You can also set the loudness of your song manually using the **Max. loudness** and **Max. true peak** settings. We will talk about these settings in *Chapter 15*, but the preset options in the drop-down menu are sufficient for almost any situation.

8. If you have effects plug-ins inserted on the Main channel of the Mix Console and you send the mix to a mastering house, check the **Bypass master effects** checkbox in the **Options** section. This will bypass those effects so that they don't interfere with the effects that will be applied during the mastering stage.

9. Click **OK**.

Studio One will bounce the mix, adjust its loudness level, and create the files you specified, as you take a sip from a well-deserved cup of coffee.

Exporting stems

Stems refer to individual tracks or a group of tracks that make up a song. When a song is divided into stems, each track or group of tracks is exported as a separate audio file. Depending on the intended use, these files may be delivered in their original, unprocessed form, or they may be delivered with all the effects and processing applied in post-production, such as pitch correction and audio quantization.

Songs are usually exported as stems to allow others to work on them or contribute to them. Some possible scenarios for using stems are as follows:

- You want to make your song available to others for remixing. Having stems at their disposal allows them to use parts of the song that they want to keep in the remix, and replace everything else with their own material.

- You create music for a film and want to give the rerecording mixer more freedom when mixing the film's final soundtrack. For example, if your film score comprises drums, brass instruments, and synthesizers, delivering these instrument groups in separate stems will allow the rerecording engineer to turn down the level of synthesizers that mask dialogue, while keeping the drums at full volume.

- You want to collaborate with other people, so you provide stems as raw material upon which they can improve.

The procedure for exporting stems is similar to the procedure for exporting videos. Here's what you need to do:

1. Set the left and right locators on the **Arrange** window, as described in the *Exporting final mixes* section.

2. Go to the top menu, click **Song**, and then **Export Stems**. This will open the **Export Stems** window:

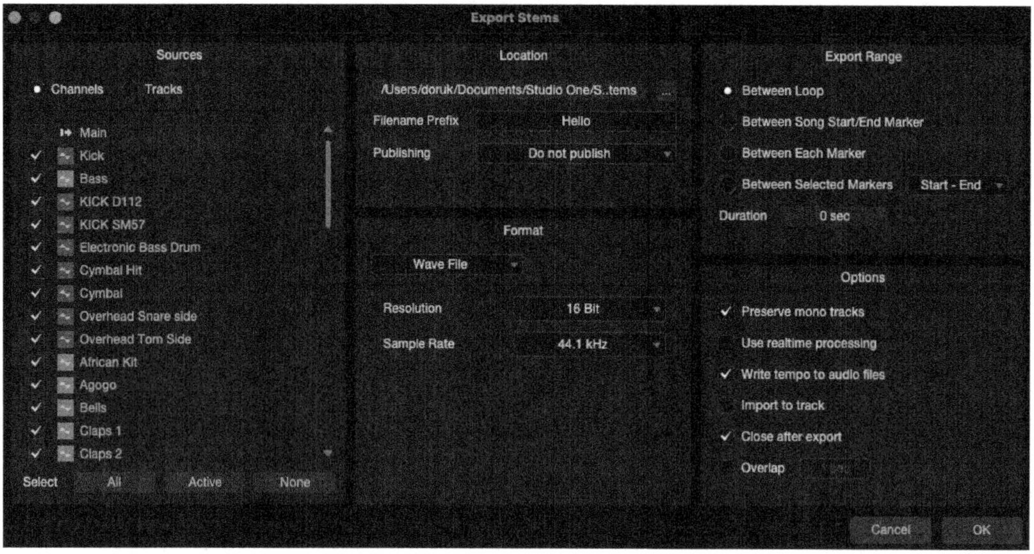

Figure 13.27: The Export Stems window

3. In the **Sources** section of this window, select the channels you want to export as individual stems.
4. In the **Location** section, select a folder for the audio files you're about to create.
5. By default, stem files will be named after their corresponding channels. If you have a channel in your song titled **Kick**, its corresponding stem file will be named `Kick.wav`. Since you will send these stems to other people, it's a good idea to add a prefix to filenames so that the people receiving the files will know which song the files are coming from. You can set this prefix in the **Filename Prefix** field. Based on my settings in *Figure 13.27*, stems will be named `Hello_Kick.wav`, `Hello_Bass.wav`, and so on.
6. The rest of the parameters are the same as in the **Export Mixdown** window, so refer to the steps we listed in the *Exporting final mixes* section to set them.
7. Click **OK**.

In this section, you learned how to export your final mixes or stems to share them with fans, clients, or collaborators. This wraps up our discussion of the mixing process in Studio One.

Summary

In this chapter, we took an in-depth look at Studio One's signal flow, discussed various methods of using effects plug-ins, and learned how to implement several advanced mixing techniques. Gaining mastery of these concepts and techniques will allow you to have complete control of your mix, develop a more efficient workflow, and facilitate creativity in mixing, helping you to meet your artistic vision.

In the next chapter, we will explore Studio One's surround sound capabilities and learn how to use them to craft immersive audio experiences.

14
Working with Spatial Audio

Spatial audio has revolutionized how we perceive and create sound, and Studio One's latest version brings this exciting frontier directly into your workflow. In this chapter, we'll explore how to harness Studio One's immersive audio capabilities to craft three-dimensional sonic experiences. Whether you're aiming to produce spatially enriched music, design compelling soundscapes for games, or create content for platforms that support surround or spatial audio formats, this chapter will guide you through the tools and techniques that make it possible.

Throughout this chapter, we'll configure Studio One for spatial audio production and cover essential workflows for mixing in immersive formats. You'll also discover practical tips for exporting your projects to ensure compatibility with various playback systems and platforms. By the end of the chapter, you'll be equipped to confidently navigate the immersive audio landscape and bring your ideas to life in ways that traditional stereo mixes simply can't achieve.

In this chapter, we will cover the following main topics:

- Getting started with spatial audio
- Creating a new Song for spatial audio
- Mixing and exporting spatial audio material

Technical requirements

To follow along with this chapter, you just need to have Studio One installed and activated on your computer. Please note that spatial audio capability has been introduced with version 7.

Getting started with spatial audio

Spatial audio, also known as **immersive audio**, is a multidimensional approach to sound that creates a sense of depth, space, and presence, going beyond the traditional confines of stereo sound. Spatial audio places sound in a three-dimensional space around the listener. This can include sounds coming from precise points within a 360-degree sphere, enhancing realism and emotional engagement.

This technology is used in various applications, from music and film to **virtual reality (VR)**, **augmented reality (AR)**, and gaming. Immersive audio formats such as Dolby Atmos, DTS:X, and Ambisonics are designed to deliver spatially dynamic audio experiences on multiple playback systems, from professional setups to consumer-grade headphones. By mimicking how we naturally perceive sound in the real world, immersive audio allows creators to craft more engaging and lifelike soundscapes that captivate and transport the listener.

In practical terms, spatial audio refers to any audio format with output channels beyond traditional two-channel stereo. This is indeed a broad definition, so let's break it down.

Understanding different types of spatial audio

Spatial audio formats supported by Studio One include the following:

- **Surround** is a general term that refers to multi-channel audio configurations where each sound is assigned to a particular channel and can be positioned anywhere around the listener using the pan control on that channel. Commonly used in home theaters, cinemas, and gaming, surround audio formats such as 5.1 and 7.1 channel setups are designed to replicate real-world acoustics.
- **Dolby Atmos** is a proprietary spatial audio format developed by Dolby Labs. It takes a more advanced and flexible approach by allowing sounds to be placed and moved anywhere in a three-dimensional space, including overhead. Dolby Atmos is scalable, meaning it can adapt to systems ranging from cinema setups with hundreds of speakers to soundbars and headphones.
- **Binaural** is a two-channel audio signal that carries spatial information and can be used to convey spatial audio imaging on headphones without the need for a multi-speaker installation.

These formats, with the exception of binaural, require the use of several speakers both during production and during playback. Once we go beyond stereo, where we simply name our speakers left and right, naming our speakers can become a bit more tricky, so let's take care of that before we dive into the deep end of spatial audio.

The naming convention for speaker configurations

Spatial audio speaker configurations describe the placement and number of speakers in a setup designed to create an immersive audio experience. These configurations are expressed as numbers such as 5.1, 7.1.2, and so on, which indicate the distribution of speakers, subwoofers, and, in some cases, the presence of height or overhead channels.

Here's how to decipher a number such as 7.1.2:

- The first number is the number of speakers placed around the listener on a horizontal plane. These are typically positioned at the front, sides, and rear.
- The second number shows the number of subwoofers dedicated to **low-frequency effects** (**LFEs**), such as bass and rumble.
- The third number, if present, indicates the number of **height** or overhead speakers that provide a vertical dimension to the audio, crucial for formats such as Dolby Atmos.

Here are some common configurations and their typical use cases:

- **2.1**: Two main speakers (left and right) and one subwoofer. This is a basic stereo setup with added bass support, offering no surround or height channels.
- **5.1**: Five main speakers (front left, front right, center, rear left, and rear right) and one subwoofer. This is the standard surround sound setup used in home theaters.
- **7.1**: Adds two additional speakers (surround left and surround right) to the 5.1 setup for more precise sound placement around the listener.
- **5.1.2**: A 5.1 setup with two height speakers, adding an overhead dimension. Ideal for entry-level Dolby Atmos or DTS:X systems.
- **7.1.2**: A 7.1 setup with two height speakers. This configuration provides both horizontal and vertical immersion, which is suitable for advanced spatial audio experiences.
- **7.1.4**: Four height speakers added to a 7.1 configuration, offering even more precise vertical sound placement for a highly immersive experience.

The sheer number of speakers mentioned in these configurations may be intimidating at first: do you really need that many speakers positioned in your home studio to work with spatial audio? That depends on what you're planning to do and your target audience. That's what we will discuss in the next section.

Hardware requirements for spatial audio

Let's start with the good news – if you're going to work in Dolby Atmos, you don't need anything more than your existing sound interface and headphones. Dolby Atmos uses a proprietary algorithm called the **Dolby Atmos Renderer**, which we will discuss in the *Mixing and exporting spatial audio material* section. Suffice it to say for now that this renderer will downmix your Dolby Atmos material and convert it to a binaural signal so that you can work with your headphones and still experience spatial audio.

And now the bad news – if you're working in any other spatial audio format, including traditional surround formats such as 5.1, Dolby Atmos Renderer will not be able to apply its magic. So, you'll need to have as many speakers as indicated by your surround configuration (e.g., five speakers and one subwoofer for a 5.1 configuration). What's more, you'll also need an audio interface that supports the same number of discrete outputs (e.g., a total of six outputs for a 5.1 configuration).

Now that we have an understanding of spatial audio formats and the requirements for each, we are ready to start working on our first immersive audio masterpiece in Studio One, and that's exactly what we're doing in the next section.

Creating a new Song for spatial audio

In Studio One, spatial audio is only supported on the **Song** page. You'll create, edit, mix, and export all your spatial material using this page only. Let's get started:

1. On Studio One's start page, click **New**. This will open the **New** document window.
2. On the left side of this window, in the **Templates** list, click on the template titled **Mix in Surround**. The right side of the window will now display the options available for creating your first Song using spatial audio (*Figure 14.1*).

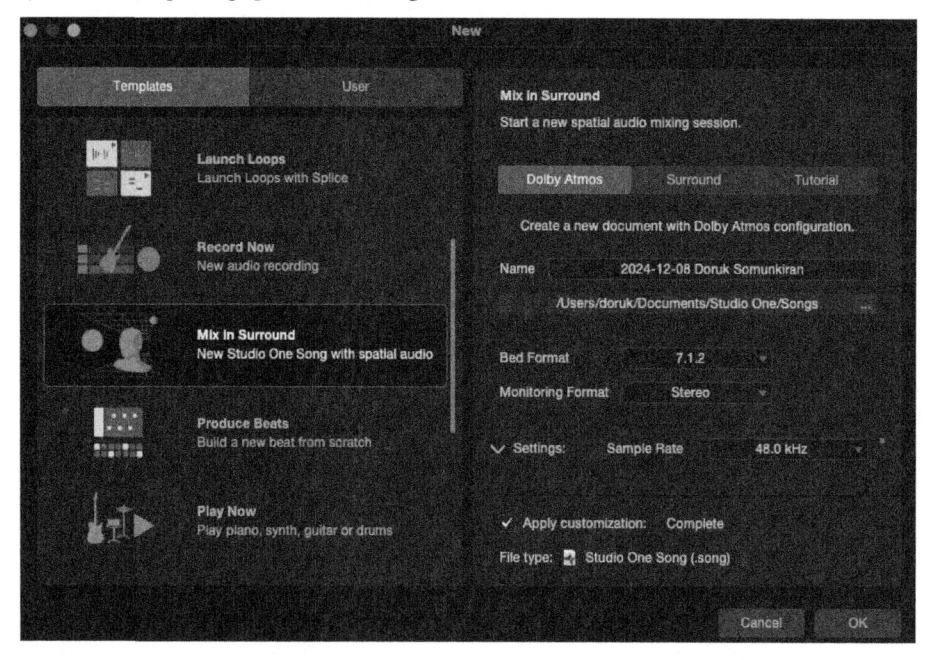

Figure 14.1: Creating a new Song for spatial audio

3. Select the type of spatial audio format you'd like to work in: **Dolby Atmos** or **Surround**. You can also select **Tutorial** to enter an interactive guide designed to help you learn about the Dolby Atmos workflow.

The options you'll see on the right side of the **New** document window will change depending on your selection of **Dolby Atmos** and **Surround**. Let's go through them one by one.

The options to create a Song for **Dolby Atmos** (shown in *Figure 14.1*) are as follows:

- **Name**: Provide a name and pick a location for your Song.

- **Bed Format**: Choose your target speaker configuration here. This is the speaker configuration that your project will ultimately play on.

- **Monitoring Format**: This is the speaker configuration that you'll be using while you do your production work. Remember we talked about the Dolby Atmos Renderer in the *Hardware requirements for spatial audio* section? That renderer will take the configuration you selected for **Bed Format** and downmix it to whatever speaker configuration you have selected here. If you're just going to be working with headphones, select **Stereo** in this field.

- **Sample Rate**: Dolby Atmos only supports sample rates of 48 kHz or 96 kHz, and those are the options you'll see here. If your audio interface does not support 96 kHz, the only available option will be **48 kHz**.

The options to create a Song for **Surround** are as follows:

- **Name**: Provide a name and pick a location for your Song.

- **Output Format**: Choose your target speaker configuration here. Note that you'll also need to have a matching speaker configuration in your studio.

- **Sample Rate**: Select a sample rate between **44.1 kHz** and **192 kHz**.

Your new Song is now configured for spatial audio. If you need to change the configuration of your Song at a later time, go to **Song** on the top menu and click on **Spatial Audio…**. This will open a dialog box where you can modify the settings we discussed previously.

Mapping speakers

Before we start working on your first Song with spatial audio, let's make sure that Studio One is configured to send each output channel to the correct speaker. This process is called **speaker mapping**, and you only need to do this once as long as you use the same speaker configuration. Let's do it:

1. On the top menu, click on **Song** and then **Song Setup**.
2. On the **Song Setup** window, click on the **Audio I/O Setup** tab.
3. Click on **Outputs**.

290   Working with Spatial Audio

4. Now, click on the field to the right of **Main** or **Main Output** to reveal a list of available output formats, as shown in *Figure 14.2*:

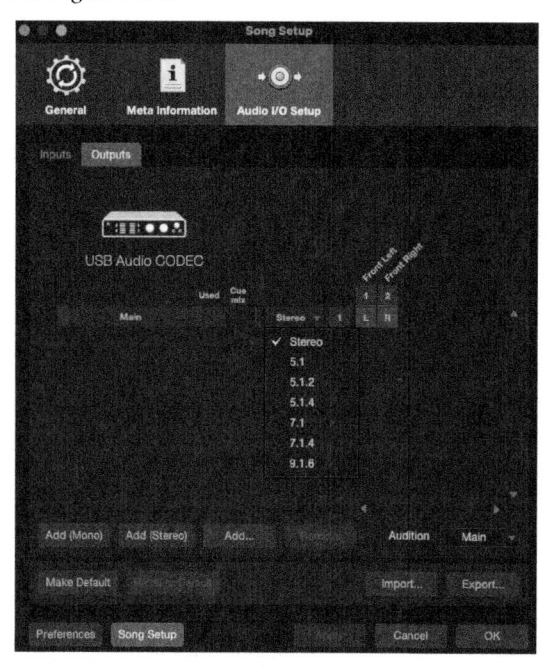

Figure 14.2: Mapping speakers for spatial audio

5. On this list, select the option that matches your Song's intended format. The window will now display the default speaker mapping for the format you selected:

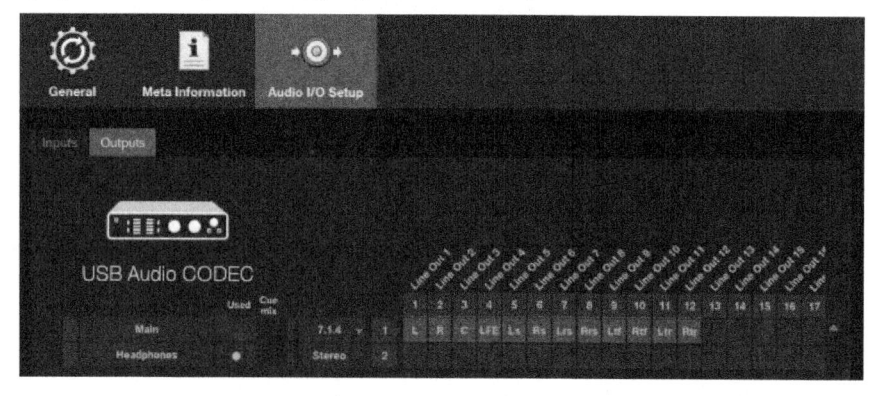

Figure 14.3: Default speaker mapping for a 7.1.4 configuration

6. Drag the speaker names (**L**, **R**, **C**, etc.) to the desired outputs on your audio interface. For example, if your subwoofer is connected to **Line Out 8** on your interface, click on **LFE** and drag it to **Line Out 8**.

7. Once you've assigned each output to the correct speaker, click on **Make Default** if you want Studio One to remember this configuration for your future Songs.

8. Click **OK**.

If you're working with Dolby Atmos and you'd like to use only headphones for monitoring, the **Headphones** section below the **Main** output (as seen in *Figure 14.3*) has got you covered. Just plug your headphones into the headphone jack on your audio interface, and you'll be good to go.

Awesome! You have just configured Studio One to work with spatial audio. Now, you're ready to create awesome three-dimensional experiences for the world to enjoy. Let's jump right in.

Formatting tracks for spatial audio

Once you are in your new Song, the workflow for creating productions is no different from what we have already discussed in the preceding chapters. The only thing you need to watch out for is to select the correct configuration when creating new tracks. Let's take care of that right now:

1. Click the **Add Tracks** button or press *Ctrl + T*/*Cmd + T*. This will open the **Add Tracks** dialog box.

2. Click on the **Audio** tab.

3. Using the **Format** pull-down menu, select the format you'd like to use for this track. For most purposes, you'll want to choose **Mono** (dialogue, vocals, a single instrument, etc.) or **Stereo** (sound effects, ambient noises, background music, etc.):

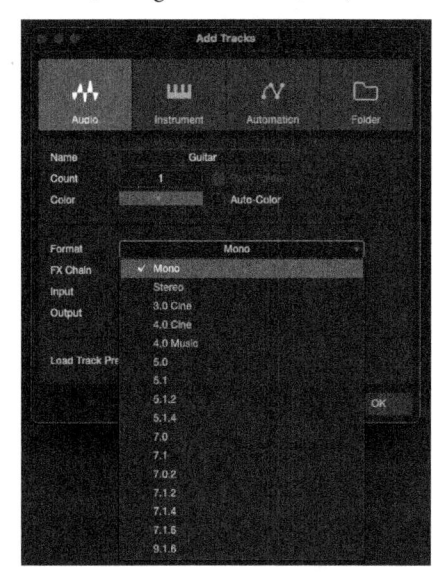

Figure 14.4: Creating a new track for spatial audio

4. Click **OK**.

From here on, continue to work with Studio One like you always have. The workflow will only change when you reach the mixing phase, which we will discuss in the next section.

Mixing and exporting spatial audio material

Traditional stereo mixing involves creating a soundscape across two audio channels: left and right. Sounds are positioned between the left and right speakers using the pan control on each track or channel. This creates the illusion of depth but it's constrained to a single dimension. Spatial audio mixing, on the other hand, involves creating a three-dimensional sound field where sounds can move around the listener. Sounds are positioned in a 360-degree sphere, offering height, depth, and width. This calls for a more intricate approach to panning, and we'll kick off this section by exploring Studio One's spatial panning capabilities.

Using the Surround Panner

Once you've created your Song and configured Studio One for spatial audio production as described earlier in this chapter, you'll notice that the pan controls for tracks and channels on the **Mix** window now look very different. This new type of pan control is called **Surround Panner**. Double-click on any channel's pan control (highlighted in *Figure 14.5*) to open the **Surround Panner** in its own window:

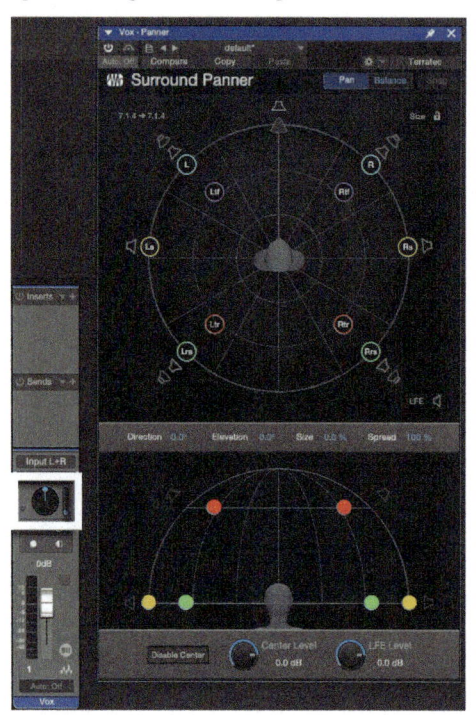

Figure 14.5: The Surround Panner window

The top half of the **Surround Panner** window shows the target speaker configuration for your production. In *Figure 14.5*, my target speaker configuration is **7.1.4**, as indicated in the top-left corner of the **Surround Panner** window. So, there are seven speaker icons placed outside the circle, representing the speaker array that will be used in the listening environment. Right in the middle of the circle stands a human figure, representing the lucky soul who gets to enjoy our production. Studio One's instruction manual lovingly dubs it **The Listener**, so we'll keep the tradition alive and call it that, too.

In order to pan the audio on a channel to any point between the seven speakers we just mentioned, all you need to do is to grab the arrow (currently extending from The Listener's nose toward the top of the circle) and point it to where you want the sound on that channel to come from. Moving the arrowhead closer to or farther away from The Listener will affect the signal's size. If you just want to change the position of the sound without changing its size, you can use the **Size** lock button at the top right (with a padlock icon) to lock the size at its current setting.

You can click on any of the bubbles on the circle (labeled **L**, **R**, **Ls**, **Rs**, etc.) and drag them to change the spread of audio on a channel. Bringing the bubbles closer together will make the sound tight and focused as if it's coming from a single spot. Spacing them farther apart will spread the sound over a wider spectrum, making the sound big and spacious.

The bottom half of the **Surround Panner** window will only be available if your output configuration has height speakers. This section of the window is used for controlling the **elevation** of the signal on a channel. You can place the sound at The Listener's ear level, on the height speakers, or anywhere in between. Just click on the bubbles and drag them to control the elevation.

Everything on the **Surround Panner** window can be automated. Just select your favorite automation mode in the top-left corner of the window (currently labeled **Auto: Off**), hit play, and get creative. We talked about automation modes back in *Chapter 11*, so you might want to visit that chapter to brush up on your automation skills.

Surround Panner is the basic tool for positioning sounds when working with spatial audio, but there are further options available if you're working with Dolby Atmos. We'll explore those options next.

Understanding beds and objects

Dolby Atmos expands the creative possibilities for sound design and mixing, enabling a more engaging and lifelike auditory experience. As we mentioned at the beginning of this chapter, part of this is achieved by adding height speakers to the equation, creating a fully immersive experience, including the vertical dimension.

Another key point in the Dolby Atmos paradigm is the introduction of two concepts: beds and objects. These are revolutionary concepts that will change the way you look at your mixes, so let's break them down:

- **Beds** are static audio channels (similar to traditional surround channels) used as a foundation for a mix. These are typically used to handle audio elements that don't require precise movement or positioning, such as background music, ambiance, or other non-dynamic sounds.

- **Objects** are individual audio elements that can be precisely positioned and moved anywhere within a three-dimensional space. Unlike traditional channel-based audio, objects are not tied to specific speakers; instead, they include metadata that tells the playback system their position and movement in the 3D environment. This allows the Dolby Atmos Renderer to dynamically adapt the mix to any speaker configuration, ensuring a consistent and immersive experience. Objects are ideal for sounds that require dynamic spatialization, such as a helicopter flying overhead or footsteps moving around the listener.

At this point, you may be thinking that since we can automate every move on **Surround Panner**, we can already make sounds move around, so what is it that makes the concept of objects so revolutionary? Let me explain. Understanding the difference between traditional surround panning and object-based motion is essential for working in Dolby Atmos, so let's dig a little deeper. Here's a comparison:

- In a traditional surround mix, a sound is assigned to specific speaker channels (e.g., front left and rear right). When automating panning, you're essentially *controlling the level distribution of the sound between these channels*. If the playback system changes (e.g., you mix for a 7.1 configuration but the end listener has a 5.1 setup), the panning information is lost and the spatial fidelity diminishes.

- In Dolby Atmos, objects are freed from fixed channels. Instead of being tied to specific speakers, objects are given 3D positional metadata that tells the playback system *where the sound should come from in space*. The system then calculates how to distribute the sound across the available speakers (or headphones) to recreate that position. Even if the playback system changes, objects are rendered to fit the existing playback system, and sounds can move seamlessly and convincingly in a sphere around the listener.

In Studio One, when you create a new track, by default, it is considered a bed. The position of beds is controlled by the **Surround Panner**, which we explored in the previous section. Objects have their own panning tool, which will be our next topic.

Using the Object Panner

The **Object Panner**, as the name indicates, controls the position of sound objects in 3D space. To work with the **Object Panner** tool, we must first let Studio One know that we want to treat a channel as an object rather than a bed. To do that, simply right-click on the pan control for that channel and select **Spatial Object Panner**:

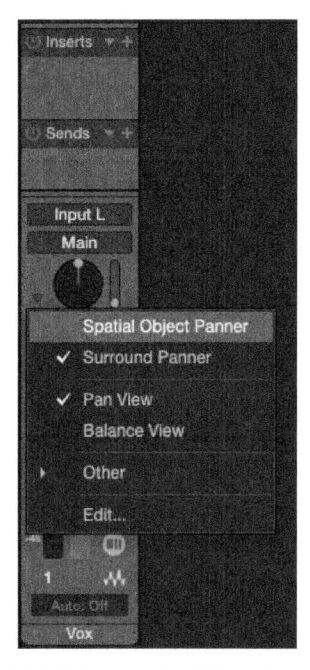

Figure 14.6: Selecting the Object Panner tool

This will designate the channel as an object in Dolby Atmos terms, and open the **Object Panner** window:

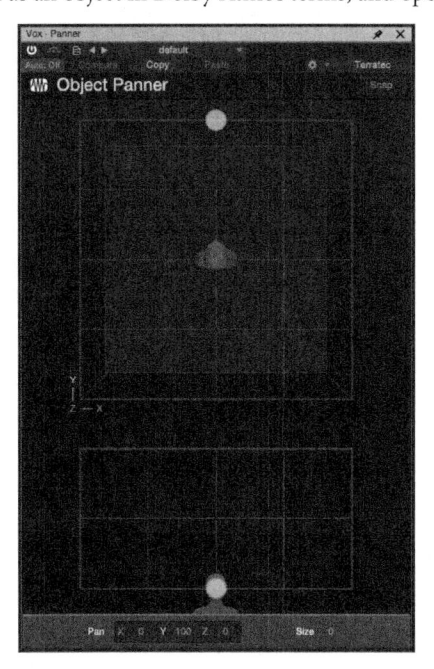

Figure 14.7: The Object Panner window

Object Panner looks like a simplified version of **Surround Panner**, and look who's back – our trusty reference, The Listener, in the center of the interface once again.

Using the **Object Panner** tool is as easy as it gets: just click on the object bubble and move it to where you want the sound to come from in 3D space. Use the top half of the window to place sound horizontally, and the bottom half to place it vertically.

It goes without saying that the movement of this bubble can be automated, so there's lots of room for creativity.

The Dolby Atmos Renderer

The Dolby Atmos Renderer is a plug-in that lets you interact with the Dolby Atmos algorithm. When you select **Dolby Atmos** in the **New** document window (as we saw in *Figure 14.1*), **Dolby Atmos Renderer** is automatically added to a special slot on the **Main** output channel. Click on this slot (highlighted in *Figure 14.8*) to open the **Dolby Atmos Renderer** interface and get ready to meet The Listener yet again:

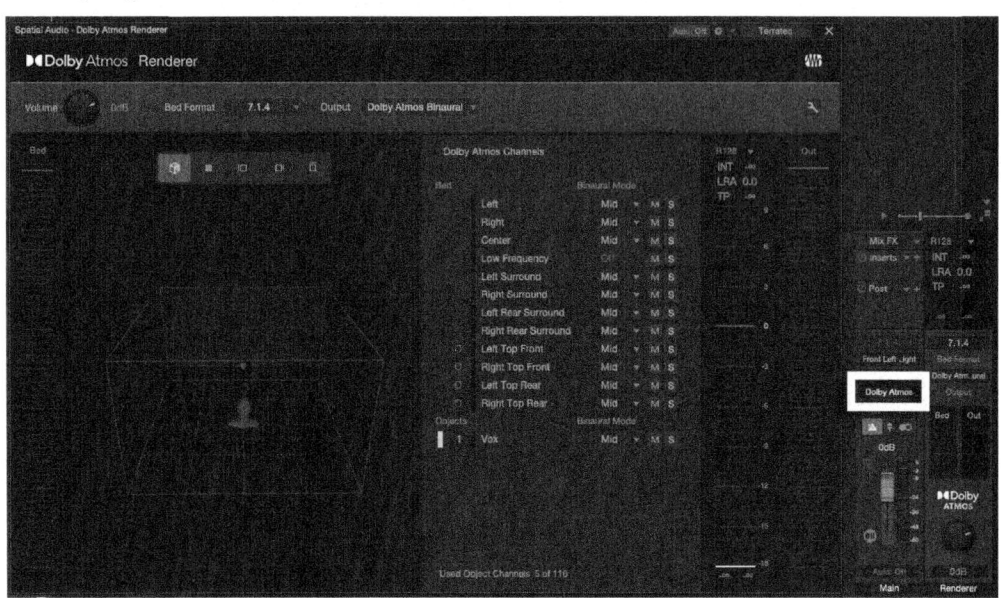

Figure 14.8: The Dolby Atmos Renderer

Two settings that we discussed in the *Creating a new Song for spatial audio* section (**Bed Format** and **Output**) appear here once again, at the top of the window. If you're going to use headphones for monitoring your production, make sure **Dolby Atmos Binaural** is selected on the **Output** pull-down menu.

The 3D room display on the left side of the window shows the positions of objects you created, as we discussed in the *Using the Object Panner* section. The center of the interface has a **Dolby Atmos Channels** list, where you can mute or solo each channel using their respective **M** or **S** buttons. Finally, the metering section on the right side of the window provides information on the loudness levels of signals passing through the renderer, so you can tell whether or not your project complies with the loudness standards set by your target listening environment. We will talk about loudness levels in *Chapter 15*.

We are now ready to move on to the final step in our spatial audio workflow.

Exporting spatial audio material

If your production involves traditional surround formats such as 5.1, export your final audio file as follows:

1. On the top menu, go to **Song** and click on **Export Mixdown…**.
2. This will open the **Export Mixdown** window, which we explored in *Chapter 13*. Set the options in this window as described therein.
3. Click **OK**. Studio One will create a multi-channel `.wav` file, adhering to the number of discrete channels in your selected format (e.g., six channels for a 5.1 configuration).

If you worked with Dolby Atmos, export your final audio file using the following steps:

1. On the top menu, go to **Song** and click on **Export Spatial Audio…**. This will open the **Export Spatial Audio** window:

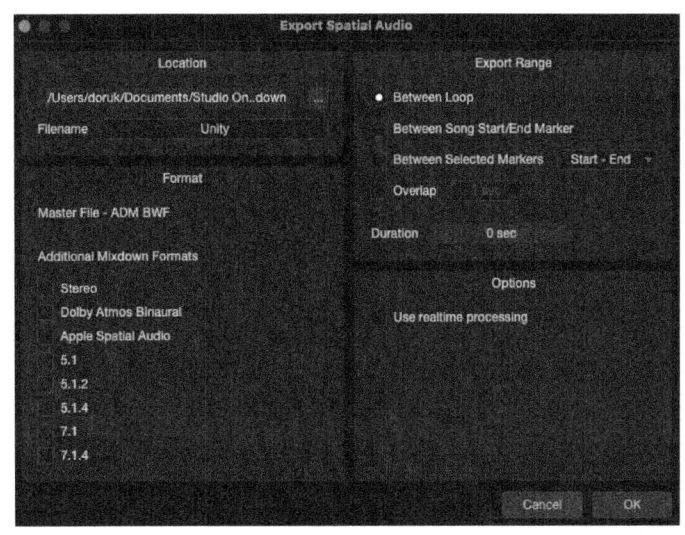

Figure 14.9: The Export Spatial Audio window

2. Adjust the **Location** and **Export Range** settings. These are identical to those in the **Export Mixdown** window.

3. An **ADM BWF** file, which is the file format required by Dolby Atmos, will be created automatically. If you want to create additional files in different formats, select them in the **Format** section of the window.

4. Click **OK**.

This is all you need to do in order to export your Song using Dolby Atmos.

Summary

In this chapter, we discussed and compared various spatial audio formats and explored Studio One's spatial audio capabilities. You configured Studio One for your production environment and target playback configuration and then created your first Song to work with spatial audio. Finally, we talked about how to mix and export your productions using Studio One's built-in spatial audio tools.

In the next chapter, we will go back to working with stereo material. We will explore the **Project** page; a unique environment that lets you perform mastering operations on your Songs.

15
Navigating the Project Page and Producing Final Masters

In the music industry, mastering is often regarded as a mysterious blend of art, science, and magic that only a few exceptional people with supernatural ears and expensive equipment can perform. While it's true that experience, a good pair of trained ears, and the right equipment will definitely have an edge, technology has reached a point where anyone in a modest home studio can create perfectly good masters of their music for publication in digital music platforms with some basic knowledge.

Studio One raises the bar in making this technology even more accessible by virtue of its **Project** page, an environment dedicated specifically to mastering. The tools available on this page put the mastering process within reach of every musician, regardless of their level of experience.

In this chapter, we will explore the **Project** page and learn how to produce final masters that meet the standards of digital music platforms. We will cover the following topics:

- Creating a new Project and navigating the **Project** page
- Mastering the **Project** page
- Rendering final masters for publishing and delivery

Technical requirements

In order to follow along with this chapter, you will need to have Studio One activated on your computer.

> **Important note**
> Most of the tools available on the **Project** page are also available as plug-ins on the **Song** page, so most of the methods we will cover in this chapter can be performed on the **Song** page as well.

Creating a new Project and navigating the Project page

Mastering is the final step in the music production process. It involves the preparation and enhancement of a mix for distribution on various platforms, such as streaming services, CDs, vinyl, or digital downloads.

Our goal in mastering is to optimize the sound of a mix to ensure that the final product sounds great on a wide range of playback systems, from high-end studio monitors to tiny earbuds. This is certainly not an easy task, but Studio One makes the entire process as streamlined as possible with the **Project** page, an innovative approach that is not available in any competing music production software at the time of writing.

The **Project** page is a mastering environment that is tightly integrated with the **Song** page to create a unified, efficient workflow that covers all stages of music production, from recording to mastering. It is similar to the **Song** page in many ways, so most of the tools and features will be familiar once you start working with it.

Let's start by creating a new Project and exploring the **Project** page interface.

Creating a new Project

There are two possible scenarios in which you would want to create a new Project:

- You have one or more songs that were previously mixed and rendered as stereo .wav files, and you want to work on those files to create a final master for distribution
- You have a Song, a work in progress, that you've mixed on Studio One's **Song** page, and you are now ready to take it through the mastering process

The procedure for creating a new Project is different for these scenarios. Let's take a look at each.

Creating a new Project for existing .wav files

If you have one or more songs that have already been mixed and rendered as .wav files, follow these steps to create a new Project for them:

1. On the **Start** page, click on the **New…** button, which will open the **New** window:

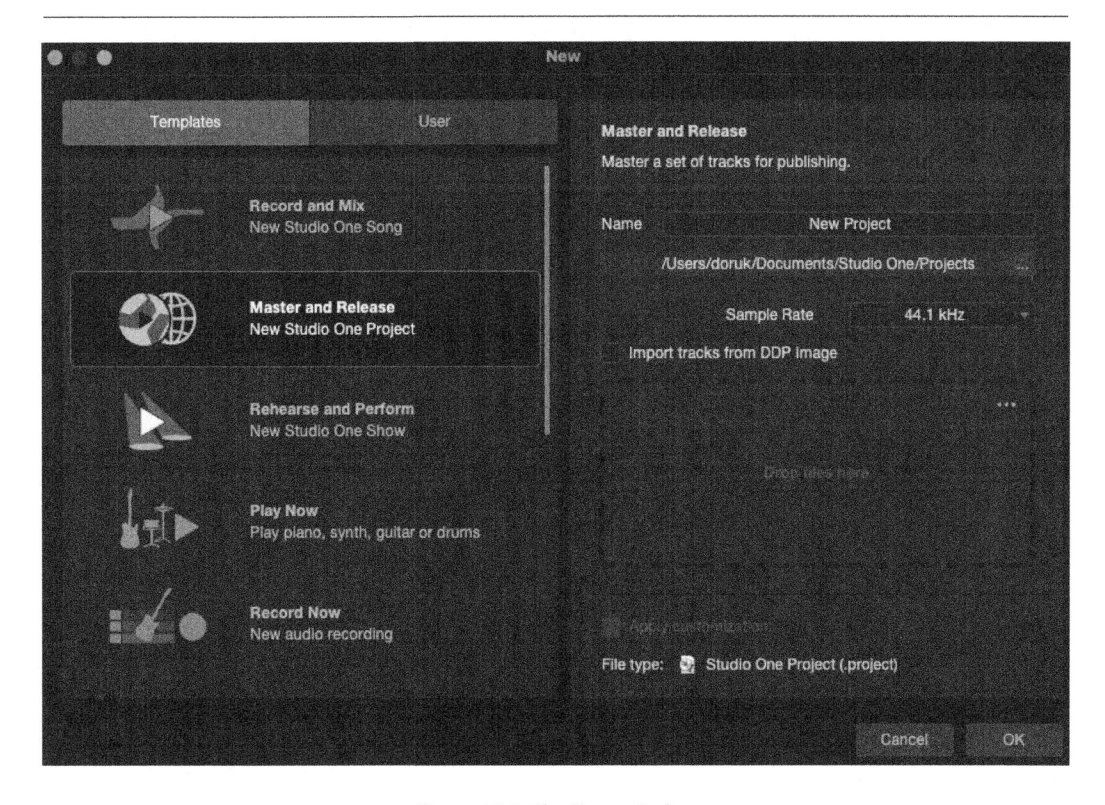

Figure 15.1: The New window

2. On the left side of this window, select **Master and Release**.
3. On the right side of the window, type a name and select a folder for the Project you're about to create.
4. If your final masters will be uploaded to streaming services and digital music platforms, set **Sample Rate** to **44.1 kHz**. If they will be used in video post-production, set it to **48 kHz**.
5. Open Explorer (Windows) or Finder (Mac) and locate the .wav files you'd like to work on. Drag and drop these files into the box labeled **Drop files here**.
6. Click **OK**.

This will create a new Project, with your .wav files laid out across the timeline in the **Project** window.

Creating a new Project from the Song page

If you've finished mixing a Song on the **Song** page and you're ready to start mastering it, you can send it directly to the **Project** page from within the **Song** page. Here's how to do it:

1. On the top menu of the **Song** page, go to **Song** and select **Add to Project**. You'll be prompted to create a new Project with the current title of your Song. Here, I'm about to create a new Project for my Song titled `Pole Star`:

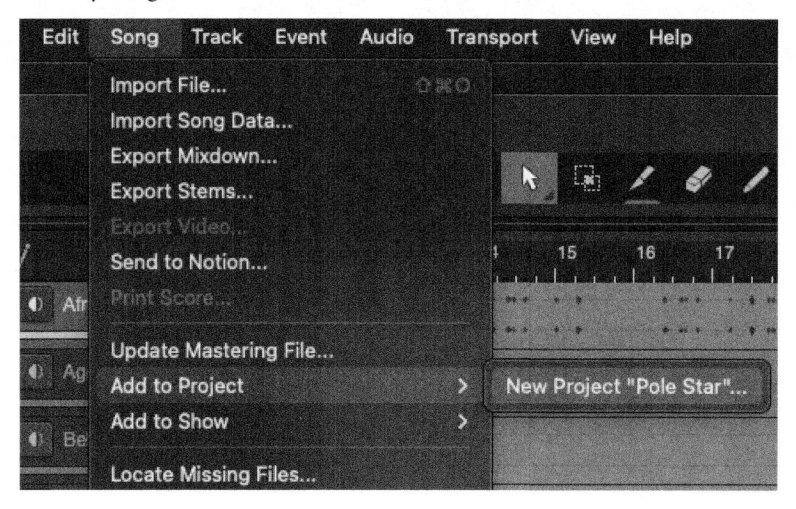

Figure 15.2: Creating a new Project on the Song page

2. Once you click on the prompt to create a new Project, you'll be taken to the **New Project** window:

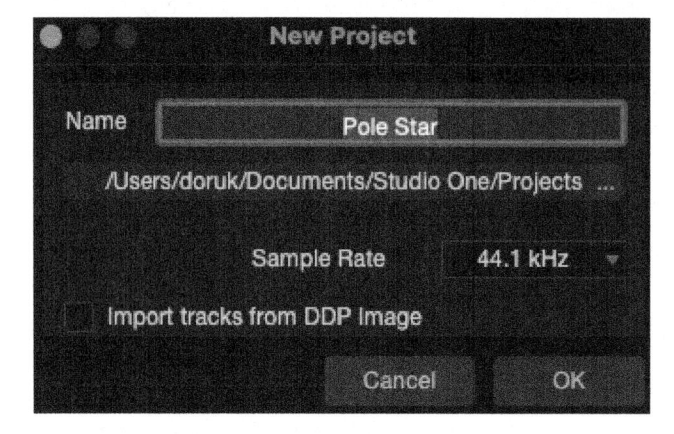

Figure 15.3: The New Project window

3. Give your Project file a name and select a folder that you want to save it in.

4. If your final masters will be uploaded to streaming services and digital music platforms, set **Sample Rate** to **44.1 kHz**. If they will be used in video post-production, set it to **48 kHz**.

5. Click **OK**.

Studio One will automatically bounce your Song to a stereo file, create a new Project, and place the bounced file on the new Project's timeline.

Now, let's explore the **Project** page and become acquainted with its set of mastering tools.

Navigating the Project page

The **Project** page looks like a stripped-down version of the **Song** page, so it shouldn't be too unfamiliar:

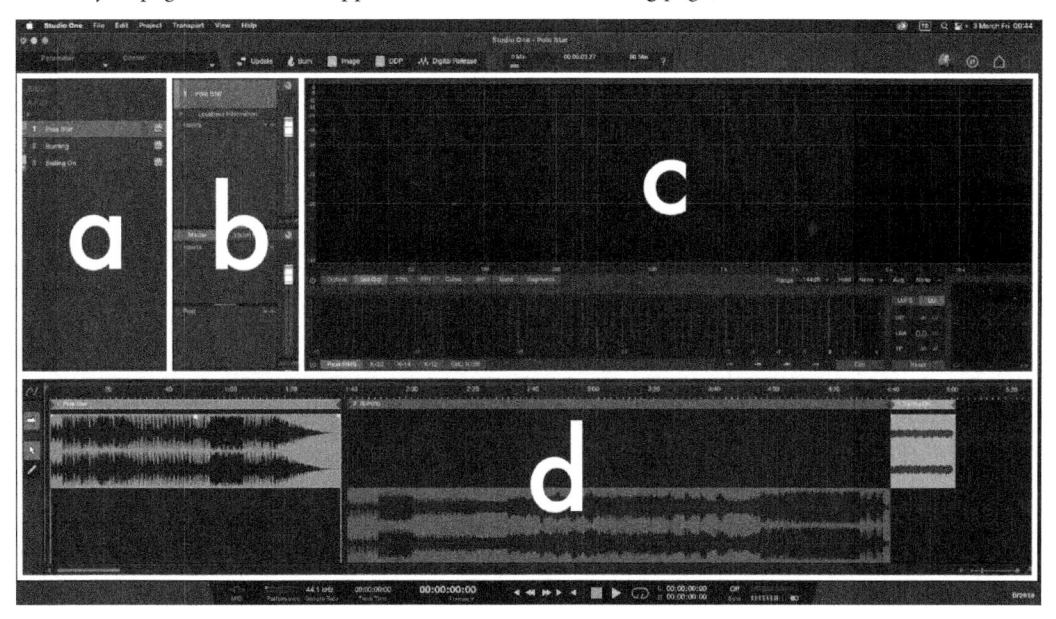

Figure 15.4: The Project page

Let's break it down:

- **Track column** (**a** in *Figure 15.4*): This column lists all the Songs you've added to your Project. Change the order of your Songs simply by dragging them up or down in this list.

- **Effects racks** (**b**): These work just like the **Inserts** racks in the **Song** window and allow you to add effects to individual tracks or the entire Project. We will talk about working with effects in the next section, under *Adding effects plug-ins*.

- **Metering tools (c)**: This section is home to three measurement tools that are essential during the mastering process: Spectrum meter, level/loudness meter, and phase meter. We will discuss these tools in the *Using the metering tools* section.
- **Track lane (d)**: This section displays the waveforms for the Songs in your Project and allows you to perform basic editing operations on them.

The similarity between the **Project** page and the **Song** page is not a coincidence. There is a tight integration between the two pages, which may forever change the way you master your music. Next, we'll explore this integration and see how it can enhance your production workflow.

Integration between the Song and Project pages

In a traditional music production workflow, mixing and mastering are two distinct processes:

- You finish mixing, bounce the final mix to a single file, and start mastering that file
- If the song needs to be revised, you go back to the mix, revise it, render the file again, and bring it back to your mastering environment

When you work on an album with several songs, keeping track of these revisions can quickly become overwhelming. You may find that you end up mastering an old version of a song because you forgot to bring the updated version into your mastering session.

Studio One takes care of this problem by introducing close integration between the mixing and mastering workflows. The **Song** page and **Project** page are intelligently aware of each other so that changes you make on one page are known to the other. This allows Studio One to keep track of all revisions and always keep your mastering Projects up to date with the most current versions of your Songs, without you having to update your mastering files manually.

To illustrate how this integration works, let's go back to my Song, `Pole Star`. This was a Song I created and mixed on the **Song** page, and as you will remember from *Figure 15.2*, I used the **Add to Project** command to add this Song to a new mastering Project. Using this command allowed Studio One to create a link between the two versions of `Pole Star` on the **Song** page and the **Project** page.

Let's say that halfway through mastering `Pole Star` on the **Project** page, I find that something is not right in the arrangement of the Song, and I decide to go back to the **Song** page to fix it. Here's how to do that easily:

1. In the **Track** column, click on the **Edit** button (marked by a wrench icon) next to the name of the Song:

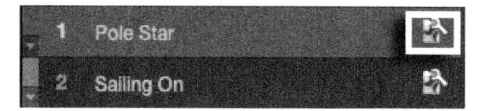

Figure 15.5: The Edit button on the Track column

2. This will automatically open the **Song** page for `Pole Star`, where I can revise it to my heart's content. When I'm done with revisions, I save and close the **Song** page.

3. The next time I open the **Project** page to continue mastering `Pole Star`, Studio One will ask whether I want to update the mastering file to reflect the revisions that I've made:

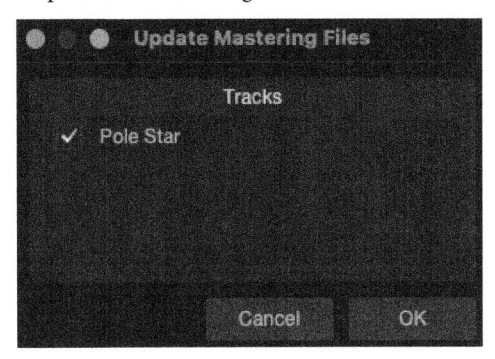

Figure 15.6: The Update Mastering Files dialog box

4. When I click **OK** in this box, Studio One will open the **Song** page for `Pole Star`, bounce the revised version of the Song, and update the mastering file to reflect my revisions. Now, I can keep working in the **Project** window, safe in the knowledge that I'm working on the most current version.

This level of integration streamlines the workflow and saves you the trouble of keeping track of different versions of your Songs, allowing you to focus on what really matters – presenting your music in the best possible light.

Now that we know the basics of the **Project** page, let's dive in and start mastering our Songs to perfection.

Mastering the Project page

Once you add your Songs to a Project, they will be listed on the **Track** column and displayed as events on the **Track** lane, as we saw in *Figure 15.4*. Now, let's walk through the process of mastering these Songs, from start to finish.

Entering metadata

Metadata is the essential information about a music track that includes, among other things, its title, artist, album, genre, and year of release. This information is embedded in the final audio file and helps music distribution platforms categorize and distribute the music correctly. It also helps with royalty collection and ensures that the artist receives proper credit for their work. If you're planning to release your songs, you'll definitely want to have metadata embedded in them, so let's take care of this before we go into deeper topics.

To enter metadata for a track, locate the track on the **Track** column and click on the **Show/hide more** button (a tiny white triangle, highlighted in *Figure 15.7*) next to its title. This will open the metadata window for that track:

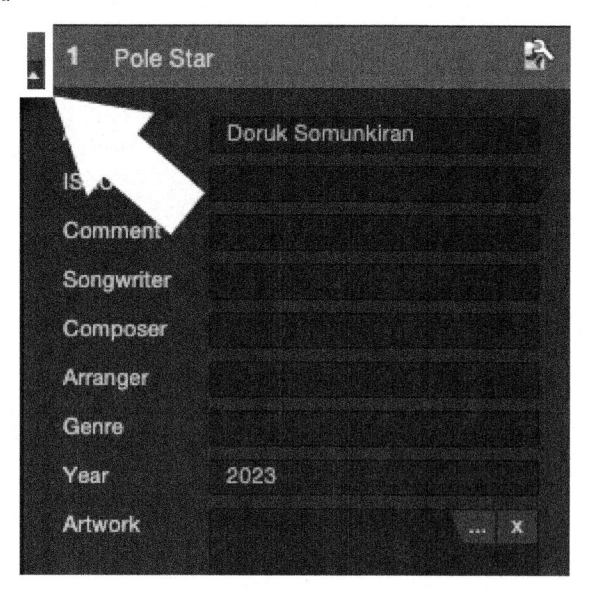

Figure 15.7: The metadata window

Fill out the fields in this window so that distribution platforms get to know your song better.

If you already have an **International Standard Recording Code** (**ISRC**) for your song, type it in here. ISRC is a unique identifier that is issued by music publishers. It will be used by distribution networks to keep track of how many times your song has been streamed or downloaded.

You can also add artwork to your Song, which will be displayed on its page on music streaming platforms (the maximum image size is 1,400 x 1,400 pixels).

Once you've completed all the applicable fields, minimize this window by clicking the **Show/hide more** button once again. Metadata will be saved next time you save the Project.

Sequencing tracks

When you add tracks to a Project, they appear on the **Track** lane and the **Track** column in the order that you add them. The sequence of the tracks is not a big deal if you plan to export them individually for streaming platforms, but it will be important if you want to release the tracks as an album on a CD. (Remember CDs? Yes, we still use them!)

To change the sequence of your tracks, simply drag them up and down in the **Track** column to put them in the right order. The changes you make here will be reflected on the **Track** lane as well.

When you listen to an album on a CD, you will notice that there is usually a brief pause when going from one song to another. If you're releasing an album on CD and want to have that type of pause between your tracks as well, follow these steps:

1. On the **Track** column, click on the **Normal** button (**a** in *Figure 15.8*) to expand the tracks:

Figure 15.8: Inserting pauses between tracks

2. Use the pause field (**b** in *Figure 15.8*) to enter a value, in seconds, for the length of the pause you'd like to have between a track and the track preceding it. You can set this value to anything between 0 and 10 seconds. Two seconds is a commonly used value. If you're working on an album where one song blends seamlessly into the next, set this value to zero seconds. That way, playback will continue without any pauses but listeners will still be able to jump to the beginning of tracks using the controls on their media players.

Now, we are ready to dive into the deeper end of mastering.

Editing tracks on the Project page

The **Project** page allows you to edit your tracks before packing them for final delivery. While the set of tools available for editing is not as extensive as on the **Song** page, the modes of operation are similar, so if you've skimmed over our discussion of editing tools in *Chapter 7*, now is a good time to take a closer look at that chapter to brush up on your editing skills.

308   Navigating the Project Page and Producing Final Masters

The **Arrow** tool is the only editing tool available on the **Project** page. Pick it up by pressing *1* on your keyboard or by clicking on its icon on the left side of the **Track** lane:

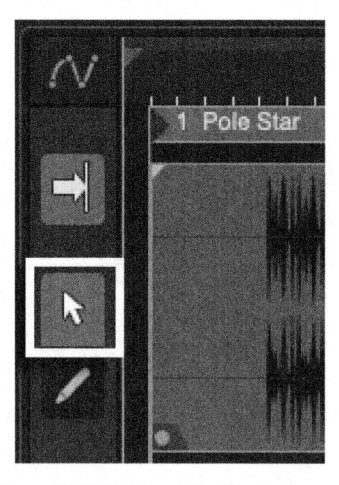

Figure 15.9: Tools on the Project page

Here are the editing operations you can perform with the **Arrow** tool on the **Project** page:

- Drag tracks to move them on the timeline. This can be useful to arrange the sequence and positioning of tracks.
- Resize tracks to trim gaps of silence at their beginning or end. To do so, hover your mouse at the left or right edge of a track; the mouse cursor will turn to a double-headed arrow:

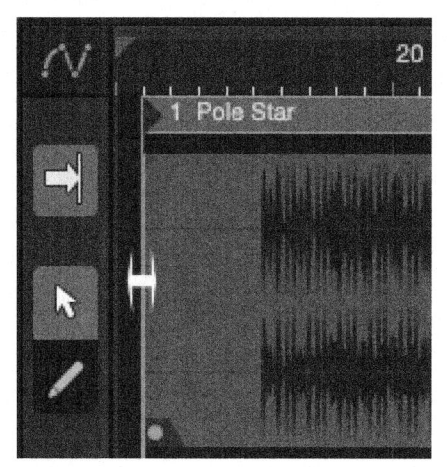

Figure 15.10: Resizing a track

Click and drag this double-headed arrow to resize the track and trim the gap of silence at the beginning.

- Perform fades at the beginning and end of tracks. Here is a fade-out happening at the end of a track:

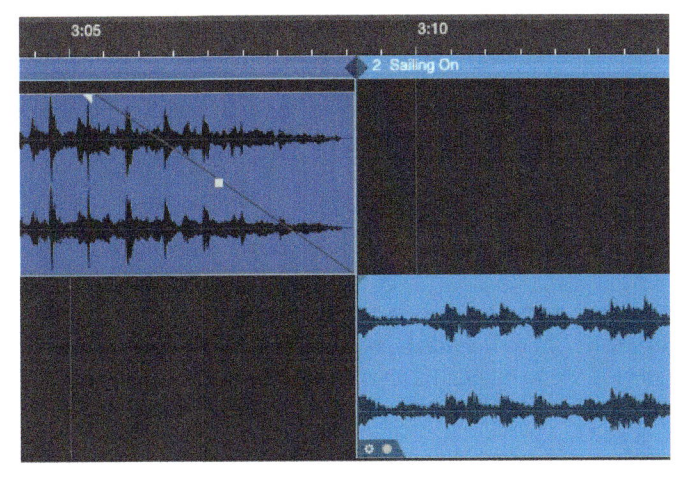

Figure 15.11: Adding a fade-out

To perform an automatic **crossfade** between two tracks so that one fades out as the other fades in, do the following:

I. Arrange the tracks on the timeline so that the end of the first song will overlap the beginning of the first song.

II. Select both tracks.

III. Press *X* on your keyboard. This will add the crossfade:

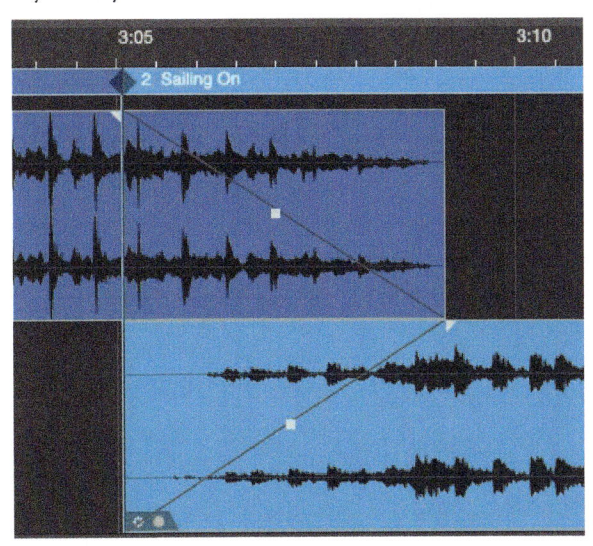

Figure 15.12: Adding a crossfade

Although the **Split** tool is not available on the **Project** page, you can still split a track into two separate tracks. This can be useful to apply different effects plug-ins to different sections of a song. To split a track, simply place the playback cursor where you want to split it and press *Alt + X* (Windows) or *Option + X* (Mac) on your keyboard.

Now that we've edited our tracks and arranged them the way we want them to be, we are ready to enhance them to make sure they sound great in any playback environment. We will do that by using effects plug-ins.

Adding effects plug-ins

The purpose of using effects in mastering is to create a final product that sounds great and accurately represents the original mix, while also enhancing its overall sound quality and making it as engaging and enjoyable as possible for the listener. Effects can be used to correct any issues with the mix, give it warmth and character, and ensure it conforms to the specifications required by streaming platforms.

The following is a list of the most common uses of effects in mastering:

- **Equalizer**: Use this to adjust the tonal balance of the song. If some frequency ranges in your mix are too dominant and others are weak, this will disrupt your song's tonal balance and make the whole production sound unprofessional. Dynamic equalizers such as **Pro EQ**[3] are excellent tools to fix such problems in mastering because they only kick in when a certain threshold is reached, staying out of the way for the rest of the song.

- **Compressor**: Use this to even out the dynamic range of the song and make it more consistent. Plug-ins that emulate vintage analog compressors are usually preferred in mastering because their slower response times make them more gentle; aggressive amounts of compression can suck the life out of a song by taking away too much of its dynamic range. Emulated analog compressors such as the **Tube**, **Everest C100A**, and **Brit Comp** options in **Fat Channel** also add some upper harmonics and other artifacts to a song, which may cause the instruments to blend better together. A compressor used to achieve this blending effect is sometimes referred to as a **glue compressor**.

- **Stereo imaging**: Stereo imaging refers to the perception of the sound's placement and width across the stereo field. A well-controlled stereo image can create a sense of depth, width, and separation. Use an imaging plug-in to enhance the stereo image and create a more immersive listening experience. On the **Project** page, this can be achieved by using the **Binaural Pan** plug-in.

- **Limiter**: Use this to optimize the volume of the sound without exceeding a certain level. **Limiter**[2] is perfect for this task.

For more information on these effects, see *Chapter 12*.

One important thing to note when working with effects in mastering is that you have to be subtle. When you're mixing a song, you can insert an equalizer on the guitar track and boost a certain frequency by 10 dB if that serves your purpose. However, if you try to boost that much in mastering, you will end up boosting that frequency range for all the instruments in the song, and it will sound horrible. So, use broad brush strokes in the mix, but only apply minor finishing touches in mastering. The same logic applies to all other plug-ins as well.

Now, let's take a look at how you can add effects when mastering your songs in Studio One. The **Effects** rack on the **Project** page is divided into two parts:

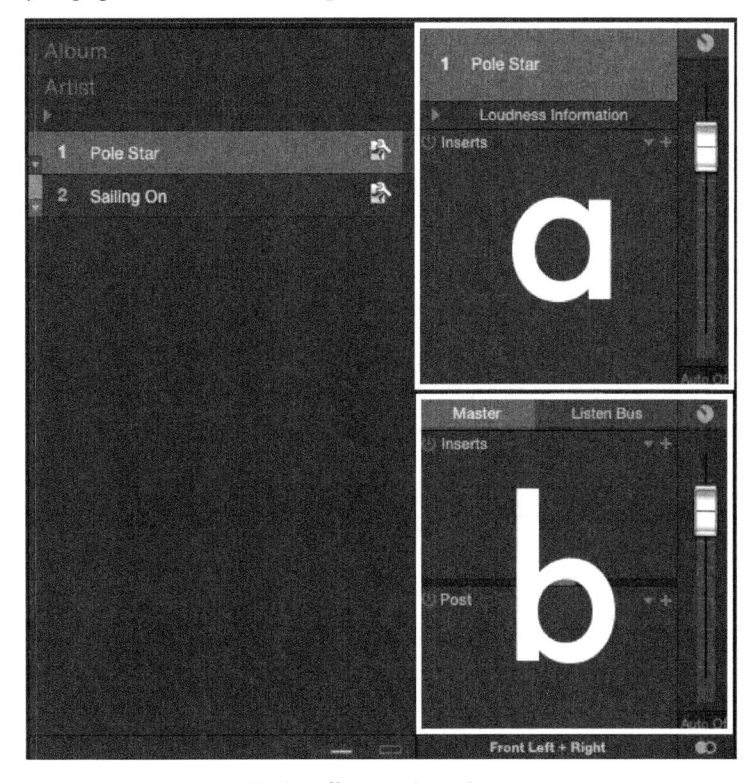

Figure 15.13: The Effects rack on the Project page

The first rack (**a** in *Figure 15.13*) is called the **Track Device** rack and allows you to add effects to the song that is currently selected in the **Track** column on the left. You can use the **Track Device** rack to add effects on a per-song basis; this is especially useful when you're mastering several songs for an album because you have the added goal of maintaining consistency when going from one song to the next.

For example, if a song sounds brighter compared to the others and you feel that this will deviate from the overall *sound* you're trying to achieve on the album, select the song in the **Track** column, insert an equalizer in the **Track Device** rack, and tame the offending frequencies. The equalizer will be applied to that song only, making it more consistent with the other songs.

The second rack (**b** in *Figure 15.13*) is called the **Master Device** rack. The effects you insert here are applied globally to all the tracks in the Project. Use this rack for effects that are meant to add an overall sonic character to all of the songs (such as plug-ins that add analog color and saturation), and for effects that optimize and control the global loudness of the entire album (such as **Limiter**[2]).

Both the **Track Device** rack and the **Master Device** rack are insert racks, just like the ones we saw on the Mix console of the **Song** page. Adding plug-ins to these racks works the same way – just drag a plug-in from the **Browse** window and drop it on the rack you want to use.

It is worth noting once again that the order of these plug-ins is important. Think of the signal as flowing from the top of each rack to the bottom. What comes before a plug-in will significantly alter the way it responds, so keep this in mind when creating your signal chain. You can click and drag the plug-ins inside a rack to change their order.

Using the metering tools

Metering tools are audio analysis tools used to measure and display various aspects of an audio signal. These tools are included in mastering because they help us make accurate and informed decisions, which ultimately result in a higher-quality final product.

In a typical home studio, where the acoustics are less than ideal, relying solely on your ears for mixing and mastering may be misleading. In such cases, having access to accurate metering tools is a great advantage since these tools provide visual feedback, with precise and detailed information about the audio signal.

It's not surprising that metering tools take up most of the space on the **Project** page (marked **c** back in *Figure 15.4*). There are three metering tools on this page, with several customization options to fit different usage scenarios. Let's explore each of them.

The spectrum meter

The **spectrum meter** displays the frequency content of your songs. It helps you identify any frequency imbalances or problems that need to be addressed, such as resonant frequencies or excessive low end. If you're mastering several tracks for an album, you can also use the spectrum meter to compare their frequency distributions with each other. For example, if you have tiny speakers in your home studio and cannot hear too much of the bass frequencies, the spectrum meter will let you know whether one of the songs has way more bass content compared to the other songs.

The spectrum meter has several options at the bottom of its interface, allowing you to fine-tune its display format for your needs:

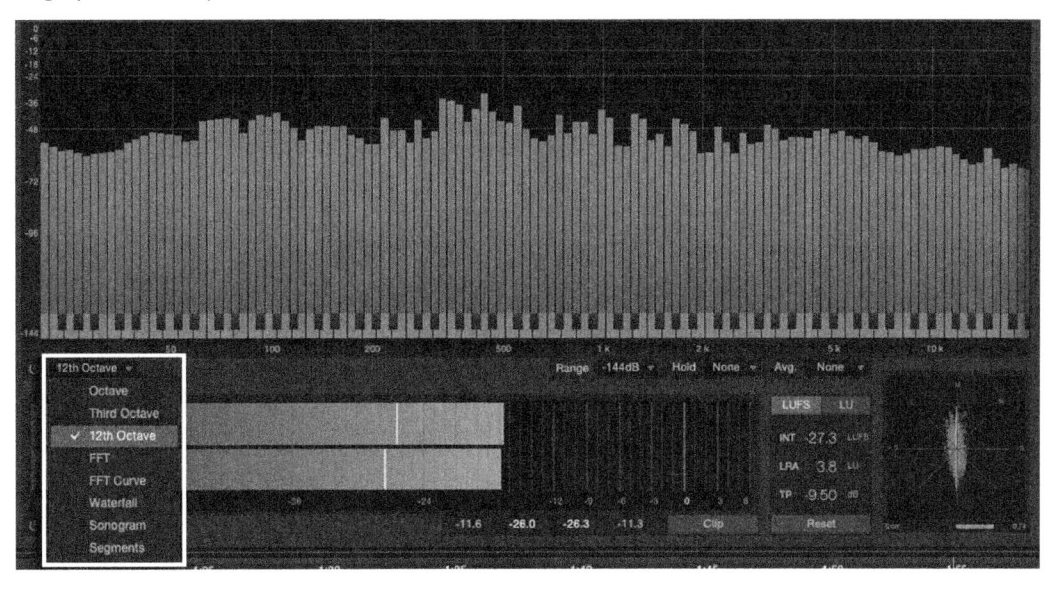

Figure 15.14: Spectrum meter

Let's take a look at some of the options:

- The **Display Mode** selector (highlighted in *Figure 15.14*) in the bottom-left corner offers several different display modes. A discussion of these modes is far beyond the scope of this book; however, we can create a shortlist of the options that you're most likely to use:

    - If you come from a musician background, and musical notes make more sense to you than frequencies expressed in Hertz, then use the **12th Octave** option. When you select this option, a piano keyboard will be overlaid below the spectrum display, allowing you to see the musical notes that all frequency bands correspond to.

    - If you want to get more detailed and responsive feedback for the frequency distribution of your songs, use the **FFT** (**Fast Fourier Transform**) option. This is a very precise frequency analysis mode that will help you pinpoint problem frequencies at a glance.

- Use the **Hold** option to hold the peak values for each frequency band so that you don't miss a momentary spike when you blink.

- Use the **Avg.** (**average**) setting to add a continuous line that shows the average level of the signal in each frequency band. This continuous line shows the perceived loudness of a frequency band, whereas the rapidly moving bars in the spectrum display show momentary values.

If you're just starting out with the spectrum meter, just add several reference tracks to your Project page, play them, and observe how the Spectrum Meter looks. (A reference track is a piece of music that's been mixed and produced professionally.) Go for tracks that you are familiar with. That way, you'll learn how to read the Spectrum Meter in no time.

The level/loudness meter

The **level/loudness meter** displays the amplitude and perceived loudness of your songs and helps you ensure that your songs are at the appropriate level, with no distortion or clipping. It has several display options as well, which can be found in the lower-left corner:

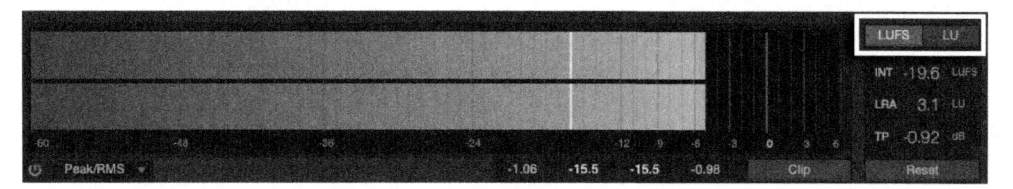

Figure 15.15: The level/loudness meter

For a great majority of music production, you can leave this at **Peak/RMS**, its default value.

On the right side of the Level/Loudness Meter, you'll see the **loudness display**, which provides essential information that will affect how your songs are delivered to your fans. Let's clarify two vital readings shown in this display:

- **INT** is short for **Integrated LUFS**, the latter of which is short for **Loudness Units Full Scale**. This is a measure of the average loudness of an audio signal over a certain period of time. In simple terms, it's a measure of your song's perceived overall loudness.
- **TP** stands for **True Peak**. This is simply the highest level the audio signal reaches during your entire song, measured in decibels.

We will discuss how to work with these readings in the *Creating final masters for digital release* section.

Phase meter

The **phase meter** displays the phase relationship between the left and right channels of your mixes. This is important to detect phase-related issues such as phase cancellation.

Let's illustrate this with an example. In *Figure 15.16*, the signal on the left channel is identical to the signal on the right channel. The peaks and dips of the waveforms align perfectly; in technical terms, the two channels are **in phase**.

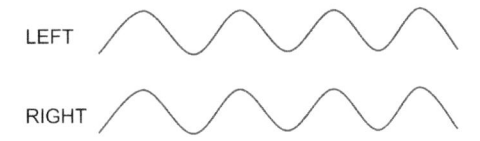

Figure 15.16: The two channels are in phase

Now, if we were to nudge one of the channels ever so slightly, this would change the phase relationship between the two channels. In *Figure 15.17*, the right channel is nudged by a small amount. Now, the dip on one channel is aligned with a peak on the other channel, and vice versa; these two channels are now **out of phase**:

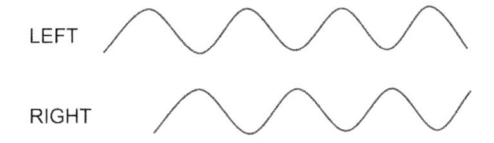

Figure 15.17: The two channels are out of phase

This is a big problem since these two channels now move in opposite directions at exactly the same frequency. Their vibrations will cancel each other out. This is called **phase cancellation**. When it happens in your mix, your song will sound thinner. In extreme cases, some sounds may disappear completely.

The Phase Meter allows us to spot these issues. The easiest way to use it is to keep an eye on the **Corr** (correlation) indicator at the bottom of its interface:

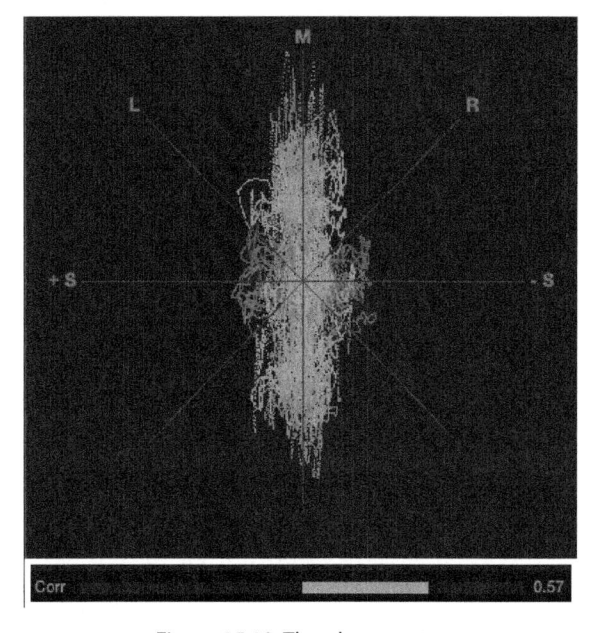

Figure 15.18: The phase meter

When the left and right channels are in phase and perfectly identical, as in *Figure 15.16*, the **Corr** indicator will show a value of **+1**. In a stereo mix, the left and right channels are not identical, so the **Corr** indicator hovers somewhere between **+1** and **0**. This is perfectly normal.

When the left and right channels are out of phase, the **Corr** indicator will begin to display negative values:

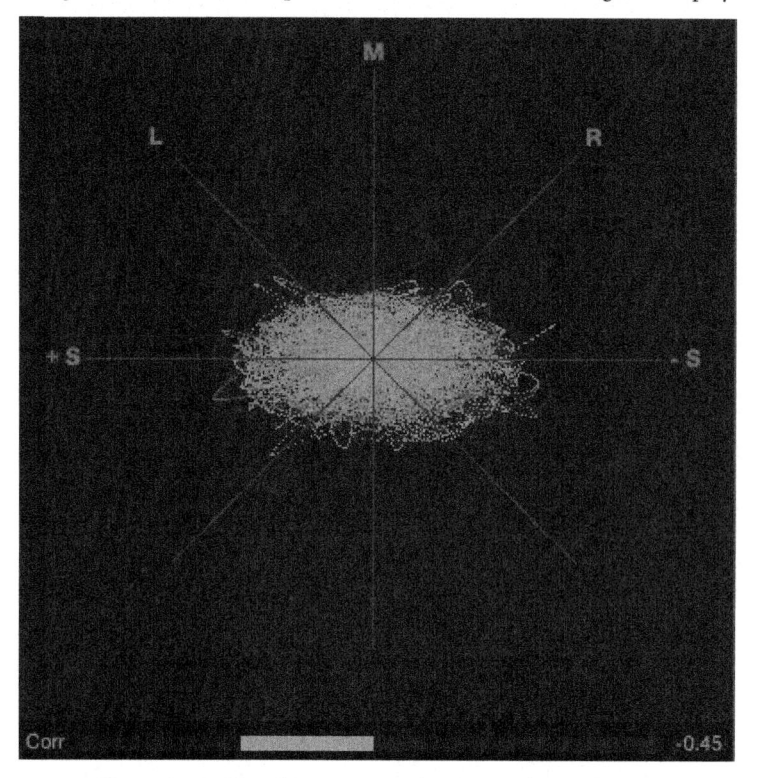

Figure 15.19: The phase meter indicating phase problems

This is a red flag, warning you that there is phase cancellation going on in your mix. Phase cancellation can occur for a variety of reasons. The most common causes are as follows:

- Wrong microphone placement during the recording. Let's say you're recording an acoustic guitar with two microphones. If the sound of the guitar reaches one microphone a bit late compared to the other microphone, you'll end up with the same situation as in *Figure 15.17*.
- Excessive use of stereo-widening effects; these effects tend to introduce phase issues as artifacts.

Every Project is unique, so it's up to you to track down the cause of the problem. If it's a stereo-widening effect, you can usually solve the problem by lowering its settings. If it's caused by microphone placement, go back to the mix and try inserting a **Mixtool** plug-in on one of the offending channels. Use the **Phase Invert** button on **Mixtool**; that should solve the problem.

Using automation on the Project page

Almost every parameter on the **Project** page can be automated. We talked about automation in *Chapter 11*, and the procedure for applying automation is similar, so you might want to visit that chapter for a refresher on how automation works in Studio One.

To start using automation on the **Project** page, click on the **Automation** button, highlighted in *Figure 15.20*.

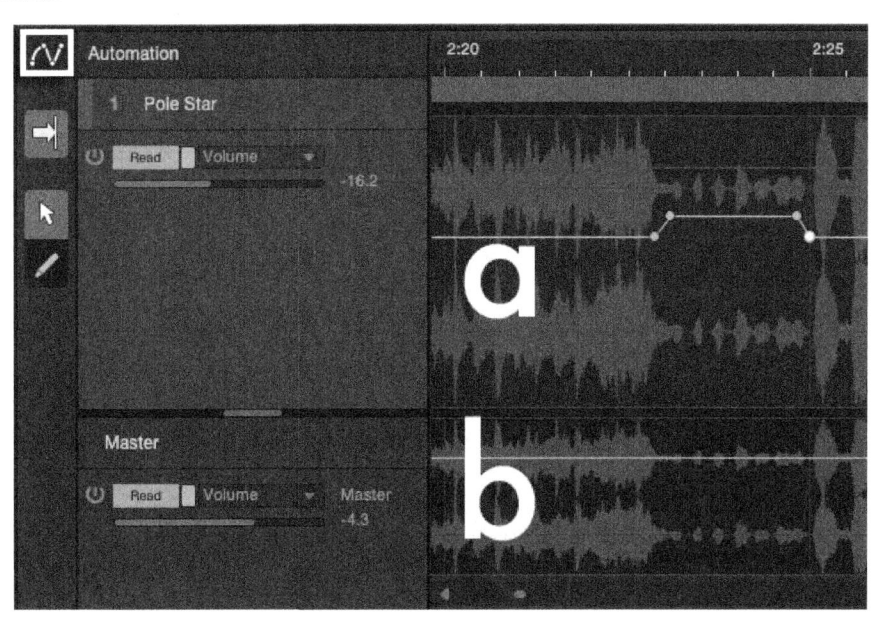

Figure 15.20: Using automation on the Project page

The **Project** page has two separate automation lanes:

- The automation lane at the top is called the **Track Automation** lane (**a** in *Figure 15.20*). This lane allows you to set automation for plug-ins in the **Track Device** rack.
- The automation lane at the bottom is called the **Master Automation** lane (**b** in *Figure 15.20*). This lane allows you to set automation for plug-ins in the **Master Device** rack.

Having these two separate layers of automation running simultaneously gives you greater control and allows you to get creative with your mastering process.

In this section, you learned how to use the **Project** page to put the final touches on your tracks by editing them to perfection and applying some final mastering effects. Your songs are now ready to be discovered by the world, and in the next section, you'll learn how to export the final masters of your songs so that you can deliver them to your fans.

Rendering final masters for publishing and delivery

Part of what makes the mastering process intimidating to many people is the abundance of delivery formats and the standards associated with them. Digital distribution networks, streaming services, and CD manufacturing plants all have unique standards that they expect you to conform to when delivering your final masters. If you fail to comply with these standards, in the best-case scenario, you'll be required to submit your masters again, this time with the correct settings. In the worst-case scenario, your songs will be published as is, resulting in sub-par sound quality.

Fortunately, the **Project** page makes it easy to render final masters that comply with all applicable standards, even if you don't have any experience or technical knowledge in mastering. Using the **Project** page, you can create final masters of your songs for the following formats:

- **Digital distribution**: This is by far the most popular channel to release your music. This method allows listeners to stream and download your songs.
- **CDs**: Although diminishing in popularity, the CD still has a place in the music market, especially if several songs are presented together in an album format.

Now, let's take a look at how you can render your final masters for each of these formats.

Creating final masters for digital release

You can export the final masters of your songs directly from the **Project** page, which can then be uploaded to platforms such as **DistroKid**, **TuneCore**, or **CD Baby** for distribution. Here's how to do it:

1. At the top of the **Project** page, click the **Digital Release** button. This will open the **Digital Release** window:

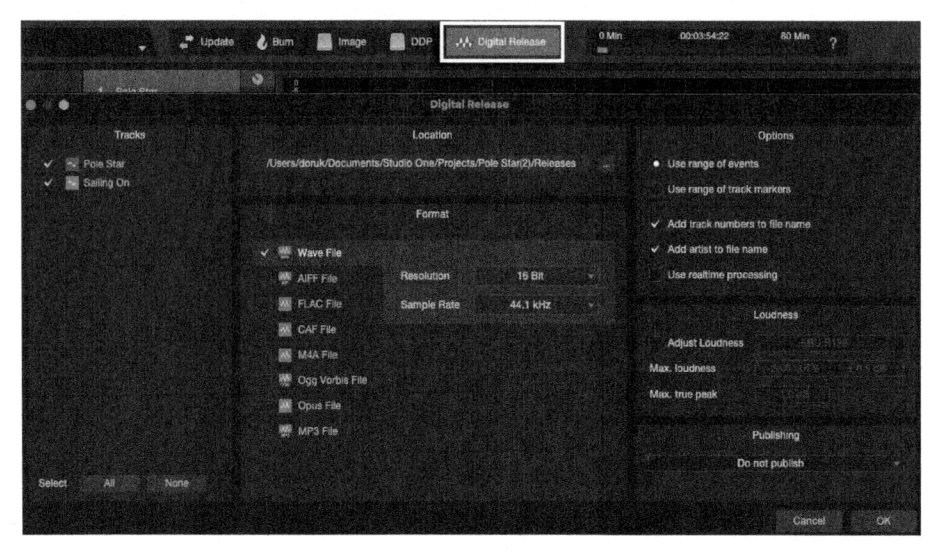

Figure 15.21: The Digital Release window

2. On the left side of this window, select the songs that you want to export as final masters. Note that even if you have several songs on the **Project** page and you want to combine them as an album, these songs will be exported as separate individual files. You will then upload these files to a distribution platform and use that platform's own set of tools to combine them as an album.

3. In the **Location** section of the window, select a folder that the files will be exported to.

4. In the **Format** section of the window, select the format for the files that you'd like to export. For music distribution platforms, you'll want to select **Wave File**, with a **Resolution** setting of **16 Bit** and a **Sample Rate** setting of **44.1 kHz**. For more information on these settings, see *Chapter 13*.

5. In the **Loudness** section of the window, check **Adjust Loudness**. This will activate the drop-down menu next to this checkbox. Use this menu to select the platform on which you'd like to publish your music. Studio One will analyze the loudness of your songs and optimize them to comply with the loudness standards required by the platform you select here. In *Figure 15.22*, I have selected **Apple Music** as my target platform, and all the fields in this section of the window have been populated automatically to reflect Apple Music's loudness standards.

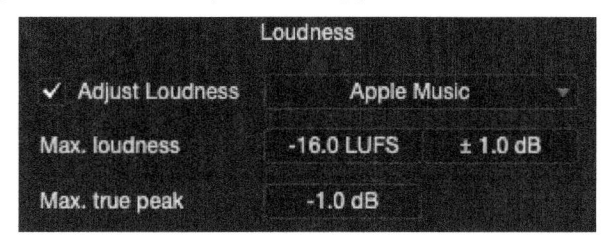

Figure 15.22: Adjusting the Loudness settings

This is a great way of optimizing your songs for digital platforms, even if you have no experience or technical background in working with their standards.

6. Click **OK**.

Each song on the **Project** page will be rendered as a separate file to the folder you have just selected, waiting to be uploaded for the final release.

Creating final masters for release on a CD

While not quite as popular as digital distribution, the CD still enjoys a solid market share in the music industry, so you might want to consider releasing your songs in this format. The procedure is a bit complicated – you need to create a single **Disc Description Protocol** (**DDP**) file that contains all the songs you want to have on the CD, and that file must conform to the Red Book standard, developed in the 1980s, which goes into some very specific details about the production of audio CDs.

Confused? That's totally understandable. You'll be glad to know that on the **Project** page, you can create a Red Book-compliant DDP image in just two clicks. Here's how:

1. At the top of the **Project** page, click **DDP**. This will open a simple dialog box, asking whether you really want to create a DDP image:

Figure 15.23: Creating a DDP image

2. Click **Yes**. Studio One will create a DDP image and place it in a folder with DDP appended to its name. Here is the folder created for the Project in *Figure 15.23*:

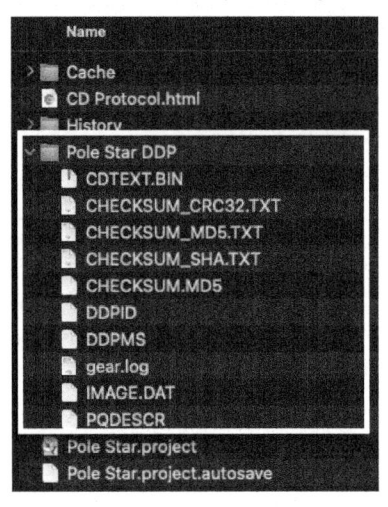

Figure 15.24: The folder containing the DDP image

3. Now, all you need to do is send this folder, along with all of its contents, to the CD pressing plant, and they'll take care of the rest.

In this section, you learned how to export the final masters of your songs to upload them to digital platforms or send them to CD pressing plants. This completes our tour of the music production process; your songs are now ready to meet your audience.

Summary

In this chapter, we explored the **Project** page, Studio One's unique environment dedicated to mastering audio. We talked about the integration between the **Song** page and the **Project** page and discussed how you can use this integration to maximize your production workflow. Then, we saw how you can edit and enhance your songs on the **Project** page to add some finishing touches. Finally, we explored how to export your masters for final delivery to your audience.

This was the final step in our coverage of the music production process, starting with the first recording and going all the way to the final delivery. In the next chapter, we will take a look at features in Studio One that do not correspond to standard steps in the music production process but offer added value and functionality, which may be invaluable additions to your workflow.

16
Using Additional Studio One Features

So far in this book, our coverage of the features available in Studio One has followed the steps of a typical music production workflow. We started by creating a new project and worked all the way up to exporting the final masters. However, there are some features in Studio One that don't fall within this classic workflow, and they merit special coverage. That's what this chapter is about.

In this chapter, we will explore three features that add extra value by expanding the scope of the already amazing list of things you can do with Studio One. By learning how to use these features, you'll be able to bring the sound processing power of Studio One to your live performances, express your ideas using musical notation, and use powerful sound design technology to create your very own unique sounds.

We will cover the following topics:

- Using Studio One in live performances with the **Show** page
- Using the Score Editor
- Creating and manipulating samples with SampleOne XT

Technical requirements

In order to follow along with this chapter, you will need to have Studio One activated on your computer.

Using Studio One in live performances with the Show page

The **Show page** is a dedicated live performance environment that allows you to use the power of Studio One to run live shows directly from your computer. If you have a band or a solo act, you can use the **Show** page to prepare and organize all the audio material for an entire concert in advance. When it's show time, Studio One will take care of running all the technical stuff in the background while you concentrate on your performance. It's like having a live sound engineer right inside your computer.

Using Additional Studio One Features

Before we begin to set up your next concert, let's clarify a couple of important terms that we'll use on the **Show** page:

- A **Show** refers to a document that contains and organizes all the audio assets for an entire concert, event, or performance. Just like we create a new Song to work on the **Song** page, we create a new Show to work on the **Show** page.
- A **Setlist** is a list of all the songs you'll be performing during the Show.
- A **backing track** is a pre-recorded musical accompaniment that you'll be using to support your live performance.

Now, we are ready to prepare for your next concert.

Creating your first Show

To get started using the **Show** page, we must first create a new Show. Here's how to do it:

1. Head over to Studio One's **Start** page and click on the **New...** button. This will open the **New** window:

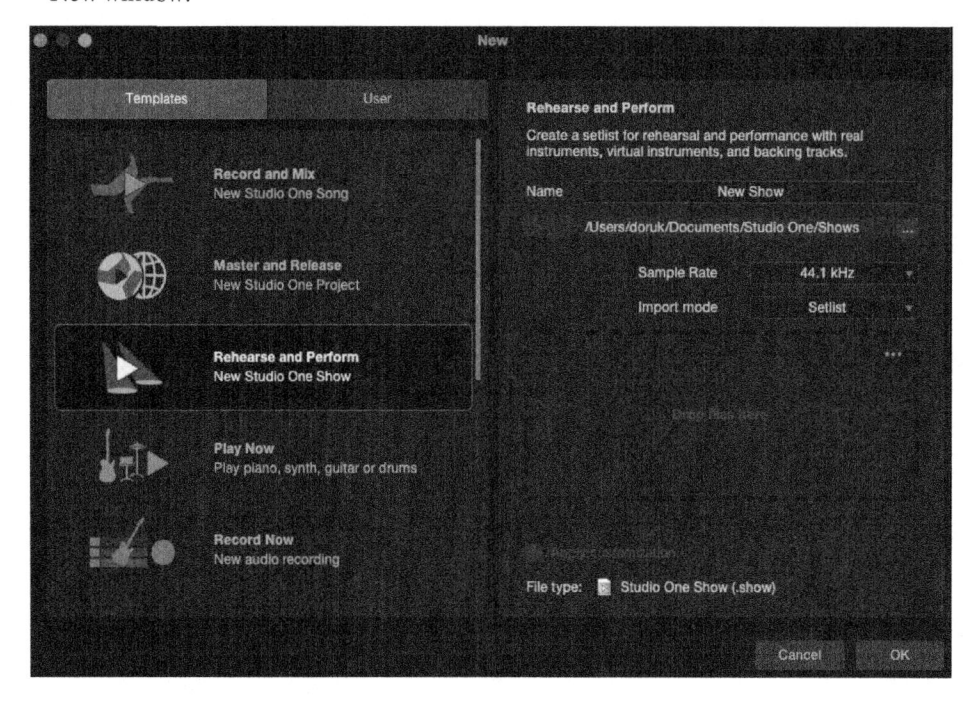

Figure 16.1: Creating a new Show

2. On the left side of this window, select **Rehearse and Perform**.

3. On the right side of the window, type a name for the Show you're about to create.
4. If you already have the backing tracks for the songs you'd like to play, drag them from Explorer (Windows) or Finder (macOS) and drop them in the audio drop zone (titled **Drop files here**). Don't worry if your backing tracks are not ready just yet; you can always add them later.
5. Click **OK**.

This will create your first Show in Studio One and take you to the **Show** page, which is what we'll be exploring next.

Exploring the Show page

The **Show** page looks like a simplified version of the **Song** page, so it will not be too unfamiliar.

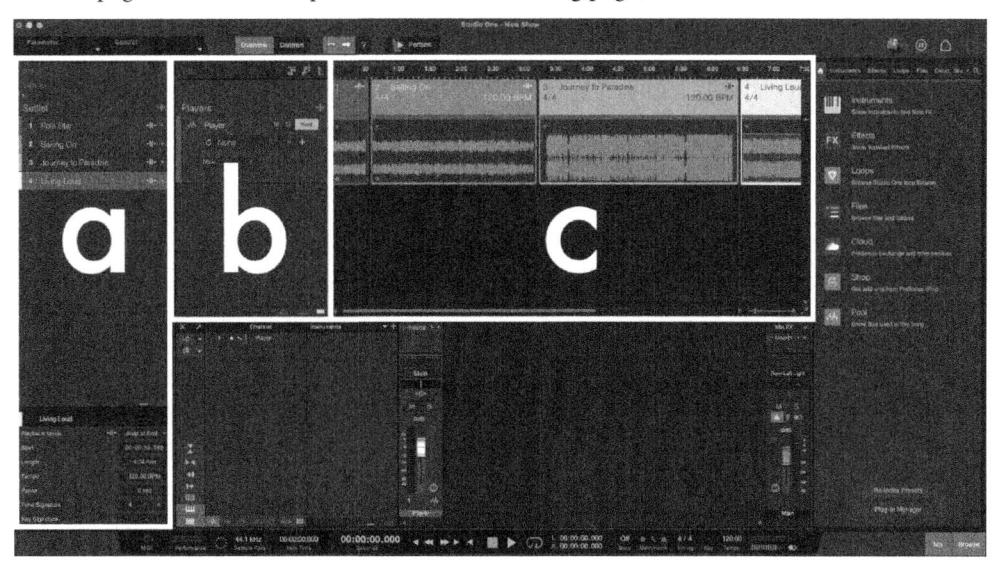

Figure 16.2: The Show page

There are three sections that are unique to the **Show** page. Let's take a look at each of them:

- **Setlist** (**a** in *Figure 16.2*): This section holds a list of all the songs that you will be performing during your live Show. If you imported any backing tracks using the audio drop zone in *Figure 16.1*, they will be listed in this window. During your live performance, these songs will be played back in the order in which they appear here. You can easily reorder the songs by dragging them up or down in this list.

- The **Players** column (**b** in *Figure 16.2*): This column holds a list of all the players that will be active in your show. We'll talk about players shortly, in the *Working with players* section.

- **Overview** window (**c** in *Figure 16.2*): The songs in the Setlist are laid out horizontally as events in the Overview window. We will use this window to set up and organize your Show.

Now, we're ready to dive into the deep end of the **Show** page and learn how to set it up to run your next live performance.

Working with players

A song performed in a concert may comprise several musical elements:

- Singers
- Musicians playing physical instruments such as guitars and drums
- Musicians playing virtual instruments such as Studio One's Presence
- Backing tracks supplementing the performance

On the **Show** page, each of these elements is represented by a corresponding device called a **Player**. Just like we have a different track for each instrument on the **Song** page, we have a different Player for each instrument on the **Show** page. There are three types of Players:

- Backing Track Player
- Real Instrument Player
- Virtual Instrument Player

Now, let's explore each player type and see how you can add players to populate your Show.

Adding a Backing Track Player

A **Backing Track Player** simply plays back an audio file, just like an audio track on the **Song** page. During your live performance, a Backing Track Player will play back any prerecorded audio files that you'd like to use for accompaniment.

While creating a new Show in *Figure 16.1*, I dropped four audio files on the audio drop zone. Studio One created a Backing Track Player and placed those files back to back across the Player, as we can now see here:

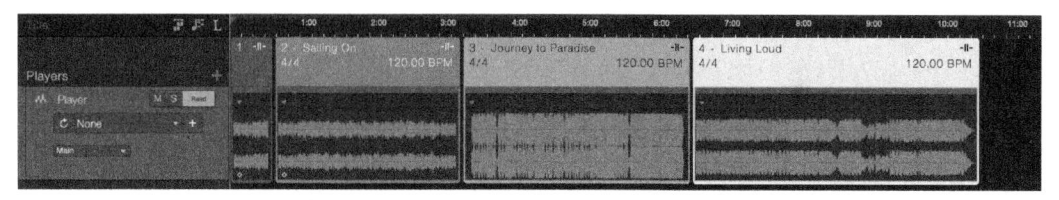

Figure 16.3: Backing Track Player

If I want to play more songs during my concert, here's what I need to do:

1. Locate the backing tracks for the new songs in Explorer (Windows) or Finder (macOS).
2. Drag the new backing tracks and drop them into the empty space at the right side of the Backing Track Player:

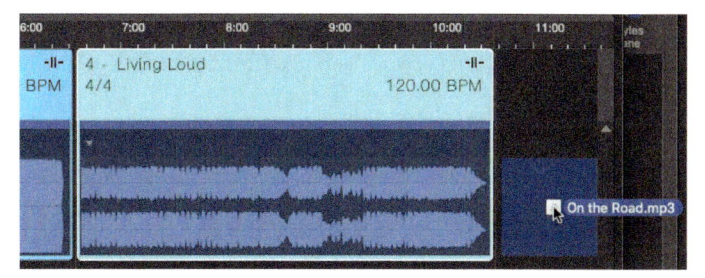

Figure 16.4: Adding new files to a Backing Track Player

3. Once I add the new tracks, I can easily reorder them by dragging them here in the **Overview** window or the Setlist.

You may also want to have several audio files playing simultaneously during a song in your performance. For example, you may want to import various elements of a song in the form of stems – one stem containing drums, another containing guitars, and so on – and have the ability to control each of these stems separately during your live performance. To do that, simply drag the audio files from Explorer (Windows) or Finder (macOS) and drop them into the empty space below the Backing Track Player. Studio One will create a new player for each audio file and place them under the same song:

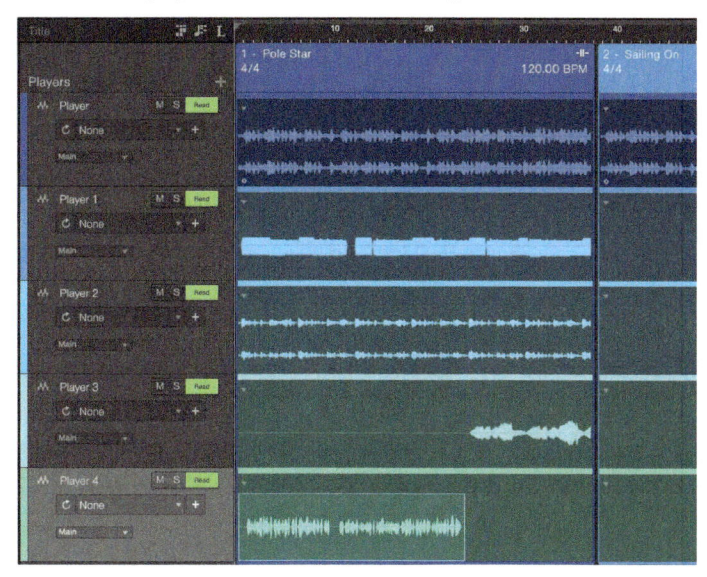

Figure 16.5: Adding new files to a song

This flexible setup allows you to control your backing tracks on a more granular level, such as applying different effects plug-ins to different elements of the song.

Adding a Real Instrument Player

If you or your band members will be playing physical instruments or delivering vocal performances during the concert, you can add them to your Show using **Real Instrument Players**. This allows you to process the sound of those instruments or vocals in real time by using Studio One's effects plug-ins.

To add a Real Instrument Player, follow these steps:

1. Click on the **Add Player** button in the **Players** column. This will open the **Add Player** window:

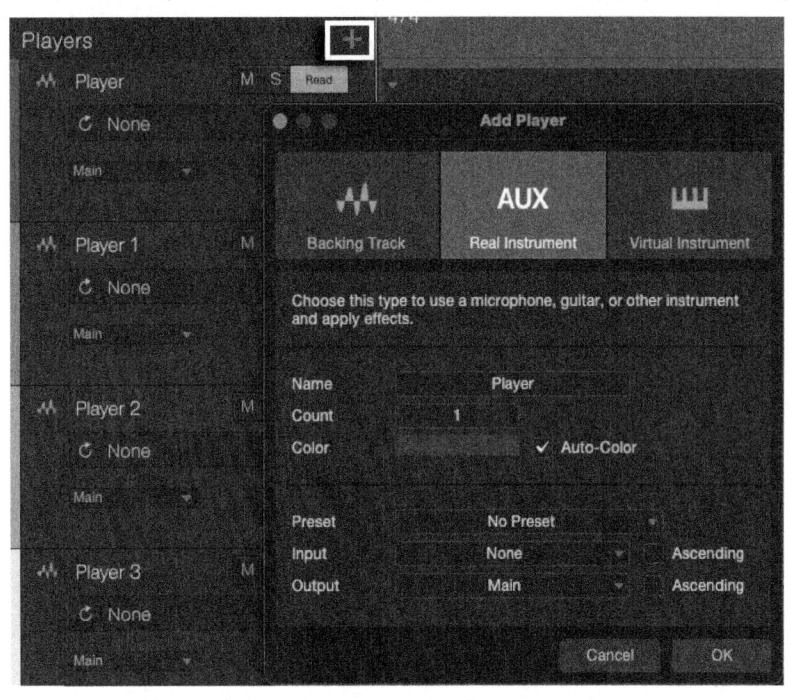

Figure 16.6: The Add Player window

2. Click on the **AUX** tab.
3. Give a short, descriptive name to the player you're about to create so you can recognize it easily among other players in the **Players** column.
4. In the **Input** field, select the physical input on your audio device that this player will be connected to. For example, if you're creating a Real Instrument Player for an electric guitar, and that guitar is connected to input 2 on your audio device, select **Input 2** here.
5. Click **OK**.

You'll want to create as many Real Instrument Players as there are performers in your band, so you can process them separately by applying different effects to each of them.

Adding a Virtual Instrument Player

A **Virtual Instrument Player** lets you add a virtual instrument such as **Presence** to your Show and play it during your live performance. If you want the sound of a virtual instrument to change from one song to the next, you can program these changes in advance and let Studio One take care of implementing these changes for you during your concert while you concentrate on your playing.

To add a Virtual Instrument Player to your Show, do the following:

1. Open the **Browse** window and select the **Instruments** tab.
2. Locate the virtual instrument that you'd like to add to your Show.
3. Click the small triangle to the left of the virtual instrument's name. This will open a list of the available presets for that instrument:

Figure 16.7: List of presets for Presence

4. Drag the preset you'd like to use and drop it into the **Overview** window. This will create a new Virtual Instrument Player and load the preset you have selected:

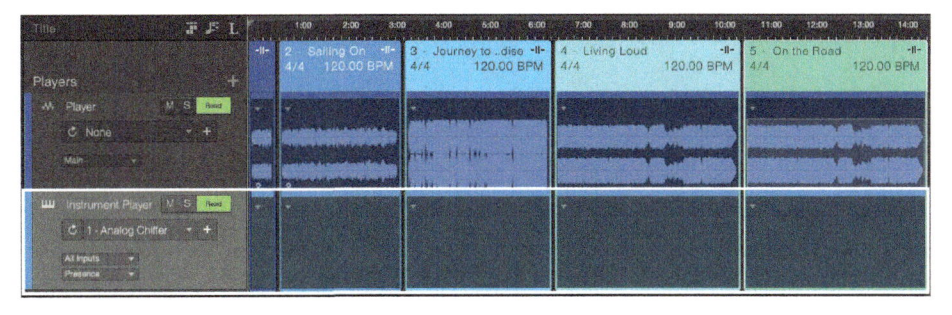

Figure 16.8: A Virtual Instrument Player

5. You can now play this virtual instrument using your MIDI keyboard.

The Show in *Figure 16.8* has five songs, as seen at the top of the **Overview** window. Currently, the Virtual Instrument Player we created will play the same preset on all of these five songs. However, most of the time, you'll want to use a different sound for each song – an acoustic piano for the first, an electric piano for the second, an organ for the third, and so on. To do that, simply drag the preset you'd like to use for each song and drop it on the corresponding slot on the Virtual Instrument Player. In *Figure 16.9*, I have loaded different presets for each song. You can see their names displayed on their respective slots:

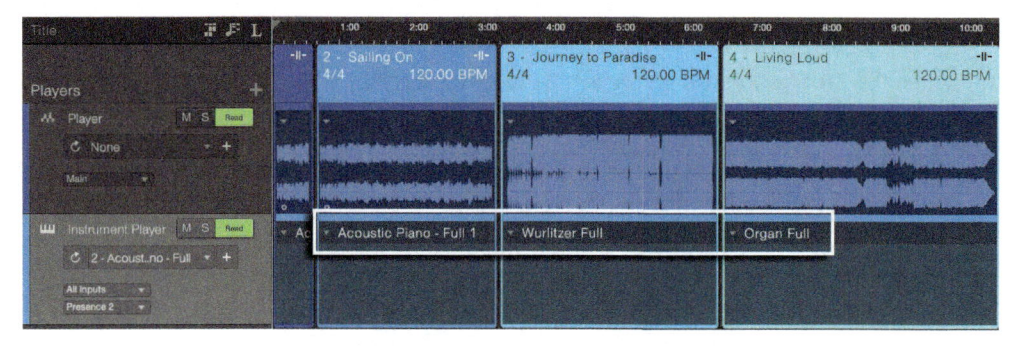

Figure 16.9: Adding a different preset for each song

Now, during your live performance, Studio One will automatically switch from one sound to another as you go from one song to the next. That's one less thing to worry about when you're on stage!

Adding effects to a live performance

Now that we've added our backing tracks and instruments, we will want to embellish them using effects plug-ins. This will allow us to use Studio One's sound processing capabilities during live performances.

True to Studio One's drag-and-drop interface design, adding effects plug-ins is as easy as it gets. Let's take a look:

1. Open the **Browse** window and go to the **Effects** tab:

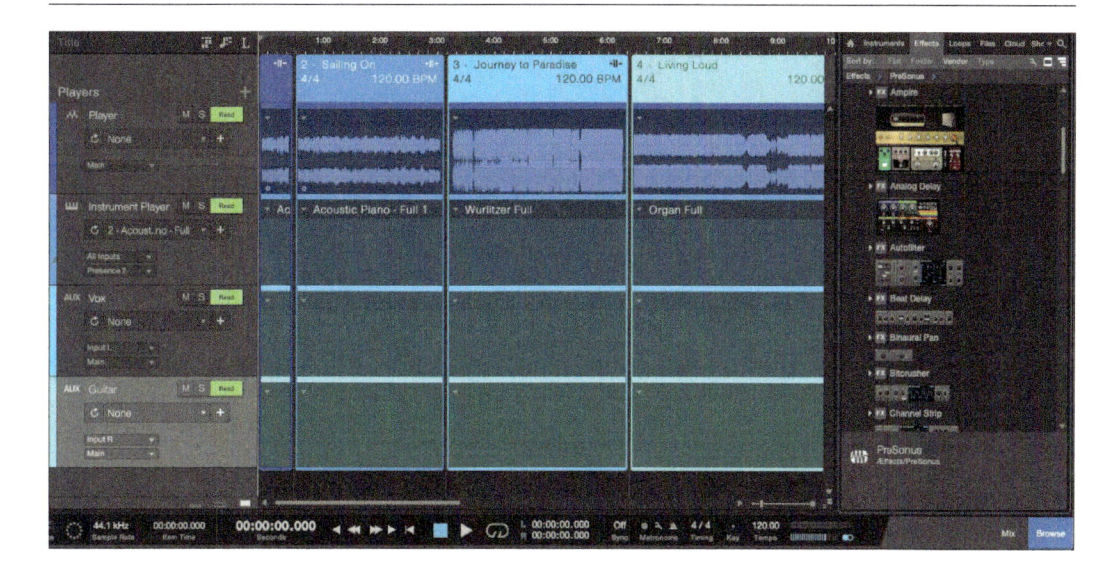

Figure 16.10: Adding effects plug-ins to a Show

2. Drag an effect you'd like to use and drop it on a slot in the **Overview** window.

This method allows you to add effects combinations on a granular level. For example, *Figure 16.11* shows a Real Instrument Player I created for my electric guitar. I added the **Ampire** plug-in to the slot that corresponds to the first song because I want a distorted guitar sound for that song. For the next song, I added **Analog Delay**, and for the third, I added **Room Reverb**. During a live performance, as the timeline moves from one song to the next, Studio One will automatically switch from one effects plug-in to the other, and my guitar tone will be ready, waiting for me to play.

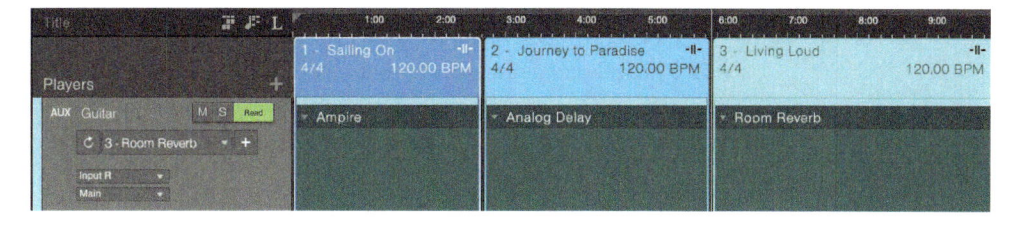

Figure 16.11: Adding different effects to a player

You can add as many effects plug-ins as you like into each slot, allowing you to build complex effects chains for each song.

Using the Arranger Track to define sections of song

So far, we've created a roadmap for our concert and told Studio One exactly what to do during each song. When it's showtime, we'll put Studio One on autopilot and it will take care of all the technical stuff for us. This kind of strict planning may bring a sense of safety when you're on stage, but it will also take away the fun and excitement of spontaneity that we associate with live performance. What if you find that the audience is really enjoying your guitar solo and you just want to keep playing a bit longer than you originally planned? Do you have to end your solo and move on, just because the timeline on the **Show** page has no idea about the reaction from your audience and just keeps moving?

Fortunately, the answer is no. You can divide the song in your Setlist into sections and then freely jump from one section to another, repeat a section, or drop it altogether. We do this by using the **Arranger Track**, which we have already seen on the **Song** page.

Here's how you can use the Arranger Track to divide your song into smaller sections:

1. Click the **Open Arranger Track** button at the top of the **Players** column. This will display the Arranger Track:

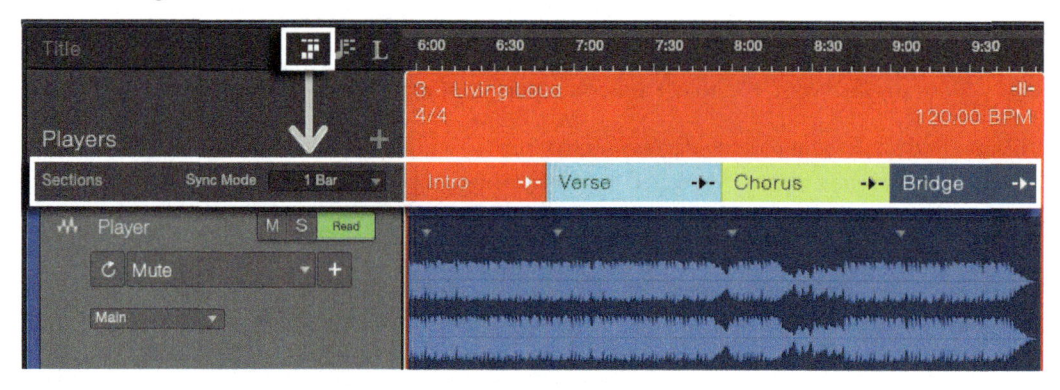

Figure 16.12: Arranger Track on the Show page

2. Double-click on the Arranger Track to create a new section. Studio One will name each section automatically.
3. Right-click on a section to change its name and color.
4. Drag the left and right edges of a section to align it precisely to the beginning and end of the corresponding section on the track.

You can see that I added four sections to my Song in *Figure 16.12*. Now, Studio One knows where each section begins and ends. This will come in handy when we're performing on stage, which will be our next topic.

Performing live with the Show page

Now, we're ready to perform! Believe it or not, at this point, all you have to do is press the spacebar on your keyboard to start the Show, and Studio One will take care of all the details for running it, leaving you and your bandmates free to focus on your performances.

While you can use the **Show** page during a performance, Studio One offers a separate environment, called the **Performance View**, which is optimized for use on stage. The Performance View is a simple interface that only contains the basic controls you'll need during a performance. Everything is large and easy to see, so at a glance, you can find what you're looking for, even if you're using a small laptop computer on a stage with poor lighting.

To switch to Performance View, click the **Perform** button at the top of the **Show** page:

Figure 16.13: The Perform button

This will open the Performance View:

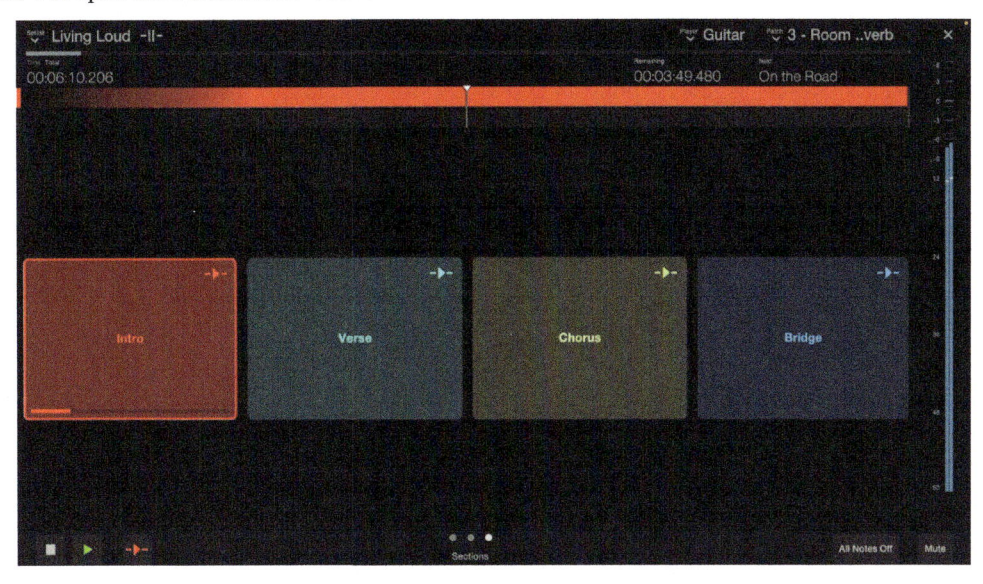

Figure 16.14: Performance View

The Performance View is as simple as it gets. Let's take a quick look:

- The top of the window shows your position on the timeline.
- In the center of the window, you can see the sections we created on the Arranger Track earlier. If your audience is enjoying a section and you want to repeat it, simply click on it. If you'd like to jump to a different section, just click on that one.
- There are two buttons in the lower-right corner, which are there for emergencies:
  - Sometimes, virtual instruments get stuck while playing a note and will keep playing even if you let go of the keys on your MIDI keyboard. In such cases, clicking on the **All Notes Off** button will send a **NOTE OFF** command to all virtual instruments, forcing them to stop playing whatever they are playing at that moment. Clicking this button will not affect the playback of backing tracks, so there will not be an awkward silence, and you can return to playing your virtual instruments immediately. Usually, the stuck note problem is a simple glitch and will not be repeated.
  - Speaking of awkward silence, the **Mute** button is reserved for extreme cases when things get out of control and the only solution is to turn off all audio. This is especially handy for protecting people's ears from that nasty ringing feedback sound that sometimes happens on stage.

Congratulations! Your first Show is now ready. When it's show time, all you need to do is hit **Play**, and Studio One will take care of the rest.

Now, let's take a look at the Score Editor, another great feature in Studio One.

Using the Score Editor

The **Score Editor** allows you to view and edit MIDI data in musical notation form. It's great for people who are not comfortable using the standard, piano-roll-style MIDI editor, which we discussed in *Chapter 9*. The Score Editor also comes in handy when you need to print out music scores of your projects to share them with fellow musicians.

Opening the Score Editor

To get started using the Score Editor, follow these steps:

1. Create an Instrument Track, as we discussed in *Chapter 6*.
2. Double-click on the Instrument Track to create an empty MIDI event.
3. Double-click on the MIDI event to open it in the **Edit** window.

4. On the left side of the **Edit** window, click the **Score View** button (marked as a treble clef):

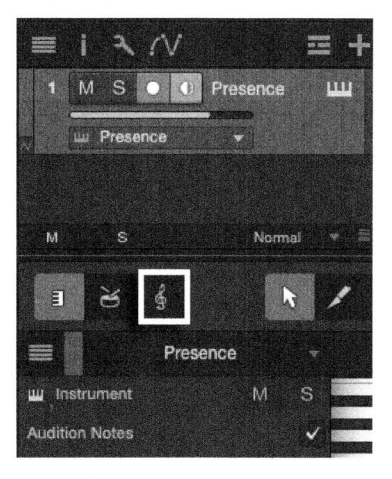

Figure 16.15: Score View button on the Edit window

This will switch the **Edit** window to display the Score Editor.

Exploring the Score Editor

By default, the Score Editor displays an empty staff using the treble clef:

Figure 16.16: Score Editor

At the top of the Score Editor is the **Score Editor** toolbar, which allows you to enter and edit notes on the staff.

Using Additional Studio One Features

On the left side of the window is the **Score Editor Inspector**, which allows you to add musical expression marks to your notes and change the format of the displayed staff.

Entering notes in the Score Editor

You can enter notes in the Score Editor by using any of the following methods:

- Playing the notes live with a MIDI keyboard
- Using **Step Input** to enter one note at a time with a MIDI keyboard
- Entering notes with the **Paint** tool

We discussed these methods in *Chapter 6*, and the first two methods work exactly the same way in the Score Editor. Therefore, in this section, we will just focus on the third method.

Follow these steps to enter notes in the Score Editor using the **Paint** tool:

1. On the Score Editor, press *2* on your keyboard to pick up the **Paint** tool.
2. Go to the **Score Editor** toolbar and select the note value you'd like to enter. You can select any value between a whole note and a 64th note.
3. Now, when you hover your mouse over the staff, the cursor will turn to a pencil, with a gray note shape following it:

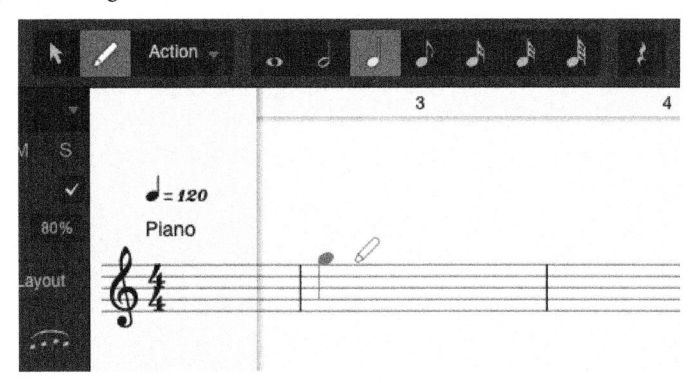

Figure 16.17: Entering a note with the Paint tool

4. Bring the gray note to the desired position on the staff and left-click to place the note there.
5. To add a rest, click on the **Rest** button on the **Score Editor** toolbar.

Note that you can work much faster if you learn the keyboard shortcuts for note values. Here are the keyboard shortcuts that you'll need:

- *1* selects the **Arrow** tool
- *2* selects the **Paint** tool
- *3* selects a whole note
- *4* selects a half note
- *5* selects a quarter note
- *6* selects an 8th note
- *7* selects a 16th note
- *8* selects a 32nd note
- *9* selects a 64th note

With these shortcuts, you can fill a score in no time, using just a mouse and your computer keyboard.

Editing notes in the Score Editor

Once you've entered your notes, you can easily edit them using the **Arrow** tool. Here's how to do it:

1. Press *1* on your keyboard to pick up the **Arrow** tool.
2. To change a note's pitch, left-click on it and drag it up or down till you find the correct pitch. Studio One will play the note as you drag it up or down to help you find the pitch you're looking for.
3. To change a note's length, select the desired note length in the **Score Editor** toolbar and then left-click on the note.

Note that the Score Editor and Piano Editor are dynamically linked; any changes you make on one window will be reflected on the other.

Adding musical expressions and formatting the score

The Score Editor Inspector helps you fine-tune the look of your score so that you can convey your musical ideas much more clearly. There are three tabs on the Score Editor Inspector, each specializing in a different part of the score. Let's explore them one by one.

The Symbols tab

The **Symbols** tab lets you add accidentals and musical expressions to your notes. To apply any of the expressions on this tab, select the expression and then click on the note or group of notes to which you'd like to apply the expression.

338 Using Additional Studio One Features

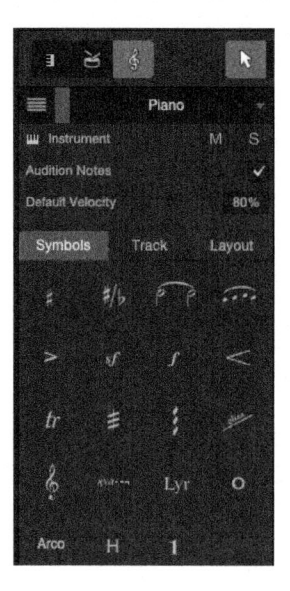

Figure 16.18: The Symbols tab of the Score Editor Inspector

Most of the buttons on this tab will show a small triangle in their lower-right corners when you hover your mouse on them. Clicking on these triangles will open pop-up windows that reveal further options. For example, here's the pop-up menu for the **Dynamics** button:

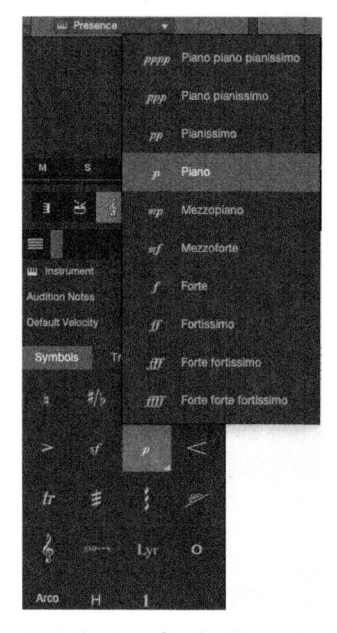

Figure 16.19: Options for the Dynamics button

These options allow you to add a wide variety of expression marks to your scores, helping you communicate your musical ideas clearly.

The Track tab

The **Track** tab helps you select the right staff type for your instrument. Open the **Staff Type** drop-down menu and select the type of staff you'd like to use:

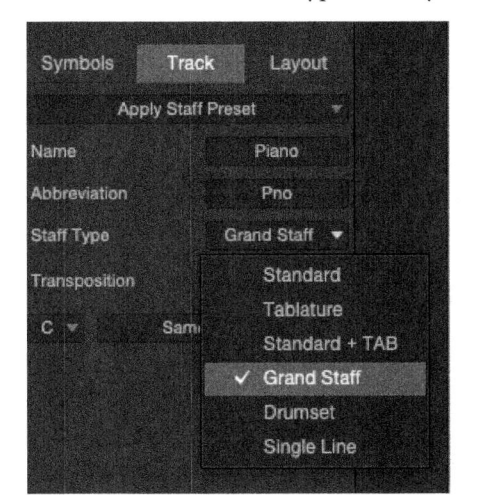

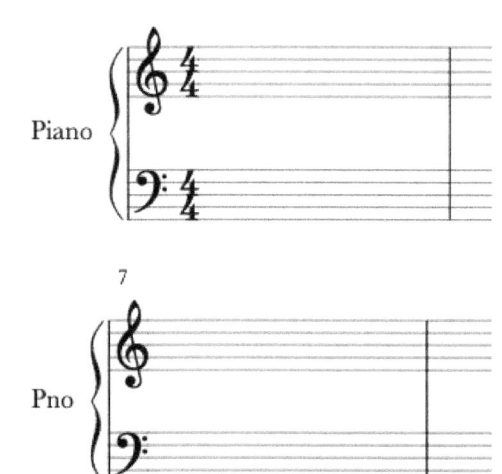

Figure 16.20: Selecting a staff type

Use the **Name** and **Abbreviation** fields on this tab to give a descriptive name to your instrument. The **Name** field is used at the beginning of the score; what you type in the **Abbreviation** field is used for labeling all subsequent lines.

The Layout tab

The **Layout** tab lets you adjust what your score will look like when it's printed. You can nerd out and adjust every fine detail, but Studio One does a pretty good job of formatting a score to fit on a page, so the default values should be fine for most cases.

340　Using Additional Studio One Features

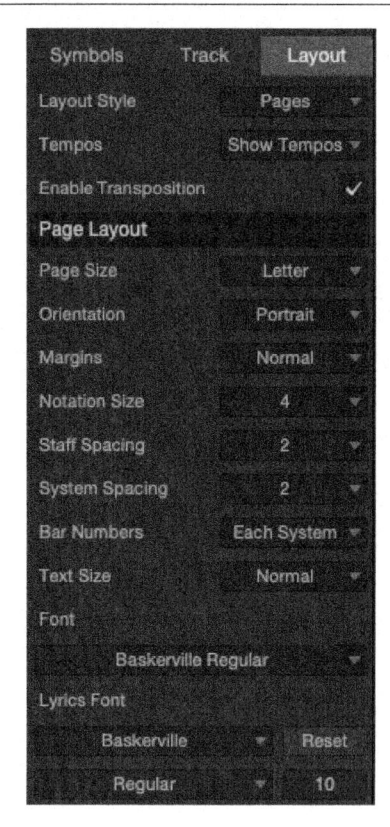

Figure 16.21: The Layout tab of the Score Editor Inspector

Here, just make sure that **Pages** is selected for **Layout Style**; this will tell Studio One to neatly divide your score into as many pages as necessary.

Finalizing and printing a score

Before we print our score to share with the rest of the world, let's make sure that the score gives credit where credit is due. When you first open the Score Editor, Studio One populates the **Title** field of the score with the name of your Song file and the **Artist** field with your name. If you'd like to change these or supply additional information, just click on the Song title. It will open the **Song Setup** menu:

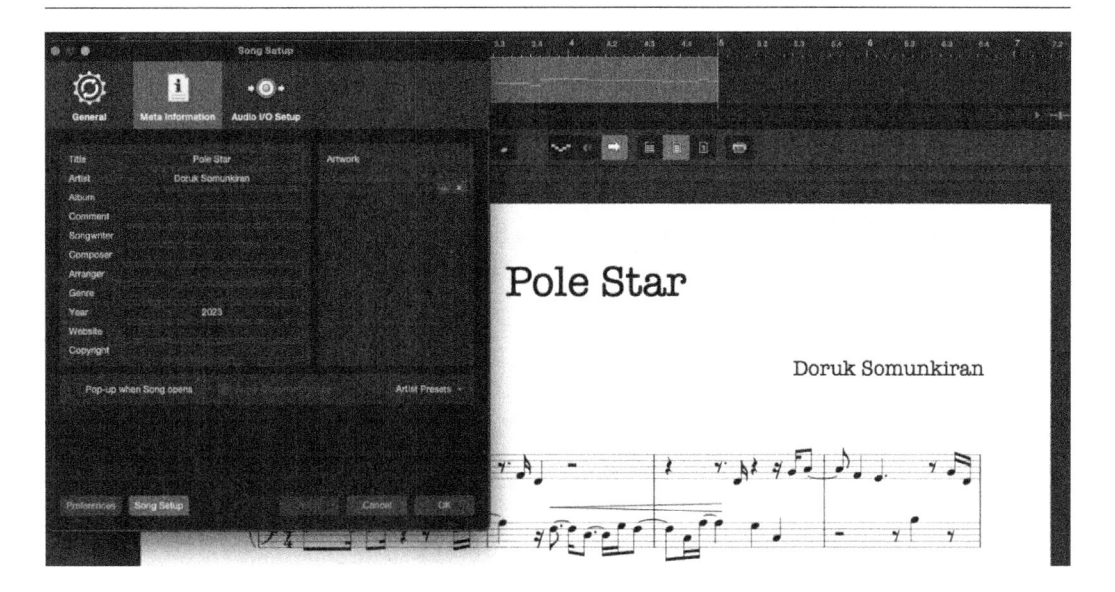

Figure 16.22: Entering Song information

Here, you can change the Song information as needed.

Once you're happy with your score, click on the **Print** button on the **Score Editor** toolbar. This will open the standard printing dialog box for your operating system, where you can select your printer and print away.

This concludes our coverage of the Score Editor. Now, let's move on to an extremely fun feature in Studio One's toolkit: SampleOne XT.

Creating and manipulating samples with SampleOne XT

SampleOne XT is a full-featured sampler that ships with Studio One. A **sampler** is a device or software that can record and manipulate audio samples. A **sample** is a short recording of a sound, such as a drum hit, a guitar chord, or a vocal phrase.

In plain terms, SampleOne XT is an extremely fun piece of software that allows you to create your very own virtual instruments from any sound you can get your hands on – your dog's bark, that broken toy piano in the attic… you name it. If you can record it, SampleOne XT can turn it into a playable instrument for you.

To get started using SampleOne XT, you'll need to add an instance of it to your Song. Proceed as follows:

1. Open the **Browse** window and go to the **Instruments** tab.
2. Drag **SampleOne XT** and drop it on the **Arrange** window.

3. Say hello to SampleOne XT:

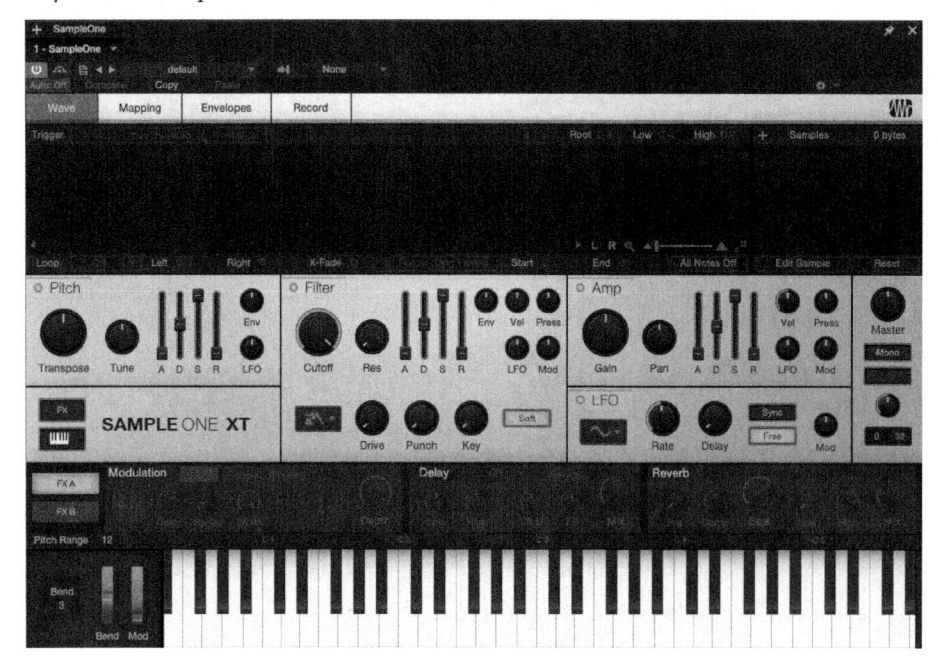

Figure 16.23: SampleOne XT

If the interface looks intimidating, it's warranted. SampleOne XT is a powerful tool that allows you to go into the deep end of creative sound design. But don't worry, we will get you up and running with the basics in no time!

Adding a sample

Now, we need to give SampleOne XT a sample to work with. There are two ways of adding a sample to SampleOne XT:

- If you already have a recorded sample, in the form of a `.wav` or `.mp3` file, you can drag it from the **Arrange** window, the **Browse** window, Explorer (Windows), or Finder (macOS), and drop it on SampleOne XT.

Creating and manipulating samples with SampleOne XT   343

- If you don't have a sample recorded yet, you can record directly into SampleOne XT. Here's how:

    I. Click the **Record** tab at the top of the SampleOne XT interface. This will open the **Record** view:

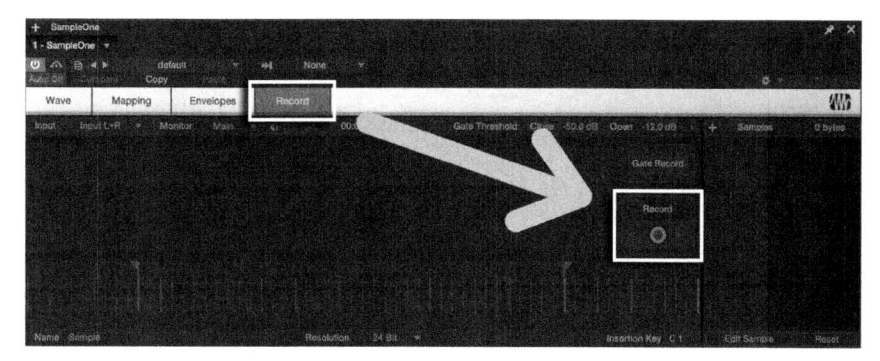

Figure 16.24: Recording into SampleOne XT

  II. Click the **Record** button in this view.
 III. Click the same button once again to stop recording.

Now that we've got our sample loaded into SampleOne XT, it's time for the fun part!

Editing a sample

Play any note on your MIDI keyboard, or click on any note on the virtual keyboard on SampleOne XT's interface. You will hear the sample that we've just added. SampleOne XT will automatically transpose the sample to the notes that you're playing, so you can already start to play your sample like a musical instrument. But let's take this a step further.

If you've recorded a sample right into SampleOne XT, there may be a gap of silence at the beginning of the sample, so you may have to wait for a bit after playing a note. Let's fix that:

1. Click the **Wave** tab at the top of SampleOne XT's interface. This will open the **Wave** view:

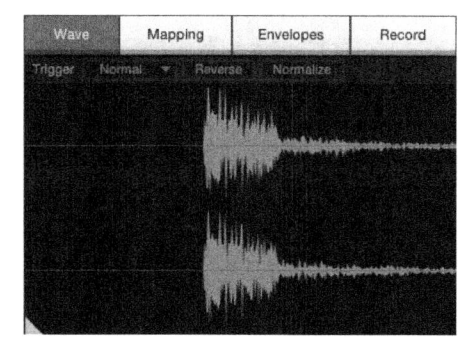

Figure 16.25: A gap at the beginning of a sample

344 Using Additional Studio One Features

2. In *Figure 16.25*, you can see that there is a gap at the beginning of the sample. Grab the small triangle in the lower-left corner of the window and drag it to the right until the beginning of the sample. This will trim out the gap:

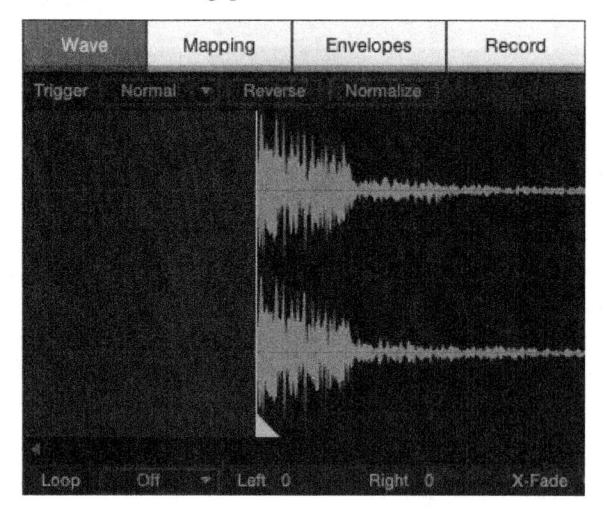

Figure 16.26: No gap at the beginning of the sample

Now your sample will be much more responsive; it will be triggered the moment you play a note on your MIDI keyboard.

Selecting Trigger modes

The **Trigger** setting determines how SampleOne XT will play back a sample when you play a note on your MIDI keyboard. There are three available options, which can be accessed by clicking on the drop-down menu:

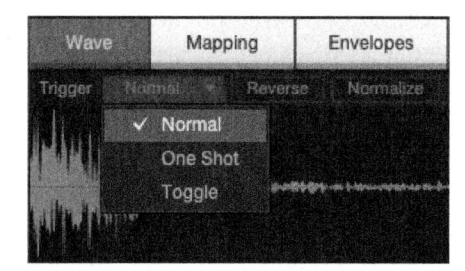

Figure 16.27: Trigger modes

Let's explore these options:

- **Normal**: When you play a note on your MIDI keyboard, the sample will play back. When you let go of the note, the sample will stop.

- **One Shot**: When you play a note on your MIDI keyboard, the sample will play back and it will keep playing until the end of the sample, regardless of when you let go of the note. This is the preferred **Trigger** method for drum and percussion samples; you don't want them to sound chopped off if you let go of the note a bit too early.

- **Toggle**: When you play a note on your MIDI keyboard, the sample will play back, and when you play the same note again, it will stop. This is the preferred **Trigger** method for long samples such as sound effects, pads, or drones.

Selecting the correct **Trigger** mode for your sample will allow you to gain a better command of your sample and make your new virtual instrument much more playable and enjoyable.

Integrating SampleOne XT into your production workflow will open the door to a whole new level of creativity, allowing you to design your very own sounds and instruments. It's the gateway to developing your signature sound in music.

Summary

In this chapter, we covered three important features in Studio One that fall outside the standard music production workflow. First, we took an in-depth look at the **Show** page and discussed how you can harness the power of Studio One to augment your live performances. Then, we explored the Score Editor, which provides a much more intuitive interface for people who are comfortable with using music notation. Finally, we looked at SampleOne XT, a powerful sampler with deep sound design capabilities, opening the door to endless creative possibilities.

And with this chapter, we have come to the end of the book. Through its pages, I hope to have provided you with a comprehensive guide to using Studio One. Music production is a constantly evolving field that requires a combination of technical skill, creativity, and passion. Whether you are just starting out or have been producing music for years, there is always something new to learn and explore.

Go forth, learn, create, and share your music with the world!

Appendix
Customizing Studio One and Following Best Practices

As you know by now, Studio One makes music production as simple as possible by streamlining your workflow. In this appendix, we'll take this a step further by discussing several methods to customize Studio One so that you can avoid repetitive tasks. We'll also explore Studio One's file management system and discuss how to optimize your workflow to avoid some common problems. Finally, we'll talk about the best practices to share your projects with others for collaboration.

Following the methods that we'll discuss here will allow your overall music production experience to run even more smoothly.

We will cover the following topics:

- Customizing Studio One
- Understanding the file and folder system
- Sharing your files with others

Technical requirements

In order to follow along with this section, you'll need to have Studio One activated on your computer.

Customizing Studio One

As you go from one project to another, some procedures become muscle memory and you find yourself doing them over and over again. Maybe you have a special combination of effects plug-ins that work like magic on your vocals. Or maybe you created a killer sound by layering three virtual instruments on top of each other, and that sound has become such a part of your sonic signature that you want to use it on all your projects.

If you find yourself launching the same plug-ins or virtual instruments frequently, it's a good idea to save them as templates and presets. This will allow you to jump right into the creative process without spending time setting up the same elements every time.

Studio One offers several methods that allow you to customize your workflow for more efficiency and consistency. In this section, we will explore these methods in detail.

Creating your own Smart Templates

In Studio One, a **Smart Template** is a preconfigured Song file that includes settings, preloaded virtual instruments, effects, and other elements that can be used to jump-start a new project. Templates create a consistent starting point for new projects and save time by eliminating the need to configure the same elements each time a Song file is created. Templates can also be shared among collaborators, allowing for a standardized approach to music production.

If you find yourself adding the same instruments and effects and creating the same routings and mixer configurations for every project, you can easily create your own Smart Templates to skip these steps on your next projects and jump right into creating. Here's how to do it:

1. Open a typical Song file that contains the elements you routinely add to your projects.
2. Tweak all effects and instruments and set them up the way you want to find them when you create your next Song file.
3. Configure all routing settings and mixer configurations as best fit your workflow; this includes setting up FX channels, creating buses, and applying sidechains between channels.
4. Customize the user interface to include only what's relevant to you, as discussed in *Chapter 3*.
5. Delete everything inside the **Arrange** window – you don't want to save the content in your template.
6. Now, head over to the top menu, click **File**, and select **Save As Template…**, which will open the **Save As Template** dialog box:

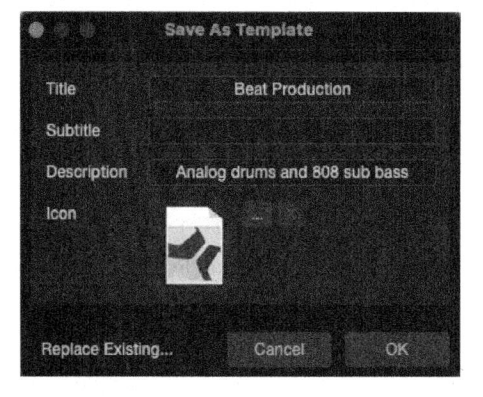

Figure A.1: The Save As Template dialog box

7. Use the **Title** field to give a short name to your template.
8. In the **Description** field, provide a brief description of your template. As you create more and more templates, this will help you remember what this template is about.
9. Click **OK**.

Now, the next time you start Studio One, your new template will be ready, waiting for you to start working on your new Song. You can open it as follows:

1. On the **Start** page, click on the **New…** button. This will open the **New** document window.
2. Click on the **User** tab.

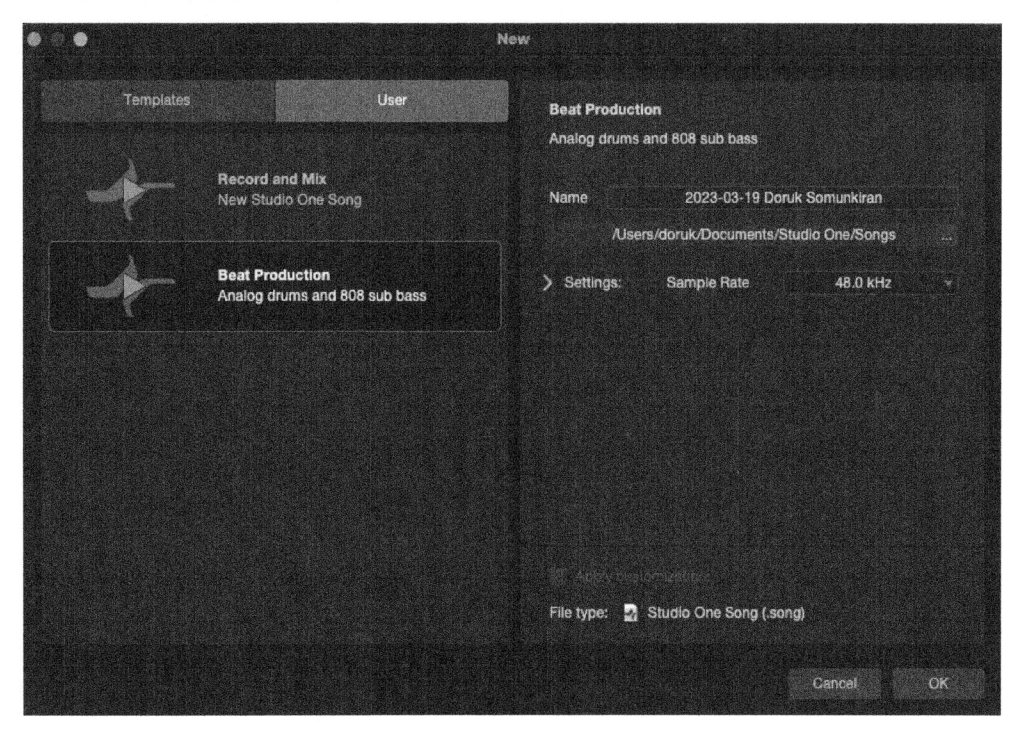

Figure A.2: Opening a User template

3. Select your template.
4. Click **OK**.

Create as many Smart Templates as you need for various workflow scenarios. This will free up mental bandwidth that would otherwise be devoted to the mechanics of music production.

Working with Track Presets

Track Presets allow you to save and recall frequently used track configurations, so you don't have to recreate these settings every time you create a new track.

A Track Preset saves and recalls every parameter that pertains to a track. For example, let's say that for every new Song, I set up my lead electric guitar track like this:

- Name the track `E Gtr Lead`.
- Use red as the track color.
- Insert **Ampire** on the track, with my own custom settings.
- Use the track's **Sends** rack to send a signal at -9 dB to an FX channel, with **Room Reverb** and **Pro EQ**.
- Route the track to a bus titled `E Guitars`.

Instead of having to create a track with the preceding settings on every new project, I can just save that configuration as a Track Preset and recall it on my next projects. Studio One will automatically recreate the same combination, saving me time and streamlining my workflow. It's very easy to do:

1. In an existing Song, set up your track the way you want it:

    I. Give it a name.

    II. Assign a track color.

    III. Insert any effects plug-ins and adjust them the way you want to find them.

    IV. Create an FX channel and add any additional effects by using the **Sends** rack (optional).

    V. Create a new bus channel and route the output of the track to that bus (optional).

Here's my lead electric guitar track, configured as I just described:

Figure A.3: Preparing a track for a Track Preset

1. Right-click on the track and select **Store Track Preset…**, which will open the **Store Preset** dialog box:

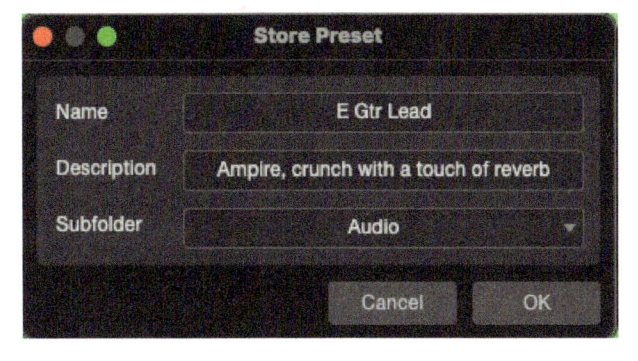

Figure A.4: The Store Preset dialog box

2. Type a name and description for your preset. Providing a thorough description here will help you remember what this preset is about.

3. Click **OK**.

Now, let's see how you can recall this track preset in your next project:

1. Click on the **Add Tracks** button. This will open the **Add Tracks** dialog box:

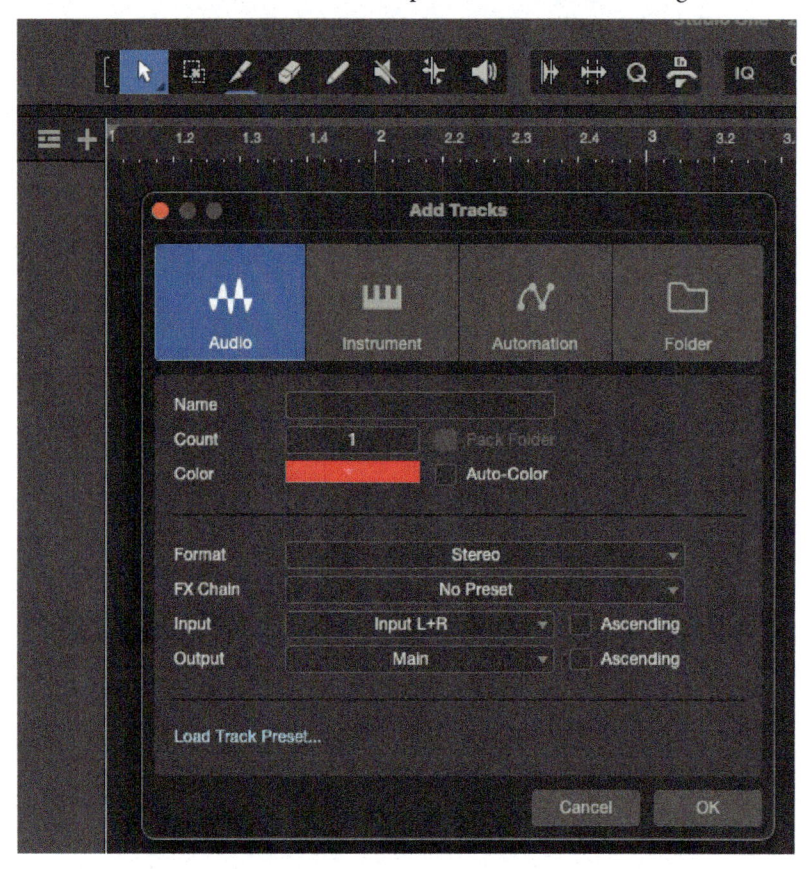

Figure A.5: The Add Tracks dialog box

2. Click on **Load Track Preset…**. This will open the **Load Track Preset** window:

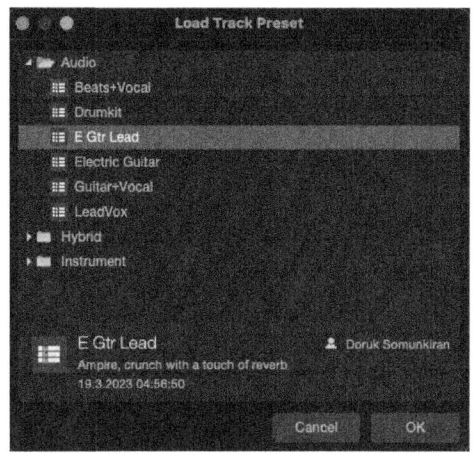

Figure A.6: The Load Track Preset window

3. Locate your preset and click **OK**.

In *Figure A.7*, I loaded my `E Gtr Lead` track preset on an empty project. Note that an FX channel and a bus channel have been created and all routings have been made automatically, just like the configuration of the original track in *Figure A.3*.

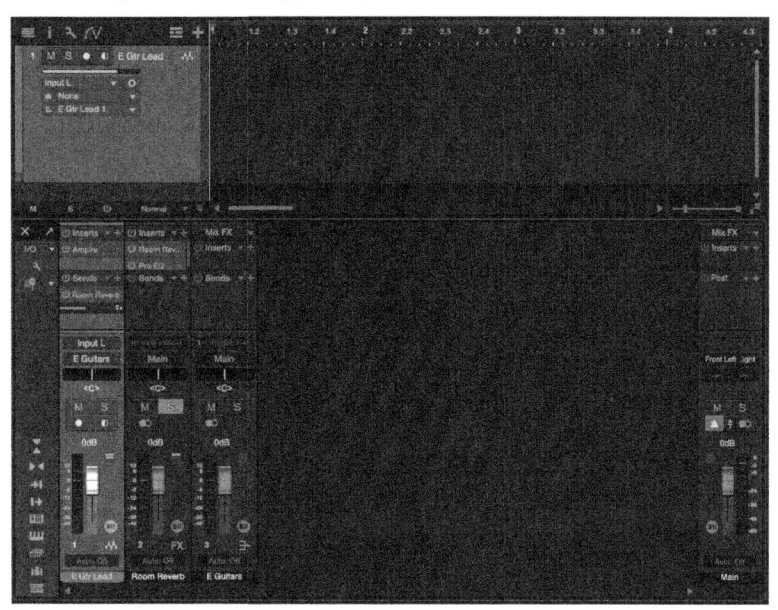

Figure A.7: A track, an FX channel, and a bus channel created by recalling a track preset

Studio One comes with several preconfigured track presets, and many more can be downloaded for free at PreSonus Exchange (which we discussed in *Chapter 2*). Feel free to explore these presets to get an idea of how other people set up their tracks. It's like watching over a fellow producer's shoulder as they work, and it will be an excellent learning experience.

Using effects chains

An **effects chain**, also known as an **FX Chain** in Studio One, is a series of audio effects that are applied in sequence to an audio signal. By combining several effects plug-ins in a specific order, you can create a unique and distinctive sound, which can be used to enhance sound quality or achieve a particular artistic effect.

If you frequently use the same sequence of effects in your projects, you can save them as an FX Chain and recall it in your future projects with a single click, with all the effects parameters set up the way you want them to be. Here's how:

1. On the **Inserts** rack of a track, set up your FX Chain. Adjust all effects parameters the way you want to find them.
2. Click on the small triangle next to the **Inserts** label. This will open the **FX Chain** menu:

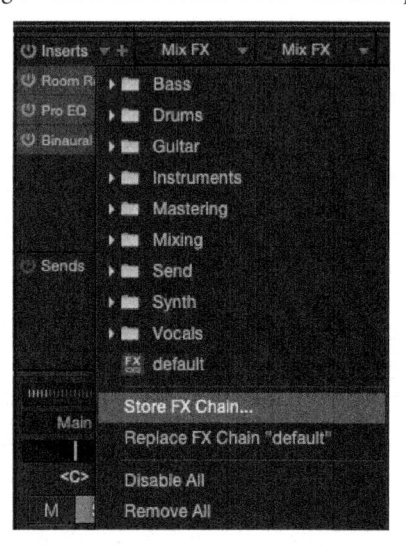

Figure A.8: The FX Chain menu

3. Select **Store FX Chain…**. This will open the **Store Preset** dialog box:

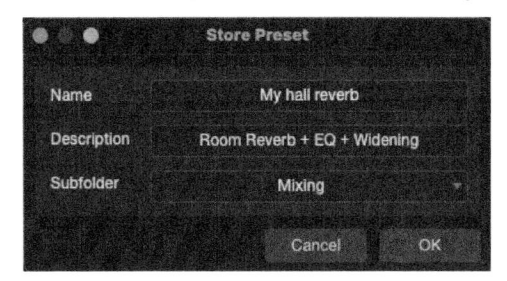

Figure A.9: The Store Preset dialog box

4. Type a name for your FX Chain and give it a brief description.
5. Studio One tries to keep FX Chains organized by grouping them into folders. Select the subfolder that this FX Chain should be listed under.
6. Click **OK**.

In your future projects, when you want to recall your FX Chain, proceed as follows:

1. Go to the **Inserts** rack of the track where you want to load your FX Chain.
2. Click on the small triangle next to the **Inserts** label.
3. Locate your FX Chain in the folder that you saved it to, and click it to load it.

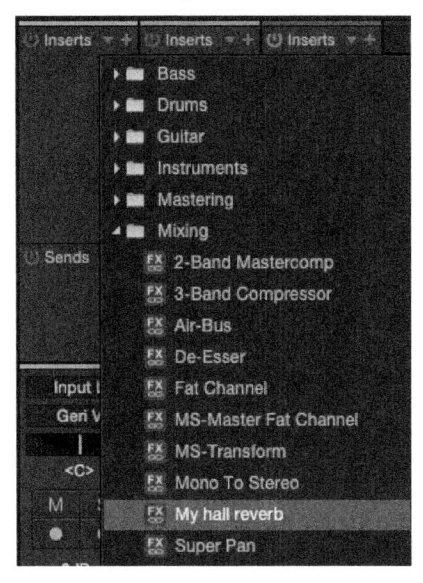

Figure A.10: Loading an FX Chain

Just as with track presets, Studio One ships with a big collection of FX Chains, and many more can be downloaded from PreSonus Exchange. Feel free to explore them to see what fellow producers use for different sound-shaping scenarios.

In this section, you have learned how to save time and streamline your workflow by automating repetitive tasks, by creating templates and presets. In the next section, we will talk about best practices that will help you make the most of Studio One's file management system.

Understanding the file and folder system

When inspiration strikes and you're in the mood to create your next hit, you can just go with the flow and bring in material from all kinds of different sources – grab an audio file from an earlier project, use a loop that's on an external drive, extract audio from a YouTube video to use as a sample… you name it.

Behind the scenes, Studio One does an excellent job of keeping track of these audio assets, so you can keep creating without being distracted. For a modest project, Studio One's file management capability will be more than enough; however, as your projects grow, there will come a time when Studio One will need a little assistance on your part to keep things organized and running smoothly. That's what we're aiming for in this section.

Let's start by discussing how Studio One handles files and folders.

Exploring Studio One's file management system

When you install Studio One on your computer, it creates three folders that will be home to your future Songs, Projects, and Shows, respectively. Here are those folders on my computer's Studio One installation:

Figure A.11: Studio One user data folders

Collectively, these three folders are referred to as **user data**, and we talked about how to customize the location of these folders in *Chapter 2*.

As you start creating new Projects, Shows, and Songs, Studio One will create separate subfolders for each of these under their respective folders. Here's a subfolder for one of my Songs:

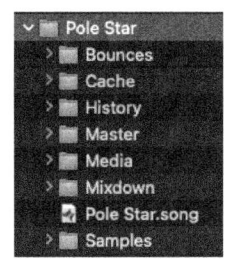

Figure A.12: The contents of a subfolder for a Song

When I created the Song, Studio One created the file with the `.song` extension. All other folders were created and populated automatically by Studio One as I continued working on my Song. That's the beauty of working with Studio One: it does all the housekeeping behind the scenes, allowing you to focus on creating. You don't have to know what's inside these folders; you don't even have to know that these folders exist… until you do.

Locating and copying missing files

Let's go back to that joyful moment when you were in a creative mood, working on your new Song. You work on it for hours, and it sounds like a hit already. So, you call it a day and shut down your computer. However, when you come back to your Song the next day, you get a message like this:

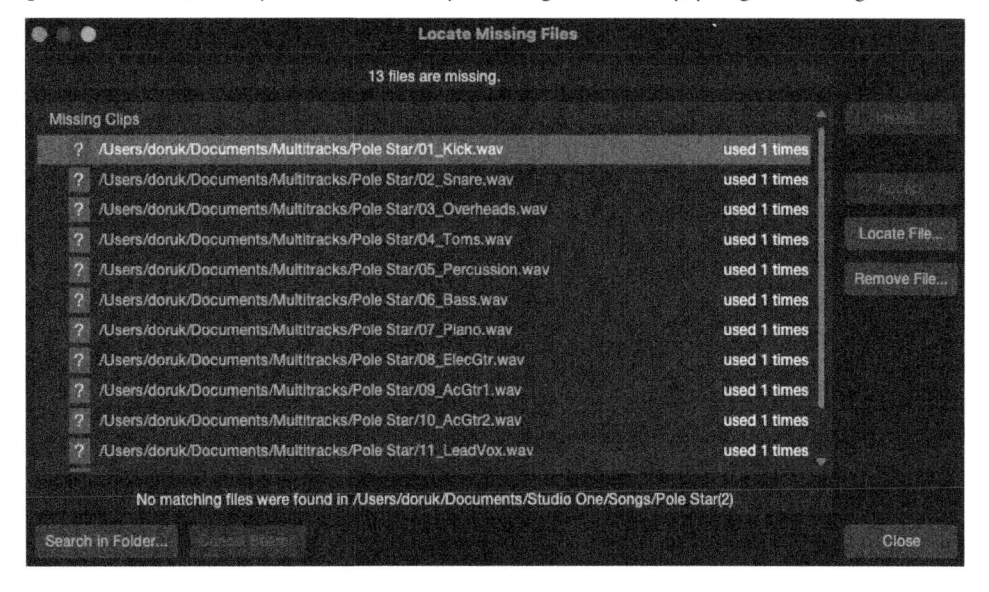

Figure A.13: The Locate Missing Files dialog box

Remember that audio file you dragged into the Song from a removable drive? Now that drive is not connected to your computer, so Studio One cannot find the audio file.

The quick solution is to connect the drive, click **Locate File…** on this window, and point Studio One to where it can find the file. However, that's only a temporary fix; you will have the same problem again the next time you open this Song unless the external drive is always connected.

A permanent solution is to bring all such external files home by copying them under this Song's own folder, which is very easy to do:

1. Make sure all external drives used in the Song are connected.
2. Open the Song.
3. On the top menu, go to **Song** and select **Copy External Files**.

Studio One will copy all the external files into their respective places inside the Song's folder. You will no longer get missing file warnings, and you will no longer have to go hunting for files on other drives.

Removing unused files

As you work on your Song, you will create lots of files that you will not end up using. For example, if you record several takes of a vocal performance and end up using just one of them, files for the other takes will still sit on your drive, occupying valuable storage space.

Studio One can automatically detect these unused files and delete them for you. It takes only three clicks:

1. Open the Song.
2. Go to **Song** on the top menu.
3. Select **Remove Unused Files**.

It's a good idea to make a habit of issuing this command once your Song is complete. If you do lots of recording, you'll be surprised to know how much storage space is wasted by unused material.

Be aware, though, that if you're using these assets on other Songs, deleting them will make them unavailable for those other Songs as well. So, here's a best practice – run **Copy External Files** on all your Songs first, and then select **Remove Unused Files**. That will eliminate any risk of deleting used files by mistake.

Using autosave and recovery

By default, Studio One will save your Song automatically every five minutes. These autosaved files are stored in the **History** subfolder of your Song's main folder. That's a blessing because if, for some reason, you are unable to save your Song (due to a system crash, power failure, etc.), you'll lose no more than five minutes of your work.

When you try to open a Song file that has crashed before, Studio One will ask you whether you want to continue with the most recent autosaved version. Click **OK**, and you can continue as if the crash never happened.

If you experience a lot of crashes, though, it may be time for some troubleshooting. Studio One has a **Studio One Safety** window that may help to diagnose the cause of the crashes, through some trial and error.

When Studio One crashes, the **Studio One Safety** window will open automatically the next time you launch the program. You can also force it to open by holding the *Shift* key on your keyboard when starting Studio One.

Figure A.14: The Safety window

Usually, crashes happen due to conflicts with third-party plug-ins, particularly older ones. Using the **Studio One Safety** window, you can temporarily disable certain plug-in types, start Studio One, and see whether that solves the problem. This will help you narrow down the suspects through trial and error. Once you find the culprit, you can try updating or replacing it with an alternative that plays well with Studio One.

Saving incremental versions

Here's a best practice that will save you a lot of headaches – save your files with different version names every half hour or so. The easiest way to do this is to add a number to the end of your filename and increase it with each version, like this:

Figure A.15: Saving a Song file with incremental versions

When you're working on a Song, especially if you've been grinding away for a while and you're tired, you may find that your latest actions take away from your Song rather than add to it. You may find yourself saying, "This did not work. I wish I could go back." Studio One does have an **Undo** feature, but just like in real life, some moves just cannot be undone.

In such cases, it's a lifesaver to have a version of your Song that was saved half an hour ago, when things were still sitting pretty. Just close this version, open the previous one, and enjoy a second chance to make things right.

Studio One makes this easy to implement. Here's how to set it up:

1. While you're in your Song, go to **File** on the top menu and select **Save New Version…**. This will open a dialog box:

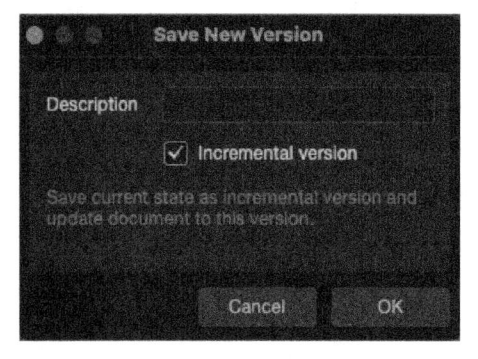

Figure A.16: The Save New Version dialog box

2. Check **Incremental version**.

3. Click **OK**.

Now that the **Incremental version** checkbox is selected, you don't have to open this dialog box to save a new version anymore. Next time you want to create a new version, simply use the keyboard shortcut for the **Save New Version…** command – *Ctrl* + *Alt* + *S* (Windows) or *Option* + *Cmd* + *S* (Mac) – and Studio One will create a new version automatically.

In this section, we explored how Studio One handles all the files that make up our Songs, and we discussed several best practices to keep this filesystem organized, avoid missing file warnings, troubleshoot for crashes, and go back to previous versions of our Songs. Next, we will talk about best practices to share your Studio One files with others for collaboration.

Sharing your files with others

Whether you're collaborating with other producers, swapping ideas with bandmates, or sending tracks to a mixing studio, sharing files you created within Studio One is an important skill set that comes with its own set of best practices.

In this section, we will take a look at different scenarios where you'd want to share your files, considering the most effective method of sharing in each scenario.

Sharing with a collaborator who has Studio One

If you're collaborating with a fellow producer who also has Studio One, you will get the best mileage by sharing your Song folders with them. That way, your collaborator will be able to work directly on the document and send it back to you, eliminating the need for any conversion or rendering.

To share a Song folder with a collaborator, do the following:

1. Open your Song.

2. On the top menu, go to **File** and select **Copy External Files**. This will make sure that all the files used in your Song will be included in its folder when you share it, preventing any messages about missing files.

3. Again, on the top menu, go to **File** and select **Remove Unused Files**. This will eliminate any clutter caused by files you no longer need, reducing the size of the folder and making it easier to share over the internet.

4. Locate the folder for your Song and share it with your collaborator.

If you only share the file with the `.song` extension, your collaborator will not be able to load the media files, so sharing the entire folder is essential.

Versions of Studio One are backward compatible, so Studio One 7 can open Song files created in Studio One 6. However, it doesn't work the other way around; if you have Studio One 7 and your collaborator has Studio One 6, they will not be able to open your Song.

Also, if you used third-party plug-ins in your Song and your collaborator does not have them, the Song file will open fine on their computer but they will not be able to hear the effects created by those plug-ins. If these effects are indispensable during the collaboration phase, render the audio files (as explained in *Chapter 13*) before sharing the folder.

Sharing with a collaborator who does not have Studio One

If you're sharing a Song with a collaborator who does not have Studio One, your best bet is to share a MIDI file. MIDI files can be opened in any **digital audio workstation** (**DAW**) software, so your collaborator can just drop the file into whatever program they're using and keep working.

To create a MIDI file from your project, do the following:

1. Open your Song.
2. Go to **File** on the top menu, hover on **Convert To**, and select **MIDI File…**.
3. In the dialog box, give a name to your MIDI file.
4. Click **OK**.

MIDI files have the added advantage of being tiny in size, so they can be shared easily even across mobile devices.

Sharing tracks for mixing

If you're hiring the services of a mixing engineer to mix your Song, you need to send them the Song's individual tracks. Here are some best practices that will save time for both you and the mixing engineer:

1. Open your Song and disable all effects plug-ins, except for those that are essential components of an instrument's characteristic sound. For example, if you have a unique guitar sound that you achieve by using **Ampire** or a similar plug-in, leave it on. Disable all other plug-ins you've added to your Song; these are now the responsibility of the mixing engineer.
2. Export all the tracks in your Song by using the **Export Stems** command, as we discussed in *Chapter 13*.
3. Go to the folder containing the stems and give them short, descriptive names. Don't add long prefixes, such as `MySongTrack07_Bass`. The mix consoles on all DAW software display only the first few letters of track names, and having the same prefix on all stem names will mean that the mixing engineer will see the same thing on every channel of the mixer.

4. Create a text file that includes your name, contact details, the Song's name, the sample rate and bit depth of the exported stems, and the Song's tempo.
5. Combine all the stems and the text file in a single ZIP folder.
6. Rename the ZIP folder to contain your name and the Song's name.

Following these best practices will allow the mixing engineer to start working on your Song immediately without having to do any additional work or call you with questions.

Summary

In this section, we discussed several methods of customizing Studio One to match and accelerate your workflow. Then, we explored Studio One's file management system to help you keep track of various assets in your Songs. Over time, this will become more and more important as you need to do housekeeping on your computer, reduce clutter and archive finished Songs. Finally, we explored various methods for sharing your finished and unfinished Songs with colleagues and collaborators. Following these best practices will make life easier for you and other people on your team.

Index

A

Ableton Live 44
Additional Content 12
ADM BWF file 298
Ampire 18, 81, 245, 246, 258
Analog Delay 243
analog to digital converter 59
analysis tools plug-ins 254
Arpeggiator 179
  interface 179, 180
  Pattern Sequencer, using 180, 181
Arranger Track 130, 188
  for editing song 130
  using, to define song section 332
  working with 130, 131
arrange window 40
Arrow tool 114, 115
  alternative tool, selecting 120
  events, looping 116
  events, sizing 115
  fades, applying 118, 119
  gain, adjusting 119
  slip editing 119
  time stretching 116, 117
Audio Bend tool
  used, for fixing errors manually 144, 145

audio editing tools 136
  audio events, transposing 136
  audio events, tuning 136
  editing commands, using 140-142
  performance, taking to next level 139, 140
  Strip Silence command 137, 138
audio equalizer (EQ) 237
audio event
  isolating, with stem separation 154, 155
  transposing 136
  tuning 136
audio recordings
  Audio Bend tool, using 144, 145
  audio quantization 146, 147
  quantizing, to custom grooves 147, 148
  timing, enhancing 143
  timing, fixing 143
  transients 143, 144
Audio Sub-Track 203
audio-to-MIDI-conversion
  with Melodyne 107-109
Audio Tracks
  setting 194
augmented reality (AR) 286

automation 228
  adding, to create dynamic mix 230
  editing 230-232
  examples 228
  modes 229
automation envelope 230
Automation Lane 168
Auto Punch feature 84, 85

B

background harmony vocals
  creating, with Melodyn 153
backing track 324
Backing Track Player
  adding 326, 327
Beat Delay 243
beds 293
bend markers 124, 125, 144
Bend tool 124
binaural 286
Binaural Pan 276
binaural panning 227
Bitcrusher 246
bits 60
browse window 40, 41
buffers 23
bundled plug-ins 233
buses 263
  channels, controlling 263-265

C

cardioid pattern 71
CD standard 279
Celemony 148
Channel Strip plug-in 250
chord detection
  failure 195

Chorder 181, 182
  interface 182
  programming, to use custom chords 182
chords
  adding, by drag and drop 192
  detecting 188, 189
  entering, manually 190, 191
  extracting, from audio recording 189
Chord Track 187, 188
  using 188
Chorus plug-in 247
clipping 219
combined mix plug-ins 250
  channel strips 250
  Fat Channel XT 250, 251
  Mix Engine FX 252
comping 139
compressor 234
Compressor plug-in 81
condenser microphones 70
continuous controller messages (CCMs) 172
control surface
  adding 30
convolution reverb 241
customization editor 47

D

decibels relative to full scale (dBFS) 218
Deep Flight One 10, 11
de-esser 236, 237
delay plug-ins 242
  Analog Delay 243
  Beat Delay 243, 244
denominator 62
digital audio workstation (DAW) 3, 362
digital data 59
Disc Description Protocol (DDP) 319

distortion effects 244
distortion plug-ins 244
   Ampire 245, 246
   Bitcrusher 246
   Red Light Distortion 246
Dolby Atmos 286
Dolby Atmos Renderer 287, 296, 297
drag and drop
   chords, adding 192
Dropout Protection 214
DVD standard 280
dynamic microphones 70
dynamic range 60
dynamics plug-ins and equalizer
   level and frequency, controlling with 234
dynamics processors 234
   compressor 234
   de-esser 236, 237
   expansion 236
   gate 236
   limiter 235, 236
   Multiband Dynamics 237
   Pro EQ3 237-239
   Tricomp 237

E

editing 113
editing tools
   Arrow tool 114, 115
   Arrow tool, for performing editing tasks 158
   Bend tool 124, 125
   Eraser tool 121
   exploring 114
   Listen tool 125
   Mute tool 123
   Paint tool 121-123
   Range tool 120
   Select Notes window, using for precise selection 159-161
   Split tool 121
effects chain 354
effects plug-ins 233
elevation 293
Eraser tool 121
expansion 236
exporting 278
external devices configuration
   control surface, adding 30, 31
   instrument, adding 30
   keyboard, adding 29

F

fade-in 118
Fade In to Cursor command 141, 142
fade-out 118
faders 223, 224
Fast Fourier Transform (FFT) 313
Fat Channel XT 18, 250, 251
file and folder system 356
   autosave, using 358, 359
   file management system, exploring 356, 357
   incremental versions, saving 360, 361
   missing files, copying 357, 358
   missing files, locating 357, 358
   recovery, using 358, 359
   unused files, removing 358
file sharing 361
   for mixing engineer 362, 363
   with out Studio One collaborator 362
   with Studio One collaborator 361
final masters for CD release
   creating 319-321
final masters for delivery
   rendering 318

final masters for digital release
  creating 318, 319
final masters for publishing
  rendering 318
final mixes
  exporting, from Song 278-281
Flanger plug-in 247
folders 221
Follow Chord menu 195, 196
Follow Chord parameter
  setting 192-194
FX Chain 354
  creating 276
FX channels
  using 260-263

G

gain 119, 217
gain staging 217
gate 236
Gear Acquisition Syndrome (GAS) 12
glissando 151
global tracks 63, 187
glue compressor 310
groove 147
Groove Delay 243, 244
groove quantization 147
groups
  using 273, 274

H

Handbrake
  URL 202
hard disk drive (HDD) 31
hard quantizing 147

hardware setup, for recording 70
  instrument, setting up 72, 73
  microphone, setting up 70
headroom 219
hi-hat rolls 105

I

immersive audio 286
impact 7, 8
impulse response 241
in phase 314
Input Filter 184, 185
Inserts rack 258, 259
instrument
  adding 30
instrument-level source 72
Instrument Tracks
  setting 191
International Standard Recording Code (ISRC) 306
IR Maker 253

K

keyboard
  adding 29

L

large-diaphragm microphones 71
latency 23
Launcher 131
  using 131-134
Lead Architect 10
level/loudness meter 314
Limiter2 plug-in 235, 236

line-level source 72
Listen tool 125
live performance recording, with MIDI 96
   computer keyboard, using 96
   loop recording 98, 99
   walk-through 97, 98
loop mode 244
loop recording 85, 86, 98, 99
loops and sounds 12, 13
lower panel, Song page 41
   edit window 42
   mix window 43
low-frequency effects (LFEs) 287
Lyrics Display 201
Lyrics Track
   using 200, 201

M

Mai Tai 8
Marker Track
   using 198, 199
mastering 300
mastering effects
   compressor 310
   equalizer 310
   limiter 310
   stereo imaging 310
Melodyne 107
   audio material, selecting 107
   audio-to-MIDI conversion 107-109
   used, for fixing out-of-tune vocal
      performance 149-152
   using, to create background
      harmony vocals 153
   using, to fix vocal recordings 148
Melodyne Essential 19, 148
metadata 305

meta tags 21
metering tools 312
   level/loudness meter 314
   phase meter 314-316
   spectrum meter 312
   using 312
metronome
   setting up 81, 82
microphone
   accessories 72
   condenser microphone 70
   dynamic microphone 70
   large-diaphragm microphone 71
   positioning 71
   setting up 70
   small-diaphragm microphone 71
MIDI instruments
   hardware instrument, adding 93-96
   software instrument, adding 92
MIDI notes
   drawing, with Paint tool 100-102
   half-time or double-time, applying 163-165
   inputting, manually 99
   lengths, adjusting 163-165
   patterns, creating 103-107
   quantizing, to change timing
      of performance 161
   step recording 102, 103
MIDI performance
   data, adjusting 166
   modulation, adjusting 172
   modulation data, editing 173, 174
   modulation data, recording 172
   notes, transposing 166-168
   velocity, adjusting 168-171
MIDI quantization
   freezing 163
   restoring 162
   stiff performances, humanizing 162

mid-side processing 228
Mix Console 256
Mix Engine FX 252
mixer channel
   anatomy 256
   audio event 257
   fader 257
   Inserts rack 257
   live input 257
   Main channel 257
   Monitor button 257
   Sends rack 257
mixing 213, 255
Mixtool 253
Mixverb 239
modulation 172
   data, editing 173, 174
   data, recording 172
modulation effect plug-ins 246
   Autofilter 247
   Chorus 247
   Flanger 247
   Phaser plug-in 247
   Rotor 247
   vocoder 248, 249
   X-Trem 249
modulation wheel 172
Mojito 8
Monophonic audio material 107
MP3 files 280
mud 137
Multiband Dynamics 237
multiband imagers 270
multi-tap delay 243
Musical Instrument Digital Interface (MIDI) 89, 90
   devices, connecting to Studio One 91
   live performance, recording 96

MIDI controller 90
MIDI device 90
MIDI notes, inputting manually 99
music production 57
Mute tool 123

N

New Document page settings, Song
   external files, adding 63
   Song Length 62
   Tempo 62
   Time and key signatures 62
   Timebase 61, 62
New York compression 261
Note FX 176
   plugins, loading 177-179
   using 176
Notion 4
numerator 62

O

Object Panner
   using 294-296
objects 294
online resources
   exploring 19
Open AIR 241, 242
out of phase 315
out-of-tune vocal performance
   fixing, with Melodyne 149-153

P

pages 36
Paint tool 121-123

panning 225, 226
   modes 226-228
parallel compression 261
parallel processing 260
Pattern Editor 104, 174
   drum mode 104
   melodic mode 104
   using 175, 176
pattern programming 103
pattern sequencers 103
Performance View 333
Perpetual license 4
phantom power 70
phase cancellation 315
phase meter 314
Phaser plug-in 247
pitch correction 149
pitch detection algorithm 136
pitch-shifting 195
Player 326
plug-ins
   adding, to Favorites category 275
   customizing 275
   FX chains, creating 276, 277
   presets, adding 277
polar pattern 71
presence 6, 7
Presence XT Core Library 6
PreSonus 3
   loops and sounds 12, 13
   reference link 5, 16
PreSonus additional content 5
   stock plug-ins 11
   virtual instruments 5
PreSonus Sphere 4
Pro+ 12

production kits 12
Pro EQ3 237-239
Project page 36, 43, 44
   automation, using 317
   creating 300
   effects plugins, adding 310-312
   integrating, with Song page 304, 305
   mastering 305
   metadata, entering 305, 306
   metering tools, using 312
   navigating 303, 304
   Project, creating 300
   project, creating for existing .wav files 300, 301
   project, creating from Song page 302
   tracks, editing 307-310
   tracks, sequencing 306, 307
pulses per quarter (PPQ) note 164

Q

quantization 146, 161

R

Range tool 120
   using 120
Real Instrument Player
   adding 328, 329
recording
   best practices 86-88
   hardware, setting up 70
   Studio One, setting up 73
recording modes 83
   Auto Punch feature 84, 85
   basic recording 83
   loop recording 85, 86

Redlight 81
Red Light Distortion 246
Repeater 183, 184
return to zero 52
reverberation 239
reverb plug-ins 239
　Mixverb 239
　Open AIR 241, 242
　Room Reverb 239, 240
Room Reverb 239, 240, 276
roundtrip latency 24
Ruler Track
　using 197, 198

S

sample 341
　adding 342, 343
　editing 343, 344
Sample One 9
SampleOne XT
　used, for adding samples 342, 343
　used, for creating samples 341
　used, for editing samples 343, 344
　used, for selecting Trigger modes 344, 345
sampler 341
sample rate 59
Score Editor
　exploring 335
　musical expressions. adding 337
　notes, editing 337
　notes, entering 336, 337
　opening 334, 335
　score, finalizing 340
　score, formatting 337
　score, printing 340
　using 334

Score Editor Inspector
　Layout tab 339, 340
　Symbols tab 337-339
　Track tab 339
Setlist 324
setting levels 223, 224
Show page 36, 44, 45, 324
　Arranger Track, using to define song section 332
　effects, adding to live performance 330, 331
　exploring 325, 326
　players, working with 326
　show, creating 324, 325
　Studio One, using in live performances with 323
　used, for performing live 333, 334
sibilance 236
sidechain compression 268
　implementing 268, 269
sidechain processing 267, 268
signal flow 255
Signature track 188
　used, for changing Song's key or time signature 66-68
slap-back delay 244
slip editing 119
small-diaphragm microphones 71
Smart Template 348
Snap 126
　modes 126
　Relative Grid 127, 128
　Snap Event End 128
　Snap To Cursor & Loop 128
　Snap To Events 128
　Snap To Grid 126
　Snap To Zero Crossings 129, 130
snare rolls 105
solid-state drive (SSD) 31

Song
  setting up 57
song editing
  with Arranger Track 130, 131
Song, for mix session
  gain staging 217, 218
  hardware and software, optimizing 214
  instrument tracks, converting to audio 215, 216
  tracks, editing for perfection 217
Song page 36-38
  arrange window 40
  browse window 40, 41
  integrating, with Project page 304, 305
  lower panel 41
  top menu 38, 39
  track window 39
Song settings 57, 58
  Name field 59
  New Document page settings 61
  Resolution field 61
  Sample Rate 59, 60
  Save location field 59
sound card 59
SoundCloud 41
Sound Sets 6
spatial audio 285, 286
  binaural 286
  Dolby Atmos 286
  hardware requisites 287
  Song, creating for 288, 289
  surround 286
  tracks, formatting 291, 292
spatial audio material
  exporting 297, 298
spatial audio mixing 292
spatial audio speaker configurations
  naming convention 286, 287

speaker mapping 289, 290
special tools plug-ins 253
  IR Maker 253
  Mixtool 253
  Tone Generator 253
  Tuner 253
spectrum meter 312
  options 313
Splice 41
Splitter 270
  using 271-273
Split tool 121
stems 154, 281
  exporting 281, 282
stem separation
  using, to isolate audio events 154, 155
step recording 102, 103
stock plug-ins 11, 233
  Perpetual license 12
  Pro+ 12
Strip Silence command 137, 138
Studio One 3
  additional content, installing 18
  configuring 20
  customizing 347, 348
  effects chain, using 354-356
  extra content and plugins 18
  included sound sets 18, 19
  installing 16, 17
  Melodyne Essential 19
  MIDI devices, connecting 91
  Smart Template, creating 348, 349
  Track Presets, working 350-354
Studio One+ 4
Studio One configuration
  artist profile, filling 21
  audio device 22, 23
  Audio Device tab 24, 25

Index

buffer size 23, 24
external devices, configuring 26-29
language, selecting 21, 22
latency 23, 24
Processing tab 25, 26
Studio One environment
 navigating 46
 navigation tips 51-53
 project page 36
 show page 36
 Song page 36
 user interface 37
 windows management 46, 47
 zoom levels 48-51
Studio One Pro
 Annual subscription 4
 Monthly subscription 4
 Perpetual license 4
 subscription plan, selecting 5
Studio One setup, for recording 73
 audio track, creating 73-76
 effects, applying 78-81
 metronome, setting up 81-83
 recording levels, setting 76, 78
surround 286
Surround Panner
 using 292, 293
system optimization 31
 file locations, configuring 32-34
 multiple disks, working with 31, 32

T

taps 244
Tempo track 188
 used, for changing Song's tempo 64-66
The Listener 293
Timebase selector 206-208

time stretching 60
Tone Generator 253
tool selection panel 40
Track Automation Lane 173
Track Presets 350
tracks
 formatting, for spatial audio 291, 292
 optimizing, for better control 220-222
track window 39
traditional stereo mixing 292
transient detection algorithm 136
transients 144
tremolo 249
Tricomp 237
Trigger modes
 selecting 344, 345
Tuner plug-in 81, 253

U

USB microphones 71
user data 356
user interface
 navigating 37
 Project page 43, 44
 Show page 45
 Song page 38

V

VCA fader
 adding, to channel 266
video
 audio and MIDI events, synchronizing 204-206
 editing 203, 204
 exporting 208, 209
 importing 202

Video Player 203
Video Track 202, 203
Virtual Instrument Player
  adding 329, 330
virtual instruments 5
  Deep Flight One 10, 11
  impact 7, 8
  Lead Architect 10
  Mai Tai 8
  Mojito 8
  presence 6, 7
  Sample One 9
virtual reality (VR) 286
vocoder 248, 249
Voltage-Controlled Amplifier (VCA) channels 266
  volume, controlling 266
volume 119

W

Wave File 279

X

X-Trem 249

Z

zero crossings 130

⟨packt⟩

packtpub.com

Subscribe to our online digital library for full access to over 7,000 books and videos, as well as industry leading tools to help you plan your personal development and advance your career. For more information, please visit our website.

Why subscribe?

- Spend less time learning and more time coding with practical eBooks and Videos from over 4,000 industry professionals
- Improve your learning with Skill Plans built especially for you
- Get a free eBook or video every month
- Fully searchable for easy access to vital information
- Copy and paste, print, and bookmark content

Did you know that Packt offers eBook versions of every book published, with PDF and ePub files available? You can upgrade to the eBook version at packtpub.com and as a print book customer, you are entitled to a discount on the eBook copy. Get in touch with us at customercare@packtpub.com for more details.

At www.packtpub.com, you can also read a collection of free technical articles, sign up for a range of free newsletters, and receive exclusive discounts and offers on Packt books and eBooks.

Other Books You May Enjoy

If you enjoyed this book, you may be interested in these other books by Packt:

The Music Producer's Ultimate Guide to FL Studio 21

Joshua Au-Yeung

ISBN: 978-1-83763-165-0

- Get up and running with FL Studio 21
- Compose melodies and chord progressions on the piano roll
- Mix your music effectively with mixing techniques and plugins, such as compressors and equalizers
- Record into FL Studio, pitch-correct and retime samples, and follow advice for applying effects to vocals
- Create vocal harmonies and learn how to use vocoders to modulate your vocals with an instrument
- Create glitch effects, transform audio samples into playable instruments, and sound design with cutting-edge effects
- Develop your brand to promote your music effectively
- Publish your music online and collect royalty revenues

The Music Producer's Creative Guide to Ableton Live 11

Anna Lakatos

ISBN: 978-1-80181-763-9

- Understand the concept of Live, the workflow of recording and editing Audio and MIDI, and Warping
- Utilize Groove, MIDI effects, and Live 11 s new workflow enhancements to create innovative music
- Use Audio to MIDI conversion tools to translate and generate ideas quickly
- Dive into Live's automation and modulation capabilities and explore project organization techniques to speed up your workflow
- Utilize MIDI Polyphonic Expression to create evolving sounds and textures
- Adopt useful techniques for production and discover the capabilities of live performance

Packt is searching for authors like you

If you're interested in becoming an author for Packt, please visit `authors.packtpub.com` and apply today. We have worked with thousands of developers and tech professionals, just like you, to help them share their insight with the global tech community. You can make a general application, apply for a specific hot topic that we are recruiting an author for, or submit your own idea.

Share Your Thoughts

Now you've finished *The Ultimate Studio One Pro 7 Book*, we'd love to hear your thoughts! Scan the QR code below to go straight to the Amazon review page for this book and share your feedback or leave a review on the site that you purchased it from.

`https://packt.link/r/1836200978`

Your review is important to us and the tech community and will help us make sure we're delivering excellent quality content.

Download a free PDF copy of this book

Thanks for purchasing this book!

Do you like to read on the go but are unable to carry your print books everywhere?

Is your eBook purchase not compatible with the device of your choice?

Don't worry, now with every Packt book you get a DRM-free PDF version of that book at no cost.

Read anywhere, any place, on any device. Search, copy, and paste code from your favorite technical books directly into your application.

The perks don't stop there, you can get exclusive access to discounts, newsletters, and great free content in your inbox daily

Follow these simple steps to get the benefits:

1. Scan the QR code or visit the link below

    `https://packt.link/free-ebook/978-1-83620-097-0`

2. Submit your proof of purchase
3. That's it! We'll send your free PDF and other benefits to your email directly

Printed in Great Britain
by Amazon